A HISTORY
OF THE
THEATRE

A HISTORY OF THE THEATRE

Glynne Wickham

Second Edition

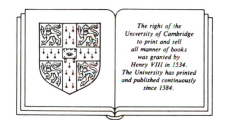

The right of the
University of Cambridge
to print and sell
all manner of books
was granted by
Henry VIII in 1534.
The University has printed
and published continuously
since 1584.

CAMBRIDGE UNIVERSITY PRESS

CAMBRIDGE · NEW YORK · PORT CHESTER
MELBOURNE · SYDNEY

To those actors and actresses, designers, directors, playwrights and theatre technicians who as artists or students (and often in both capacities) have given me the benefit of their experience and friendship.

Published in North America by the
Press Syndicate of the University of Cambridge
The Pitt Building, Trumpington Street, Cambridge CB2 1RP
40 West 20th Street, New York, NY 10011-4211, USA
10 Stamford Road, Oakleigh, Victoria 3166, Australia

© Phaidon Press Limited 1985, 1992
Text © Glynne Wickham 1985, 1992

This edition first published 1992

Printed in Hong Kong

Library of Congress Cataloging-in-Publication Data applied for

ISBN 0-521-43733-4 paperback

Unless otherwise indicated all dates of plays are the dates of
first performance.

FRONTISPIECE: *Barbara Kellerman in the Royal Shakespeare Company's
production of Calderón's* Life's a Dream *(Stratford and London, 1983).*

Contents

1. *Dionysus on a couch with a satyr holding a jug and situla, and a maenad with a wreath and tambourine; above, a female mask. Apulian red-figure bell krater by the Dijon Painter, 380–360 BC. Vatican Museums.*

Preface and Acknowledgements

To discuss drama as if it were simply dramatic literature is about as sensible as trying to drive a car with only one cylinder in working order. Drama—and the theatres in which it is presented—embraces actors and actresses, painters and paintings, architects and craftsmen, costumiers and engineers; it also extends to encompass composers and musicians, choreographers and dancers, acrobats and athletes, poets and journalists, and—perhaps the most significant of all its elements—audiences. In short it is a group experience based on interaction.

In the theatre no performance can ever be identically repeated. The actors are human: they remember their lines and moves one night and forget them or mistime them the next. Nor is the composition of the audience ever exactly the same. Each performance is thus a shared experience unique to those actually present at the time. Anyone who has tried to describe an actor's rendering of a particular line of verse to someone else not present at the time, or an actress's death-bed sigh, or some especially striking lighting effect, knows the truth of this.

How, then, can one explain this special and intimate relationship within the group? Clearly, audiences have first got to be persuaded that it will be worth their while to attend the performance; that requires an act of faith, repeated every time they exercise their right of choice in deciding how to use their free time.

Once an audience, however, has made this decision, it becomes the actor's prime task to woo its members, to gain their confidence, to persuade them to accept in their hearts as real what they know in their minds to be fiction, pretence. It is like courtship and just as treacherous; for if, at any time, the actor loses his concentration and becomes careless, the audience can become offended, take umbrage, and withdraw its confidence. This happens when actors cannot be heard, allow themselves to be hidden from view by other actors, or indulge in narcissistic posturing that reveals the real man or woman behind the character. It is for such reasons that critics come, on occasion, to damn on its first night a play which posterity later comes to recognize as great: more often, great acting can lead critics to believe that a play of little genuine merit is a considerable work of art—a view quickly dispelled once the play is presented by other and less distinguished casts.

What is not so often recognized is that every member of an audience (ourselves included) spends a large part of every day acting out some chosen role (often an imposed role), giving a daily 'performance'. Those people whom we encounter in the course of the day are our 'audience'. We wear clothes or 'costume' we consider to be appropriate to that role, and we use the words and speech rhythms (technical jargon for the most part) which we regard as likely either to conform with the role or to help us to define it in other people's eyes; and in all our behaviour, above all in our use of our feet, hands and eyes, we give constant signals to those around us indicating how we wish them to interpret our actions and our utterances. Unhappily for us, we can also be transmitting signals by these same means, unknown or only partly known to ourselves, which can betray to perceptive spectators feelings which we are seeking to hide. In short, whether in arguing with our colleagues or in more relaxed social conversation, we strive, like actors, to capture and to hold the attention of an audience, to make it laugh with us, or to appreciate our personal anxieties and sorrows.

In doing all of this we rarely regard ourselves as actors; yet every now and again—when we get home, and are having a bath or pouring ourselves a drink—we recognize that we have changed one persona for another. We have ceased to be actors and become ourselves.

This phenomenon is one of the most vital factors in explaining the group experience unique to dramatic art since it links, through mimetic action, each and everyone of us with those rare and exceptional individuals whom we label as actors. Yet they, like us, are human beings, but the role that they have chosen to play in life consists of putting this whole process into reverse. The major difference lies in the subjectivity of the role-playing in our own daily lives and the objectivity of a professional actor's public theatrical performance. The latter is invariably a demonstration, a show, whereas the former is only rarely self-conscious, and is employed as often to conceal as to display. This link, which we carry with us from the cradle to the grave, between our own and the actor's motivation and technique, goes far towards explaining the enduring fascination of the theatre the world over, and its ability so to adapt itself to change that even when apparently sick and dying it is at that very moment in the process of renewing itself in some novel, challenging and more appropriate form.

All theatre is make-believe, a world of marvels and illusion, pretended actions, game or play; yet this fairy-tale world of artifice must be firmly anchored in the real world (sometimes the dream-world) either through its characters—their speech and behaviour—or through the action represented, if it is to be recognized by audiences and to awake any emotional response. Our minds and our hearts are called upon to respond simultaneously, the one in step with the other. If, in our minds, we lose track of which character is which, or of what is supposed to be happening, we rapidly lose interest and cease to care which character is praised and which maligned, who lives or who dies. In other words, the illusion of credible human actions or relationships has collapsed; we can no longer believe in what we are seeing or hearing; and when that happens our emotional involvement in the predicament represented vanishes. In extreme cases our response becomes the opposite of what is expected of us: we laugh at what we should be taking seriously and yawn at what is intended to make us laugh. The author of the play may be among the finest of poets and the designer may have provided the most convincing of landscapes or interiors; and the director and stage-manager may have done their best to orchestrate the scene as an ensemble; but if the actor fails to convince us that he is what he claims in his costume and make-up to be, we, his audience, will actively resist his pretensions; and if we refuse to allow him to penetrate our emotional

defences, everyone else concerned has effectively wasted their time.

What audiences consider to be acceptable has varied from one period to another and is to a large extent dependent on their expectancies—upon conventions. The spectrum of theatrical illusion is itself exceptionally wide, including as it does at one extreme an almost photographic degree of realism in both acting and scenic representation, and at the other a reliance upon emblems, symbols, images and allusions which seem far removed from any behaviour or environment encountered in everyday life (see Figs. 179 and 191). In the early Middle Ages, for instance, actors were not expected to speak, let alone use conversational prose; they were expected to sing, in verse and in Latin: that was the convention. Yet in the sixteenth century actors were expected to speak, normally in verse but sometimes in prose, and almost invariably in the vernacular. In our own time, to write a play in verse is virtually to invite managements to reject it.

Audiences can be educated to change their approach and attitude to stage conventions. This usually occurs first in universities, schools, or in 'fringe' groups where experiment is encouraged, and then extends outwards into society at large. Thus what at first had seemed outlandish and unintelligible to the play-going public comes to be received as natural, welcome, and ultimately taken for granted. When this happens, the pioneering initiatives have usually been taken by amateur enthusiasts who are not dependent on the financial results of their experiments for their livelihood; but once it has become obvious to professionals that a particular experiment is attracting substantial public attention and support (as was the case with changeable scenery during the seventeenth century, and again with ensemble acting in the early years of this century), they have normally adopted this change for themselves and have then gone on to execute it better than the original, amateur exponents.

The many illustrations in this book are there to remind readers that audiences enter theatres with eyes as well as ears, and that a play is never simply a written statement like a philosophical treatise or an epic poem or an academic lecture or a political harangue. Pictures which hang in a gallery or on living-room walls are static; stage-pictures are not. Play texts and the theatrical representation of them are thus inextricably linked. Audiences are always juxtaposing what they see happening on the stage with what the actors are saying, and then weighing the two impressions in the scales of their own hearts and minds. It is in this way that they arrive at judgements about the characters and on their respective actions. And herein, precisely, lies the thrill and enjoyment of theatre as an art form; the open invitation which it accords to us to make judgements on human motivation and action in situations which we have either experienced for ourselves or can at least imagine ourselves as being confronted with.

This ability to juxtapose and contrast verbal statements with visual images is a quality denied to the other arts and is unique to theatre. It is a property that every playwright has to learn to handle before his work is likely to be of much interest to actors and actresses; but it is also one which can, unfortunately, serve to separate audiences who have been educated to appreciate complicated verbal debate and sophisticated witticisms from those who have not. Shakespeare was aware of this when stating in *Coriolanus* (III, 2, 76–7): 'Action is eloquence, and the eyes of the ignorant more learned than the ears.' What is dangerous in this for the playwright is that spectacle can come to eclipse verbal sense for many playgoers, particularly when it is linked to violent action. Once this happens, or is encouraged to happen, dramatic art can dwindle into a variety of entertainments ranging from glamorous revues and strip-tease on the one hand to military tattoos and every kind of athletic competition on the other at the expense of plays of social and literary merit (see Figs. 87, 159 and 181).

The theatre's capacity to juxtapose verbal with visual imagery confronts dramatists with another difficulty. Since changes of direction in the theatre can rarely occur in advance of similar changes of direction in related arts, stylistic problems arise during the interval between the first expressions of dynamic change in poetic vision, or in the visual arts, or in music, and the ultimate arrival of a new yet harmonious accord between them all. This generally results in a lack of commitment, self-assurance or sense of direction (sometimes all three) which shocks or bewilders playgoers and provokes critics into writing funeral obsequies for a decadent and moribund art. On the other hand, a strong sense of nationhood has often served to resolve these stylistic problems in itself and thus to inaugurate a great period of dramatic achievement. This was as true for Periclean Athens as it was for Louis XIV's France or Ibsen's Norway.

I shall try in this book, therefore, as I advance from one period and style of theatrical performance to another, to preserve and highlight the essentially organic and evolving character of the changes discussed; but in adopting this approach for the sake of clarity, I hope I shall have avoided making it appear that every change noted was itself an unqualified *improvement* on the past, for it is true to say that every distinct change of style, while seen by its contemporaries as an improvement, involves some element of loss.

The chapters are grouped within five, separate sections, each section corresponding to a major shift in society's view of itself which, down the centuries, the theatre sought to reflect. Each of these sections is equipped with its own general introduction, chronology and recommended further reading.

The first section surveys the origins and development of dramatic art in Western and Eastern countries in the five centuries both before and after the birth of Christ. The second traces its renewal within Christian Europe. The third examines the radical changes wrought in the emerging nation-states by the Italian Renaissance and the Protestant Reformation. The fourth views theatre from the standpoint of the princes of commerce and industry who acquired the power during the eighteenth and nineteenth centuries to shape its further philosophical, social, economic and political development within existing moral and aesthetic forms. The final section surveys the disintegration of both the subject matter of dramatic art and the forms of its theatrical expression which has accompanied the adoption in the West of a predominantly scientific approach to life, including the advent of cable and satellite television, but not beyond.

These five sections are framed by a Prologue and an Epilogue. The Prologue is designed to alert the reader both to the ambiguity that has always characterized public attitudes towards actors and actresses as well as towards dramatic art itself, and to the shifting nature of artistic priorities and responsibilities within the theatre where actors, writers, designers and composers are concerned, since each of these factors has contributed to (and at times occasioned) major changes of direction in the course of the theatre's long history which cannot otherwise be accounted for. The Epilogue is offered to assist readers to arrive at a considered response to the unprecedentedly wide range of dramatic genres and modes of expression (which now extend broadly into 'pop' concerts and a range of spectator sports at least as numerous as those on offer in Imperial Rome) that have competed with plays and films increasingly since television relieved the public of any obligation to stir out of their own homes for entertainment.

Not every well-known dramatist, actor, actress or designer will be discussed (or even referred to) since the criterion for selection for inclusion in this relatively short book must be the impact made by performances of a play upon audiences in its own time, and its subsequent influence as a model for others. This principle of selection extends during the seventeenth century and after to the advent of opera and ballet and, late in the nineteenth century, to that of cinema which, in its turn, has been supplemented during this century with a virtually non-stop supply of entertainment offered to the public on radio, television and, most recently of all, video-cassettes.

Lastly, I must express my thanks to those colleagues and friends who have given up time to read chapters of this book while it was still in draft form and again when it was in proof stage, and whose expert knowledge and care have rescued me from many errors of fact, emphasis or both which would otherwise have been present in it. The list is a long one: Professor John Gould, Dr Oliver Neville, Professors W. D. Howarth and Hans Reiss, Dr John Golder, Dr O. B. Hardison jun., Emeritus Professor J. C. Metford, Mr George Rowell, Miss Ann Brooke Barnett, Mr Christopher Robinson, and not least my long-suffering wife.

No less important to the style and appearance of the book have been the patient labours of Marie Leahy and Caroline Lucas in bearing with my many uncertainties and changes of mind about what to include, what to omit, what to expand and what to contract or amend as the book took shape in the course of its preparation for the printers.

Bristol, October 1984   G.W.

PREFACE TO THE SECOND EDITION

Seven years on from the publication of the first edition, revisions have been made both within the text and to the List of Further Reading to take account of new plays, writers, productions and recently published books about the theatre.

Coverage of the twentieth century in particular has been greatly extended. Chapter 14 is now devoted exclusively to events between the start of the First World War and the end of the Second, and a new Chapter has been added to cover developments from the 1950s to the 1990s.

Illustration of this period has likewise been enlarged by the addition of 20 new pictures.

Bristol, 1991   G.W.

Prologue

Theatre is the most dangerous of all arts. Banned throughout Christian Europe for four centuries following the sack of Rome by Alaric the Goth in AD 410, dramatic art was suppressed in India for nearly twice as long after the Islamic conquest of the tenth and eleventh centuries AD. It was banned again for nearly twenty years in Britain by Act of Parliament, even while memories of Shakespearean 'first nights' were still the subject of parental reminiscence. In America too it was banned by the founding fathers throughout all the New England States in the north until after the Revolution; and in Soviet Russia, since 1934, it has been tolerated only under strict censorship and State control until very recently. The theatre has thus been a constant source of anxiety the world over to leaders of Church and State alike (Fig. 2). That is a central fact of this story.

Actors and actresses, on whom this dynamic and provocative art relies for the breath of life, emerge from world history in no better state. Worshipped at times like gods and royalty, and frequently transmuted into icons of physical beauty and sexual allure, they have nevertheless been despised and scorned at other times as parasites, whores and vagabonds. They have usually eclipsed painters, sculptors, musicians, architects, and poets in the degrees of love, envy or hatred which their profession and conduct have aroused in society: only their professional relatives—singers and dancers—can claim to have been their serious rivals in these respects. In oriental countries, as in the West, while some actors and actresses could be welcomed into temple precincts and into princely households and amass private fortunes, the majority have always been required to reside in the red-light districts of the towns in which they sought to work.

This ambiguity in social attitudes towards actors has, not surprisingly, coloured public attitudes towards dramatic art itself. Even supposedly rational men of letters have quarrelled over drama, allowing only its strictly literary values to possess much merit, and frequently dismissing all forms of theatrical action and spectacle as irrelevant or, if that charge could not be made to stick, as ephemeral. Plato banished actors and acting from his ideal Republic in the fifth century BC; so did Alaric the Visigoth in the real world of the Roman Empire in the fifth century AD. Only in the 1980s have a film actor and a playwright been trusted to assume the duties of a Head of State (see p. 262).

These incontestable facts should warn us against

2. *Banned! A scene from Wole Soyinka's Brother Jero's Metamorphosis, a play about military dictatorship in Nigeria, which was given its first performance in white face at the New Vic, Bristol, by students in the Drama Department of Bristol University, directed by the author, in 1974. The play is still banned in Nigeria.*

approaching the story of theatre as if it consisted merely
of a roll of honour of distinguished dramatic poets, or some
classroom reading-list of prescribed texts: for if that were
true, then dramatic art could not have provoked governments so frequently into taking action against it: nor could
churchmen and academics have consistently adopted such
an austerely cautious (if not positively hostile) attitude
towards it. Even the public has been fickle, sometimes risk-
ing the penalties of absenteeism—like football fans today—
to be sure of a seat, and sometimes permitting managements to face bankruptcy for lack of their support.

To understand these conflicting stances, we must constantly remind ourselves that theatre is essentially a social
art enhancing and reflecting religious and political beliefs
and moral and social concerns as well as literature, music,
painting and dance. Indeed, so wide are its terms of reference that theatre has often been used as a metaphor for
life itself (see pp. 57 and 157). As such, the theatre is itself
a language, coupling verbal with visual images, which
assists humanity to understand itself—to define its
culture—rather than a craft for the gifted few or a recreation for a privileged elite.

Where then should we begin? With dramatists? With
actors? Or with audiences? Theatre's origins are wrapped
in mystery. Like all mysteries, this one is capable of a
variety of solutions, all of them speculative and hypotheti-
cal; none of them subject to proof. Where the most primitive of societies are concerned, drama rarely if ever comes
to be accepted as an organized art-form without first gradu-
ating from community rituals involving song, dance, or
both together. Indeed, in some African, Asian, and
Polynesian countries, drama remains firmly anchored
today in folklore and is expressed through highly stylized
chant, dance and instrumental accompaniment rather than
in scripted plays—in short, it remains a symbolic language
that helps the community to understand itself (see Plates
1 and 2 and Figs. 3, 4, 5 and 9). Even in the Christian Europe
of the early Middle Ages (which can hardly be described
as primitive) folk-dance and the choral liturgies of the
Roman Catholic Church supplied the dynamics out of
which all forms of scripted drama which have since become
familiar in the Western world were forged. Here, then, we
find our starting point in a world altogether without texts.
When these are added, they arrive as odes or hymns for
solo voice, for choric unison, and finally for antiphonal
exchange between soloist and chorus. It is where the words
of these antiphonal exchanges come to relate legendary or
historical events *which are then re-enacted* that we find ourselves finally confronted with dramatic art—an art that is
able both to instruct and entertain (see Fig. 11).

3. *Villagers at Mahekuku on the river Asaro, Papua, New
Guinea, pay homage in ritual dance to the God of the River who
saved their ancestors from disaster in battle. Legend relates that
when forced to retreat into the river, their pursuers at first thought
they had drowned; but when they emerged covered in grey mud,
they were assumed to be avenging ghosts. Terrified, their enemies
fled. The head-masks are carefully preserved, fresh mud being
applied each year to seal up cracks.*

It is at this same moment in time, when we first find
a narrative text being superimposed upon the skeletal structure of dance and song, that dramatic art begins to become
a contentious art-form as well as an obligatory social ritual,
both where public responses are concerned and in the
growth of rivalries between the performing artists themselves. Texts and the manner in which they are represented,
at least to the minds of the ruling caste, can quickly become
salacious, blasphemous, even subversive; and if this threat
to the status quo once starts to attract public suport, action
is taken to control or even to suppress them, together with
the actors who perform them, through threats of fines,
imprisonment and the closure of playhouses. Since the
play-text can quickly become an *agent-provocateur* by
operating as an instrument of propaganda for particular
moral crusades or for strictly political ends, it can thus as

easily become a divisive force in society as a unifying one. The public says that it knows what it likes, and this usually means it likes what it knows—the familiar, the safe, the soothing; it is disconcerted, if not actually frightened, by the unfamiliar, and especially by subject-matter (verbal and visual) which provokes, disturbs or shocks. It is usually at this point that leaders of Church and State alike take fright and seek to intervene through censorship and legislation (see Fig. 2).

Among the performing artists themselves, controversy normally arises out of disputes and rivalries about the balance to be aimed at, or to be maintained, between the component elements of dramatic art, and above all about who among the actors, playwrights, painters and musicians working in and for the theatre is entitled to take control of the direction in which dramatic art should move if it is both to keep pace with changing public attitudes and moods yet avoid interference (and the risk of suppression) from the ruling caste.

Aristotle, when writing his *Poetics* in the fourth century BC, placed spectacle at the bottom of his list of priorities for the composition of a tragedy. Since then, most actor-managers have tended to agree with him, not least because the provision of spectacle is invariably very expensive. There have been times, however, when the public has persuaded them to think otherwise. This occurred during the Renaissance when a group of Italian architects and painters (stretching from Brunelleschi and Leonardo da Vinci to Palladio and the Bibiena family) persuaded all the courts of Europe to replace open, thrust stages with proscenium-

5. *Polynesian Face Mask, 'Ocean Spirit', made out of fibre from tree bark and large leaves. The wearer does not self-consciously 'represent' the supernatural being since, for the community, that being exists and becomes embodied in the mask whenever it is animated by the performer. The mask is thus inviolable and strict rules govern its use.*

arched theatres equipped with changeable scenery. While this startling change must be attributed in part to these artists' own genius, the fact that most of the actors and writers whom they were serving were amateurs and theorists must also be reckoned with, since the degree of control which they could exercise over their scenic collaborators was far more hesitant and tentative than that normally imposed by professional actor managers (see pp. 103, 108). Another example, however, is to be found in the nineteenth century when change was actively promoted by professional actors and managers alike: this was occasioned by the steady advance of technology, especially in respect of stage-lighting and machinery. In this instance, spectacle was permitted to take precedence over almost everything else in the service of both popular melodrama and revivals of Shakespeare's plays (see pp. 182 and 195). This development, accompanied by further progress in optical science, led inexorably towards the invention of the motion-picture camera and projector, and thus to the advent of cinema as a rival to the theatre itself.

Musicians and composers have rarely challenged the dominance of actors and dramatists in the theatre; but when they did so during the seventeenth century their action resulted in the creation of two new dramatic genres as distinct from one another as from spoken drama—opera

4. *A village masquerade near Ibadan, Nigeria. Daytime masquerades are used to promote goodwill and to encourage social solidarity. Night-time masquerades are used to seek out evil and to prevent its extension by threatening or punishing guilty individuals.*

and ballet. Yet these innovations may justly be regarded as a reversion, derived from sixteenth-century attempts to revive Greek tragedies, to the primacy of song and dance within primitive dramatic ritual rather than as a deliberate escape from the tyranny of contemporary playwrights or actors (see pp. 102–3 and 152–3). Perhaps more influential on the subsequent development of theatre itself were the music-dramas of Richard Wagner during the latter half of the nineteenth century which caused every contributor to dramatic art, both at Bayreuth and elsewhere in the theatre, to re-evaluate his own position. This resulted in a succession of debates and practical experiments which in their turn led to the rejection of realistic pictorial scenery, and to a return in our own time to the frequent production of plays on thrust and arena stages instead of behind picture-frame proscenium arches (see Figs. 189, 202 and 204).

This leaves us with the claims of the playwright and the actor for pre-eminence where ultimate control of the theatre is concerned. Those of the dramatist must by any standards be considered as strong. The greatest names, from Aeschylus and Aristophanes onwards to such relatively recent figures as Ibsen, Chekhov, Shaw, O'Neill and Beckett, regardless of period, national frontiers, or language, provide the corner-stones of the whole complex fabric of theatrical art: editions and translations of their plays continue to proliferate: revivals continue to serve as challenges to actors, actresses, and directors. 'The play's the thing' as Hamlet so memorably remarked. Yet Hamlet, we must recall, also thought it necessary to discourse at some length on the art of acting and held the view, by implication if not overtly, that the play will fail if its actors lack talent or self-discipline, or at least fail to reveal its full potential. And who can honestly say that his creator, Shakespeare (himself a trained actor), was not correct in this assessment? Exponents of mime tell their own story in their own way, without words, in silence: a Marcel Marceau can hold any audience's attention for at least an hour with no help from anyone else, and with only a few suggestive items of costume and scenic properties to assist him. The *Commedia dell'Arte* troupes, who took the courts of Europe by storm in the seventeenth and eighteenth centuries, improvised their dialogue around the most rudimentary of scripts (see pp. 110–12); and in our own time it is again becoming customary for many 'fringe' groups to work from improvisations on a chosen theme and towards a final script with an author in attendance as recorder, rather than to wait for plays to be submitted to them which have to be rejected because of casting difficulties, scenic costs, or other problems outside that company's control (see p. 260).

To the layman, therefore, it may seem that the respective claims of dramatist and actor for dominance in the theatre's development are finely balanced; but there is another factor to be taken into account, and that is the constant rivalry, bordering at times on ill-concealed hostility, which has characterized their mutual dependence, one upon the other, over more than two thousand years. In general, it would seem that actors have rarely cultivated the allegiance of dramatists for their merits as poets, philosophers, moralists, or satirists; rather have they judged them on their abilities as story-tellers and as portrayers of characters: this is particularly true of oriental drama (see Chapter 1). Since actors need self-confidence above all else, it is understandable that the dramatic potential of leading parts has frequently outweighed other considerations in determining in Western countries whether a play is accepted for production or rejected. A dramatist can only hope to turn the tables on the actors when the previous success and reputation of several of his earlier plays is such that managements feel obliged to compete against each other to secure the right to perform the next one: as a novice he must depend upon the actors' judgements and accept such cuts or other adjustments to his text as they elect to make with as good a grace as he can. Modern copyright laws have made his position more secure than it used to be; but against that he has to reckon on the ever-increasing repertoire of earlier plays on which no copyright fees are payable—as far as both actors and audiences are concerned, many of these, having stood the test of time as proven successes, contain none of the risk elements that accompany the first production of a new play.

These factors, in my view, finally tip the scales in the actor's favour; and for this reason, within this book the primary viewpoint adopted throughout will be that of actors seeking to collaborate with writers ranging from poets to journalists, with musicians, dancers, painters and technicians, and often with businessmen, in a constant attempt to forecast what audiences hope for from the public forum that is the theatre. This will not resolve any of the debates surrounding the primacy of the text, of interpretation of a title role and character relationships, or of pictorial illusion; but it will at least offer the reader a consistency of approach (impossible from any other viewpoint) to the organic development over the centuries of shifting theatrical forms and conventions which, when single aspects are taken separately, often appear to be contradictory and confusing.

Since actors, however, depend on audiences to support their performances, the last word must be reserved for them. Their reactions, which range, as already remarked, between idolatry and contempt, are the most delicate of all theatrical commodities and can never be taken for granted. Since all audiences are called upon to interpret what the performers are attempting to convey, dramatic art, whether in terms of simple mimicry or of more complicated action accompanied by dialogue, requires the awakening of imaginative powers in those who watch and listen as well as within the performers: otherwise this entire game of make-believe appears idiotic.

Here, marked differences arise between individual members of the same audience: what is funny to one can fail to amuse another, and what evokes tears in one can be dismissed as trite or pretentious by yet another. Slowly, as society develops, its receptive powers and standards change: more is demanded of the performers in direct proportion to the experience of the spectator and listener. Ultimately, what audiences come to expect of actors is virtuosity: and this applies both to characterization and to technique, the manner in which characterization is conveyed. And here we reach the frontier that separates the amateur from the professional.

Amateurs are wholly free to experiment in any direction they wish, since their livelihood is not dependent on the reward; what they need is a fellow enthusiast who is sufficiently affluent to finance their performances without regard to profit or loss. Whether that patron is a king, a bishop, a banker, a businessman, a university or a subscription list of interested well-wishers is immaterial. It is amateurs, therefore, who most frequently have pioneered those radical changes of approach to theatre practice that have resulted in what posterity has recognized to be major shifts in direction. However, many amateur groups lack the talent or the leadership to do more than copy professional example, and consequently achieve little more than pale imitations of standard professional practice despite the time and energy devoted to rehearsal.

Whereas amateurs normally prepare a performance either to put some theory to the test of practical enactment or in the expectation that friends and neighbours may be persuaded to attend and enjoy it, the professional by contrast assesses both what he elects to do and how he does it in terms of what he knows from long experience his audiences have come to expect of him. He is always conscious that his personal reputation and future employment are at stake, since he is aware that anything wholly new may displease, or disappoint, or shock his audiences and thus transform tested supporters into disenchanted or even hostile absentees. He must thus experiment, if he so chooses, with care.

Amateurs often castigate professionals for their conservatism and their failure to take risks with audiences or to experiment with new styles of writing and production, but fail to take any serious account of the economic factors that determine their position. Professionals, likewise, often fear and despise amateurs because they seem able to indulge themselves and their fantasies by presenting plays for the fun of it without any risk to their personal security or standard of living. The truth is, where audiences are concerned, that the one has been as necessary to society as the other in the past, and will continue to be so if standards of performance are to be maintained or improved.

It is in this way that theatrical representation itself is supplied with fresh dynamics to keep it closely in touch with changing patterns of religious, political, social, and aesthetic thought in daily life. It will therefore be my major objective as the story of theatre unfolds within this book to illustrate this principle in action. To do so, it will be necessary first to consider primitive societies the world over, where dramatic art did not exist but had to be formulated as a means to answer practical needs that could be met in no other way.

PART I

COMMUNITIES AND THEIR GODS

Introduction

. . . creation of new aesthetic forms, including those of worship, has been the most fundamentally productive of all forms of human activity.

Whoever creates new artistic conventions has found methods of interchange between people about matters that were incommunicable before. The capacity to do this has been the basis of the whole of human history.

(Prof. J. Z. Young, *An Introduction to the Study of Man*, 1971, p. 519.)

Faced with the terrors of the supernatural—volcanoes, typhoons, hurricanes, plagues, floods, drought—or any other threat to the normal cycle of birth, growth and pro-creation, primitive communities the world over have turned their own instinctive response to rhythm and melody to use as a channel of communication between themselves and the mysterious intangible forces in nature whose help and protection they strive to enlist and whose ill-will and anger they fear and hope to deflect. Song and dance thus come to be employed to summon these awesome beings, whether conceived of as spirits, gods or devils, into the presence of the community, to present them with suitable gifts as thank-offerings or propitiative sacrifices, and then to release them again.

These spirits are endowed with forms appropriate to their environment. Thus the Yoruba tribe in Nigeria see the two great rivers which flow through their region, the Ogun and the Oshun, as a god and a goddess respectively, the former epitomized by a python, the latter by a fish. Jupiter, the Roman equivalent to the Greek Zeus, assumed the forms of a bull, an eagle and a swan to seduce the ladies he sought to possess, but he was as often to be seen in thunder, lightning and mountain-tops. The Germans and the Celts, like the Japanese, regarded large trees as the home of the gods—a feature still preserved in the reverence accorded to the pine tree which invariably stands brooding over the stage in Noh plays (Fig. 14).

These beings and many others, normally aloof and invisible yet ruling over human destiny through the annual courses of the sun, moon and stars, and the alteration of day

and night, of summer and winter, cannot be invoked at will. As the witches in *Macbeth* observe, the time must be right and the place fitting. Mere mortals must also prepare themselves for the exceptional honour of a visitation and organize an appropriate reception. Thus rituals, being functional, take shapes specifically designed to invoke, to receive and to dismiss; and these rituals deploy action—movement, gesture and song—to achieve their objectives. These actions are thus, in an important sense, descriptive. In other words the design of the ritual is strictly practical and is choreographed intuitively with the aim of magic simulation, first to obtain the attention and then to retain the interest of the particular god or goddess whose help is wanted. Strongly accented rhythmic drumming accompanied by stamping dance steps is a frequent feature of the initial invocation. Circular dances reflect the proper continuity of the natural order, while reversal or other changes of pattern within the cyclic dance simulate regular and natural changes from dry to wet seasons, day to night, and so on. Among the most striking examples of this process is the simulated death, revival and resurrection of a god or hero which was central not only to the cult of Osiris in ancient Egypt but to the king-games and May-games of Western Europe which underpin the so-called mummers' plays (Fig. 6). This phenomenon will be more fully dealt with in Chapter 4. The whole body is put to use in creating these rituals. This may include use of the voice but not necessarily language, human words often being deemed too trite and banal to impress a god.

No texts accompany dance drama among the tribes of

6. *The Marshfield Mummers' Play, Gloucestershire, performed annually in the village High Street on 26 December. The costumes consist of strips of paper (frequently newspaper) attached to sackcloth. The headdresses serve to conceal the identity of the villagers who perform it. This scene depicts the death of the hero, who will shortly be revived by the doctor.*

Papua, New Guinea, or that of Indian communities in North and South America today: nor did they ever form a significant component of the folk-festivals of European countries in the centuries immediately preceding or subsequent to the birth of Christ. Yet like all communities in a similar state of development in the remoter parts of the third world today, they could sing, they could dance and they could disguise themselves; and indeed they did so in order to celebrate special occasions which they regarded as being of paramount importance to their survival. Their hopes and fears within a hostile environment were predominantly reflected in war and hunting games and in courtship and fertility games (Figs. 3, 7 and 9). These reflections can still be seen in the sword-dances, morris dances, plough and king games of European folk-festivals. With the passing of time some primeval enemies with supernatural power and godlike attainments may have been transmuted into more tangible opponents; but others, in the shapes of ghosts, demons, devils and witches culled from a world of imaginative fantasy, were very real for country people, and persisted everywhere as hauntingly alluring presences: some of them still do in horror films and space epics on television screens today, albeit in rather different forms and attire.

Moreover, dance drama in primitive communities fulfilled another function, for there was a great sense of pleasure (and subsequently of well-being) which derived from participation in these propitiatory rituals. This stemmed in part from preparation and anticipation and in part from a sense of release and relief. Both provided strong incentives for annual repetition. This offers an instance of familiarity, far from breeding contempt, inviting careful preservation and transmission from parent to child, and so to grandchild. Within this family chain-response the ultimate objective which inspires and informs all these dance dramas time out of mind thus comes ultimately to be fulfilled.

Interpreting the wishes and intentions of the unseen and unpredictable presiding deities towards humankind calls for special skills. Here guesswork has to be tempered by an inner sensitivity or tact. Given an individual endowed with this quality in special measure, the figure of the witch-doctor, guru or priest emerges; an individual trusted to formulate the rituals and to conduct them; and, dependent on success, such an individual may be permitted to articulate the wishes of the group in what we call prayer, but which in the context of the dance might better be described as chant or song. And once this has been allowed, and found to be effective, it is natural enough for the other dancers to articulate key-words or phrases in repetitive unison. When this happens a balance comes to be struck between soloist and chorus; and a ritual that has reached this degree of sophistication warrants description as a dance drama. At this level the drama is likely to be evident in the story-line and in the several levels of meaning, both

7. *Horn dance, Abbots Bromley, Staffordshire, performed annually on the first Monday after 4 September. Despite the presence of such 'characters' as the bowman, the fool and the hobby-horse (centre, in cloak) this is a Morris Dance, not a play, as there is no text.*

explicit and implicit, that it expresses; but the verbal component will still be eclipsed by dance.

As I have already remarked, appropriate times and places are essential ingredients of sympathetic magic; so are costume and facial disguise. Nature itself will, therefore, dictate to any community wholly dependent on local agriculture for its survival the time, place and costume best suited to the performance of the ritual. In this way certain springs, pools, forest glades, caves and mountains acquire a special significance and are thought of as themselves possessing magic properties as the home of a *genius loci* or benign spirit and thus as 'holy'; or, if the spirit is regarded as spiteful, then as 'demonic' or 'bewitched'. In time, these 'holy' places come to be regarded as shrines within the local community—sacred groves in Italy and holy wells in Wales and Ireland are typical examples—and even become places of pilgrimage for other communities living at a distance. 'Bewitched' places are regarded as dangerous and are shunned.

Similarly, it is the moments of significant balance in time—the winter solstice when lengthening night gives way to lengthening daylight (and the opposite in summer), and the vernal and autumnal equinoxes—and the key moments in an agrarian calendar, when ploughing starts, seed is sown, and crops are harvested and marketed, that are chosen as requiring the blessing of the gods or as being suitable for rendering thanks to them (Fig. 8).

In such ways time, place and activity combine into a shared sense of occasion expressed by recourse to a festival with its own rituals. Holy day and holiday become synonymous: work ceases and the whole community joins in a common celebration distinguished by the performance of a dance drama specifically designed to reveal the significance of the occasion to participants and spectators alike.

The gods are summoned. They are informed of what is wanted and thanked in advance with gifts for their assistance. They are then formally released. The community returns to the normal routines of daily life and awaits the answers to their prayers and offerings (sacrifices). In Asia, Africa, Europe and the Americas enough evidence has been supplied by anthropologists to show that these ceremonies were broadly the same and represent the start of the story of theatre throughout the world (see Plate 14 and Figs. 3, 4, 5 and 9).

In the following four chapters the theatre's development

from these festive beginnings will be considered separately in Asia, Greece, Italy, and in Western and Northern Europe before and after the birth of Christ. Asia is taken first, not only because dance drama appears to have acquired a self-consciously theatrical shape in several eastern countries before it did so in Europe, but because its origins survive in India, China, South-East Asia and Japan in so easily identifiable a manner within its more modern forms.

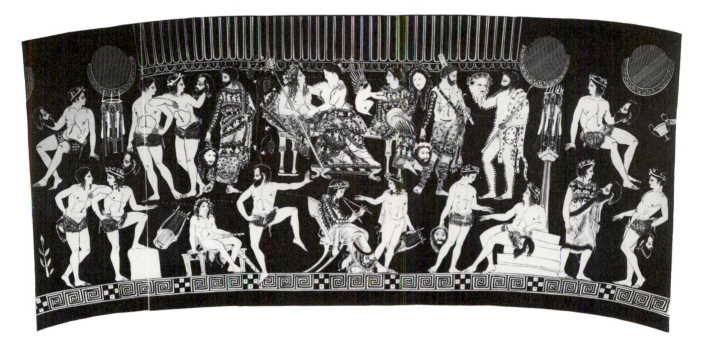

8. *Attic red-figured Pronomos vase, c.400 BC, depicting actors in a satyr-play carrying their masks and surrounding Dionysus and Ariadne (top centre). Among other characters are Heracles (holding a club), musicians, and the chorus of satyrs wearing fur trunks with phallus in front and tail behind. Naples, National Museum.*

9. *Warriors dancing at a cremation ceremony in Bali. High priority is accorded in all the animist religions of countries in or bordering the Pacific Ocean to honouring ancestors (whether long or newly deceased) and to initiation ceremonies: the former protect the community, the latter grant admission to it.*

	ASIA	EUROPE
10th century BC 9th	Hindu temple rituals embrace dance drama in India	(?) Dance dramas in Egypt and the Hittite Empire
8th	Establishment of secular theatrical entertainment in India	(?) Dance dramas introduced at agricultural festivals in Greece
7th 6th	(?) Indian dance drama reaches Persia, Egypt, Israel and Turkey	
5th	Confucius establishes Buddhism in China	Cleisthenes introduces democratic government to Athens (510) Thespis active at City Dionysia First prize at City Dionysia awarded to Aeschylus (484), Sophocles (464), and to Euripides (441) Lenaea established in Athens (*c*.460) Production of Aristophanes' *The Clouds* (423), *Lysistrata* (411) Athens defeated by Sparta in Peloponnesian War (431–404)
4th	Composition of *Artha Sāstra* in Sanskrit	Philip of Macedon conquers Greece (338) Aristotle writes the *Poetics* (*c*.330) Menander introduces New Comedy (*c*.310)
3rd	Indian drama reaches China	Atellan farce reaches Rome (*c*.250) Plautus writes his plays (*c*.210–184)
2nd 1st	Indian drama reaches Burma	Terence writes his plays (*c*.170–159) Pompey builds first public theatre in Rome (*c*.80) Horace writes his *Art of Poetry* (*c*.10)
1st century AD	Indian drama reaches Sri Lanka and Indonesia	Death of Augustus, first Emperor, in Rome (14) Seneca writes his plays (*c*.25–65) Vitruvius writes his ten books on architecture (*c*.70)
2nd 3rd	Composition of *Nātya Sāstra* in Sanskrit	Tertullian writes *De spectaculis* (*c*.195)
4th 5th		Conversion of Emperor Constantine to Christianity (313) Roman legions quit Britain (409) Alaric the Visigoth sacks Rome (410); theatres closed St Augustine writes *The City of God* (*c*.420)
6th		Christianity reaches Scotland from Ireland (563) Gregory the Great elected Pope (590) Christianity reaches Southern England (597)
7th 8th	Emperor Ming Huang establishes a training school for actors in China, the Pear Garden Muslim invasion of India begins	Moors defeated at Poitiers (732) and retreat into Spain
9th 10th	Public playhouses established in Chinese towns Sanskrit drama suppressed in Northern India	Charlemagne crowned Roman Emperor (800) *Concordia Regularis* of St Ethelwold, Bishop of Winchester, prescribed for use in all Benedictine monasteries (975) First liturgical music drama presented as Introit at Mass on Easter Sunday (*c*.975) at St Gall, Switzerland
11th 12th 17th	Zen Buddhism reaches Japan Emergence of Nōh drama in Japanese temple rituals Emergence of Kabuki theatre in Japanese towns	Norman Conquest of Britain (1066)

1

Oriental Drama and Theatre: Origins, Experiment and Development

1 FOUNDATIONS

As in Europe, so in India and China the first records of dramatic art are to be traced in a context of religious observances. There, however, its primary features can still be seen to lie in dance, song and gesture with a clarity and certainty now altogether missing from the historical debris out of which the origins of drama in both Hellenistic and Christian Europe have had to be reconstructed. This has occurred because the cultural life of all societies in the Eastern hemisphere (with the exception of Japan which was penetrated by Jesuit missionaries late in the sixteenth century) was protected against confrontation with that of Christian industrialized societies in the West until relatively late in the nineteenth century; and eager though Eastern countries have been since then to acquire Western technology, they have reacted far less positively—indeed, in many respects have shied away from, or elected to shun— the accompanying behavioural patterns of Western peoples, including those relating to all the arts. In the case of dramatic art, spoken and written language have provided another, far more tangible and effective protective barrier since it is hardly worth substituting Western theatrical forms for native ones when the content remains unintelligible and untranslatable: and attractive as Westerners have found oriental drama when actually confronted with it, its conventions have remained strange and unfathomable to all but specialists. Much Eastern drama, therefore, has survived with many of its earliest elements safely preserved, like some animated museum treasure, which today's spectator may still view swaying, gyrating and gesticulating, notwithstanding the many alterations and additions that the passing of some two thousand years of local history has imposed upon it and its practitioners.

In all parts of the East nature and ancestor worship formed the basis of religious observance, and the dance drama that developed in its service was regarded in part as a votive offering and in part as a celebration of major seasonal festivals. Its forms, moreover, evolved from an ideal of attempting to interpret existence by recourse to aesthetic imagery rather than by representation. The earliest initiatives appear to have been taken in India some two thousand years before an organized theatre was established in Athens. From India, models then spread slowly southeast through Burma into Indonesia, and northwards through China to Korea and Japan. Hindu in origin and an essential component of Indian temple ritual, dance drama had already reached a sufficiently high degree of sophistication in China by the time of Confucius (551– 479 BC), and was classified and codified within his system of being; but it only reached Japan late in the twelfth century AD in the wake of a Buddhist revival associated simultaneously with the Zen sect and with the cult of the sun goddess, Shinto. In the West an increasing body of scholarly opinion is becoming convinced that it also spread north-west from India into the Middle East and Egypt at least as early as the sixth century BC, and was firmly rooted there for the armies of Alexander the Great to encounter and absorb when they occupied all those countries stretching from Turkey through Syria and Iraq to Persia and Afghanistan late in the fourth century BC. Some revision of received opinion on the development of drama in the West during the Hellenistic era and throughout the later Roman Empire may become necessary if this notion is translated from speculation into proven fact.

2 INDIA

Everywhere in the East, dance drama was an aristocratic activity. Its rituals were prescribed by literate and elite patrons, and their practice was consigned to a section of the community, or caste, dedicated to total mastery of this art. This situation has been succinctly summed up by A. C. Scott:

> Dance and drama in India were the dynamic accessories of a culture entirely dependent on a grand scheme of hierarchical ritual affecting every phase of living and given total realization in the community through the institution of caste. As the supreme celebration of ritual it can be said without exaggeration that dance has there attained qualities of dramatic intensity unsurpassed in any civilization.
>
> (*The Theatre in Asia*, 1972, p. 29)

Within Hindu culture Brahmin theology had decreed that a divine creator had divided society into four distinct castes—poet-priests, warrior-chiefs, ordinary people (including artisans, farmers and soldiers) and slave-workers. Dancers, actors and musicians thus came to be regarded as slave-workers in the service of the priests and warrior-chiefs, but could also claim to be 'married to a deity' (Fig. 10). This qualification, however, did not rescue them from being regarded as the social inferiors of virtually everyone else and tolerated, along with beggars, pimps and whores, as necessary evils within society.

While still in temple service the dancing girls, given this status, had no option but to accept the role of courtesans; but in that capacity they enjoyed the protection of their patrons, lived in relative luxury and could acquire wealth. Their training was rigorous, often starting at the age of five or six and lasting some seven years. In this way alone could they hope to master a sign-language of footsteps, body movement and gesture accompanied by specific instrumental music and songs comprehensive enough to communicate through emotional experience the secrets of existence itself. This endeavour altogether to transcend the bonds of normal terrestrial existence and to free the mind and the spirit to enter into direct communion with the creative and controlling forces of nature itself is perhaps the most important of all differences between both the objectives and the methods of Eastern and Western dramatic art.

In India most of these requirements and accomplishments were set down in writing in two Sanskrit books that have survived, the *Artha Śāstra* (The Doctrine of Prosperity) and more especially the *Nātya Śāstra* (The Doctrine of Dramatic Art): both are of great antiquity, the former dating from the fourth century BC and the latter from the second century AD, but both are actually compilations by several hands assembled over several centuries. The *Nātya Śāstra* is divided into thirty-six sections which include discourses on the origins and architecture of theatres; religious rites accompanied by dramatic observances; the nature of the transcendental aesthetic experience aspired to; melody, rhythm and instrumentation; speech and metre; choreography; characterization; and a final explanation of how actors fell from the highest to the lowest caste in society. It is a very difficult document for Westerners to read and interpret since written language itself becomes a barrier between what its authors aspired to express and what they succeed in expressing: for all that, its survival supplies a vitally informative manual for anyone today who attempts to account for, and to explain, the growth of dramatic art in both classical and medieval Europe where the nearest equivalent documents are Aristotle's *Poetics*, Vitruvius's *De Architectura* and St Ethelwold's *Concordia Regularis*, which will be discussed in Chapters 2, 3 and 4 respectively.

In India, as in Europe, what was fashionable in courtly circles spread slowly outwards into society, a fact which accounts for the growth of a more popular style of dance drama, carried by itinerant families of dancers, musicians and actors into villages to assist in the celebration of local festivals and to permit men of high caste to entertain their

10. *Nataraja. South Indian statuette of Siva, Lord of Dance, portraying the creation and dissolution of the cosmos in the rhythms of dance. Eleventh century AD. Paris, Musée Guimet.*

friends on festive, domestic occasions. In this context the dancers allied themselves with the ever-popular and highly professional local story-tellers, and allowed one particular artist, the clown, a degree of freedom scarcely imaginable within the environments of the temple or the palace. From the story-teller derive the heroic and romantic elements of Indian popular drama, and from the clown the elements of comedy, farce and satire (Fig. 11). Episodic narrative thus came to be universally accepted as a norm, together with a mixture of tragi-comic and melodramatic incident drawn from myth and legend. Strict differentiation of dramatic genre along Greek or Roman lines was neither known nor sought after. Happily a large number of plays in ancient Sanskrit survive to corroborate this, most of which have marked affinities with Greek myths and German fairy stories. In Bengal all dramatic art came under attack as the Muslim invaders from the North succeeded in retaining their hold on the territory they had begun to occupy from the eighth century AD onwards, since Islam would not tolerate representation of the human form in art. The salient traditions of northern drama, however, survived in the song-dance drama known as *Kathakali*, associated with the temples of Kerala in southern India which most recent scholars now regard as having been more deeply rooted in popular folk art than in the more sophisticated poetic drama of northern palaces and temples (see Plate 2 and Fig. 18). This took its present form in the seventeenth century, and is now a major tourist attraction.

British rule in India brought with it, late in the eighteenth century, a revival of interest in ancient Sanskrit drama. Antiquarian research, however, became confused during the nineteenth century with Western ideas about playwriting and theatrical representation. This confusion arose in part because English-educated Indians themselves preferred to experiment with Shakespeare's plays in Bengali translation which they presented to high-caste audiences in wealthy homes. It also arose among thousands of less well-educated Indians who flocked to crude adaptations of Victorian melodramas (see Chapter 12) which had a more obvious visual appeal. Thus when modern India's most distinguished philanthropist-philosopher-poet, Sir Rabindranath Tagore (1816–1941), started to write plays in 1892, it was within a strange hybrid tradition of ancient, native dance-drama flavoured by Sanskrit plays and more modern Western imports. Two of his later plays, *The King of the Dark Chamber* (1910) and *The Post Office* (1912), attracted considerable attention in the West; but his efforts to found a school of indigenous Indian drama had to face the competition of imported British and American films.

Since Independence, the rapid growth of an Indian film industry has come to pose a severe threat to the survival of any live theatre other than dance drama.

3 CHINA

In China concubines were regarded as acceptable additions to the extended family, itself the sheet-anchor of Confucian society. As a justification for their existence, most were trained to serve their masters as musicians and dancers, professions banned to ordinary women. The practice of foot-binding of women in infancy, however, became a desperate impediment to success in acting, thus allowing men, whose muscular control over their bodies was inevitably far better, to dominate the theatrical profession at an early date. Although originally dedicated to the service of the Buddhist temples, actors (as in India) were welcomed by agricultural communities in China, notwithstanding their degraded social status, to adorn major festivals and provide them with a sense of magic and excitement that exactly matched the nature of the occasion celebrated. Chinese festivals were geared to the lunar calendar, starting with the New Year and proceeding through the Spring Festival (dedicated as much to ancestors as to fertility) and the Midsummer or Dragon Boat Festival, to the Festivals of August and September Moons which corresponded with harvest and the marketing of its fruits. This engendered a competitive spirit among villages, the relative wealth of each thus determining to some extent the status and calibre of the troupe of actors it could afford to invite.

As in Athens in the fifth century BC, the rich footed the bills; the poor attended as of right (see p. 39). To this extent at least, the despised caste of actors can be said to have fulfilled the transcendental ideals of their profession by uniting whole communities that were normally sharply divided, both in rank and role in daily life, in a common act of celebration. Standards of professional discipline and corresponding virtuosity in their craft compensated, in the eyes of popular audiences, for any misgivings entertained about the moral probity of actors. Provided the entertainment offered lived up to expectation, all else was forgiven—even privately admired and envied as has often been the case elsewhere.

Tradition played a dominant role in shaping the Chinese theatre, as one might expect given Confucian respect for ancestors and heads of families in real life. The extended family, moreover, helped to stereotype character roles in a manner that made each familiar and instantly recognizable to audiences. Some of these resemble those stock types familiar to Western audiences from Plautine farce and the *Commedia dell'Arte*—the government official (Dottore),

11. *Chinese story-teller made up as a clown.*

Rome; but the Chinese, like the dancers of southern India, came to admit painted faces (*hua lien*), where the choice and use of colours was codified to illustrate character—white, for example, for cowardice or cunning, black for fierceness and crudity, red for vigour or loyalty. Gods had gold faces, devils green ones. Several colours could be used on a single face, each chosen to depict an aspect of a complex character (see Plate 3).

Granted a clear-cut cast-list of typed character roles, each of whom was instantly identifiable without recourse to literacy because recognizable through stage-costume and make-up, the stories which these characters peopled and narrated took second place to the degree of virtuosity with which the actors fulfilled their respective functions in these stories. Very little has survived therefore of what we might

12. *Japanese nomadic acrobats and musicians. A page from Hokusai's* Manga *(vol. 10) in the library of the University of Bristol.*

the warrior (Capitano), the patriarchal merchant (Pantalone), the clever peasant Harlequin (Arlecchino), the flirtatious maid (Columbine) (see pp. 45–6 and 110–12): others were particular to Chinese society, most notably the matriarchal mother-in-law, the courtesan and the demons.

By the eighth century AD training schools had been established in China with regimes as taxing as those in India and embracing likewise the skills of the story-teller and the clown as extensions to the basic training in music, dance and gesture (Fig. 11). Acrobatic and pugilistic skills acquired a special pre-eminence in Chinese theatres, but these too required long and arduous practice (Figs. 12 and 13). The most famous training school in China was that established by the T'ang Emperor Ming Huang in 720 and known as the 'Pear Garden'.

The narrative component of Chinese drama was sub-divided into categories, the earliest being devoted to stories of gods and ancestors with a patriotic flavour: later, plays devoted to more recent history were admitted to the repertoire, these being sub-divided into those dealing with military events and those concerned with civil affairs. Use of masks characterized the earliest plays, as in Greece and term great dramatic literature. Pantomimic skill was called upon to define place, time and predicament; song, dance, gymnastics and swordsmanship to define sentiment and emotion. What Chinese acting set out to portray above all else was the very essence of being the human or supernatural character whom the actor sought to impersonate.

In such circumstances scenery was neither needed nor supplied. A few basic stage-properties—a table, a stool, a chair, a hobby horse, a sword, a pole to serve as broom, oar, agricultural implement, or cudgel—sufficed: the use made of them in terms of bodily control, and consequent definition of both action and motivation, was what counted. Music was important but simple. A small orchestra of a drummer, a flautist, and players of castanets, gongs and a stringed instrument sat on the stage, as did the suppliers of stage properties who introduced and removed them as the story required (Fig. 13).

As in medieval Europe, most aristocratic families in China had come by the thirteenth and fourteenth centuries to possess private troupes of actors, many of whom had been recruited from amongst their own servants and then handed over to a professional especially hired to train them (see pp. 87, 88). This practice spread later to those merchants who had invested their wealth in land. These developments led directly to the building of theatres both in private houses and in the brothel districts of the towns.

With the establishment of these theatres during the thirteenth and fourteenth centuries came the development of structured plays conforming to acknowledged rules of composition and involving familiar, stereotyped characters; but the siting of these theatres in the pleasure districts of the cities also ensured that the appeal of these plays

---

13. *Detail from an early Chinese painting* A City of Cathay *depicting a theatre built in a temple courtyard by Chin Ying. Taiwan, Collection of the National Palace Museum.*

would remain rooted in hedonistic recreation rather than develop along literary lines into dramas of political or social criticism. Tea, wine and food were served throughout performances which began around midday and lasted until evening.

As trade and industry provided the merchant class during succeeding centuries with the funds to finance training schools in association with the theatres (admission being restricted to boys), so distinctive regional styles began to emerge, like those of regional cuisine. The most highly reputed were those of Soochow in central China, Canton on the eastern seaboard, and the capital, Peking. The Peking style finally achieved pre-eminence in the nineteenth century, and it was in this form that it began to attract the attention of Western travellers.

What mattered to Chinese theatre-goers then remained what had always stimulated their passion for play-acting—the virtuosity of the performers. All the conventions of costume, make-up, posture, gesture, singing, dancing and gymnastics were intimately known to play-goers. They thus attended every performance as highly informed critics, and their interest lay primarily in the actors' success in co-ordinating all the skills required of them into an aesthetically refined, harmonious and exciting ensemble.

4 JAPAN

Japan remained isolated from continental Asia until late in the twelfth century. Between two and three centuries later it had absorbed as much of Chinese culture (which it had for long greatly admired) as it felt it needed and was ready to establish a culture particular to its own history, local environment and climate. This process was grounded on Japan's own preference for a military oligarchy governing under the formal, but largely powerless, figurehead of an Emperor. It was hastened in part by the missionary zeal of the Zen Buddhists whose faith rested on intuitive enlightenment achieved through both meditative and physical exercises, and whose ethic favoured the advancement of a philosophical basis for the claims of the ruling warrior class; and in part by the growth of the cult of the sun goddess, Shinto, with its simple reversion to nature worship. Of these two activating forces, Shintoism was the more important to the development of theatrical art since it appealed primarily to the isolated imperial court in Kyoto while leaving the more pragmatic *Shogun*, or warrior governor, and his henchmen in Edo (the modern Tokyo) impervious to its refinements. A compromise was found in a general acceptance of Confucionism with its emphasis upon the family and, as a variant peculiar to Japan, on

14. *Japanese Noh stage with pine-tree and an actor in the play* Shoki. *Print by Kogyo (1869–1927) published in 1899. University of Bristol Theatre Collection.*

loyalty to kith and kin. Out of these warrior aesthetics the Noh drama was later to be born in the fifteenth century (Fig. 14). This represents an improbable but actual fusion of sincerely devotional court ethics with irreligious urban values—values which accorded the status of high priests to the courtesans, dancers and puppeteers of a folk-religion as popular and pervasive as the modern American cult of Hollywood or Elvis Presley at Gracelands, Memphis, Tennessee. It is worth noticing here an interesting correspondence between East and West in a similar fusion of the monastic and secular cultures that had been achieved in Christian Europe some three centuries earlier (see pp. 90-4).

Noh, like its Indian and Chinese antecedents, was temple based; but its development was matched by the growth of an uninhibited secular theatre more pertinent to the bourgeois hurly-burly of city life; and out of this sensual, mercantile ethic the rival popular drama known as Kabuki evolved alongside a puppet theatre which, on grounds of relative costs alone, proved to be a tough rival in attracting public audiences.

Long before the fourteenth century, however, the stratification of Japanese society which accompanied the adoption of neo-Confucian social theory resulted, as in China, in dancers, musicians and actors being classed with courtesans and brothel keepers, and segregated by law from performing or residing in areas of town favoured by the other classes—notably the military and civil administrators and the artisans and merchants. Noh actors, however, by their attachment to a temple, freed themselves from this degraded social status. Training schools and family protectionism helped further to bestow a sense of professional pride upon them, an elitist tendency in itself that could only be enhanced by imperial patronage. Women were finally banned from the stage in Japan at the start of the seventeenth century and so, shortly afterwards, were boys. Thenceforth all acting, in both Noh and Kabuki plays, became a profession exclusive to adult males (Fig. 15a, b).

Kabuki, as a theatrical form, developed in the seventeenth century, and out of the merchant classes' taste for female impersonations (Fig. 16). The virtuosity of the deception, down to the minutest of mannerisms, quickly became all important: the rest of the troupe of actors existed to support the impersonators. Although treated by the government as social outcasts, Kabuki actors (provided they lived, trained, and worked within their own class) were idolized by their audiences.

Kabuki theatres, although adapted from Noh models, were soon equipped with a distinctive runway projecting obliquely from the stage into the auditorium and known as the Flower Walk (Fig. 17). Machinery followed, including a revolving stage and stage-traps.

Kabuki companies maintained a team of resident playwrights (and assistants) all of whom knew the actors intimately and were expected to provide material that suited their respective talents. Each had his particular duties (from compiling the script to copying actors' parts) prescribed for him. This is understandable once it is appreciated that a play was expected to last for some seven or eight hours and to incorporate up-to-the-minute topical material. Given the virtually unchanging nature of the stage-conventions and audience expectancies, it proved relatively easy to compose new scripts or to alter and adapt old ones at speed, since what mattered was always that the team of writers should provide the actors with an appropriate vehicle within which to display their virtuosity.

The most serious threat to the survival of both Noh and Kabuki during our own century has arisen from the determination of the Japanese to emulate the West as a modern commercial empire: but in today's commercial world few people have the time to devote whole days and evenings to watching plays. With production costs constantly rising and reflected in seat prices, attendance figures

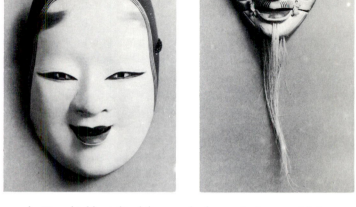

15a, b. Two highly stylized face-masks for use in Japanese Noh plays. Note the string-hinged mouthpiece for the male character. University of Bristol Theatre Collection.

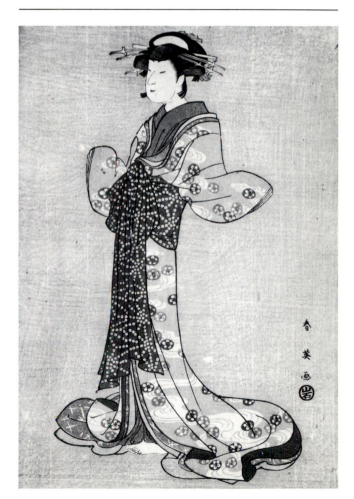

16. The actor Nakayota Tomisabur impersonating a courtesan, O'Karu, in a Japanese Kabuki play, 1795. Hawaii, Honolulu Academy of Arts, Michener Collection.

17. *Japanese Kabuki theatre. Note the projecting thrust-stage with spectators on three sides; the musicians and property-men at the back, and the 'flower-walk' giving access to the stage from the dressing-room through the audience at the front. Print by Toyokouni. (Compare Fig. 204.)*

encountered on arrival in the fifteenth century and after (Fig. 9). Once again it was the temple rather than the market-place that provided the principal environment in which this art developed in all these countries. And once again it was a Buddhist view of life which this art was direc-

18. *Cobra-capped, one-eyed, devil dancer's mask from Sri Lanka (Ceylon). London, British Museum.*

have fallen proportionately. This has produced a financial crisis which industrial sponsorship and government subsidy have thus far combined to contain. Films, television and sport, however, have also combined to make the conventions of both styles of theatre appear old-fashioned and irrelevant to the young. This is the most serious threat of all, since this is a theatre that has always depended on the active engagement of audiences in its conventions and in the careers of the principal performers.

5 SOUTH-EAST ASIA

During the early centuries AD, the influence of Indian dance drama spread slowly south-east through Ceylon, Burma and Cambodia to Malaysia and Indonesia, there to be grafted onto existing, indigenous cultures. Once again dance, rather than a written text, emerges as central to the varied forms of dramatic art which European explorers first

ted to serve and to express. These were the common factors that led to a refinement of native, but primitive, folk arts in the first instance, and which subsequently paved the way towards recognizably different natural expressions of this cultural inheritance. The prime movers in popularizing it were once again the story-teller and the clown, the former by supplying narrative and the latter by adding both a farcical and a satiric dimension to existing possibilities (Fig. 11).

Of all forms of dance drama derived from Indian models much the most popular proved to be *chaya-nataka*, shadow play. Here the story-teller usurped to himself all the skills of narrator, dancer, singer and mimic through the use of puppets or marionettes which he animated behind a silken screen (Fig. 19). All he had to do was to plunder such mythological epics as *Ramayana* or *Mahabharata* and bring episodes from them to life through figures, many of which were grotesque caricatures rather than characters, observed as shadow silhouettes in the auditorium, and to acquire an assistant to help out with intrumental music, songs and, on occasion, particularly difficult technical manipulation of the puppets or marionettes.

This genre of theatre began to develop in the seventh century AD alongside more courtly pantomimic plays for live actors; but the examples of both types of theatre which survive to us cannot be traced back further than the thirteenth century. Most of them, together with the styles of theatre in which they are performed, whether of Burmese, Thai or Javanese provenance, are of a much later date.

19. *Grotesque character in a Javanese shadow-puppet play, nineteenth century. London, British Library.*

6 CORRESPONDENCES IN EARLY ORIENTAL AND EUROPEAN THEATRICAL PRACTICES

Historical analogies are always dangerous and should never be used as direct parallels: nevertheless when affinities are clearly recognizable, it is useful to take note of them. In this case the affinities between religious observances on the one hand and social attitudes on the other in respect of actors and acting in Asia and in Europe before AD 1000 are both numerous and clear enough to warrant comparison. The results, when this is done, must remain speculative; but, at the very least, it can only be helpful to know that the ambivalent attitude adopted by the Christian Church towards actors and play-acting in Europe was not a unique phenomenon; that the classification of actors as social outcasts within the aristocratically organized regimes of Western nation-states along with 'rogues, vagabonds and sturdy beggars' (and even as 'caterpillars of the Commonwealth' or social parasites, as

they were described in Elizabethan England) was directly paralleled in all Asian countries from the outset, notwithstanding the major divergencies of particular national cultures; that the association of sexual licence and deviant practices with European entertainers of all descriptions likewise stigmatized dancers, musicians and actors from the earliest times in Asian countries; and that, in the East as well as in the West, a popular puppet theatre flourished alongside live theatre, which, while it tended to escape much of this moral opprobrium, was nevertheless still regarded as likely to be politically and socially subversive if not kept under constant surveillance, and its activities carefully regulated.

These common factors which are observable in the attitudes adopted by the governing classes towards dramatic art in both Europe and Asia are matched by others among the protective devices adopted by actors in self-defence. These include a direct turning of the tables by the oppressed on their oppressors as represented by temple service in the East and by working for the Roman Catholic Church in the West (see Chapters 4–6); by the assiduous cultivation of court patronage in the first instance and then that of the rival merchant princes when the balance of power began to shift (see Chapters 7–12); by the exploitation of festivals and fairs to win popular support for nomadic groups of performers; and by the formation of professional guilds (see Chapters 5 and 6). Comparison also opens up the fascinating possibility that the Asian poets and story-tellers whose recitals were accompanied by illustrative dance and mime had their counterparts in medieval Europe in the composers of the great romantic and chivalric romances and the troubadours who chanted or recited them at festive banquets in the Great Halls of palaces, castles and priories, accompanied by their dependent jongleurs as the fifteenth-century English poet, John Lydgate, suggests that they did (see pp. 86–7).

What early medieval Europe certainly lacked was any equivalent to the training schools established in the vicinity of Indian and Chinese courts and temples. It must be presumed, therefore, that acting in Christian Europe was at once a more fluid and dynamic art than in Asia since it was both more severely restricted to Calendar Festivals (and thus more likely to be intuitive and amateur) yet less severely restricted by years of disciplined apprenticeship (and thus freer to experiment with new ideas). When, therefore, we come to consider European theatre of the Early Middle Ages, it may prove rather easier than might have been otherwise the case to comprehend how the transition, after centuries of the barbarism which virtually obliterated all organized forms of theatre from the Graeco-Roman world, to those new forms of dramatic art cast in unmistakably Christian moulds was actually effected (see Chapter 4).

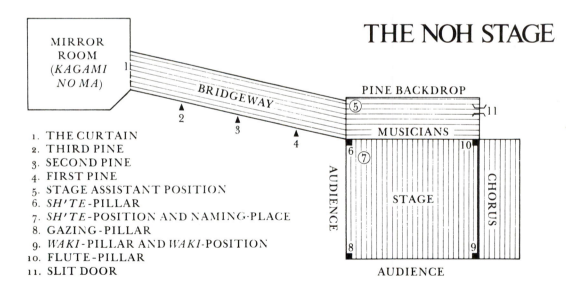

THE NOH STAGE

1. THE CURTAIN
2. THIRD PINE
3. SECOND PINE
4. FIRST PINE
5. STAGE ASSISTANT POSITION
6. *SH'TE*-PILLAR
7. *SH'TE*-POSITION AND NAMING-PLACE
8. GAZING-PILLAR
9. *WAKI*-PILLAR AND *WAKI*-POSITION
10. FLUTE-PILLAR
11. SLIT DOOR

2

Ancient Greece
and the Hellenistic World, 500–200 BC

1 FACTS AND SPECULATION

(a) **Facts:** The story of theatre in ancient Greece, at least as we have received it, is essentially that of the city of Athens in the fifth and fourth centuries BC. It is a story, moreover, dominated by five dramatists—three tragic and two comic—and by one theorist and critic.

It starts late in the sixth century with the authorization by the populist leader, Peisistratus, of a competition for the performance of tragic plays (rounded off by a satyr play devoted to lighter subject matter) as an integral part of the festival held each spring in honour of Dionysus, god of wine, youth and fertility—mythic spirit of energy, violence and action (Fig. 1). It then proceeds to the overthrow of Peisistratus's son, Hippias, and the introduction by Cleisthenes c.510 BC of a truly democratic form of government in Athens. In the course of his reforms, this festival quickly acquired a civic and political dimension to rival

its earlier religious significance, warranting formal recognition as the City Dionysia. It is against this background that the spectral figure of Thespis (was he a writer, an actor, a priest, or all three?) emerges from obscurity into the world of recorded history by winning the play competition in 534 BC.

Behind Thespis lay a number of agricultural festivals widely scattered over the whole country marked by singing, dancing, and mystic ceremonies that were in part religious and in part sexual and ecstatic, and possibly by satirical comic sketches (Fig. 8). No recorded facts, however, verbal or visual, about Thespis himself or any of these earlier activities can compare with the evidence supplied by the surviving texts of actual plays by Aeschylus (525–456 BC), Sophocles (496–406 BC), Euripides (c. 480–406 BC), Aristophanes (c. 448–380 BC), and Menander (342–292 BC), and by the writings about some of those plays by the philosopher and teacher Aristotle (384–322 BC): the evidence of

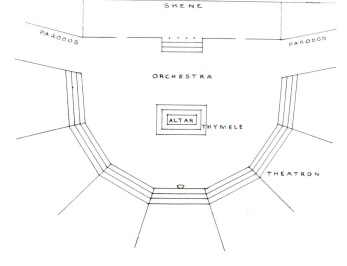

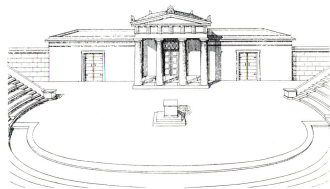

20a, b. Ground plan and elevation of a Greek theatre in Sophocles' time: reconstruction.

these texts is supplemented by a number of mosaics, vase-paintings and inscriptions, and by our knowledge that Athens was about to become the leader of an empire when these plays began to be written.

All these plays were acted, as we know from surviving inscriptions recording their production. All of them were associated with particular calendar festivals—notably those in honour of Dionysus—and thus look back in some sense towards a more primitive past: yet as all of them were first produced as entries to the annual competitions, they were thus products of a politically and socially sophisticated urban society, aware of its own identity and proud of it.

No less impressive as indicators of rapidly evolving change within progressive Athenian society are the sharp differences of style and content between the plays of Aeschylus and those of Sophocles, and between those of Sophocles and those of Euripides. Where comedy is concerned, Menander's plays differ just as radically from those of Aristophanes although written within a hundred years of them.

(b) Speculation: What still baffles us today is how Aeschylus, Sophocles, Euripides and Aristophanes were able to rely upon the Athenian public to stand or sit in arenas, terraced with wooden seats and accommodating thousands of spectators apparently eager to watch their plays, since this facility appears to have arrived in Athens and other Attic centres of religious culture in the fifth century without recorded precedent. At first, such arenas amounted to little more than a level area at the base of a hillside or cliff which had been conveniently hollowed by natural erosion into semi-circular shape; but by the fourth century stone seating was provided on these slopes (Fig. 21). What is even more puzzling is that the Greeks, within a single century, should appear to have brought to birth not only a formal code of dramatic genres (tragedy, comedy, satyr play)—like Pallas Athene jumping fully armed out of Zeus's head—but one so definitive as to have been taken as the required point of reference by which to assess any subsequent variants. In this respect the pronouncements of Aristotle have exercised a Moses-like authority over subsequent generations and are even now a force to be reckoned with in academic circles.

In attempting to explain these mysteries it is useful to recall that parallels exist where theatrical art is concerned in Philip II's Spain and in Elizabethan England: for there too, dramatists, theatres, actors, audiences and critics appear to have blossomed in full maturity without a recognizable childhood or adolescence, as does a definable

style of playhouse to contain them (see Chapters 8, 9). Yet we now know that behind this astonishing florescence lay some five hundred years of experiment and development in the churches, schools and market-places of the Middle Ages: in short, the forging of a strong dramatic tradition grounded upon widely accepted theatrical conventions which only required a shift of emphasis from specifically religious to broadly secular subject matter, and from amateur and occasional to professional and regular conditions of production, to thrive as it did. We thus have strong grounds for suspecting that a similar story of experiment and growth lies behind the phenomenon of Athenian drama. What clues to its true nature survive for us to ponder?

A vital one reposes in the three words, theatre, drama and acting. Theatre and drama are both derived from Greek words meaning respectively a place in which to witness some form of action or spectacle and a particular kind of action or activity, game or play, so ordered and articulated as to possess a meaning for participants and spectators alike. Our word acting implies activity, action, some form of practical doing. Dance is the most primitive form of this kind of activity since it disregards literacy and is itself a natural, human response to rhythm. Granted a drum and a pipe or flute, any individual can respond to the rhythms and melodies offered by the players of these simplest of instruments (see p. 16).

As in other primitive societies, it is within the rituals particular to the agricultural festivals marking the death of one year in autumn and winter and the birth of another in spring and summer that an explanation must be sought for the origins of dramatic art, otherwise missing in ancient Greece, and of the circumstances that enabled fully scripted poetic plays to flower at Athens in the hands of Thespis and Aeschylus late in the sixth century BC and early in the fifth while still rooted in the celebration of a public festival dedicated to Dionysus, mystical source of energy, action and thus of drama.

It is hard to determine which of the later dramatic genres—tragedy, comedy, satyr-play—developed first. Aristotle has the weight of the literary evidence on his side in asserting as he did that tragedy not only established itself before comedy, but was regarded in Athens as its superior and accorded precedence where formal recognition in official circles was concerned. Yet comedy, at least in its simplest forms of brief, farcical or satirical mimicry—spontaneous and improvised rather than scripted—normally appeals more readily to peasant and bourgeois audiences than tragic drama which itself tends to invite parody among people not pre-disposed to take it seriously.

21. *The ruins of the theatre of Dionysus in Athens, fourth century* BC. *Note the remains of the sculpted frieze at the foot of the skēnē and the specially carved seating still visible in the centre of the front two or three rows. The encroachment of an enlarged skēnē upon the orchestra dates from the first century* AD.

That parody at least co-existed with early Athenian tragedy is something we can be sure of since records prove that the three tragedies that each competing author was expected to submit for performance at the City Dionysia had normally to be accompanied by a satyr-play. Only one complete text of this genre survives—Euripides' *Cyclops*—together with fragments of a few others: but this meagre evidence at least suffices to indicate that this genre was devoted to burlesque and to parody, and that the subject matter mocked could be drawn from one or more of the three tragedies which had just been performed; and an ability to laugh at oneself normally denotes maturity and self-confidence.

Where comedy is concerned, the truth may therefore be that it simply took longer for comic characterization and incident to evolve into a sustained and recognizable art form of sufficient length and narrative content to warrant direct comparison with tragedy and to merit description as a separate dramatic genre in its own right. This moment appears to have arrived early in the fifth century (*c*.485 BC) when Aeschylus was at the height of his poetic achievement and some thirty years before Aristophanes was born.

2 TOWARDS A PRESUMPTIVE CHRONOLOGY

If we now broaden this enquiry from the narrow limits of the city of Athens in the fifth century BC to embrace comparison with what is known of the beginnings of dramatic art in other countries, then such evidence as survives to us not only from Greece and Rome, but also from India, China and Japan, indicates clearly that as society achieves greater stability and coherence, depending less on hunting (or on farming as was the case in Greece) and more on industry and trade—in short, as it acquires social, political and military self-awareness and self-confidence—so it turns increasingly away from dance and towards language as a more flexible medium through which to formulate and express its views of itself in action. And consequent upon this change in attitudes, the story-line of archetypal legend or myth, still presented in ritualized and emblematic forms, comes gradually to be substituted as the basis of dramatic representation for the simpler and strictly non-narrative rituals of earlier dance drama. Many of the old characteristics are retained and remain discernible beneath the developing textual elaboration of festive drama —soloist and chorus, dance and song, and a vivid consciousness of the gods as ultimate controllers of human destiny. Yet the increasing number of actors called upon by the playwrights, the corresponding decrease in the size and role of the chorus and a dwindling respect for supernatural agencies all testify simultaneously to the steady submergence of older values and techniques under innovative and experimental developments. This is the process, where Athenian drama is concerned, which we can observe in action with some precision during the course of the fifth and fourth centuries BC, from the plays of Aeschylus to those of Euripides and, ultimately, Menander.

The conclusions reached from this admittedly speculative approach receive substantial corroboration from what we know of the physical conditions of performance in Athens, during and after the time of Pericles. For instance, the architecture of the great stone theatres of the fourth century BC at Epidaurus and in Athens, still dedicated like temples to the gods, nevertheless catered increasingly as time passed for the comfort of spectators in ways not contemplated by the communities who surrounded the circular threshing floors and wine presses of country villages for festive dance in an earlier Attica (see Plate 4). No less significant is the strictly ordered competitive element of fifth-century Athenian productions, undreamt of when dance drama was still an intuitive and obligatory response from village communities to the most significant moments of the solar, lunar and agricultural year, yet a natural enough development given a larger, wealthier and more highly structured and articulate urban society.

When considering the City Dionysia in Athens, therefore, we should not be surprised that the theatre prepared for the annual presentation of the festive plays in March or April should have been situated at the foot of the Acropolis adjacent to the temple of Dionysus and equipped both with an altar in the centre of the acting-area and (at least from the fourth century onwards) a seat reserved in the centre of the front row for the priest of Dionysus. Nor should we be worried by the subsequent provision of a raised stage, scenic buildings, and stage-machinery; nor by evidence of rising production costs and the imposition of an admission charge. All these features bear witness to a drama passing out of adolescence and into full maturity. The appearance late in the fourth century of a comedy of manners (called New Comedy) marks the final stage of this protracted evolutionary process. By then the gods and goddesses, whose original grandeur had derived from their being created within men's imaginations as metaphors to describe the great universal truths about the human condition, and who could be brought to life as forces at work in the world by recourse to dramatic art, had lost most of their awesome and frightening aspects. On their way to being rationalized into recognizably human figures, they came to be depicted as mortals among mortals in paintings on walls and vases, and identified by their own, particular emblems—Athena by her spear, shield and helmet for example, or Dionysus by his long hair, vine leaves, and escort of prancing satyrs and Bacchants (see Figs. 1 and 8). This does not imply that all respect for them had vanished, but it does mean that society had become sufficiently tightly organized and self-conscious to be able to stand back and question the man-made principles and special conventions on which it rested, and even to expose them to gentle ridicule.

3 TRAGEDY

(a) **Aeschylus**: The journey I have just charted is a long one, but the principal landmarks are clearly recognizable. Starting with the plays of Aeschylus, who began his dramatic career some fifty years after Peisistratus inaugurated the competitive dramatic festival, or City Dionysia, in Athens, we find a form of drama static enough—to borrow E. F. Watling's phrase—to resemble oratorio and verse that gives precedence to lyrical rather than dramatic values. By adding a second actor and thus creating dialogue between characters, Aeschylus advanced the histrionic possibilities of the drama, allowing character and plot to grow through conflicting desires and actions at the expense of exchanges with a meditative chorus. By linking the three obligatory tragedies required for entry to the competition to a single theme, he preserved the opportunity to handle majestic concepts—concepts that required firm structural control over time, distance and personal relationships if any sense of unity was to be achieved. The gods lower over his plays ready to reward human arrogance with disaster and prepared to allow a return to stability and security in society

22. *A chorus scene from the National Theatre's production of Aeschylus'* Agamemnon, *1982.*

only after due atonement for those thoughts and deeds which had provoked the initial calamity. Justice, war, revenge and retribution provide him with his themes: while his characters pursue their ends with single-minded intensity and narrow blinkered vision, Aeschylus uses his chorus to comment actively and lyrically on their actions in odes of singular force and beauty. In this sense his plays were as political as they were religious.

Only one of his trilogies has survived complete, the *Oresteia*. In this case the theme is justice and the initial crime adultery—the seduction by Thyestes of his brother Atreus' wife. The first of the three plays picks up the story in the next generation at the point where Atreus' son, Agamemnon (having sacrificed his daughter, Iphigenia, in order to reach Troy), is about to return home as a conquering hero. On doing so, he is murdered by his own wife, Clytemnestra, in revenge for the death of their daughter;

in this she is assisted by her lover, Thyestes' son Aegisthus. In the second play both of these murderers die at the hands of Agamemnon's and Clytemnestra's son, Orestes, assisted by his sister Electra. The house of Atreus can thus truly be said to be accursed, and its terrible story serves, as it unfolds, to raise with ever increasing intensity a cry for justice (Fig. 22). The third play seeks to supply a resolution that will bring this calamitous blood feud to an end. Where may this be found when all human attempts to obtain a final answer appear doomed to end in further crimes? Aeschylus supplies his answer through Athena, goddess of wisdom, who persuades a jury of Athenian citizens to acquit Orestes.

Terror, horror and pity are all words which describe an audience's emotional response to a drama on this scale presented as it is in poetry of the first order. There is no sub-plot; and neither extraneous characters nor superfluous comic scenes or dialogue to interrupt the forceful thrust of its theme. All is conducted with a single-minded intensity that serves to focus attention firmly on the moral issue which the story illustrates, namely that human beings

36

must learn to acknowledge their humanity if they are to enjoy the fruits of peace and prosperity.

(b) **Sophocles**: Aeschylus' initiative in expanding the histrionic component of lyric drama by using two actors certainly won the approval of his audiences. Use of a third actor, by recourse to doubling and trebling of roles, allowed him six characters in the *Agamemnon*. It was his much younger rival, Sophocles, however, who had boldly decided to add a third actor, a step which Aeschylus chose to copy in his later plays. Only seven of over a hundred plays which Sophocles was reputed to have written have survived. It is known that he beat Aeschylus in the competition in 468 BC, but the earliest text that we possess is the *Ajax*, which was written around 450 BC: *Antigone* was written at least a decade later: then *Oedipus Rex c.* 425 BC. These plays coincide with the high point of Athenian imperial power.

Sophocles' addition of the third actor enabled him to humanize his dialogue, and thus to develop an interplay between characters, or between a character in conflict with circumstances, and even between conflicting aspects of an individual's own character. If there is no resulting loss of dramatic intensity, there is a noticeable reduction in scale and, with it, a reduction in the function of the chorus. Its odes are also much shorter. It remains as an actor in the events of the drama, but more detached from them; while still serving as a major structural device in supplying unity, it does so in a less subjective and more objective capacity. It witnesses the events and comments on the characters' responses rather than responds directly. The great advantage in this technique is that it serves to make the sufferings of the protagonists *our* sufferings in the auditorium. Since neither we nor the stage chorus can alter the course of events depicted, we find that what the chorus says in its odes reflects our double vision of a conflict of principle with right on both sides which, when no quarter is given, no compromise offered or allowed, must end in disaster for both parties to the argument, and for all who depend on them.

In *Antigone*, for instance, Sophocles contrasts individual conscience with political expediency. King Creon represents government, and it is he who decrees that the corpse of a rebellious traitor should be left to rot without burial rites as a public example. The corpse in question is that of Antigone's brother and it is she who treats this decree as blasphemy and flatly disobeys it. Neither is wholly right; neither is wholly wrong; yet neither will yield up one particle of the principle which each defends. As this battle of wills develops, the chorus serves to alert the audience

23. *Apulian volute-krater, c.325 BC, inspired by Euripides'* Medea, *but possibly depicting scenes from a later adaptation. These include the death of Creon's daughter (centre top), Medea's murder of one of her own children (bottom left) and the snake-chariot of the sun (bottom centre). Staatliche Antikensammlungen und Glyptothek, Munich.*

to the dangers ahead and to the ultimate catastrophe which will envelop and destroy both contestants together with Haemon who, as Creon's son and Antigone's lover, is trapped in the middle between them.

(c) **Euripides**: Euripides was Sophocles' near contemporary, winning the competition for tragedy five times, while Sophocles won it eighteen times. Yet the world of his plays has a far more human and radical atmosphere about it than that of his rival (Fig. 23). Credited with more than ninety plays, we know him by eighteen of which one, *The Cyclops*, is a satyr-play (Fig. 8), and another, *Helen*, is often regarded today as a 'dark' comedy; several more resemble what we might prefer to call melodramas and tragicomedies rather than tragedies. All of them were, in one way or another, contentious in their time. In this Euripides was a realist and possibly entertained a more prophetic vision than Sophocles of the imminent disintegration of Athenian democratic culture under the pressures of the long war with Sparta which started in 431 BC and ended in defeat in 404 BC, shortly after his death. For Euripides the gods remain useful as personifications of forces in nature which mortal men must recognize and come to terms with if they are to survive in society. As absolutes (Aphrodite and Dionysus in particular) they characterize the irrational in human nature which, no matter what merit rational counter-arguments may have in any situation, exists within us as a force capable of demolishing them all. Thus in the *Bacchae*, while both Pentheus the doctrinaire moralist and Cadmus the patronizing politician may regard sobriety and chastity as needful requirements in a well-ordered society, by ignoring or challenging the existence of passion (Dionysus) each invites his own, ultimate destruction, and thus that of the principles he has voiced. It is tragic but inevitable, since the existence of Dionysus (as a symbol of 'ecstasy', or that which is above and beyond reason) can only be denied in human affairs with tragic consequences.

In his own lifetime Euripides enjoyed the reputation of an *enfant terrible* whose concentration on issues of private rather than public concern, and on personal psychology and scientific thought, marked him out as a disruptive and subversive poet, however skilful and witty his plays were judged to be. The other charges levelled against him (and he was a frequent target of parody for Aristophanes) can be summed up by the word 'theatricality' as used today in its pejorative sense. Yet what, to his enemies, seemed sensational, morbid and rhetorical won him a degree of popular favour which was destined during the next three centuries to make posterity regard his plays as the peak of Athenian dramatic achievement. It was his plays that Seneca chose to translate and adapt for Roman listeners, and it was these Latin versions that scholars of the Renaissance would first turn to when seeking to translate them into modern European languages in the sixteenth century.

Euripides retained a chorus, but his use of it suggests a shift towards ornamentation rather than the compulsion of structural necessity. This idea gains substance from his invention of a formal prologue—an opening speech charged with informing the audience at the outset of the point in the story at which the dramatic action to follow would begin. The precedent, once set, is clearly capable of extension as a bridging mechanism elsewhere within a play and as a device to provide a final summary. The most enduring of his tragedies have been those which dealt with women—*Medea, Hippolytus, Andromache* and the *Trojan Women*. In our times this group has been joined by frequent revivals of the *Bacchae*. Only *Alcestis* among his tragicomedies has encountered equal favour.

Change within Athenian society played a major part in persuading all tragic dramatists during the fifth century BC to alter their style. What this required of them was first to gauge the scale and quality of changes in political and social outlook, and then to choose either to stand by traditional values or to move forward with those advocating new stances. It is significant that both Aeschylus and Sophocles were born into aristocratic families and played an active role in public life: Euripides may have come from humbler stock and appears to have held no civic or military office. If this is true, it would go far to explain the major differences between his plays and those of his predecessors; and also to cast light on his notoriety as an egotistical and opinionated rebel among his own contemporaries.

4 COMEDY

(a) **'Old' Comedy**: Turning to comedy we encounter an immediate problem. On the one hand we have to accept as fact that a festival characterized by a contest for comic writers was not established in Athens until some fifty years after the contest for tragic writers: although it too was associated directly with the cult of Dionysus, it was linked with the winter festival, or Lenaea, not the major spring festival. On the other hand we should not ignore what has already been said about parody as a major component of satyr-plays, which were normally regarded as an obligatory conclusion to tragic trilogies at the City Dionysia.

(b) **Aristophanes**: A probable resolution of the problem rests in the nature of Greek comedy as received from the early plays of Aristophanes. These appear to have been deliberately constructed to integrate two separate approaches to comedy—the one, rustic and choreographic, the other verbal and sophisticated—into a single and innovative style of drama governed by verbal disputation, but heavily dependent on personalized mockery and topical satire. The older component of rustic ritual survives in the titles of such plays as *Wasps, Frogs, Birds* and *Clouds* and more visibly in the use of corresponding disguises for the choruses (Fig. 24): the newer component of literary satire emerges in the verbal ridicule (frequently libellous, blasphemous and obscene) heaped upon prominent figures in government, and in legal and military circles alike; but this verbal mockery was undoubtedly reinforced by such visual effrontery as could be projected through mime and gesture. It is inconceivable that this could have been tolerated by

24. *Attic black-figured amphora, painted c.545 BC, depicting a chorus of knights. A flute-player (left) wears a long chiton. The actors, wearing short chitons, horse-head masks and tails, carry riders wearing crested helmets. This suggests that Aristophanes' Knights (424 BC) had antecedents in comic performances of a much earlier period. Berlin State Museums.*

Athenian society as an everyday occurence. What made it acceptable was, in part a civilized and humane acknowledgement that the animal instincts and passions in man's nature cry out for recognition as forcefully as the more rational and spiritual elements, and in part the formal restrictions automatically imposed on these licensed occasions by limiting them to a single major festival each year.

Of all Aristophanes' plays it is *Lysistrata* (first staged in 411 BC)—where women deny sexual intercourse to their husbands in order to bring the war to an end—which has been most frequently revived in modern times. This is undoubtedly because its theme, 'Make love, not war', has corresponded so closely with modern sentiment; but it is also true that this play, in containing less material extraneous to its principal theme and fewer topical allusions than Aristophanes' other plays, is the easiest for actors to handle within stage-conventions familiar to audiences today. Not the least of its modern attractions is the large number of good parts it offers to actresses.

(c) 'Middle' and 'New' Comedy: As with tragedy, changes within Athenian society brought recognizable changes in comic form. Where, to start with, plot was minimal, characterization two-dimensional and situation paramount (that situation being highly topical in a political, military or social sense), a gradual shift becomes observable towards a greater emphasis on plot with a corresponding decline in the role of the chorus, and a softening of the original harshness of the ridicule aimed at personalities into a more generalized lampooning of men and manners. This phase is illustrated by Aristophanes' *Women in Parliament*

and *Wealth*, both written early in the fourth century BC, and is referred to by classical scholars as Middle Comedy: what it marks is a transition from Old to New Comedy.

(d) Menander: New Comedy is principally represented, in terms of surviving plays, by the comedies of Menander. Late in the fourth century, when he came to write his first play, Athens had lost most of the power that it had enjoyed a century earlier. Its culture had likewise suffered a loss of robustness and had declined into a provincialism which we associate with bourgeois city life and which prefers sentimentalism to satire. A form of romanticism thus enters into Greek comedy and an increasing emphasis comes to be placed on niceties of style at the expense of fantasy, farce and bawdry. In Menander's plays the old Aristophanic choruses have dwindled into little more than a song and dance troupe to provide the *divertissements* in the four intervals which punctuate the five parts of the action. His characters have become stereotypes of professional men and their domestic entourage. By comparison with its antecedents, New Comedy is elegant, delicate and decadent—in modern parlance, 'situation comedy'.

Four or five of Menander's plays have come down to us (only *one* intact), but they rarely inspire actors and directors today to attempt revival; yet in his own time his fame was universal—as much, perhaps, because he did not have to face any serious competition from writers of tragedy (which by then had lost its popular appeal) as for any other reason. His subsequent influence on Roman drama was far greater than that of anyone else, including Aristophanes (see pp. 44–5 and Figs. 31 and 33).

5 ATHENIAN DRAMATIC FESTIVALS

(a) **Play Production**: Events as prestigious and elaborate as the dramatic contests in Athens required a high degree of organization, preparation and discipline in execution. Regarded as community events and not as commercial enterprises, responsibility for them was shouldered directly by State officials on behalf of the citizens and visitors from neighbouring districts and states. Doubtless farmers and traders, the keepers of shops and hostelries and the manufacturers of souvenirs reaped a substantial commercial reward from the influx of visitors to these festivals; but, if so, this was a by-product of these occasions which, in the fifth century, were still rooted in the religious calendar of Attic life. Participation in the contests both for the authors and for the actors and spectators was then regarded primarily as a civic duty and only in a secondary sense as an entertainment or pastime, though this order of precedence came slowly to be reversed. Accordingly the contests were heavily subsidized with no attempt made to recoup costs by admission charges until the end of the fifth century: even then the charge was nominal and free places continued to be held back for those unable to meet it.

Government and wealthy individuals between them agreed on the appointment of a *choregos*—the equivalent of the pageant master of the Middle Ages, or business manager of the modern theatre—to supervise the production of each group of plays accepted for the contest. Once allocated, he became responsible in both an artistic and a financial sense for organizing the preparation and presentation of the plays, although the author normally claimed his right to direct rehearsals. The *choregos* did not have to hire the theatre nor reward the principal actors: the former was free, and the cost of the latter was borne by the state: after 449 BC actors became eligible, like authors, for the award of prizes. What remuneration the authors received, if any, beyond the prizes on offer is not known.

(b) **Actors and Acting**: As in the Far East, acting was a profession restricted to men, who thus invariably played female roles as well as male ones, a fact which suggests that the style employed was still far closer to ritual (as it still is in Indian Kathakali dance drama or Japanese Noh plays, see pp. 23 and 26) than realism in any modern sense of that word. Throughout the fifth century, moreover, the same actor was called upon to perform several different roles (some male, some female) within the same play. The verse forms employed also suggest a declamatory style of speech. We are probably not far from the truth, therefore, when trying to visualize in our mind's eye what audiences witnessed in a Greek theatre, if we see sequences of animated icons moving rhythmically before us which serve to cast an hypnotic spell, reinforced by music, dance and incantation, over the whole auditorium, thus inducing a trance-like response echoing that accorded to the dance dramas of an earlier epoch. This response is admirably depicted, in terms of Japanese Noh, by F. T. Imoos:

> Intoxicated by the rhythmic circling and swinging, the dancer experiences a feeling of liberation, of release from the fetters of personality; he enters into a wide-reaching communion with his fellow dancers and with the whole clan [i.e. the audience]. He is beside himself in the full sense of the words. The circle grows wider. The elements are taken in, water and wind join in, plants and trees, tame animals and wild animals, the stars in heaven, all join in the all-embracing dance. The walls collapse between things of this world and things of the beyond.
>
> (*Japanese Theatre*, Studio Vista, London, English ed., 1977, pp. 14–15)

Against this transcendental aspect of a performance has to be set the demanding rhetoric of Greek tragic dialogue and the swift repartee of Old Comedy.

(c) **Theatres**: The vast size of classical Greek theatres seating between 15,000 and 20,000 spectators, open to the sky and provided with nature's own backcloth of mountains, valleys, seascapes and trees, makes it relatively easy for anyone who, as a tourist, has visited their ruined remains to recapture something of that state of heart and mind, transcending normal possibilities, which the tragic playwright sought to induce for his auditors and which would win him the prize were he to be successful in this quest. A further factor within this equation is the diminutive size of the characters represented by the actors, whether standing on the raised platform or in the circular orchestra as seen from the ranks of seating towering above them. All performances took place in daylight.

Greek actors wore face masks (Fig. 25). It has often been argued that it was this sense of remoteness created by the size of the theatres that caused the Greeks to supply their actors with masks (equipped with amplification devices for their voices) and with the high-soled boots known as *kothornoi*, and to endow male characters in comedies with a large, artificial phallus; in short, that such devices were needed to distinguish one character from another and to conceal the fact that the same actor was playing several roles. It must be remembered, however, that some of these costume devices only came into being as extraneous additions accompanying the approach to theatrical representation typified in New Comedy of the fourth and third centuries BC; certainly the bas-reliefs, vase paintings, terracotta figures and other archaeological treasures which actually depict them throughout the Hellenistic world all are artifacts of a much later epoch (Fig. 26).

The acoustics of theatres surviving from the fifth and fourth centuries are near-perfect; magnification of sound seems unnecessary; the fact that human actors look very small in this environment only serves to emphasize the supremacy of the natural world that surrounds them, solid and unchanging except for those differences of light and shadow on the landscape occasioned by the passage of the sun across the heavens during the action of the plays (see Plate 4). This can only serve to relate human ambitions, and the frequently disastrous results which flow from them, more closely and realistically to nature's own abilities to curb or humble pride. *Hybris* was the word coined by the Greeks to describe pride expressed in gratuitously aggressive or insulting behaviour towards others; *nemesis* the word to describe the anger this pride provoked: in tragedy *hybris* is applied by modern critics to men's overreaching desires and uncontrolled passions; *nemesis* to the gods' retributive responses.

---

25. *Actor holding a tragic mask. Vase fragment from Tarentum, mid-fourth century BC. Würzburg, Martin von Wagner Museum.*

(d) **Stage settings:** The diameter of the *orchēstra* in a Greek theatre measured between twenty and twenty-five metres. Outside Greece itself good examples survive as far west as Syracuse in Sicily and to the east at Aspendos in Turkey. Those remaining on the eastern and southern shores of the Mediterannean are of a much later date, most of them being subject to Roman colonial influences and designed to serve different needs. The actors' changing room or *skēnē* (hence our word scene) was originally a simple structure of a strictly functional character brought into being by the actors' need to change their masks and costumes to match each change of role; but once set up on the circumference of the *orchēstra* and facing the audience, it could be elaborated to provide such elementary machinery as was needed to display and remove corpses in accordance with Greek ideas of decorum, or to project gods and goddesses downwards into the mortal world of stage-action and hoist them up out of it again. A single door, for similar utilitarian reasons, came to be replaced by three, two of which flanked the central door: two more were added later and were placed in the *paraskēnia*, or wings projecting at right angles from the façade of the structure. The Chorus came and went though the gates linking the *skēnē* to the auditorium (*parodoi*: see Plate 4 and Fig. 21). Later convention decreed that one should be deemed (actor's right) to lead towards the harbour and the other (actor's left) towards the marketplace: the central doors remained allocated to the palace, temple or some other dominant locality as each particular text decreed. For New Comedy the several sections of the *skēnē* were regarded as representing houses in the city, and at an uncertain date a second storey was added to it. Provision was also made for thunder, lightning and instrumental music. Only brief snatches of Greek music have survived and next to nothing of the choreography or dance notation.

(e) **Costume:** Costumes were elaborate and colourful, and became more distinctively theatrical as time passed, notwithstanding increasing textual realism. The stage costumes which figure most frequently in Athenian vase-paintings and sculpture are the ankle-length dress and the short, sleeveless tunic normally worn by citizens in daily life (see Figs. 23 and 24). Comic actors wore the *chitōn*; actors in tragedy a long, heavy sleeved robe called, in Hellenistic times, a *syrma*. Foreigners were distinguished from Greeks by the use of elaborately woven and embroidered long-sleeved tunics, and by realistic features in the ornamentation of their clothes, armour, hair-style, hats and helmets. Gods were distinguishable, as already observed, by their insignia—Hermes, for example, by his winged boots and caduceus or mace; Herakles by his lion skin and

26. *Paestan kalyx-krater signed by Asteas, c.345 BC, depicting a scene from Middle Comedy. A miser, sleeping on his money chest, is rudely awoken by two thieves while his servant stands ineffectually out of harm's way. Berlin State Museum.*

27. *Three of a set of seven Attic terracotta statuettes of actors in Middle Comedy, 375–350 BC. Figures like these were popular souvenirs and were widely exported in the Hellenistic world. New York, The Metropolitan Museum of Art, Rogers Fund, 1913 (13.225).*

his club (Fig. 8). All these stage-conventions were destined to survive the collapse of the Greek and Roman civilization and to spring to life again in the theatres of medieval Europe and those of the Renaissance.

6 HELLENISTIC THEATRE

Following the conquests of Alexander the Great in the fourth century BC, Greek became the indispensable common language of most countries bordering on the Mediterranean. This explains why the culture of the next two centuries is normally referred to as Hellenistic (i.e. pertaining to Greece, *Hellas*). Attic theatrical example thus came also to be copied and absorbed into the social life of the neighbouring countries stretching from Turkey and the Lebanon via Alexandria, Tripoli and Carthage to Spain and Provence; most importantly, Greek farces (as performed in Sicily and southern Italy) spread north to Rome. Play texts found their way into foreign libraries where they were copied and used as models for imitation. Copyists and imitators used these originals for purposes of adaptation,

diluting them in the process with a wide variety of popular folk entertainments native to these other countries to make them acceptable for performance there. Theatre buildings, exposed to these influences, were steadily 'modernized' and eventually 'Romanized'. Spectacle acquired a higher priority in public esteem than that which Aristotle had permitted to it, as did acting itself. Troupes of mimes (some known as *Phlyakes*) combining farce with dance, acrobatics and juggling, found that by travelling from one theatre to another (and thus acquiring new audiences) they could translate their art into a profession, living off their earnings and importing women into their ranks—especially as dancers (Fig. 27). A few distinguished actors acquired the status of star performers deemed worthy of having statues erected in their honour and epitaphs inscribed on their tombs.

The great casualty of this new and cosmopolitan era was dramatic literature. What had started as a writer's theatre at the dawn of the fifth century had, by the end of the fourth century, become an actor's theatre. Only in southern Italy, and not then until the second and first centuries BC, is any evidence forthcoming of a conscientious effort to recreate in another language types of comedy and tragedy where the provision of plot, character and dialogue again became the prerogative of a dramatic poet, allowing the theatre to be regarded as an educational force within society instead of simply as a source of entertainment.

3

Rome and the Hellenistic World, 200 BC–AD 500

1 THE EUROPEAN HERITAGE OF ROMAN DRAMA AND THEATRE

If the drama that survives to us in Latin has been generally dismissed by posterity as inferior to that in Greek, the most obvious reason is that Roman drama was so largely derived both in respect of play scripts and theatre buildings from Greek models as to allow little scope for genuine originality. On the other hand, as Roman colonization spread much further north and west than its Greek antecedent, and as Latin both superseded Greek as the *lingua franca* of the Western world and held that position for 1,600 years, posterity devoted much more attention to Roman theatres and Latin plays than to Greek equivalents. For these reasons Roman drama and theatre practice have exercised a more lasting and far-reaching influence upon all subsequent European drama than Greek. It is thus important not to dismiss it too peremptorily.

The most substantial claim that can be made for Latin drama in its own right is that it influenced all subsequent forms of farce and what we have come to describe as melodrama. To the Romans must also go the credit for the invention and erection of stone-built amphitheatres and arenas of which the Colosseum in Rome itself is both the most notorious and the most familiar example. It is also to the Roman engineer Vitruvius that we owe the most detailed description of theatre architecture in the first century AD; and it was his work, rediscovered early in the fifteenth century, that provided Italian architects of the Renaissance with most of their ideas of what a theatre should look like and how it should be built (see p. 103ff. and Figs. 39 and 40).

Another debt which posterity owes to Rome is the nomenclature given to these buildings and their uses since the Latin words chosen established concepts of theatrical recreation and appropriate environments for differing forms of entertainment which were destined to outlive the Empire and to supply the basis of the vocabulary coined to describe the mimetic and athletic pastimes of Europe in the new vernacular languages of the early Middle Ages. The most obvious example is the Latin word *theatrum*, which although derived from the Greek θέατρον, in Italy slides into *teatro*, in France becomes *théâtre* and in England *theatre*. Less obvious, but ultimately more important, is the Latin *ludus*, the literal meaning of which is recreation, game or play, but which in the Middle Ages was brought back into general use in the same broad theatrical context, and then translated into vernacular equivalents (see Chapters 4 and 6). Another Latin word *jocus* (lit. word-game or jest) later came to be applied more generally to verbal wit and thus to those forms of mimetic entertainment largely dependent upon it: hence the derivation of the French words for play and actor, *jeu* and *joueur*, still in use today, and the near equivalents similarly used in Italy and Spain. The English-speaking world has inherited the words joke and joker.

2 COMEDY

(a) **Atellan Farce:** As in Greece, drama in southern Italy emerges from the celebrations marking religious festivals; but there they were associated with the New Year and harvest time. These festivities, however, were characterized by an important difference—the impact on indigenous folk custom of far more sophisticated Greek mimes (*Phlyakes*) who had imported the farce and buffoonery associated with satyr-plays from Athens into Sicily by the fourth century BC. Particularly active in this respect was the city of Atella, situated between Capua and Naples in southern Campania. Atellan farce became noted for its brevity and topicality, and was itself imported into Rome in the third century BC.

28. *Three terracotta statuettes of actors in Atellan farce. Paris, Louvre.*

Its most distinguishing feature, derived from Greek precedents, was the group of stock characters whose masks and costumes were standardized along with their names—*Pappus* (Old Fool), *Manducus* (Ogre or Glutton), *Bucco* (Fat-cheeks), etc.—whose clowning was loosely linked to some intrigue or other (Fig. 28). They thus bear a marked resemblance to their sixteenth-century successors in northern Italy, the *Commedia dell'Arte*, whose special skill lay in improvisation and whose special claim on the affections of audiences rested on their familiarity. It is to be doubted, however, whether our knowledge of what the actors of the *fabulae atellanae* actually presented or how it was performed will ever be more precise than those fragmentary descriptive accounts that survive from such authors as Diomedes, Livy and Juvenal, and such pottery, sculpture and mosaics as archaeologists have dug up and placed on view in museums.

(b) *Fabula Palliata* and *Fabula Togata*: Drama with a written text reached Rome itself around 250 BC; it is thus possible that it first appeared in Latinized versions of Atellan farces, but the probability must also be accepted that these were preceded, at least in academic and aristocratic circles, by translations into Latin of Greek comedies by Menander and later authors. This style of drama came to be known as *Fabula Palliata*. The first individual whose name is attached to it is Livius Andronicus (a Greek slave

of a Roman master), one of whose plays was acted at the public games in 240 BC. A third form of drama—a crossbreed between the two—appears in the second century BC: this was described as *Fabula Togata*, implying native rather than foreign origin. It is significant that *toga* was the standard form of Roman dress while *pallium* was the word used to describe normal Greek dress. As such, this offers us a broad hint about the major difference between popular (plebeian) Roman taste and that of the patricians and their protégés among the Roman intelligentsia (Fig. 29). Three names of authors and the titles of some seventy plays survive from the second and first centuries BC, all of which serve to confirm an impression that the writers and actors of a *Fabula Togata* felt obliged to provide their audiences with situation comedy of domestic and business life of a standard comparable to that offered on television screens today.

(c) **Terence**: The author whose surviving plays best represent intelligent and creative advances within the tradition of *Fabula Palliata* is Terence (c.190–159 BC). As William Beare has remarked, he set his own artistic standards and attempted to improve on his Greek models. This stance, as we know from the defensive prologues to his six surviving comedies (all written between 166 and 160 BC), earned him critical abuse from some of his contemporaries. His answers afford us at least a glimpse of the narrowness of vision and generally pedantic approach to 'imitation' adopted by other playwrights of his time as well as by his own critics.

Terence, like Ben Jonson in Jacobean England, responded sharply (notably in his prologues to *The Eunuch* and *Andria*) by claiming that such charges missed the point. His purpose—or so he claimed—was never slavishly to copy but to improve upon his originals, taking only what he needed from them as the basis on which to graft his own ideas in a language commonly employed by his own audiences. All Terence's plays possess a refinement of literary style, and a broad humanity and charm comparable with that of such eighteenth-century writers of comedy as Goldsmith, Marivaux and Goldoni (see Chapter 11): while they treat of domestic life and business affairs, virtually ignoring politics, they appear studiously to avoid farcical situation, buffoonery, obscenity and personalized satire. We should not therefore be surprised that Terence's plays came to be far more highly rated by men of letters in later generations than they seem to have been amongst the boisterous and fickle Roman audiences of his own time.

His most creative departure from past precedent was the use of a sub-plot coupled to a plot, a device that enabled

29. *A Roman actor wearing a toga and studying a tragic mask. Naples, National Museum.*

him to contrast the reactions of several different characters to the same set of circumstances and thus to develop his characters in terms of these varied responses. It is one that Shakespeare eagerly adopted and which was followed by most English playwrights throughout the seventeenth century: it found favour again among writers of melodrama in the nineteenth century and has proved a seemingly indispensable device to the writers of Hollywood filmscripts.

(d) **Plautus:** If Terence is the only accessible representative of the refined writers of *fabula palliata*, Plautus (?c.250–184 BC), who was already eight years dead but at the height of his fame when Terence wrote his first surviving play, represents those dramatists who appear to have been willing to temper allegiance to strict *fabula palliata* with features borrowed freely from the more popular *fabula togata* or native tradition. Of the 130 plays attributed to Plautus after his death, twenty have survived as complete

texts and one more, *Vidularia*, in fragmentary form. Practically nothing is known of his early life beyond the fact that he came from Umbria to Rome as an actor and attracted attention as a clown. His career as a playwright began when he was about forty, and such was his success in this capacity that he was accorded Roman citizenship. Whether he set out to establish himself as a translator, in the literal sense of the word, or whether—like Terence after him—he merely borrowed what he wanted and adapted or invented the rest is a subject of endless argument among classical scholars: lacking virtually all the Greek originals against which to check any of his texts, no definite answer is ever likely to be forthcoming. Here Plautus' dialogue is probably our best guide, since this has an unmistakably Roman flavour to it both in its racy topicality and in its self-conscious Latinism as expressed in puns and other word-games: it thus seems sensible to assume that he translated as freely as his fancy directed, lacing what he took over from Greek originals with whatever in his own experience of Roman people and social customs he regarded as relevant to audiences of the Republic.

That Plautus could, when he wanted to, follow the high moral tone, tinged with sentimentality, of bourgeois New Comedy may be seen in *The Captives* where the conduct of a faithful and courageous slave results in his master's escape from his captors; the master then recognizes this slave to be his own son. For the most part, however, Plautus preferred broad farce of a kind that appears deliberately to invert all the norms that governed Roman attitudes to political and domestic life. Thus the prevailing moral order—as if under the special licence of a public holiday—is seen on the stage to be reversed. Sons and daughters, far from treating their parents with the respect owed to them, regard them as tiresome bores and restrictive obstacles to the fulfilment of their own desires: slaves view their masters as pompous fools who deserve to be outwitted and fleeced of their money and possessions. Laughter here results from surprise, not to say shock, a conjunction which serves to mock the solemnity and pretensions symbolized by the all-enveloping togas of Roman daily wear, just as a similar conjunction in French 'bedroom farce' of the late nineteenth century served to expose the hypocrisy concealed beneath Victorian top-hats, frock-coats, and crinolines. It is here above all that the Dionysiac world of Atellan farce can be seen to have been integrated with the formal plots of Greek New Comedy and thus to have brought to birth a new and dynamic style of drama that would itself become a magnet that would attract the serious attention of future generations of translators and adapters. This path will lead from such later writers as Machiavelli

30. *The Braggart Captain, the* Miles Gloriosus *of Plautine farce, refurbished as* Il Capitano *of the* Commedia dell'Arte. *He wears Spanish military uniform and is instantly recognizable by his sword and moustache. Paris, Bibliothèque Nationale.*

and John Heywood on to Ben Jonson and the *Commedia dell'Arte*, and so to Chekhov, Feydau, Pinero, Buster Keaton, Charlie Chaplin, Ben Travers and the Marx Brothers. Shakespeare found in *Amphitryo* and *Menaechmi* the raw materials out of which to fashion *The Comedy of Errors*. Yet of all Plautus' plays it is arguable that the *Miles Gloriosus* (Braggart Captain) has proved to be the most influential. This is a play in which the title role offers audiences a self-proclaimed heroic character who, no matter what changes in methods of waging war and in styles of military and naval uniform time may have brought with it, remains a constant figure of ridicule when his claims to be the confidant of powerful and influential people, a cause of heartbreak for women the world over and a rival to Hercules and Hannibal for courage on the battlefield are all exposed as the idle boasts of an upstart, a coward and a cuckold. Thus the Plautine prototype re-emerges throughout history in different stage costumes, speaking different languages; as King Herod in medieval

mystery plays; as Sir John Falstaff; as Parolles in Shakespeare's *All's Well that Ends Well*; as Il Capitano of the *Commedia dell'Arte*; as Captain Brazen in Farquhar's *The Recruiting Officer*; as Major Sergius Saranov in Shaw's *Arms and the Man*, and in many other disguises (Fig. 30).

(e) Later Comedy: Deduce what we may from the collected plays of Plautus, and those of Terence (all written within the first forty years of the second century BC), it becomes as difficult (and dangerous) to determine what followed as it is to be precise about what preceded their work for the stage. For once again we are confronted with a smattering of names of dramatists, fragments of texts, and confused reminiscences supplied by such later men of letters as Cicero, Horace and Donatus as our only guide to what took place. By the first century BC even these sketchy signposts fade from view. The silence that then descends is so complete as strongly to suggest that serious writers of comedy failed thereafter to attract audiences into theatres and had to content themselves with regarding their plays as literary works written for private circulation, like books and poems, among the patrician class alone.

3 ROMAN TRAGEDY

Tragedy seems to have suffered the same fate at about the same time with the death of Lucius Accius, *c*.86 BC. He was the last of a long line of writers for the stage starting with Ennius (239–169 BC) who imitated Greek tragedians, but for whom rhetoric and melodrama took precedence over natural utterance and conflicting characteristics in human personality. He is himself credited with forty plays, none of which has survived as a complete text; nor is there a figure equivalent to Terence or Plautus standing behind him among earlier writers of tragedy against whose extant plays we may compare his work and thus gain a fuller critical appreciation of the quality of Roman tragedy at its best. Indeed, our only yardstick for comparison with Plautus or Terence is the work of Lucius Annaeus Seneca (3 BC–AD 65), the Stoic philosopher and tutor to the Emperor Nero, who represents Imperial rather than Republican Rome. Even then, as the texts of his nine tragedies were patently prepared for readers rather than actors, they survive as examples of a tradition already far removed from that confronting dramatists who conceived texts in terms of presentation on a stage. It is for this reason that Seneca's characters frequently appear to exist as presences rather than to make specific entrances and exits: it also explains such extraordinary occurrences as the failure of Phaedra's husband even to notice that she has killed herself—a scene which, had it ever been put into rehearsal, the actors would instantly have asked the author to rewrite for them. Seneca's readers, for their part (whether as listeners at a recital or as students in private perusal), might well reply that their primary interest lay in matters of style—the language, its sentiment, its versification, its atmospheric quality—and in the refined portrayal of treachery, brutality, grief, and stoic fortitude when faced with Fortune's fickleness: whether such 'tragedies' could or could not be staged and acted was immaterial. Viewed from this standpoint it becomes relatively easy to understand why Seneca's reputation grew as the years passed, and why such plays as his *Medea*, *Hercules*, *Oedipus* and *Phaedra* (or *Hippolytus*) should have been regarded as archetypes for imitation by humanist playwrights in Italy, France and England during the Renaissance (Figs. 23 and 38). Not only did he write in Latin, the lingua franca of the Western Empire, but with a command of Latin that lifted both the situations and the emotions he depicted into an imaginative world that made them as melodramatic as they were intelligible. Only the acid test of attempted revival on a stage, and before an audience, could serve to alter this assessment. This had to wait until late in the sixteenth century, and even then something of this quality survived the shock of disenchantment to colour the composition of such English plays as Thomas Kyd's *The Spanish Tragedy*, Shakespeare's *Titus Andronicus*, and John Webster's *The Duchess of Malfi*. By the dawn of the seventeenth century, however, the plays of the Greek tragedians had become well enough known to topple Seneca from this pedestal of critical adulation and replace him with authors whose plays were evidently both more dynamic in their treatment of human suffering and more plausible in their representations of it on the stage.

4 CRITICAL EVALUATION

(a) Shortage of Surviving Texts: The predicament which thus faces the modern critic who tries to be objective in his approach to Roman drama is how to appraise the theatrical worth and achievement of a mere three playwrights (one of whom is generally acknowledged to have written for readers rather than audiences), who survive as the isolated representatives of a period that spans some seven hundred years, against their Greek predecessors and against the many dramatists who have succeeded them in Western Europe and America. Each reader of Roman plays, whether in Latin or in translation, must be his or her own judge; but having considered the legacy which these writers inherited, it is pertinent to ask why, within an empire that embraced half of what we call Europe and most of the

31. *Mosaic from Pompeii, signed by Dioskourides of Samos, 100 BC, thought to depict a scene from Menander's* Theophoroumene. *Naples, National Museum.*

Middle East and North Africa as well, they should have had no successors of any consequence to posterity?

The answer to that question can only be sought within the context of imperial society—its tastes and its demands upon the theatre on the one hand, and the responses of the actors and managers on the other. Clearly the latter saw little prospect of earning a living, or of gaining any reputation worth having, in continuing to commission poets to provide them with scripts of serious, literary merit. English poets in the nineteenth century such as Shelley, Coleridge, Wordsworth or Browning, we might remember, found it just as difficult to convince actor-managers that they had anything to offer that was likely to interest the audiences on whom the acting companies depended for their livelihood (see p. 200). Instead, both managers and actors chose to retreat into the mimetic resources of their own profession—mime, song, dance, spectacle and the positive exploitation of popular responses to melodramatic situations and to stereotyped characterization. The descent to what in Britain has come to be described as music-hall,

32. *A Sicilian puppet of Charlemagne. Puppet plays remain very popular in Sicily today, although many are based on chivalric romances and date back to the Crusades.*

front of public audiences in a theatre (see pp. 166–7). We must not assume, therefore, that the absence of dramatic literature of consequence implies that Roman audiences had abandoned all interest in theatrical entertainment: there is ample evidence to the contrary. As part of an inherited pattern of cultural life, the public continued to seek it, and did so, moreover, increasingly *as of right*: hence the mounting pressure upon successive emperors to provide 'bread and circuses' to ensure their personal survival in office, whatever the state of a deteriorating economy. Thus spectacle, and all the technical expertise and equipment that goes with it, increased in inverse proportion to the State's ability to afford it. Nevertheless, some interest in literary forms of drama must have survived the transition from Republican to Imperial times since Horace could still see fit *c*.10 BC to write his *Art of Poetry* in the form of a letter in hexameter verse to a father and his sons which includes a passage containing rules for dramatic composition which are more dogmatic and less analytic than Aristotle's: to these he added some notes on the history of Greek drama and theatre.

(b) Horace's *Art of Poetry*: Where comedy is concerned, lacking familiarity with plays by Aristophanes or other writers of Old Comedy (which he claims to have been suppressed by censorship), Horace takes New Comedy as his model. He thus emphasizes the need to use character types and to suit their diction to their nature and status in life: this is the top priority.

> Listen now and let me tell you what I, and the world with me, expect. If you wish an applauding audience that will stay for the curtain and sit on till the flute-player gives the signal for applause, you must note the manners of each several age, and their fitting hue must be given to the tempers which change with the years. A boy, from the minute when he talks and sets firm steps upon the ground, loves to play with his young companions, grows passionate and cools again as lightly, and changes every hour. The beardless lad . . .'

Thereupon follows the classic definition of the seven ages of man. He turns next to stage-action.

> Action is either performed on the stage, or its performance is narrated. What finds entrance through the ear stirs the mind less actively than what is submitted to the eyes.

(Trans. E. C. Wickham,
Horace for English Readers, 1903, pp. 340–63)

revue or cabaret, and in America as vaudeville or burlesque, is in fact plainly charted from the first to fifth centuries AD. An offshoot of this decline was the growth of a flourishing puppet theatre in Sicily (Fig. 32).

An important clue to the cause of this literary decadence lies in the studied avoidance by the three major Roman playwrights of any overt concern with politics and religion. The fate of Gnaeus Naevius, a playwright of the second century BC who suffered both imprisonment and exile for daring to pillory politicians of his own day, strongly suggests a form of personal revenge bordering upon censorship in Republican Rome. This, of itself, suffices to restrict any serious, literary treatment of topical events and personalities on the stage to a world in which the subject matter is no longer perceived by audiences to be relevant to their own lives. One has only to look at the relative poverty of eighteenth-century drama in England and France to appreciate how circumscribed the subject matter permitted to dramatists becomes when any serious discussion of religion, politics and sex is legally banned as inadmissible in

Horace then proceeds to list the sort of actions that are to be narrated and not acted: for 'anything [i.e. of this kind] you thrust upon my sight I discredit and revolt at.'

Next comes insistence upon five-act structure. These and his other 'rules' were destined during the Renaissance to assume the absolute authority accorded to the Bible, especially in Italy and France (see pp. 101–3 and 156–7).

Aware of tragedy, he says little about it; but he does devote space to his views on the satyr-play, probably more heavily dependent on his own acquaintance with some Roman entertainment than on any close knowledge of Greek originals. These views would become just as influential on the development of Renaissance pastoral poetry and drama as those on comedy were destined to do.

Following Horace's death no Roman author (the rhetorician Quintilian of the first century AD and Donatus the grammarian of the fourth century excepted) seems to have regarded either dramatic literature or dramatic theory as a topic worth serious attention.

5 PANTOMIME

Allied with drama in the Roman world was pantomime. This was an art form original to southern Italy and welcomed into Rome during the reign of the Emperor Augustus. Its nucleus was dance rather than acting, although gesture was its salient characteristic. Facial expression was denied by the invariable use of a mask. Movement was synchronized with musical accompaniment, not unlike Japanese Noh where a chorus and musicians are as much in evidence as the actors (see pp. 26–7). Surviving descriptions give rise to the belief that Roman pantomime may have been the true lineal descendant of Greek tragedy, with emphasis shifted from language to music and choreography, since the subject matter was normally serious—myth, legend, history—while the performers excelled in the depiction of human passions, especially that of love. We should thus try to envisage a single, trained orator reciting (possibly intoning or chanting) a tragic or melodramatic story as a monologue while his fellow pantomimes depicted the emotional responses of the characters as the action unfolds, but silently in symbolic gestures and dance, accompanied by music. And here, the possibility must be entertained that the Romans acquired the essentials of pantomime through contact with Indian dance drama as practised in the south-eastern provinces of the Empire—Persia, Syria and Egypt—just as they had borrowed their ideas of comedy and tragedy from Greece.

Socially, the performers could not escape from the infamous reputation of the mimes from whose ranks female dancers and singers had entered the theatre as actresses; but such was the esteem which some of them earned, particularly among patrician ladies, that they found themselves welcomed into private houses and able to amass personal fortunes. In Byzantium a female performer of the sixth century (in our terminology a strip-tease gogo dancer), Theodora, so bewitched the Emperor Justinian as to be made his Empress: yet it was Justinian who issued the order to close the theatres in the eastern Empire. They were later reopened and survived those in the Western Empire by nearly two hundred years until finally swept away in the Saracen invasions of the seventh and eighth centuries.

6 ROMAN THEATRES

(a) **Spectacle and Spectator Sports:** If what Aristotle had felt able authoritatively to describe as tragedy and comedy

---

33. Mosaic from Pompeii, signed by Dioskourides of Samos, 100 BC, thought to depict a scene from Menander's Synaristosai.

34. *Mosaic depicting games in a Roman circus in southern France, with scaffolds (left) for privileged spectators. First century* AD. *(Compare Fig. 43.) Lyons, Musée de Civilisation.*

in Athenian theatres of the fifth and fourth centuries BC had degenerated by the first century AD into what the Romans described as pantomime and mime with spectacle as the common denominator—and the lack of any dramatic literature for stage performance from Imperial Rome confirms this impression—then the lure of the circuses and amphitheatres designed to accommodate racing, pugilism and aquatic sports can be more easily understood. These athletic, as opposed to mimetic, games or *ludi* were, like stage-plays, imported from Greece but swiftly modified to suit Roman tastes. Described generically as *Ludi Circenses* as opposed to *Ludi Scenici* (Circus Games in contrast to Theatre Games) they provided the staple fare of major festivals marking both religious and civic special occasions in Republican Rome (Fig. 34). They were introduced by a procession in which it was normal to carry statues of the gods to whom the festival was dedicated. Apollo, Jupiter, Neptune, Juno, Proserpine and Pluto were all honoured in

this way, and most of the festivals were celebrated in high summer and in the autumn. Under the late Republic and the Empire they came also to be associated with major triumphs personal to the donors, usually the Emperor or wealthy generals and senators, and not least with such domestic events as weddings and funerals. As this occurred, so the general title of these events came to be sub-divided into six specific categories. First there was the *Cursus* covering all forms of running and racing, but especially chariot racing. Next pugilistic sports simulating warfare, some on horseback and some on foot, known as the *Ludus Trojae* and the *Pugna Equestris et Pedestris*: some inkling of what was on offer may be gained from attending a modern Military Tattoo. Then there were the athletic and gymnastic contests including boxing and wrestling known as *Certamen Gymnicum*: these included the famous contests between gladiators (see Plate 5 and Fig. 39). The two other forms of sporting event associated with amphitheatres and arenas were outstandingly spectacular—mock sea-battles, *Naumachia* and the *Venatio*, the display and baiting of wild animals—the latter being as sadistic as it was exotic (Fig. 47).

(b) Amphitheatres, Arenas and Circuses: As these *ludi* came to be categorized, so the buildings constructed to contain them had to be modified and provided with special equipment appropriate to the nature of the sport and the entertainment on offer. Thus, where the *Venatio* was concerned, the safety of the audience became a priority, just as an adequate supply of water became an essential precondition for the staging of a *Naumachia*.

It may seem that these assorted recreations are so far removed from drama as we understand it as scarcely to warrant mention in the story of theatre. Yet all of them in one way or another survived, or were later revived, and played an important part in fashioning another style of dramatic entertainment, both within Italy itself and in other countries during the fifteenth and sixteenth centuries, on which our own ideas of what drama is, or ought to be, are grounded. It is to be doubted whether gymnastic sports ever wholly disappeared since many of them—especially acrobatics—became the special preserve within a context of popular entertainment of the nomadic troupes of mimes long after the theatres and amphitheatres had been closed, and remain recognizable in the repertoire of the medieval minstrels in the banquet halls of the nobility (Fig. 39; see also Figs. 49, 50 and 51). The fights on horseback and on foot re-emerge in the tenth century in all the spectacular panoply of tournaments and jousts, become associated with King Arthur and 'round tables' in literary romance, and still figure as jousts-at-barriers in Stuart masques penned by Ben Jonson and dressed by Inigo Jones, and in French *ballets de cours* of the seventeenth century (see Plate 9 and Fig. 130). The *Naumachia* likewise re-emerges in the sixteenth century in the court entertainments of the Medici and the Borgias, and even as far north as Elizabethan England at Elvetham and Bristol (see Figs. 90, 91, 107 and 133): its most recent variant is the nineteenth-century aquadrome prepared for melodramatic sea-battles or, in our own time, frozen over for the staging of musicals on ice. The *Venatio* also lingered, although cut down in scale to the baiting of single bulls and bears; nevertheless it survived and inspired the 'rings' built to accommodate spectators which were a vital component in the design and construction of circular Shakespearean playhouses (see Fig. 97).

The largest and most elaborate stadium in Rome itself was the Circus Maximus, often described simply as *The Circus*, but this is now scarcely visible: others, however, have been restored to sight by archaeologists, at least in ground plan, of which one of the best preserved is that on the Via Appia. Many amphitheatres have survived around the seaboard of the Mediterranean, the best-preserved in Rome itself being the Colosseum. In Britain the best-pre-

35. *Ruins of the amphitheatre built for the entertainment of the Roman legionaries stationed at Caerleon, near Newport, South Wales.*

served Roman amphitheatre is that at Caerleon, near Newport in South Wales (Fig. 35).

(c) Theatres: Spectacularly well preserved are those at Orange in Provence (Fig. 37) and at Leptis Magna in Libya: so are those on a much reduced scale at Pompeii and Taormina. From these we know that the raised stage and ornately decorated wall rising behind it had come to eclipse the by now semi-circular orchestra in importance, and that behind the several large arches in this façade some effort was made to provide scenic vistas in receding

36. *The amphitheatre and theatre at Arles in southern France.*

37. *The Roman theatre at Orange in southern France, first century* AD. *Although badly damaged, vestiges remain of the elaborate decoration of the* frons scenae. *The tall buildings on either side housed rehearsal and storage rooms. (Compare Figs. 38 and 80.)*

perspective, and to accommodate machinery which facilitated surprising and magical stage-effects (Figs. 21 and 38). No less important was the provision made for the comfort of spectators including roof-awnings to protect them from the heat and glare of the sun (Fig. 39). None of these improvements would have become possible, granted the occasional nature of performances (for they remained relatively rare events in the annual calendar), without lavish individual patronage and government subsidy: yet this was forthcoming and accounts for the provision of stone-built

38. *A scene from a Roman adaptation of Euripides'* Iphigenia in Tauris *depicted in a wall-painting in a house at Pompeii. Compare the ornamentation of the* frons scenae *with that in the ruined theatre at Orange (Fig. 37).*

theatres as far away from Rome itself as those in Britain, Germany and Jordan (Fig. 40).

Most theatres were huge. The three in Rome itself—those of Pompey (the first to be built in stone, c.80 BC), Balbus and Marcellus—all seated about 20,000 people, and whenever one of the sterner emperors like Tiberius exerted personal authority in the name of reform by banishing the actors, popular clamour frustrated it by enforcing their swift return from exile. Nor could actors have earned themselves the high reputations—bordering upon the idolatory accorded to today's pop stars—and the fortunes that went with them without some special virtuosity acquired from outstanding skill within a recognized tradition: and it must have been this sort of artistry that recommended the celebrated Roscius in the first century BC to as sober and judicious a critic as Cicero. Even so, observant, serious writers like Livy, Tacitus, and Juvenal, together with the Emperor Marcus Aurelius, felt obliged to reprove the stage on ethical grounds for its mindless frivolity and for the lascivious life-style of most of its representatives.

(d) **Actors and Acting:** It is a mistake to generalize about the status of Roman actors; and it is rash to think of them as professionals, at least in any modern sense. That even the best of them were several rungs down the social ladder from the position occupied by the performers familiar to Aristotle in fourth-century Athens seems certain; but the actors whom Plautus and Terence could call upon were just as certainly regarded with far more respect than either the mimes of their own day or any of the entertainers who appeared before the public in Imperial Rome. The former are represented by the masters (*domini*) of small troupes five or six strong—not unlike the early Tudor companies of four men and a boy—who could hire 'extras' for non-speaking roles when wanted (see p. 120). These 'masters', having first acquired social respectability as reputable tradesmen, or artisans, then superimposed upon this relatively firm base both their histrionic talent and the supplementary income which it earned for them and their fellows (Figs. 33 and 41). Just such a person was Ambivius Turpio who bought Terence's plays and presented them. Between the companies and their patrician sponsors there existed a number of middlemen—the Roman *choragi*—who arranged the bookings and the scenic and costume necessities for the production, and who paid the bills. The bridge that the Roman *choragus* offered in his person between the patron and his patrician friends on the one hand and the *dominus* and his companions on the other was a vital factor, since this permitted the finest artists among them to acquire the sort of respect accorded two thousand years later to Victorian actor-managers while still relegating those of indifferent talent to a status scarcely more elevated than slaves: some almost certainly were slaves.

As the Roman public lost interest in literary drama, so the integrity and skills previously required of the *dominus* were devalued, thereby allowing personality and popular acclaim to become the sole criteria regulating an actor's

39. *The riot in the amphitheatre at Pompeii,* AD 59, *depicted in a fresco of* c.AD 75. *Because several supporters of the visiting team of gladiators from Nuceria were killed, the Senate in Rome closed the amphitheatre for ten years (compare football fans today). Note the roof-awning rolled back behind the arena and the small shop under a canopy in the foreground. Naples, National Museum.*

40. *The Roman theatre at Amman in Jordan. Similar theatres were found in all Mediterranean countries and were subjected to substantial alteration and improvement between the first and fourth centuries* AD.

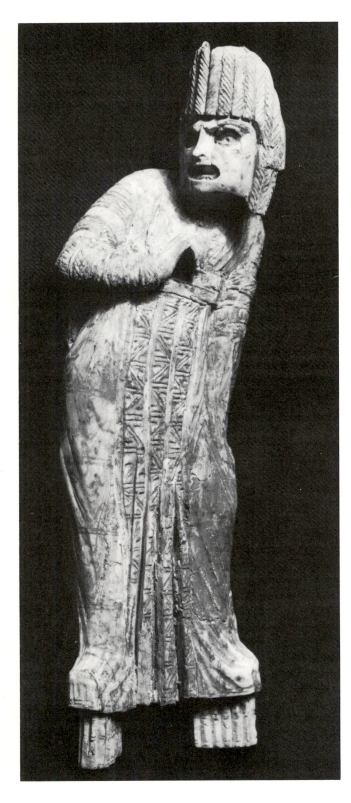

41. *A Roman actor wearing a tragic mask, a long chiton and high-soled boots ('buskins'). c.AD 150. Paris, Musée du Petit Palais.*

reputation and rewards in Imperial society. Apart from seats reserved near the stage for senators, admission was on a first-come-first-served basis with thieves and prostitutes as able to claim a place as those patricians brave enough and keen enough to face a noisy, jostling crowd in holiday mood which was just as liable to boo actors who failed to arrest and maintain their attention as to applaud those who amused them. In such conditions—once they had become the norm—it is easy to understand how the serious-minded intelligentsia, more especially the professed Christians among them, chose to abandon theatre-going and tried to persuade others in their writing and their preaching to share their viewpoint.

7 CHRISTIANITY AND THE THEATRES

These strictures served to lay firm foundations for much more sweeping and scathing attacks on all forms of *ludi* launched by Christian converts. These reached a climax in Tertullian's *De Spectaculis*, c.AD 195, an uncompromising, frontal attack on mimes, singers, dancers, athletes and pugilists coupled with an exhortation to substitute for such vain and degrading pastimes the spiritual recreations provided by the Christian Church on its own high days and holidays. And here it is important to recall that this treatise was destined to become as formative an influence on Puritan attitudes to the stage in the sixteenth century as the writings of Aristotle and Vitruvius were to be in humanist circles (see p. 59–60)

As the standards of subject-matter on offer in Roman theatres declined, so did the status of the performers, at least in the opinion of the upper class. In this way, actors and acting acquired an evil reputation which, on moral grounds, was shared by the growing Christian communities within the Empire: yet the more harshly the actors were condemned by outspoken Christians, the more sharply the actors retaliated in parody and general mockery of Christian behaviour and everything Christians held to be most sacred. This widening division within society was in no way helped by the undemanding alternative of spectator sports offered in the circuses and amphitheatres of the Empire.

The Colosseum in Rome provides a grim reminder of the realities of gladiatorial combats in which Christians were expected to defend themselves against trained fighters as a sport for the spectators. Just as familiar is that variant on the *Venatio* where, instead of dogs or men baiting wild beasts, hungry lions were released to bait Christians. Tacitus provides a chilling description of Christians tarred, crucified and set alight like grotesque fireworks as a spectacular amusement for the populace. With the conversion of the Emperor Constantine to Christianity in AD 312 discernible changes of attitude became apparent in legislation; but time was running out. The Empire itself was split and fraying at its edges. While the extravagance and ostentation railed at by the Christian bishops persisted in Rome and in Byzantium, the funds and military resources needed to prevent rebellions in the colonies (and to keep the barbarians to the north and east at a safe distance) were dwindling from bare sufficiency towards exhaustion. By the start of the fifth century Rome felt compelled to withdraw its legions from Britain, thus ending more than three centuries of colonial rule. In AD 410 Alaric the Visigoth swept over the Alps and succeeded in achieving what Hannibal had tried but failed to accomplish, the sack of Rome itself. Shortly after, all theatres were closed. Thus, in the end, a new and virile paganism succeeded in doing, abruptly and with astonishing finality, what centuries of Christian protest and endeavour had clamoured for but failed to effect.

Because it is so easy to misconstrue the hostility exhibited by such early Christian leaders as Tertullian in the West and St Chrysostom in the East, and even St Jerome and St Augustine, it is important to try not to exaggerate it. The more serious thinkers and spokesmen for Christianity had never wished to lay siege to either drama or theatre: rather had they found themselves forced by the self-evident decadence of dramatic art under Imperial rule to attack what was then offered to the public on ethical grounds as a pernicious commodity and a demoralizing example to the young which, in the words adopted by their Puritan successors in Elizabeth England, should be dismissed as unhealthy and banned as 'unfitting in any well-ordered Commonwealth'. The disenfranchisement of an organized theatre, however, as a social institution does not imply the automatic extinction and immediate disappearance of all professional entertainers: rather does it suggest that, to survive, they must take to the roads as nomads, or vagabonds, and travel light, seeking audiences at markets, fairs and taverns. In view of the attitude which the Roman Catholic Church was destined to adopt towards drama in the Middle Ages, these considerations, however startling, should not be disregarded as ridiculous: indeed, as the vital link between classical antiquity and modern Europe, they merit further discussion in the next chapter.

4
The Roman Phoenix, AD 410–975

When legend becomes fact, print the legend.
(From the filmscript of *The Man Who Shot Liberty Valance*)

1 IMPERIAL VERSUS PAPAL ROME

Since no plays written and no theatres built in Europe during the five centuries between Alaric's sack of Rome in AD 410 and the reform of all Benedictine monasteries, which marks the advent of Christian religious drama late in the tenth century, have survived for us to inspect today, convenience combines with simplicity to urge acceptance of the orthodox view that theatres were closed, plays banned and actors relegated to the status of criminals (or vagrants at best) which will then permit us to move swiftly to the revival of dramatic art in the Middle Ages.

Unfortunately, such evidence as does exist for our inspection powerfully suggests that we may be dealing with a view that is legendary rather than factual, convenient rather than truthful. That Alaric closed the theatres in Rome following his arrival there must be taken as fact; but it is one thing to legislate and quite another to enforce. By then the Roman Empire itself had split into two distinct halves speaking different languages: both halves contained overseas provinces where decrees and legislation promulgated in Rome could be breached or ignored with impunity. Syria, North Africa and Britain provide the most obvious examples: and drama, in its many forms we must remember, survived for much longer in the Greek-speaking Eastern Empire of Byzantium than it did in the West.

Another factor of equal importance is the opportunity which the collapse of strictly Roman control over the Western Empire offered to the Christian Church to advance its own claims on men's spiritual allegiance throughout the civilized world. Once the former centre of government and cultural initiative had lost credibility, the Christian bishops could seize on the chance to offer the faith they represented as the sole surviving unifying force among socially disoriented and deeply disillusioned communities stretching from Antioch and Alexandria to Dublin and Gibraltar. This they

did. And as this movement developed momentum, it became necessary to convene councils and synods in order to focus opinion, to control deviants and to promote missionary zeal. If we choose to listen to the voices that spoke up and were recorded at these meetings, then we will quickly recognize that over the next three to four centuries actors, *ludi* and *spectacula* remained as irritating and threatening as ever throughout the erstwhile empire.

How are we to interpret these records? They have to be accepted as facts and not as legends: moreover, they have to be grappled with if we are to comprehend how an organized form of drama and theatre came to re-establish itself as a vital cultural and educative presence in Christian Europe, and if we are to gain any true understanding of the foundations on which this new drama was based. It is thus worth devoting a little space here to try to resolve the apparent contradictions between official legislation and actuality which the evidence exposes.

For instance, we have got to explain the paradox of how the same Christian Church of Roman Imperial times that had striven to suppress acting and to close theatres came to admit drama five centuries later to a place close to the heart of its own most sacred liturgies. We must also explain how it became possible for churchmen of the early Middle Ages to condone the existence of such self-evidently dramatic rituals as mummings and tournaments despite their secular provenance, and even borrow from them for their own teaching purposes in the later miracle cycles, morality plays and saint plays.

Perhaps the most important clue to an answer to both questions lies in the assertive insistence of the natural rhythms of the seasons within all agriculturally orientated communities: for that is what all European countries were until the return of relative stability (political, social and economic) made possible the development of trade and industry, and with them the growth of towns. With the regular and adequate supply of food and drink remaining the priority for mere survival, as it had been through the seventh, eighth and ninth centuries, nothing could shake the pre-eminence of festivals associated with procreation and harvest; and both were as inexorably anchored in the winter and summer solstices and the vernal and autumnal equinoxes as ever they had been in classical antiquity. The continuing relationship between a sense of occasion and the festive celebration of it is thus one topic to which some space must be allotted in this chapter: and to this I will return later.

Another clue that helps to provide an answer stems directly from this relationship. This is the triumphant Christian Church's own philosophical struggle to reconcile the civilized but pagan past and the barbarous present with its own future as the dominant civilizing force in the new Europe. Slowly and painfully the Roman Church reached an accommodation with the classical philosophers and writers; then with architecture, music, sculpture and painting; and finally with the playwrights and the actors. To this rapprochement there is no better guide than St Augustine, bishop of Hippo in North Africa (AD 354–430).

2 TOWARDS AN ACCOMMODATION WITH PAGAN CULTURE

Described by E. K. Rand as 'a Carthaginian roisterer who became a Christian Saint', Augustine was responsive to the festive spirit and, until his conversion in AD 387, addicted to every form of *ludus* on offer on public holidays. 'In my time I had a violent passion for these spectacles, which were full of the images of my miseries and of the amorous flames which devoured me' (*Confessions*) (Figs. 42 and 43). Indeed, so steeped was he in all aspects of the actor's art as practised in his time that even after his conversion he returned imaginatively to his experience of it as a treasury of metaphor to depict, in sermons and in books, men as acting roles in the great theatre of the world: 'we too are acting in life this mime of ours'. As a professional rhetorician, he must surely here be referring to the Roman art of pantomime (see p. 49). When, after his conversion, he joins the ranks of those who had felt obliged to deny Christian baptism and burial to actors, to excommunicate Christians who on holy days were to be found at the theatre instead of in Church, and to condemn the traditional celebrations of social inversion dedicated to Saturn at the start of each New Year as works of the devil, what was he attacking and what did he fear?

Before his conversion Augustine left North Africa for Italy, where he quickly attracted attention. At the age of

42. *Exterior of the Roman amphitheatre at El Djem, Tunisia, looking very much as it did to St Augustine when he frequented it in the fourth century* AD.

thirty he was appointed principal teacher of rhetoric in Milan, in which capacity he was not only able to exercise his histrionic talents (for rhetoric then embraced eloquence in oratory as well as a command of grammar and other literary skills), but also came to acquire a mastery of Roman literature. It was the latter that was to present him with his greatest problem following his baptism, just as it had already done for other outstanding Christians like his predecessors Tertullian and St Cyprian and his near contemporaries St Jerome and St Ambrose, who was his bishop in Milan at the time of his conversion. How was it possible to reconcile admiration of pagan poets and philosophers of the reputation of Virgil, Horace, Cicero or Quintilian among the Romans, or Plato and Aristotle among the

43. *Bas-relief on a marble sarcophagus depicting a chariot-race in the Circus Maximus, Rome. (Compare Fig. 34.) Foligno, Museo Civico.*

44. *Devils in Hell Castle take up arms against the angels defending the City of God. Sixteenth-century wood-cut illustration to St Augustine's* City of God. *Avranches, Municipal Library.*

Greeks, with loyalty to the Christian faith? This was a question above all others that the leading thinkers and spokesmen for the new religion had to isolate and resolve. They themselves spoke and wrote in either Latin or Greek. How could they make themselves masters of either language without becoming closely acquainted with the principal works of the acknowledged masters of both? And the extant works of these masters included in the West manuscript copies of some plays of Plautus, Terence and Seneca and in the East various writings of at least Aristotle, Euripides and Menander. Content as well as style thus came inevitably to engage the minds of the new school of Christian writers. The solution to the problem, once it had been recognized and isolated, lay in reconcilement through argument. Take the pagan authors for what they were; give them their due; they were not gods but mortals; mortals, moreover, living in darkness but awaiting the enlightenment of the new faith; the certainty of a single universal creator, redeemer, judge and saviour instead of a pantheon of vaguely defined and erratically behaved gods, goddesses and demons. Then consult them in order to build on them. If your viewpoint represents a radical departure from cherished, traditional beliefs, then present it as progressive, as a logical and necessary step forward into a new and better society. Allegorize, translate, improve.

To this extent, at least, it is possible to recognize in Augustine someone who was fully aware of the continuing existence of dramatic art in Christian Europe, and a writer to whom, in the centuries to come, churchmen might turn for assistance in coming to terms with an art form with such loudly proclaimed and indeed self-evidently pagan origins as drama (Fig. 44).

3 PAPAL AUTHORITY AND HERETICAL OPINION

Reverting now to the sixth century AD, where *all* the arts were concerned, what was needed following the reconciliation finally achieved by Augustine (after some three centuries of endeavour and dispute between Christian progressives and representatives of the conservative, reactionary past) was an administrator with adequate executive authority to systemize it throughout the old Empire.

In the West this was forthcoming with the accession of a former Prefect of Rome itself, Gregory the Great, to the Papacy in AD 509, equipped with all the temporal power which by then accompanied that office. It was he who asserted the supremacy of the Roman See over all the Churches in the western world and laid the foundations for the ultimate triumph of the Latin liturgy. It is to him that we owe the establishment of the see of Canterbury in England, and the *Antiphonarium* of plain chant that still holds currency throughout the Christian world today. What was still lacking as the sixth century gave way to the seventh was military strength sufficient to protect the nascent culture of the new era against barbarian attack. Just as Imperial Rome, by the end of the fourth century, had exhausted its strength to control its own future, so by the close of the sixth century Christian Rome had squandered most of its own energies in endless committee meetings, councils, debates and attacks on deviant (heretical) groups and opinion. The most virulent and persistent of these groups was the sect led by Arius, bishop of Alexandria in the fourth century, who insisted that Christ, as God's son, was *not* God but only the most godlike of God's creatures. This view was roundly condemned at councils in Nicaea in AD 325 and again in Constantinople in AD 381, but it proved to be particularly attractive to barbarian settlers within the whole Empire and flourished for two hundred years, arising like brushwood fires in one place as quickly as it was extinguished in another. Exhausted by its battles against heresy, the new culture, which by the seventh century might otherwise have been expected to flower from its newly won self-confidence and security, found itself called upon to endure a battering of unparalleled ferocity. Saracens, Huns and Norsemen swept with ease across the former Imperial frontiers which by then were frequently protected only by recently converted barbarian mercenaries.

The Islamic attack on the Eastern Empire began early in the seventh century, with Palestine, Syria and Egypt all yielding to the invaders shortly after the death of Muhammad in AD 632. Within a hundred years the Muslims had absorbed the whole of the North African provinces and Spain and had entered France: thereafter they were slowly pushed back across the Pyrenees, but not out of Spain. Byzantium, besieged by the Persians in 626 and again by the Arabs in 721, stood firm. It was then the turn of the Northern and Western provinces to undergo the same experiences.

4 BARBARIAN INVASIONS AND SOCIAL INSTABILITY

What is material to the state of all the arts—dramatic art in particular in this context—is not so much the historical facts, names and dates that punctuate three centuries, but rather the political, economic and social instability that such facts represent. Mere survival at subsistence level overtakes cultural aspirations of any sort in such conditions. Caravans of refugees and resettlement camps become more familiar sights and experiences than the bourgeois occupations and aristocratic diversions of city dwellers, or even the traditional rhythms and patterns of farm life. It becomes more natural (because easier and more appropriate) to build in clay and wood instead of stone and plaster; alternatively to re-use the stones of empty buildings crumbling into ruins for the construction of fortifications and simple dwellings than to hack them out of quarries. The struggle to acquire enough food and clothing banishes leisure, and with it the time and inclination for artistic expression in forms other than the most utilitarian of crafts. Most deadly of all, it shatters confidence in human potential and achievement, replacing it with fear and all the dark imaginings of superstition.

5 RECONSTRUCTING CHRISTIAN EUROPE

(a) **The Holy Roman Empire and the Ninth-Century Renaissance:** What is thus truly astonishing about these terrible centuries of political and social turmoil is not so much the apparent collapse of all organized artistic life as the actual survival of so much of it in forms coherent enough to serve as a firm base for reconstruction to begin in a new world returning to some semblance of stability in the tenth and eleventh centuries. This change becomes perceptible with the coronation of Charlemagne as King of the Franks and Roman Emperor in Aachen (Aix-la-Chapelle) on Christmas Day, 800—although when recording this fact it is salutary to recall that while Charlemagne was able to read he never learned to write. Once this is appreciated, it becomes obvious that it is to the monastic libraries and classrooms that we must turn if we wish to

45. *A medieval puppet-play. Marginal illustration to the manuscript of* Li Roman d'Alexandre. *Flemish, c.1340. Oxford, Bodleian Library.*

know what aspects of Greek, Hellenistic and Roman artistic life the Christian conservationists had rescued from the barbarian holocaust, and how they re-interpreted what they had saved to their own contemporaries, as interest in learning and in the arts slowly revived.

(b) **Memories of Graeco-Roman Drama:** Salvaged for future reference and development were not only the names and plays of Seneca, Plautus and Terence among Roman authors, but also some rudimentary ideas of dramatic genre (at least as applied to literary narrative) derived from Horace's *Art of Poetry*, and the Latin vocabulary describing Roman festive recreations and places of performance. There also survived small groups of nomadic mimes, professional singers, acrobats and puppeteers (see Figs. 45 and 46). Opposed to all this, however, was the simultaneous survival of the violent denunciations by the early Christian fathers of Roman festivals and associated *ludi scenici* or *spectacula*. No less inimical to the redevelopment of theatrical life were the legendary accounts of those saints who had met martyrdom in the theatres and amphitheatres of the old Empire. Such had been the fate, for example, of St Felicity and St Perpetua—thrown to wild beasts by the Emperor Severus in Carthage in 203 to amuse his soldiers (Fig. 47).

Thus literate courtiers, churchmen and teachers of the Early Middle Ages found themselves confronted with a choice as stark as that originally presented to the Greeks by Plato and Aristotle. For Christian Europe the choice lay between Tertullian's and Augustine's approach to the theatre, playwrights and actors. If any true understanding of the subsequent development of the theatre throughout the Middle Ages and the Renaissance is to be grasped, it is essential to appreciate that this ancient Greek debate about whether poets and actors merited any place in an

46. *Musician, bear-ward and performing animals. Marginal illustration to the manuscript of* Li Roman d'Alexandre. *Flemish, c.1340. Oxford, Bodleian Library.*

47. *Bone diptych depicting the consul Anastasius holding up the prize money, thus signalling the start of the combat between gladiators and wild beasts in the amphitheatre below.* AD 517. *Paris, Musée Cluny.*

ideal society was itself among the debris salvaged from the so-called Dark Ages. But this conflict, when resumed, was to be fought out in the Christian philosophical and literary terms of reference formulated by Tertullian and Augustine and subsequently espoused by Wycliffe and Dante rather than specifically Greek or Roman ones, and to gather momentum over some six centuries to reach its climax during the Protestant Reformation and the Catholic Counter-Reformation. In other words, such notable apologists for the theatre in the sixteenth and seventeenth centuries as Erasmus, Thomas More, St Ignatius Loyola and Ben Jonson were able to derive their arguments as firmly from St Augustine as from Aristotle. The theatre's antagonists, on the other hand, could and did derive theirs as freely from Tertullian as from Plato: and they numbered in their ranks such formidable figures as John Calvin, John Knox, William Penn and William Prynne (see Chapter 8).

(c) **Pagan Festivals and Pagan Rituals:** In Christian Europe the battle began over the question of how to handle religious festivals, rites and shrines pertaining to cultures widely established and deeply rooted before the Christian missionaries arrived. Many of these customs were Roman imports, others indigenous—Celtic, Norse and Teutonic. Here are to be traced the origins of the sword-dances, battle-games or tournaments, maypoles, midsummer watches, bonfires and sacred groves and streams that figure so prominently in the social life and folk-arts of the Middle Ages. What, therefore, was to be done about these festivals and the dramatic rituals associated with them which the pioneers of the Christian faith found on their arrival in France, Germanic countries, Ireland and England during the sixth century? From Rome, Pope Gregory the Great and his successors decreed that confrontation should, where possible, be avoided. Instead, according to local circumstances, every effort should be made to persuade the local community first to consider, and then to accept, Christian alternatives. Adaptation was thus to be the answer. Transform a temple or a shrine into a church or hermitage. Translate the significance of a pagan ceremony into a celebration of a notable event in Christian history. In short, strive to convert by retaining what was already familiar and revered by transfiguring it into the service of Christian worship.

That this adaptation of existing festivals and folk customs to the service of Christian worship was the deliberate policy of the Church, decreed from Rome itself, is witnessed by Pope Gregory's instructions to Abbot Miletus in Canterbury in 601, shortly after his arrival there. Allow existing temples to stand, he says:

> Destroy the idols; purify the buildings with holy water; set relics there; and let them become the temples of the true God. So the people will have no need to change their places of concourse; and where of old they were wont to sacrifice cattle to demons, thither let them continue to resort on the day of the Saint to whom the church is dedicated and slay their beasts no longer as sacrifice, but for a social meal in honour of him whom they now worship.

This method was adopted everywhere and proved flexible enough to absorb, much later, into miracle, morality and saint plays, aspects of secular life—poetic, musical, even comic—which struck churchmen as likely to reinforce faith and to propagate it in areas where resistance was most stubborn.

(d) 'Christianizing' the Calendar: It is this approach that explains eventual agreement within the Roman Church to align the birth of Christ with the winter solstice late in December; Easter with the vernal equinox; Pentecost or Whitsuntide (and later Corpus Christi) with the summer solstice, and St Michael and All Angels (and later All Souls) with the autumnal equinox. By the same process other festivities came to be equated with the commemoration of particular apostles, saints and martyrs. In this way, the dramatic rituals of several primitive religions were absorbed into the Christian calendar. Precedence was naturally accorded to the Virgin Mary, to the twelve apostles, and to St Paul; but the popularity of particular saints also influenced the attachment of their names to the most significant dates in the agricultural year.

St Stephen, the first martyr, the Adoration of the Magi, the Massacre of the Innocents and the Circumcision of the infant Jesus *had* to be commemorated shortly after Christmas (and thus near the winter solstice) with the prophets shortly before it. The saints could be venerated at other times, but their feast days were also significantly grouped around the principal festivals of the agricultural year.

St John the Baptist, and St Peter and St Paul came thus to be commemorated annually near the summer solstice (21 June), on 24 June and 29 June respectively, thereby subsuming, as it was hoped, the old midsummer watches and bonfires of earlier cultures. Lesser figures like St Bartholomew, St Martin and St Giles came to be grouped around St Luke (18 October) and to be attached to harvest festivals and corresponding markets and fairs. Among still less substantially documented figures, legend determined that St Nicholas, St George, St Lawrence and St Catherine should be especially revered. Where a particular figure was chosen as the patron of a church, chantry or chapel, this too played an important part in transferring existing dramatic games and rituals in that locality from public holidays previously celebrated within an earlier culture to one of the new, Christian alternatives. All such changes were gradually reinforced by the formation of guilds especially constituted to ensure that the holy day in question should be adequately funded and regularly celebrated—a movement which reaches its apogee in the fourteenth century with the establishment of the Corpus Christi guilds charged with the annual production of the miracle cycles in England. Another, earlier example of this adaptation of the pagan past to Christian needs explains the use made of a manuscript copy of Terence's plays in the library of the monastery at Gandesheim in Saxony where the nun Hrostwitha wrote (*c.*970) five plays in imitation of them, extolling the virtues of Christian piety, chastity and fortitude in the face of persecution.

As this process of using old skins to contain new wine slowly advanced, some dislocation of traditional customs and calendar dates occurred: some of the most cherished among them, however, obstinately refused to be accommodated. This is most noticeable in respect of certain spring and autumn festivals, since it is there that geography and climate had the most marked effects on the time chosen to plough the fields, sow crops, inseminate flocks of sheep and cattle, harvest corn and grapes, and slaughter stock when fodder ran short. Thus superimposition of a regular, annual, Christian calendar upon existing customs in countries facing the North Sea and the Atlantic could not be kept wholly in phase with efforts to achieve the same end in countries bordering upon the Mediterranean.

Nor did the Church's own obligation to attach the date of Easter to the lunar calendar help. Itself a 'floating' feast which could be celebrated in one year as early as 25 March and in another not until 25 April, it dragged the subsequent feasts of Whitsuntide and Ascension Day—celebrated at fixed intervals from Easter—with it. Certain farming festivals of great antiquity within the former Roman

48. Swiss tapestry depicting wildmen (woderwose) and a wild woman with legendary beasts. c.1450. London, Victoria and Albert Museum.

Empire like May Day with all its vestigial fertility rites continued to be celebrated independently of the Christian Calendar (Fig. 48). Another and even more contentious festival directly descended from the Roman Kalends and dedicated to social inversion and licence, the notorious Feast of Fools, continued to be observed, notwithstanding frequent prohibitions, shortly after Christmas (Fig. 50). Two other such festivals of great subsequent importance to the story of the theatre were Twelfth Night and Carnival: both of these found a loose location in Christian observance—the former being linked, through the giving of presents, to the Visit of the Magi and thus with Epiphany; the latter with Shrovetide, notably Shrove Tuesday (Pancake Day), and thus with Ash Wednesday as an excuse for a final blow out before the annual forty days of Lenten fasting and penitence. All four festivals were reluctantly condoned by the Church as 'seasons of goodwill'; but the borderline between goodwill and excess is a thin one, as individual bishops never ceased to point out, yet seemingly with little effect.

Three of these ancient festivities evolved during the early Middle Ages into forms of particular significance to the subsequent development of dramatic art: mumming, folly or misrule, and tournaments.

6 MUMMING

The genesis of mumming (out of which developed the disguising which in its turn produced the English masque, Spanish *momeries*, French *ballet de cour* and Italian *intermezzo*) lies unquestionably in the propitiatory ritual of gift-giving. That was its *raison d'être*. In medieval times the word mumming was as closely associated with silence as it was with disguise and dance (cf. German *mumme*; Danish *mom*; closed, or sealed lips; silence; secrecy) and continued to be used in that sense by Shakespeare. A mumming harnessed the rituals of disguise and dance to a procession and visitation to the home of a social superior—normally the king or some provincial magnate to whom allegiance was in some way due—and was conducted in

49. Three of the six carved wooden panels ornamenting the upper balcony of 'The Golden Roof', Innsbruck. c.1450. On the right, princely spectators; centre and left, male acrobatic dancers with performing dogs and monkeys.

50. *Mimes or mummers disguised as animals. Marginal illustration to the manuscript of* Li Roman d'Alexandre. *Flemish, c.1340. Oxford, Bodleian Library.*

silence. This silence was a needful corollary of the polite fiction that the visitors were both strangers (which they were not) and costumed and masked so as to seem to be characters (which indeed they were) other than themselves—cardinals, for instance, or African kings, or shepherds (see pp. 85–6). Convention decreed that they should employ a herald or presenter to announce their arrival, to beg leave for their admission, and to explain the purpose of their visit. Leave granted, they then danced among themselves, but not with their hosts, presented their gifts and departed as silently as they had come. It is legitimate to view this ritual as a survival of the Roman practice of offering oblations to the goddess Fortuna (and later to the Emperor) on New Year's Day: it is just as legitimate to view it as a commemoration and imitation of the visit of the three Kings to Bethlehem and their obeisance to the infant Jesus in the crib with gifts of gold, frankincense and myrrh on 6 January, Epiphany. If mumming thus became attached to Twelfth Night—a day of especial goodwill—within the annual calendar, it was no less appropriate as a ritual to celebrate a wedding or a christening. In short, it supplied an appropriate dramatic form for a particular type of social occasion.

7 LORDS OF MISRULE

Folly, to which medieval Christendom devoted itself annually on the days immediately after Christmas and again at Carnival, celebrates Dionysus, Apollo and Saturn far more self-evidently than any obvious Christian figure. Lip-service was paid to an association between the need for humility and meekness in Christian conduct on the one hand and the three feast days prescribed for children on the other, St Nicholas (6 December), Holy Innocents (28

December) and the Circumcision (1 January), which provided some justification for festivities characterized by an inversion of social hierarchy—hence the Boy Bishop. Parody of Christian ritual and liturgy (also an inversion) to the point of obscenity and even blasphemy was altogether another matter: yet such conduct, as practised by the minor clergy, novices and their servants at this season had its own parallels, if not its own antecedents, in the secular plays of Aristophanes and in at least some scenes in those of Plautus (Figs. 50 and 51). This proved hard to control, impossible to cure! The survival of the *Carmina Burana* from the monastery at Benediktbeuern (so memorably orchestrated for modern ears by Carl Orff) proves the point. Thus, in England, Robert Grosseteste, when Bishop of Lincoln, wrote to priests in his diocese *c*.1230:

> We command and strongly enjoin you by virtue of your obedience that as regards the Feast of Fools which is replete with vanity and soiled with sensuality, hateful to God yet acceptable to devils, you absolutely forbid it to be held in future on the Feast-day of the Holy Circumcision of Our Lord in the Church.

Because Lent covers the forty days prior to Easter, Shrovetide which introduces it (including Carnival, Shrove Tuesday), unlike the Feast of Fools or that of the Boy

51. *A scene from Terence's* The Woman of Andros *as depicted in an early medieval manuscript copy of Terence's plays. Oxford, Bodleian Library.*

52. An allegorical and satiric caricature by Pieter Bruegel the Elder, closely related to his Strife between Shrovetide [Carnival] and Lent *of 1559. Copenhagen, National Art Museum.*

Bishop, which fell on fixed dates, is a 'floating' Feast. Nevertheless, it would always occur in February or March which means that it was likely to be very cold. In medieval Europe the shortages of milk, meat, fish, grain, fruit and vegetables for both human and animal consumption were perennial questions of far more serious concern than they are to us today, closely matched by the scarcity of fuel and the difficulty of travel even between towns. Carnival (literally *Carnem Vale*, or 'farewell to meat') with larder-shelves in most households at their lowest point of the year was thus as much an advance warning of a sustained period of physical austerity, danger and endurance as a season of revelry. In short, whole communities throughout Europe, clergy included, recognized a clarion call to abandon the abrasive routines of heavy physical work in favour of a brief spell of equally physical pleasure—a festival of thanksgiving for survival thus far beyond the solstice, combined with one of propitiation against whatever hazards the winter still held concealed. If ever there was an occasion to turn to the secular world and invite its active participation in these celebrations this was it (Fig. 52). Gift-giving thus formed as usual a part in the festivities as buffoonery, gluttony, drunkenness, and sexual licence: the tavern took over from the church as the true centre of spiritual life, and what followed might be described as a feast in honour of the seven deadly sins. Carnival thus offered a well-nigh unique opportunity for student entertainers—intelligent, witty and talented—to bid for the patronage of landed noblemen and wealthy merchants alike. This they did with

songs, satirical verses directed at all irksomely restrictive institutions—religious, political, social, and educational—and with mimicry directed against the more pompous and tiresome individual representatives of these institutions. Carnival thus became the nursery garden of new forms of satirical and farcical comedy within a Christian world. To this we must return in Chapter 5.

8 TOURNAMENTS

The third type of festive celebration that aroused both the continuing suspicion and the hostility of the Church, but which succeeded in re-establishing itself during the Christian Middle Ages, was the tournament. Derived from man's vital need to acquire hunting skills and the arts of self-defence with primitive weapons, these athletic games contained an innate, competitive element. The best wrestler, swordsman, runner and archer thus developed into a local champion. Such men came to be selected as natural tribal leaders—men apart, charged with the defence of a community's physical well-being, just as priests were treated as men apart, selected to safeguard its social and spiritual welfare. As these men acquired power, so they acquired the primary status symbols demonstrative of it—land and the right to call upon the services of others. Throughout the old Empire this military aristocracy adopted the motto 'might is right', at least in so far as it was allowed to by that other, literate aristocracy, the leaders of the Church, whose spiritual authority was by the tenth century frequently backed by land, wealth and serfs. Where war and diplomacy were concerned these two factions eclipsed all others in early medieval society: the battle between athletes and aesthetes had begun. In time they would be challenged by a third estate, the merchants whose wealth and power would be obtained through the acquisition of commodities and trade (see pp. 88–96); but in the tenth century this challenge had not developed into a serious threat. That could only come with political and social stability sufficient to allow cities to grow; and stability itself depended on the success of the military men in demarcating new frontiers and securing them against invaders and pirates.

It was to this end that the need for battle-schools and training grounds became apparent. And therein lay a pointed reminder of Roman example, wherever memories of it survived, in respect of those athletic games known as the *ludi circenses*, the chariot races, gladiatorial combats, and duels with wild animals that had been conducted in arenas and amphitheatres purpose-built to contain them (see pp. 49–52). These memories fused with functional needs in Christian society and account for the re-emergence of tournaments in their several forms—jousts on horseback and on foot, riding at the ring, tilting at the quintain, and the *Pas d'Armes*—as a major feature of recreational pastimes in the early Middle Ages. The competitive and heroic elements intrinsic to them quickly attracted the attention of ladies; and once that happened, as was certainly the case by the twelfth century, when the award of prizes for the victors amidst songs and dances in banquet halls at night became habitual, the promoters of these crude battle-schools were safe in the knowledge that, no matter how loudly the Church might denounce them, they had acquired allies who would ensure their continuance and development. The presence of ladies added a dimension of romance, and with it a dimension more appropriate to *ludi scenici*, or theatrical art, than to the art of war (see Plate 8 and Figs. 66 and 68). Thus a path was opened that would lead over the next six centuries to 'the soft and silken wars' exploited in the Italian courtyards of the Medici, the Estes and the Borgias, in the Whitehall banquet houses of James I, Ben Jonson and Inigo Jones, and ultimately in the gardens of Louis XIV at Versailles, and in the Spanish Riding School in Vienna which still survives for our inspection today as the last true survival of a once dynamic and noble tradition (see Figs. 92, 128, 129 and 130).

The popularity of tournaments contributed substantially to the theatrical resources open to the emergent scripted drama in Christian Europe. Above all they extended the devices available for the identification of characters in stage-costume by adding the whole visual vocabulary of the iconography of heraldry to that already in use in Church vestments. Tournaments also encouraged the provision of spectacular scenic devices and personal properties to identify the locality of the assumed action and the allegorical personages presented to spectators. The organizers and patrons who financed these spectacular combats pioneered the erection of timber-built stadiums called 'lists' with adjacent, raised stages to accommodate spectators. Primitive as these structures were compared with their Roman antecedents, they nevertheless represent a major advance in the orderly provision of theatrical entertainment to the public, and they were destined to be developed via the bull- and bear-baiting arenas of Tudor London into the famous Wooden 'O' of Shakespeare's Globe Playhouse (see Plate 9 and Figs. 97 and 102).

If the right to participate in tournaments was rigidly restricted to the nobility, and if mumming and misrule were predominantly the instinctive creations of humbler folk in the early Middle Ages, and if both were anchored in secular attitudes and aspirations, the Church occupied the middle ground. The stance that it finally adopted, having failed to tame the strains of either Dionysus or Mars in the actual behaviour of its converts, whether self-consciously or not, was once again to imitate and transform what it could not suppress. Having first harnessed architecture, sculpture, and painting to its service in the years between the conversion of the Emperor Constantine in 312 and the end of the sixth century, thereafter it proceeded more cautiously in psalmody and hymn-singing to enlist poetry and music, as advocated by Prudentius, Ambrose, Augustine and Boethius, and as regulated by Gregory the Great in the seventh century, to ornament its own liturgies. By the tenth century, at least in monasteries adhering to the Benedictine rule, it was ready on its principal feast days to flirt with dramatic art in its own interest and on its own terms.

9 CHRISTIAN RELIGIOUS DRAMA

What we now describe as liturgical music drama was the handmaid of occasion, an occasion so special in the Christian calendar as to merit exceptional celebration and explanation. These twin requirements produced elementary re-enactment of the event itself. It is not credible that this came about as a result of some 'let's-write-a-play' decision taken by committee in the chapter house; rather it will have occurred through the gradual and natural extension of existing combinations of liturgical texts cast in dialogue form with choric chants divided antiphonally—i.e. with one voice responding to another alternately: and it only

53. Quem quaeritis in sepulchro? *Text and musical notation of the troped Introit for Easter Sunday Mass from St Gall. c.975. St Gall, Stiftsbibliothek.*

---

involved stretching the existing practice of 'troping' in this particular direction. The special quality of the occasion to be celebrated provided its own additional dynamic to press art beyond existing limits into the service of praise and thanksgiving worthy of the occasion. And there, primacy of place had unhesitatingly to be accorded to Easter Sunday and the Resurrection of Christ Crucified from the Dead (see Fig. 57). It was in this context that the introit, or introductory text for Mass on Easter morning was first 'troped'— i.e. chanted antiphonally. When translated into English, the Latin text reads as follows:

1st Voice	Whom seek ye in the sepulchre?
2nd Voice	Jesus of Nazareth.
1st Voice	He is not here; he is risen as predicted when it was prophesied that he would rise from the dead.
2nd Voice	Alleluia! The Lord is risen!
All Voices	Come and see the place.

Divide these lines between the angel guarding the sepulchre and the three Marys seeking to embalm the corpse; let four priests represent these individuals, and let the altar-table represent the sepulchre, and what results is a simple re-

enactment of the historical event commemorated in the introit (see Fig. 53). The instructions for the execution of this ceremony as set down in writing by St Ethelwold, Bishop of Winchester, in his *Concordia Regularis* for the Benedictine houses in England, c.975, indicate beyond doubt that re-enactment was the desired objective, and that the reawakening of faith in the reality of the event, albeit miraculous, was the essential justification for placing it within the Mass itself for that day, at that hour, and there alone.

Although deliberately a representation of an historical event, the style of re-enactment that is prescribed in the rubrics of the service books is as noticeably Romanesque as the buildings in which it was to be undertaken, and as the mosaics and frescoes which decorated their interiors or the sculpture placed on their exteriors: direct imitation of natural behaviour is not called for, only an identifiable approximation (Fig. 54). The Latin words *quasi*, as if, and *quomodo*, in the manner of, govern the costuming, actions, and even the sex of the participants throughout. Should we call them priests? Dare we call them actors? They were both at one and the same time, and were seen and heard to be so by those assembled to participate in the Mass. Should we call the latter 'the brethren', or should we describe them as the audience? They were both: partakers of the Mass and witnesses to the enactment of the event. And in the latter capacity they are called upon directly to bear witness in the world to what they had just seen and heard when required to sing *Te Deum Laudamus . . .*, We give thanks to thee O Lord . . ., at the end of the performance. A performance it certainly was, although almost literally an amateur one-night stand: yet it was also essentially a devotional exercise, undertaken within a context of worship; but in this instance worship reinforced by art to heighten the quality of the praise and thanks offered, and that of the attendant joy and comfort received.

Once formulated, this practice could readily be adapted to fit the celebration of Christ's birth and Ascension, and of the guiding star that led three kings—men of exceptional vision, initiative, and courage—to kneel and offer gifts to a child in a manger (Fig. 58a, b). It was swiftly so adapted, and this provided the Christian Church with an initial repertory of lyric dramas of its own devising—much, one may imagine, to Augustine's liking even if inviting the stern disapproval of Tertullian in the heavenly auditorium surrounding the great theatre of the terrestrial world. Though never conceived of as 'instructive' in the first instance, this practice, once widely established, could obviously be extended into a teaching instrument of considerable emotive power and effectiveness among devout but illiterate congre-

54. *Stone bas-relief depicting the visit of the Three Maries to the sepulchre. c.1130. Gustorf, Pfarrkirche.*

gations. Surviving records indicate that the Church was ready to move in this direction early in the thirteenth century.

Such then are the foundation stones upon which our modern theatre was built. In part intuitive and natural, in part doctrinally inspired and calculated; in some respects a product of earlier pagan worlds, both highly sophisticated and barbaric, in others a Christian metamorphosis; sometimes confused and confusing, at others crystal clear. What is certain is that by the eleventh century, both in secular and ecclesiastical environments, dramatic art had returned to Europe in recognizably ordered forms. It had come to stay for another thousand years and to spread its branches to other continents.

PART II

GOD AND THE COMMUNITY

Introduction

The displacement in Europe of a bewildering variety of gods and goddesses—Greek, Roman, Celtic, Norse and Teutonic—in favour of an undivided Trinity of God the Father, Son and Holy Ghost, which had become an accepted political fact of life by the tenth century AD, not only determined the development of the theatre during the next five centuries, but has contributed significantly (if decreasingly) to it ever since.

Notwithstanding the collapse of the Roman Empire in the fifth century AD, the spiritual life of the civilized world continued to be governed from Rome; so it was by the authority of, and within the conditions prescribed by, the Bishop of Rome that four centuries later dramatic art recovered a dynamic that could again transform it from a dormant adjunct to religious ritual into forms of theatre that could both entertain and teach.

These new forms were indisputably Christian despite the intrusion of many features absorbed from secular life; but it was in fact secular pressures which, as time passed and a more stable climate of political and economic life encouraged the growth of towns, industry and trade, transformed so many aspects of medieval theatre into community events. Once they had been thus transformed internationally from Spain to Poland and from Hungary to Ireland, laymen came to share a wide measure of responsibility for financing and organizing play-production on all calendar holidays. The fact that these performances were therefore organized on an occasional rather than a regular basis ensured that drama would remain a predominantly amateur art form; and this continued to be the case until early in the sixteenth century when a clamour arose in Northern Europe for root and branch reform of all relationships between Church and State.

The decision of the Roman Catholic Church to become an active patron of dramatic art, its reasons for doing so, and the conditions it imposed upon the circumstances of all performances will be discussed in Chapter 5. The impact of lay interest, and the developments which followed from it during the fourteenth and fifteenth centuries will be considered in Chapter 6.

---

55. Eleventh-century mosaic of Christ as Pantocrator in the dome of the central apse of Monreale Cathedral, Sicily.

975	**Benedictine Reform: Drama of Christ the King**	1352	Bishop Grandisson bans performance of satirical play in Exeter
c.975–80	*Visitatio Sepulchri* performed at St Gall, Switzerland; Fleury, France; and Winchester, England St Ethelwold of Winchester writes his *Concordia Regularis*	1364	The Plague (the Black Death) assumes epidemic proportions
1066	Norman Conquest of England	c.1375	William Langland writes *Piers Plowman*
1098	Founding of Cistercian Order at Cîteaux	1377	Guild Plays performed on Corpus Christi Day at Beverley, Yorkshire
	Twelfth-century Reformation and Renaissance: Drama in Transition	1377/8	*The Conquest of Jerusalem* performed at a banquet in Paris
c.1150	*Officium Stellae* at Benoit-sur-Loire includes King Herod and soldiers Hilarius in Paris writes Latin plays about Daniel, Lazarus and St Nicholas	1380–90	Chaucer writes *The Canterbury Tales*
		c.1380	Wycliffe writes his 'Treatise against Miracles'
1164	Chartres Cathedral completed	1388/9	*The Fall of Troy* performed at a banquet in Paris
1167	Founding of University of Oxford	1390	Richard II builds Westminster Hall
1188–92	Third Crusade		**Drama of Repentance, Reward and Punishment: Interludes**
1180–1200	Anglo-Norman *Jeu d'Adam* *Play of Antichrist* performed at Tegernsee, Bavaria *Play of Daniel* performed at Beauvais, France	1415	Huss burned at the stake as a heretic in Prague
1208	University of Paris accorded formal recognition by Pope Innocent III	1418	Mummings banned in London
1209	Foundation of Franciscan Order	1425–30	Lydgate's Disguisings for Henry VI and the Livery Companies of London
1215	Foundation of Dominican Order	c.1450	*The Castle of Perseverance* written and performed in East Anglia
1200–20	Founding of Trade Guilds in large manufacturing towns		The play of *The Lives of the Apostles* performed at Bourges in France
	Drama of Christ Crucified: Secular Entertainers	1453	Constantinople falls to the Ottoman Turks
1238	Grosseteste, Bishop of Lincoln, bans celebration of the Feast of Fools	1450–60	Invention of gunpowder; invention of printing
1264	Pope Urban IV promulgates the Feast of Corpus Christi	1470	*Maître Pierre Pathelin* written in France
1298	Passion play performed in Latin at Cividale, North Italy	1486	Plautus' *Menaechmi* performed in Ferrara
c.1300	Farcical *Interlude of the Student and his Girl Friend* written in Middle English	c.1490	*Mankind* and *Everyman* written and performed in England
1319–21	Dante completes the *Divine Comedy* in Ravenna	1497	Henry Medwall's *Fulgens and Lucres* performed at Lambeth Palace, London
1325	Adam de la Halle's farces performed in Arras	1504	Dom Hadton writes the Cornish *Ordinalia* and the play of *St Meriasek*
		1509	*Mystery of the Three Saints* written and performed at Romans in Southern France
		c.1515–20	John Skelton writes *Magnyfycence*
		1517	Martin Luther posts his 95 'Theses of Protest' on Wittenberg church door

5

Dramatic Experiment in Christian Europe, 1000–1300

1 DRAMA OF CHRIST THE KING

When Europe emerged from two centuries of virtual siege economy late in the ninth century, all received traditions respecting dramatic art embracing both audience expectancies and techniques of preparation and performance had as good as vanished. The pioneers of a fresh start, therefore, were fettered only by the constraints imposed upon them by a largely agrarian society under a feudal form of government. The most compelling of these was the attitude of the Christian Church ruled from Rome and claiming ultimate authority over everyone including kings and queens.

The drama of praise and thanksgiving devoted to Christ the King which evolved within the liturgies of the Christian Church during the tenth, eleventh and twelfth centuries was governed in its development in part by the limited number of special occasions it existed to celebrate, and in part by the behaviour of the biblical characters represented in it. After the celebration of the five major feasts of Easter, Christmas, Epiphany, Whitsun and Ascension, the calendar simply did not offer occasions warranting similar treatment unless the principle be extended to the Virgin Mary and to the apostles, saints and martyrs. Nor, with one notable exception—the tyrant Herod—was the behaviour required of the characters actually represented in the liturgical music dramas anything but exemplary as judged by Christian standards. Acting roles therefore called for little more than the adoption of appropriately devout postures and gesture: speech was confined to Latin verse, chanted at that. For the most part Christian liturgical ceremonial had descended directly from that prescribed for the princes of Hellenistic courts and that accorded to the bureaucracy of the Roman Emperors of the second century AD. So, with only minor modifications, had Church vest-

ments. Church music, however, was more closely related to Jewish precedent. The most important difference between all early Christian and early Oriental practice was the emphasis placed by the Church on representation. From the outset, the joyous dramatic rituals devised to celebrate Christ's Resurrection and Nativity rested, as explained in Chapter 4, on re-enactment of the event itself, the biblical text that established the factual character of both providing the nucleus in each case: thus without reference to Aristotle, his precept that drama is an imitation of an action was exactly fulfilled. The style of this representation could hardly be other than particular to its own age and environment; and that, as we have seen, was formal and artificial in extreme: we call it Romanesque (see pp. 65–7). In other words, apart from the unique element of animation, there was little that differed in the visual *appearance* of these brief dramatic spectacles from depictions of the same scenes already long familiar in mosaic, fresco or bas-relief (Figs. 54 and 58a). The difference of consequence was that of *impact*, and that was supplied by animation of these well-known scenes. Once that had been admitted within the context of worship, there could be no looking back.

2 TRANSITION

(a) **Ritual in Conflict with Entertainment**: This had clearly been recognized by the leaders of the Church as accomplished fact by the end of the twelfth century when an Anglo-Norman poet wrote a play (more probably in England than in France) about Adam and Eve entitled *Ordo Representationis Adae* (normally known as the *Jeu d'Adam*) for performance in the courtyard outside a church rather than in it. This title is doubly significant, for it both retains the liturgical Latin *Ordo* (literally 'rite'), indicative of its origin, and adds the theatrical 'representation', indicative of the changes that had occurred in the course of two centuries. *Ordo* was liturgically virtually interchangeable with *Officium*, and it is under one or other of these rubrics that all the early liturgical music dramas were described. This entitles us to say, with some claim to accuracy, that the pioneers of these re-enactments of biblical texts were unaware of any possible conflict between dramatization of historical event and entertainment in the secular sense of that word. Yet that was just the dilemma they were called upon to face once the *Officium Stellae* (Office of the Star, or Visit of the Magi) had been added to the Offices of the Visit to the Sepulchre and the Visit to the Crib. The catalyst was King Herod from whom the three distinguished foreigners first obtained permission to visit Bethlehem: they were then asked to report to him personally what they had seen before returning home. When warned in a dream not to do so, they left by another route and Herod, in a rage, ordered his soldiers to kill all children under the age of two. Self-evidently Herod's conduct, more especially since his edict was aimed at the infant Jesus, could not be described as Christian, quite the reverse! How then does the priest charged with representing Herod in the *Officium Stellae* at Mass on 6 January each year conduct himself? How does he behave when informed by the Magi of the purpose of their journey to Judea?

The answer given in the twelfth-century *Herodes* from St Benoit-sur-Loire is clearly defined in both rubrics and text. After Herod's councillors have confirmed from the writings of the prophets that the Magi's belief in Christ's birth is there predicted, the choir is instructed to sing the hymn, 'Thou, Bethlehem, art not the least of cities . . .' There follows this stage-direction:

Then let Herod, having seen the prophecy, kindled with rage, hurl the book to the floor; but let his son, hearing the tumult, advance to calm his father, and, standing, salute him:

> Hail, renowned father!
> Hail, illustrious King,
> Who rulest everywhere
> Holding the royal sceptre!

Herod:

> Most renowned son,
> Worthy of the tribute of praise,
> Bearing in thy name
> The pomp of royal glory.
>
> A King is born stronger
> Than we, and more powerful.

> I fear lest he shall drag us
> From our royal throne.

Then let the son, speaking contemptuously of Christ, offer himself as a champion, saying:

> Against that pretty King
> Against the new-born babe,
> Bid, O father, thy son
> To begin this combat.

The Magi are then sent on their way to Bethlehem, but as they leave the rubric prescribes, 'Let Herod and his son menace with their swords.'

Both vocally and in his deportment Herod was thus called upon to behave in an unseemly, undignified and barbarous manner. Intent on committing both regicide and deicide, his actions are patently blasphemous. On the stage such emotions and decisions need to be reflected in postures, vocal delivery and gesture that is either frightening or ridiculous, possibly a touch of both. Here the temptation to draw upon the proven experience and technique of the popular entertainers at the village festivals and markets of secular life must have been great. Once the priest representing Herod had arrived at actions—pompous, threatening, out of control—that fitted the words, he had created (however inadvertently) a character that entertained; a character, that is, who was perceived (with a frisson of delight) to be terrifying and comic: and once this has happened, the gravity and decorum of an *officium* has been breached and a door opened to a return to the Roman *ludus scenicus*, or stage-play. Where the *Officium Stellae* was concerned this development reached its limit in the treatment accorded to the soldiers—brutal, licentious and (anachronistically) followers of Muhammad—and to the mothers so unequally matched against them. The ensuing massacre thus could not possibly escape transformation into a *ludus*, game or play (Fig. 56). By the end of the twelfth century, so far had this aspect of the play developed that the Abbess of Hohenburg, near Strasbourg, felt obliged to remonstrate against this exhibition of 'irreligion and extravagance with all the licence of youth'. Her complaints are vividly descriptive: 'The priests,' she says, 'having changed their clothes, go forth as a troop of warriors . . . the church is desecrated by feasting and drinking, buffoonery, unseemly jokes, play and the clang of weapons, the presence of shameless wenches . . .'

In the light of these outraged sensibilities, it is obvious that all remaining semblance of a liturgical office had become submerged in the theatricality of play-acting. Translated into literal and practical terms of reference this

56. *King Herod and his son; Massacre of the Innocents; Flight into Egypt. Detail from the tympanum over the entrance to the North transept, Notre-Dame, Paris.*

meant that the Latin *platea* of the service books—'the place'—had been transformed into what we call the 'acting area'; similarly, the Latin *sedes* (lit. seats) to accommodate the characters re-enacting the historical event had expanded into identifiable scenic locations. The complete story in this case requires three such *sedes*: Herod's palace, the manger in Bethlehem, and Egypt. To the individual in charge of the representation, this is likely to mean a throne for Herod; a crib for the Christ-child (possibly with ox and ass in attendance), and a palm tree for Egypt. As the characters travel from one location to the next, time is compressed to comply with dramatic economy, and the acting area changes its identity as one location (*sedes*) is abandoned and the next one comes into use. There is no need for a change of scenery, in our sense of the word; actions and dialogue suffice. Thus handled, words and images correspond closely enough to create a work of dramatic art capable of appealing directly to the minds and emotions

of everyone assembled to witness it; given the nature of the story and the action represented, re-enactment of holy writ serves also to entertain.

Exits and entrances were normally effected by recourse to elaborate ceremonial processions. These are graphically described in the rubrics of a relatively long choral drama about the prophet Daniel that has survived from the early years of the thirteenth century entitled simply *Ludus Danielis*. Written by the young novices at Beauvais for performance on Christmas Eve, it is scripted partly in Latin and partly in French; but this play too contains, in King Belshazzar and King Darius, characters who are disbelievers, blasphemers lacking faith—tyrants. Both are melodramatic in conception and require representation as bogeymen, threatening yet absurd; an acting style that will match these requirements, however, threatens to smash the formal, restrictive frame of a devotional icon, and to print on the minds of spectators a highly animated, credible human being in its place. Here we are witnessing a movement towards increasing realism in theatrical representation corresponding to the transition from the Romanesque to the Gothic style in art. This transition was not accomplished smoothly. The leaders of the Church became thoroughly alarmed as they came to recognize that what at first had seemed so natural and so fitting an extension to the normal forms of worship had acquired dimensions that were as uncontrollable as they were inappropriate.

(b) Compromises: One answer, a compromise, was to distance these representations away from the Mass itself to Matins or Vespers on the same day: another was to displace them from the sanctuary to some more public part of the building or even to its immediate vicinity, weather permitting: a third was to admit error in the first place and seek to turn back the clock by banning all performances in future. All three were tried in one place or another throughout the Christian world; but, as we know from the twelfth century *Play of Antichrist* from Tegernsee in Bavaria, with its extraordinary amalgam of stage battles and political propaganda in a wholly liturgical format, the process had already advanced too far to be checked by such methods. (See pp. 89–90.)

Although scripted in Latin and as ritualistic in its presentation as any liturgical *officium*, it is described as a *ludus*, mixes abstract personifications freely with named historical characters and might on that account be mistaken for a play of much later date. The script calls for at least sixty actors and seven scenic locations: it also contains four battle scenes. Moreover, the subject matter is so organized as to convince all modern critics that the play was composed as propaganda for the Emperor Frederick Barbarossa's campaign to launch the Third Crusade. The play is thus as political in its content as it is liturgical in its form, and thus takes us back to the world of Aeschylus (pp. 34–6). The *aula*, or refectory of the abbey, would thus seem a more likely locality for its performance than the *basilica*, or church.

A fourth and altogether more radical answer lay to hand however; and that was to fall back on the well-tried Christian method of seeming to accept a *fait accompli* while actually translating the offensive object into one that promoted the Church's own, missionary interests (see pp. 60–2). Thus, if an animated re-enactment of an event recorded in the Bible, or in the legendary life of a saint, could entertain as well as establish faith—liturgical plays of St Paul and St Nicholas had provided early examples—why could not such representations also be used to teach? Was not Christ's humanity as important as His divinity? Coincidentally the arrival of St Francis and St Dominic on the stage of world history at this very point in time played a vital role in ensuring that this last alternative would be the solution actually adopted.

3 THE DRAMA OF CHRIST CRUCIFIED

(a) The Advent of the Friars: Early in the thirteenth century the two Orders of preaching friars, now known universally as the Franciscans and Dominicans in their distinctive habits of brown and black respectively, obtained papal encouragement to undertake a missionary crusade, preaching the gospel from wayside pulpits and living off the charitable donations received from begging. In discharging this commission they abandoned Latin for the vernacular and followed Christ in teaching through parables, drawing for their metaphors and similes on the local occupations, pastimes, and domestic concerns of their listeners. Not surprisingly they were understood. Consequently their work succeeded in doing as much to develop modern languages as it did to restore a respect for a Christian style of living to an illiterate and hedonistic peasantry. As story-tellers they had few rivals and frequently punctuated their monologues with dramatic incident and lively characterization: nor were they afraid to include mordant social criticism of nobles, knights, bishops, lawyers and merchants in their discourses. A century or so later these satirical attacks would find their way into the dialogue of the judgement play in the miracle cycles and into both the speech and conduct of many of the vices in the moralities; so it is important to remark on the encouragement that the preaching techniques adopted by the friars gave to the development of dramatic art grounded on the realism of secular life, but deliberately sublimated to evangelical ends.

Central to their teaching was the humanity of Christ. This represented a sharp break from earlier monastic concern with Christ's divinity. Necessarily, within this context, the Crucifixion—a rather gloomy and depressing subject in itself—assumed an importance hitherto neglected or avoided. Instead, both the pity of it and its horror became topics to be stressed, since both could be relied upon to evoke a strong emotional response. It can hardly be coincidental that the best-known portrait of St Francis was painted by the same man who painted the earliest life-size representation of the Crucifixion, Cimabue.

Like the preaching friars, painters, sculptors and manuscript illuminators late in the twelfth century and early in the thirteenth found new sources of inspiration for depicting sacred subjects in the life around them, and not least in antiquarianism. Museum objects like jewelry, ornamental friezes, tomb-stones, statues, mosaic tiles and—more especially in Italy—wall paintings surviving from the days of the Roman Empire, stimulated a conscious if experimental revival of realistic techniques in the treatment of landscape and both human and animal portraiture (see

57. English alabaster relief of the Resurrection, early fifteenth century. Dramatically realistic in their detail, this and similar carvings depicting other biblical scenes are representative of the costumes and groupings found in the same scenes in the Mystery Cycles. London, Victoria and Albert Museum.

Fig. 29). This extension of visual aesthetics and possibilities was as certain to have important repercussions on dramatic art in respect of costume, settings and characterization as were the experiments of the preachers with narrative and vocabulary on dramatic dialogue and play construction (Figs. 56 and 58b).

(b) Towns, Merchants, Universities and Secular Entertainers: Several other factors contributed to the rapidly widening horizons of theatrical possibilities at about this time. One of them was the cult of tournaments among the nobility already discussed in Chapter 4; another was trade, and with it the growth of a wealthy merchant class resident in towns rather than in the country; a third was the foundation of Europe's earliest universities (Bologna, Padua, Cracow, Paris, Oxford and Cambridge) to provide trained, literate recruits to the expanding professions—theologians, lawyers, doctors and administrators (clerks). All three of these developments affected patronage of all the arts. The lords temporal provided artists of all sorts with an alternative to the lords spiritual; the merchants, envious of both and anxious to acquire the most recognizable symbols of social status, offered a third choice; and in the universities, the students themselves were quick to exploit these options for their own survival or personal advancement. As minstrels—poets, musicians and sometimes both—they had wit, skill, time and youth on their side, all of which were attractive to ladies: as impecunious, but spirited and literate students they possessed the talents needed to entertain their merchant neighbours by satirizing the pretensions of the aristocracy whom they both envied and despised: and as actors they could supplement their own standard of living through the rewards attaching to their own popularity as purveyors of romance, satire and farce with women, merchants and artisans alike (see Figs. 45, 49, 50 and 59). Not surprisingly many of them sought to translate these abilities into something more closely resembling a profession than an occasional recreation. It was from the ranks of these well-educated, footloose and restless young men (as will be seen in Chapter 6) that the musicians, poets and actors of the medieval minstrel troupes were principally recruited: and they, in their turn, enlisted the support of jugglers, acrobats and keepers of animals trained to perform tricks to give their repertoire greater variety and attractiveness to the widest range of prospective patrons (Figs. 46 and 60).

Most of these changes within the social fabric of medieval Christendom were particular to the thirteenth century and resulted in an astonishing flowering of dramatic art all over Europe during the next two centuries. Secular and

58a, b. Romanesque and Gothic visions of the visit of the Magi. Left: whalebone carving, c.1100. Below: top of ivory crozier, fourteenth century. London, Victoria and Albert Museum.

59. *King David with musicians and dancers. Manuscript illumination from the* Psalterium Aureum. *c.900. St Gall.*

60. *A golliard (student entertainer) with bells, leading a troupe of musicians and masked mimes or mummers. Illumination from the* Roman de Fauvel, *early fourteenth century. Paris, Bibliothèque Nationale.*

ecclesiastical traditions began to merge, each borrowing from the other whatever was most pertinent and useful to the advancement of its own ends. Perhaps the most eloquent surviving landmark witnessing the return of that self-confidence required to herald this new world is Chartres Cathedral which was completed before the twelfth century drew to its close (see p. 80).

(c) **A New Calendar Feast: Corpus Christi:** A century later a new Feast Day, Corpus Christi (first promulgated by Pope Urban IV in 1267), was finally instituted by Pope Clement V in 1311. It was to be celebrated on the Thursday following Trinity Sunday in commemoration of and to give thanks for Christ's redemptive sacrifice of his own life for the salvation of mankind, and for the miraculous quality and power of the Eucharist. It was thus a joyous midsummer festival well suited to its principal purpose of carrying

religion out of the confines of the Church and into the thoroughfares of daily life. What started simply as a procession had, by the end of the century, been elaborated to include plays on Old and New Testament subjects performed by laymen as well as churchmen, in the vernacular instead of Latin, and subsidized as heavily by civic promoters as by the Church itself. Christ's Passion became a central feature, frighteningly and pitiably realistic in the detail of its re-enactment (Fig. 61). The labour of preparation and performance was widely spread—as were the costs. A competitive element helped to maintain high standards of presentation, reinforced by disciplinary codes of conduct both on the stage and in the auditorium that included fines and other penalties. Out of these materials grew the passion plays in France, Germany and Spain, and the miracle cycles in England which by the end of the fifteenth century were often long enough to occupy several consecutive days (see pp. 91–3 and Figs. 65 and 74).

4 DRAMA OF REPENTANCE

Just as significant where this fusion of secular and ecclesiastical dramatic traditions was concerned were the efforts made by priests to secure a place for short plays urging repentance and reform of life among the entertainments on offer at other festivals indoors at night in the banquet halls of the nobility and merchant princes. The hall, or refectory, in palace, castle and monastery alike was provided with a roof and a fire against inclement weather: it was also the common place of assembly for all residents and guests as well as the source of sustenance in terms of the daily supply of food and drink: its mirror image in the life of a town was the guildhall, presided over by the mayor (as the king's representative), and in the cities the livery halls of the trade guilds presided over by the masters of the companies. Calendar and patronal festivals were regarded as feast days in a literal sense; and since banquets in the Middle Ages were lengthy affairs, they clamoured for the provision of entertainment in the intervals between the many courses, as much to rest the digestion as for the heightened sense of occasion and pleasure that it gave (Fig. 62). And here it was the host's prerogative to select those performers whose offerings and reputation best

61. *The Isenheim Altarpiece: Grünewald's painfully realistic portrayal of the Crucifixion and the Deposition. Completed c.1515. Colmar, Unterlinden Museum.*

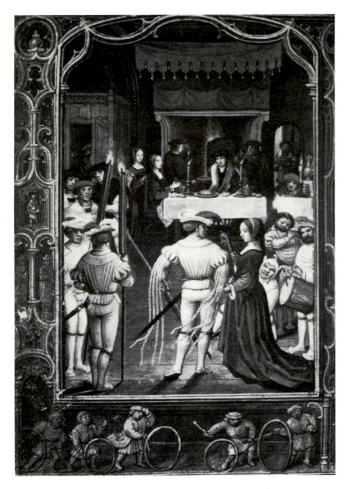

62. *Minstrels and torchbearers with a Fool providing entertainment for their patrons seated at dinner. Flemish manuscript, c.1500. London, British Library.*

matched his own (occasionally her own) personal tastes and resources. In many cases a host preferred to encourage local talent among his own servants and retainers, which called for only modest remuneration; but on others, for variety's sake, personal prestige, or some such particular reason, it was desirable to hire a troupe of visitors known to be in the vicinity. This principle also came to be adopted by parishes in the larger towns to the extent that an exchange of local 'plays' or 'games' became an established practice in the later Middle Ages, fostered once again by a competitive element grounded in local pride. In villages too small to possess a hall, where the parish church provided the only roofed building of public assembly and its yard the only alternative to the village green, these were pressed into service for both athletic and mimetic games or plays as occasion demanded under the name of 'potations' or 'church ales'. Local football matches and similar sporting fixtures preserve something of this spirit and atmosphere today, as do amateur drama festivals, at least in Britain if less frequently elsewhere.

5 PLAYMAKERS: DOCTRINE AND DRAMA

In all these environments a churchman, whether as household chaplain or as parish priest, was likely to have been called upon because of his literary and rhetorical skills to play a leading role in the provision of these entertainments, more especially when a script was needed. For this he could expect to be paid: in return he provided the single manuscript of the complete play which became the prompt-copy. As the actors only received copies of their own lines and cues, ownership of the original provided effective copyright. (One such set of actors' parts—for a shepherds play—survives from Shrewsbury, in England.) As a direct consequence of these developments, the Church came to acquire a monopolistic control over the texts of plays and thus over the doctrinal or ideological content of the script.

It is difficult to be precise about the uses to which churchmen put this authority in the Middle Ages. Criticism of actors and acting in general rumbled on; but for the most part it was confined to particular individuals in isolated places taking exception to excessive exuberance which exposed the performers to charges of blasphemy, indecency or insolence (tournaments and the Feast of Fools being particular offenders) or to overt reversion to folk customs of a kind that stirred ancient fears of pagan idolatry into new life (see pp. 57–8). That these protests cannot have been provoked without serious justification may be judged by the fact that the churchmen concerned included such outstanding humanists as Robert Grosseteste, Bishop of Lincoln, and John of Salisbury, Bishop of Chartres. Their fears, however, did not build up into an attack on religious drama itself of the sort that was to be mounted by Wycliffe and his Lollards late in the fourteenth century in England (see p. 90). Indeed there can be little doubt about the zeal with which most churchmen supported the employment of dramatic art as a teaching instrument, particularly to overcome the barrier of widespread illiteracy and when seeking to explain or to clarify difficult, abstract concepts of doctrine. To some extent, plays or stories from scripture and the legendary lives of saints and martyrs may have been regarded as simple lessons in Christian history; but their overriding purpose was to explain the mysterious ways of God to man. With the Bible still only available in Latin, these visual and dramatic representations of its contents came to assume a validity of their own for everyone who lacked access to the written word.

From this approach developed the use of typology as a control mechanism on the selection of subject matter in the extended vernacular religious dramas of the high Middle Ages. This enabled their authors to link events from the Old Testament that foreshadowed corresponding events in the New Testament as, for instance, Abraham's sacrifice of his son Isaac with Christ's crucifixion, or Noah's Flood with the Last Judgement. It also accounts for the shift from narrative to commentary upon narrative—in other words from story to argument, or debate, in the manner of a sermon—which underpinned the structure of the so-called morality plays and shorter moral interludes of the fourteenth and fifteenth centuries in which abstract concepts such as Sin, Truth, Lust, Virtue, Greed or Vice came to be personified, and then animated by recourse to costume, dialogue, verbal argument and physical combat—the City of God, or New Jerusalem, constantly at war with Lucifer's Kingdom of Hell: but that is to anticipate. What it is necessary to appreciate here is that both hell and heaven came thus to be represented in scenic terms of reference on the stage in as much realistic visual detail as the mortal world of men, and to be populated with angels and devils respectively who, while characteristically human in their sentiments and utterances, became products of the highest flights of imaginative fancy that medieval craftsmen's minds could aspire to (Plate 6 and Fig. 79): yet they still remained true to their prototypes in the early liturgical music drama with angels disporting themselves like innocent choristers, and devils (like King Herod and other disbelievers) at once frightening and comic in the eyes and hearts of their beholders (Figs. 44 and 63).

It is difficult to exaggerate the power that dramatic art in the service of the Roman Catholic Church of the early Middle Ages thus came to exercise in the imposition of orthodoxy on all ranks of society and the absorption of its tenets into all aspects of daily life. And once that is

63. *Devils carrying St Guthlac and scourging him. A twelfth-century illumination from the Scroll of Guthlac. London, British Library.*

grasped, it becomes far easier to understand why the theatre should have expanded as rapidly as it did from the thirteenth century onwards, and why it should have established its roots once again as firmly and as widely within the popular culture of urban and farming communities all over Europe as ever it had done in classical antiquity. In effect, the theatre had once again become the principal source of moral education throughout the Western world. A similar approach to the use of dramatic art to serve ideological ends may be seen in Soviet Russia both during and after the Stalinist era (see p. 227).

6

Dramatic Achievement in Christian Europe, 1300–the Reformation

Chartres is the epitome of the first great awakening in European civilization. It is also the bridge between Romanesque and Gothic, between the world of Abelard and the world of St Thomas Aquinas, the world of restless curiosity and the world of system and order.

(Kenneth Clark, *Civilization*, 1969, p. 60.)

1 THE GOTHIC STYLE IN ART AND ARCHITECTURE

If applied to the theatre, it might also be said to epitomize the transition from the Romanesque style of liturgical music drama, strictly orientated towards Christ's divinity and worship of Christ the King, to the Gothic style of vernacular drama no less purposefully orientated towards Christ's humanity and veneration of Christ Crucified.

The quotation itself is a splendid oversimplification tailored to the requirements of television; yet anyone who has tramped up the hill to the cathedral can scarcely disagree that the impact of its architecture, sculpture and stained glass on the senses is overwhelming and generates a sense of awe and mystery in a way that few other buildings can claim to surpass. Completed in 1164, this cathedral still invites its visitors to enquire what had happened to permit art on so lavish a scale to adorn the house of God— in this case more particularly the house of the Blessed Virgin Mary. Sir Kenneth answers this question by attributing the revolution that this cathedral represents, with its soaring pointed arches, its flying buttresses and its tiered rows of windows to Suger, Abbot of St Denis in Paris and Regent of France, who had argued that dull minds rise to an understanding of truth through an appreciation of material beauty and that in consequence it was the Church's duty to help men understand God by every means that art could supply. At least there can be no doubt that a century later a dramatic change had occurred throughout the length and breadth of the Christian world stretching from Cracow and Budapest to Dublin and Seville. Wherever churches were built, pointed Gothic arches and lavish space for windows replaced their rounded Romanesque antecedents (Norman in Britain) and dimly lit

interiors. Portraits of the Pantocrator (God the Father and Creator of all things) glowering threateningly from the ceiling of the sanctuary gave way to more humane images in glass and wood carvings of God the Son, hanging on the cross flanked by the weeping mother and St John whom he had instructed to comfort her (see Figs. 55, 59 and 61). Stonework was richly gilded and painted in bright, primary colours. These changes simultaneously proclaimed the Church's own power and wealth and echoed the glory of God in the temporal world, reinforced by the admission of the startlingly emotive power of *descantus* (the earliest form of polyphonic music) lifting all eyes and hearts upwards to heaven above. Drama served to advance this process still further, animating the images supplied by the painters, carvers in wood and stone, and the workers in stained glass, and by doing so made them more vivid and impressive. The more varied the musical possibilities and the more human and friendly this new style of portraiture became, so the more intimate and personal grew the relationship between these divinely appointed intercessors and the sinful worshippers who appealed to them for help with their own mundane, domestic troubles. The cults of the Virgin and of the saints grew apace, and with them the vogue for relics and pilgrimages. The outcome was the creation of a broadly international style of representation, marked by local variants of emphasis and texture. In dramatic art, the use of different vernacular dialects to convey the same biblical story offers an apt example of this characteristic.

2 EXPLAINING THE WAYS OF GOD TO MAN

Any attempt on our part today to comprehend the richly varied nature and intense emotional appeal of the theatrical

64. *The Church Militant. In this tapestry, woven in Bruges between 1373 and 1380 for Louis, first Duke of Anjou, to illustrate the Apocalypse of St John, Christ is conceived as a knight in a chivalric Romance leading a charge against infidel soldiers and wild beasts. Musée d'Angers.*

achievements of the late Middle Ages must take into account four major ideas which dominated the minds of contemporary performers and their audiences: a vivid sense of contrast, extravagant flights of romantic fantasy counterpointed by a hard-grained streak of realism, and an ability to perceive the whole natural world in terms of game or play; and it was the last of these four ideas that was increasingly drawn upon to explain to individuals of all ranks in the social hierarchy the significance of every tangible thing and every human action around them within God's creation. Nothing was too trivial to be overlooked: everything had its appointed place. By this means complicated concepts like salvation and damnation could be allegorized and made intelligible; likewise good and evil; sin, grace, redemption and atonement; pain and grief; pleasure and joy. What dramatic art was now mature enough to offer was an ability to give concrete form and recognizable shape to all such concepts, and thus to make the educational process of learning about them and how to respond to them a pleasurable experience. Thus paradise could be represented on the stage as a garden or an orchard, walled or fenced against intruders, richly scented with flowers and aglow with ripe fruit, bathed in sunshine but cooled with a stream or fountain, and with winged children hovering above to fill the air with music: and if these aspects of

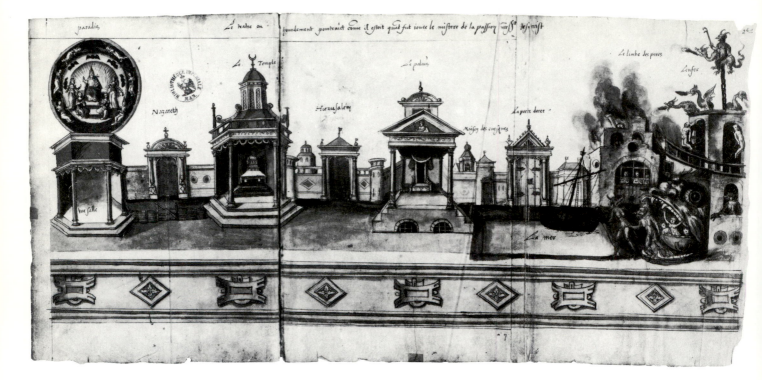

65. *Manuscript illumination of the stage and multiple emblematic settings for the Passion Play at Valenciennes, 1547. From Paradise (left) via Nazareth (fronted by a sheepfold), Jerusalem (with its temple and palace) and the Sea of Galilee to Hell Castle, no expense in craftsmanship and funding was spared for this production, which stretched over 25 days. Paris, Bibliothèque Nationale.*

human experience could be drawn upon to represent heaven, then so could thick castle walls, grimly spiked portcullises, dank, dark dungeons, greasy and cacophonous smoke-filled kitchens, cesspits and torture-chambers, and riotous taverns to represent hell (Fig. 65). The more vividly stage designers and craftsmen succeeded in endowing these visual images with a three-dimensional reality, the more desirable salvation became for the beholder as the ultimate alternative to damnation throughout eternity.

The sense of contrast implicit within these images of heaven and hell was everywhere apparent in daily life and it created a natural sense of the dramatic which the maker of plays could readily exploit. Many of these contrasts were frightening since the alternatives attendant on them were coupled with a stark choice for men and women of the Middle Ages between survival and death. The difference between night and day was far more real and threatening with no electric light switch to flick on and off; that between winter and summer far more alarming with no heating to rely on other than the wood you had yourself collected and stored (or had failed to collect in time) and with food rationed to bare subsistence level; death in infancy was a far more frequent occurrence, and in every family at that. Extremes both of wealth and of poverty abounded and with them the status symbols of rank declared in dress, from jewelled crowns, orbs and sceptres down to rags, crutches, sores and begging bowls. Possessed of eyes, any man could read this iconography for himself even if he lacked the skill to write his name, spell his neighbour's or read a letter from a friend. Travel was both difficult and dangerous, yet in the name of either chivalry or piety crusaders and pilgrims rose respectively to the challenge of adventure, even at this price, as a contrast to the monotony of grinding toil. If they survived its perils, they could hope to return home equipped with stories of exotic peoples, fabulous creatures like camels, elephants and dragons, and romantic or hazardous encounters spiced with tales of captures, ransoms and escapes sufficient to dine out on for the rest of their lives. Thus legends and miracles of bygone ages appeared to be freshly confirmed by living testimony, gleaned from places as far from home as Jerusalem, Glastonbury and Compostela, contrasting

Far left: 66. A lady in whose honour a tournament has been given bestows a prize on the victor and accords him the privilege of the first dance. French, fifteenth century. From Le Livre des Tournois du Roi René. Paris, Bibliothèque Nationale.

67. An elephant and castle: an ideal object for a Pas d'Armes. Here, the Knight-Challengers try to ward off the attacks of the Knights whose honour has been challenged. Mid-thirteenth century. (Compare the text and ground-plan of The Castle of Perseverance and Fig. 73 below.) Oxford, Bodleian Library.

sharply and strangely with the relative dullness of normal domestic life. All of these could be dramatized and offered vicariously to those less venturesome spirits who had chosen to remain at home, but who on public holidays flocked eagerly to hear and see actors perform a play.

3 TOURNAMENTS AND ROMANCE LITERATURE

At tournaments, the genesis of which has already been discussed (see pp. 64-5), knights in glittering armour riding on gorgeously caparisoned horses could be seen charging at each other with lances or hacking at each others' shields and helmets with swords and maces on foot (see Plate 9). Although still condemned by the papacy as battle schools, tournaments acquired social respectability during the twelfth century from the decision of the Cistercian monasteries (founded 1098) to recognize and support the major Orders of knighthood in Europe—Knights Templars, Knights of the Holy Sepulchre, Spanish and Portugese Orders, and the Teutonic Orders in Hungary, Poland and Livonia—as disciples of Christ crusading to defend and advance the faith against infidel attack and subversion on the frontiers of Christendom (see Fig. 64). As tournaments came thus to be endowed with an heroic spiritual dimension, many knights came to assume roman-

tic names and claimed to be present in the lists to serve some exotic lady in order to earn or preserve the hints of favour accorded to him earlier. Disguise became a necessary feature of such fiction which, in the evening, extended into the banquet hall where this lady bestowed the prizes on the victors. As well as precious stones the prizes included permission to dance with her and her attendants (see Fig. 66). In this way fictional castles came to be besieged (a form of tournament known as a *Pas d'Armes*)—Castles of Love, Gateways of Valour, Bowers of Fidelity and Beauty, an Elephant and Castle (Fig. 67). These required scenic decoration both to identify their location and to explain their allegoric meaning for the spectators. The two princelings who brought these astonishingly extravagant forms of entertainment—a mixture of the Roman *ludi circenses* and *ludi scenici* (see Chapter 3)—to their zenith in the fifteenth century with the addition of explanatory texts were René, Duke of Anjou and King of Naples and Sicily, and Philip the Good, Duke of Burgundy. Yet it was an Englishman, Edward Prince of Wales known as the Black Prince, who in the fourteenth century had come to be revered as the flower of European chivalric courtesy, and the legendary King Arthur with his assemblies of knights known as 'Round Tables' who had attracted the attention of the chroniclers and poets.

With the development of transportable cannons after

68. A Mon Seul Désir, *a tapestry from the series known as 'The Lady with the Unicorn'. Flemish, 1513. Paris, Musée Cluny.*

1450, tournaments lost the last vestiges of their earlier claim to be needed as battle schools since the armour required to resist guns and cannons proved too heavy for horses to carry while manoeuvering at any speed. Henry VIII, however, remained addicted to them and Henry II of France met his death in one as late as 1559 (see Chapters 8 and 10).

4 DANCING AND DISGUISE

Through the prize-giving ceremony which concluded tournaments, a do-it-yourself dimension came to be added to the entertainments associated with feasting in the banquet hall. This not only served to project ladies into the foreground, but on that very account introduced civilizing influences intimately related to courtship, notably dancing. It was this nucleus that was elaborated into masquerade when the martial champions of the daylight hours came into the hall at night still dressed as the fictional characters whom they had claimed to be in the lists. The vital difference was that they entered the hall at the invitation of the lady in whose honour the tournament had been arranged. The image that most perfectly represents

this change of role and status was depicted by the needle-workers who wove that great series of tapestries *The Lady with the Unicorn*, c.1470. That entitled 'A Mon Seul Desir' shows us a lady whose beauty, purity and chastity has tamed the natural aggressiveness of her knights, there represented by the lion (an emblem of physical force) and the unicorn (an emblem of lust) who patiently wait upon her, both *couchant* rather than *rampant*, pictured as her servants holding open the doors of her pavilion (Fig. 68).

Granted this refined sublimation of crude sexual impulses anchored in choreographic compliment, adorned with music, song, physical disguise and scenic ornament, and enlivened with an element of surprise, the sheer theatricality of what became known as 'disguisings' proved irresistible—the more so as expense was of no account to the wealthy amateurs who were the sole promoters, performers and recipients of these spectacular and sensual diversions (Fig. 69). Elaboration of the ornamental elements over the years led to the creation of the Venetian *ballo in maschera* early in the sixteenth century, followed by the French *ballet de cour* and the English court masques.

Disguisings, as the word suggests, were evening entertainments derived from those curious visits undertaken by

69. *A Mumming of Wild Men at the French court, 1393. The costumes of the performers caught fire when one of the torchbearers accidentally ignited them. London, British Library.*

'strangers disguised' at New Year and Carnival, and described as mummings in Chapter 4. These stemmed not from tournaments but from folk custom and ultimately from those festivals of social inversion particular to Bacchus, Fortuna and Saturn in the time of Roman rule (see Chapter 3). Of the three it was Fortuna, re-named Dame Fortune, who most strongly appealed to Christian minds in the Middle Ages; so it was to propitiate or to thank this lady, so renowned for her fickleness and mutability, that gifts continued to be given (under the convenient cover of the precedent set in Christian history by the Magi) by subjects to rulers, by retainers to their patrons, and by servants to their masters (Fig. 70).

The best-known English example of a mumming is that which the Mayor and Alderman of London prepared for the young King Richard II in 1377 when he and his court were celebrating Christmas at the palace of Kennington which occupied a site near that modern arena devoted to cricket, the Oval. On that occasion they chose to disguise themselves as popes and cardinals accompanied by a troupe of '8 or 10 arrayed and with black vizards'. Riding in torchlight procession across London Bridge they were admitted to the palace. There they asked to play a dice-game with the king. The dice were deliberately loaded to allow the king and his mother to win a gold ball and a gold ring, the gifts which these mummers had brought with them.

> And then the prince caused to bring the wine and they drank with great joy, commanding the minstrels to play[,] and the trumpets began to sound and other instruments to pipe, etc. And the king and the lords danced on the one side and the mummers on the other a great while[,] and then they drank and took their leave[,] and so departed toward London.

While the elements of mystery and surprise associated with these seemingly spontaneous goodwill visitations obviously gave pleasure—hence the drinking 'with great joy'!—they also permitted a lapse in normal security arrangements that could be used by unscrupulous schemers to introduce spies, thieves, or worse, assassins. King Henry IV took these threats seriously enough to ban mummings in London; but they appear to have survived in some provincial cities for most of the fifteenth century. They were prohibited in Bristol in 1479, but in York a 'riding' of patently pagan origin called 'Yule and Yule's Wife' still

70. *Dame Fortune, blind and holding her ever-turning wheel, sits opposite Dame Wisdom, firmly holding her mirror with its self-portrait. Early sixteenth-century French wood-engraving.*

existed as late as 1572 when the Archbishop ordered its suppression on the grounds that it was 'very rude and barbarous' and, more specifically, that Yule and his wife 'ride through the city very undecently and uncomely drawing great concourses of people after them to gaze'. Even in London, however, the Court was not willing so to be bound by its own laws as to deny itself entertainment, and a transitional phase followed during the fifteenth century that witnesses a merger between the acceptable features of the old mummings and aristocratic participation, with some assistance from professional entertainers.

In England, Chaucer's Clerk of Orleans in *The Franklyn's Tale* speaks of scenic marvels which, he says,

'subtile tregetours' make to appear and disappear in banquet halls as if by magic.

> For ofte at festes have I wel herd seye,
> That tregetours, with-inne an halle large,
> Have maad come in a water and a barge,
> And in the halle rowen up and doun.
> Somtyme hath semed come a grim leoun;
> And somtyme floures springe as in a mede;
> Sometyme a vyne, and grapes whyte and rede;
> Sometyme a castel, al of lym and stoon;
> And when hem [i.e. the tregetours] lyked, voyded it
> anoon,
>
> Thus seemed it to every mannes sights.

Although this statement occurs in a romance, scenic spectacle of just this sort accompanied two French entertainments of this period. Both are now confidently ascribed to Philippe de Mézières: *The Conquest of Jerusalem* and *The Story of Griselda*, which are dramatized versions of popular romances scripted by this gifted diplomat and traveller for presentation in banquet halls at court. Froissart in his *Chronicles* describes another Parisian entertainment, and yet others survive from Burgundy. A picture of one of these, *The Conquest of Jerusalem*, survives depicting both the ship and the castle listed by Chaucer's Clerk of Orleans (see Plate 8).

Early in the fifteenth century John Lydgate supplies us with some seven complete texts for such entertainments which he describes variously as 'mummings' or 'disguisings' as though he were himself fully aware that the genre was in transition from the former to the latter (see pp. 62–3). A presenter is invariably employed to explain the significance of the disguise adopted by the masked visitors who themselves remain silent. The characters are drawn from the Bible, more modern history, mythology and low life: in some gifts are presented, in others apparently not. Significantly some are composed for presentation at court and others for the Mayor, sheriffs, and aldermen of the City of London, one for a May Day picnic and the others for livery halls. Similar entertainments developed rapidly in Spain and Portugal (see Chapter 9).

5 MINSTRELS AND INTERLUDES

Precisely when any entertainment of a kind that we would call a play was first presented in a banquet hall must remain an open question: in the present state of knowledge sometime during the fourteenth century would appear to be the best answer, but an earlier date cannot be ruled out. In this context schools, universities and the law schools (which in England were called Inns of Court) have to be taken into account, as do the refectories of monastic houses. All were firmly ruled by churchmen, but respected normal public holidays, more especially those of the patron saints to whose service the foundations were dedicated. Founder's day feasts thus provoked yet another occasion for abnormal celebrations; and here the surviving account books frequently record payments to players, many of whom were musicians. Others, however, were actors. But what sort of actors? The clerical scribes who entered these payments in their ledgers almost invariably recorded them in Latin. The words they used embrace *ministrales*, *mimes*, *lusores*, *histriones* and *joculatores*, but it is to be doubted whether they intended any definition more precise than 'entertainer' to be applied to any of them with the possible exception of *mimes*: given the history of that word as used by the leaders of the Church from Roman times onwards, it is hard to conceive that the choice of it described anything other than movement accompanied by mimetic or pantomimic gesture and facial expression. Yet that still leaves the meaning of the alternatives obscure.

Some of the entertainers entered under one or other of these names were Northerners and thus the heirs of the Norse and Anglo-Saxon scóps (reciters of saga) and gleemen (minstrels) whose talent lay in recording the practical exploits of their masters and then reciting them (with appropriate additions and deletions) on festive occasions accompanied by a harp which they played themselves like modern folk-singers. Nothing precluded such monologues from including passages of dialogue introduced by phrases like 'He said . . .', 'She replied, . . .' or 'They said . . .', a device which, as already related in Chapters 1 and 5, was employed both by Asian story-tellers, and in Europe by the preaching friars of the thirteenth century. Nor can puppeteers be eliminated from consideration in this context since a puppet master, by simulating the different voices of all the characters in a particular story, can translate an epic or a romance into a play without the aid of human actors (see Figs. 11, 32 and 45).

Other entertainers came from the South, having first learned in Provence in the twelfth century how to translate the epic and pastoral romances of classical antiquity into a modern language which women could understand and enjoy, and then how to apply these ancient narrative techniques to describing the exploits of knights returning from Crusades. Churchmen quickly retaliated by according similar treatment to the heroic deeds recorded in Old and New Testament history and to the legendary lives of saints and martyrs (see Fig. 71). However the serious subject matter out of which all this new literature was shaped can scarcely

be expected to have retained the attention of audiences assembled at a banquet as they steeped themselves in wine, beer or spirits.

The troubadours of Provence, who were literate young men of good family—they were known as *trouvères* in the North and as *Minnesingers* in Germany—protected themselves against this fate by recruiting teams of supporting artists known as *jongleurs* (Chaucer calls them *tregetours*) whose talents were less demanding on the intellect and

---

71. *A miniature by Jean Fouquet of a scene from a fifteenth-century Saint Play about the life and martyrdom of St Apollonia. The acting area is closed off at the back with six scenic scaffolds, with Heaven on the left and Hell on the right. Note the mitred figure (centre right), with prompt-book and baton, orchestrating the dialogue and music to fit the action. The front of the stage is fenced off from the auditorium by a low hedge protected by wattle fencing. Chantilly, Musée Condé.*

appealed more directly to the emotions—acrobats, jugglers, clowns, and trainers of performing animals—where personality and virtuosity provided the sole criteria of success (see Figs. 46, 49, 60, and 62). They travelled as teams, like circus artists today, the *jongleurs* being dependent on the reputation and social status of the *trouvère* to acquire entry to a castle or priory and the *trouvère* being dependent on the varied talents of his own troupe for success thereafter. These troupes came to be described generically as minstrels, a term which by the fifteenth century was applied solely to musicians; and by then a musician's gallery had become a standard feature of medieval banquet halls (Fig. 69).

It was from the other members of the troupe that acting groups known as 'players of interludes' learned the skills needed to enliven the moralistic character of most scripts and recruited professionally experienced actors to lead them as managers. By the start of the fourteenth century awareness of the potential of dramatic art, whether in Latin or vernacular language, was widespread enough to attract the attention of an equally varied range of literate young men eager to establish a reputation for themselves as authors and to attract patrons. If the Church could by then rely on authors to expound doctrine in play form, the nobility and new-rich merchants and bankers of the rapidly growing towns were learning to recruit professional troubadours and university students to dramatize chivalric romance and short stories of a more popular and satirical character. On rare occasions the names of individuals start to reappear in Europe as authors or 'makers' of particular plays. This process appears to have begun during the twelfth century with Hilarius, a pupil of Abelard's at the university of Paris; and to him three plays can be credited written between 1130 and 1150 relating respectively to Lazarus, Daniel and St Nicholas. All three are in Latin, but an anonymous play of about the same date about the Three Kings, *Reyes Magos*, is written throughout in Catalan Spanish vernacular verse, which is notable for its conversational quality. Not long after follow two anonymous Anglo-Norman plays, the *Jeu d'Adam* discussed in Chapter 5 and a companion piece, *La Seinte Resureccion*, both written for very large casts and both referred to as 'representations' (see pp. 70–9). The latter requires a narrator, some forty actors, and at least seven scenic locations all of which were pre-set in the acting area and on view to the audience throughout the performance. No wonder the author stipulates that this play, which 'recites' the story of Christ's Passion from the Deposition to the Ascension, should be presented to the people 'in a large enough space'! Early in the thirteenth century come three more plays with an author's, or maker's, name attached: Jean Bodel's *Jeu de St Nicholas* remarkable for its realistic treatment of contemporary low life, and its affinities with tavern rituals rather than those of the liturgy; Adam de la Halle's play about Folly and his pastoral *Jeu de Robin and Marion*, both of which are topical, satirical and rooted in the life of his own town of Arras. Subsequent plays, whether anonymous (like the Flemish farce *The Boy and the Blind Man* or the fragmentary Middle English *Interlude of the Student and his Girl Friend*) or attributable to a known writer (like Rutebeuf's *Theophilus' Miracle* or Philippe de Mézière's *Presentation of the Virgin Mary in the Temple*), continue to expand both the scope of the subject matter dramatized and the treatment accorded to its staging.

By the middle of the fourteenth century this process had gone far enough to encourage the bolder spirits among the playmakers to tackle two new subjects, Christ's Crucifixion and ethical argument, both in the vernacular. The first attempt to handle the former was made in northern Italy at Cividale in Latin in 1298 and again in 1303. By the middle of the century this subject was being handled confidently in French, and from France this precedent travelled north to England and eastwards across Europe to Poland, Latvia and Hungary: significantly the French pioneer known as the *Passion du Palatinus* is derived from the *Passion d'Autun*, which in itself draws heavily for its source material (at times quoting line by line) on a famous, but much earlier romance entitled *La Passion des Jongleurs*.

6 DRAMA OF CRIME AND PUNISHMENT

The dramatization of ethical argument was suggested no less forcefully by the depiction in the visual arts of such abstract qualities as truth and falsehood, justice, chastity, gluttony or sensuality as human beings identifiable, like Greek or Roman deities before them, by their costumes and the emblems carried in their hands or on their heads; a sword and balances for justice, an olive-branch for peace and so on (Figs. 70, 72). Such persons, once vividly stamped by painters and carvers upon the popular imagination, could readily be endowed with the breath of life by actors and made to speak. Naturally, it would be assumed that they could not normally say much beyond articulating the case for conformity to the particular aspect of a Christian code of conduct which each virtue represented and against that of its opposite; or, alternatively, where vices were concerned, urging the attractions of uninhibited personal commitment to behaviour normally condemned within that same code of conduct which each Virtue represented. Nevertheless each could engage in a spirited debate. This

72. *An allegorical street-pageant of Virtues and mythological and astrological figures staged at the Chatelet in Paris, 1514, in honour of Mary Tudor and her forthcoming marriage to Louis XII of France. London, British Library.*

became the more dramatic and theatrical when modelled on that form of tournament known as a *Pas d'Armes* with the soul of a representative human substituted for the castle or gateway to be stormed and won by one of the two warring parties: and this in fact provides the structural base for *The Castle of Perseverance*, c.1450. Transition from pictorial to dramatic representation was here made the easier by depicting Christ himself as a knight crusader leading the Church militant into battle (Figs. 64, 67 and 73).

Experiment to this end had begun by the close of the twelfth century. The *Play of Antichrist* from Tegernsee in Bavaria described in Chapter 5 provides for seven such

abstract personifications—Ecclesia, Synagoga, Justice, Mercy, Gentility, Heresy and Hypocrisy—alongside of several kings, the Pope, clergy and others. It is matched by another play from a German author, this time a woman, Hildegard of Bingen, *Ordo Virtutum*, with *Felix Anima* (Happy Soul) as the central character struggling with the help of Humility, Queen of Virtue, and her assistants, to escape from the Devil. This too is in Latin and of about the same date as *Antichrist*, but the pattern of construction which it established is derived from dance drama rather than polemical debate. These early experiments are fol-

73. *Facsimile of the ground-plan of the staging arrangements for* The Castle of Perseverance *accompanying the prompt-book text, c.1450. As at a Pas d'Armes, the besieged castle is set in the middle of the arena. On the perimeter are five scaffolds accommodating the assailants and God in his capacity as judge. (Compare Fig. 74.) Original manuscript in the Folger Library, Washington, DC.*

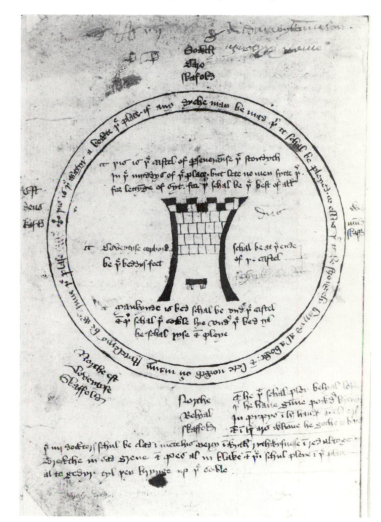

lowed in four plays of rather later date, but all written in the vernacular: two of these are French—*The Marriage between Faith and Loyalty* and *The Seven Deadly Sins and the Virtues*: the other two are English—*Dux Moraud* and *The Pride of Life*: all four belong to the fourteenth century. Further experiment is represented in this same period and shortly after in the *entremets* ascribed to Philippe de Mézières and in Lydgate's 'disguisings' already discussed.

7 AN ERA OF DRAMATIC ACHIEVEMENT

With so much accomplished, what was there left to attempt or to achieve? By the end of the fourteenth century any audience, granted a public holiday, could expect to be entertained either indoors or out of doors with dramatic spectacles ranging from circus acts to stately tournaments, from simple representations of particular stories from the Old and New Testament to much more complicated disputations on the finer points of theology, from re-enactment of the miracles of revered saints to the heroic and romantic exploits of Christian kings and conquerors, and from homely folk-dance to sophisticated farce and satire, all presented in local dialects which everyone assembled could understand. Thus Europe had once again caught up with India and China in possessing an organized and sophisticated theatre that was widely supported and enjoyed. What remained for creative minds to aspire to?

8 DOUBTS AND INNOVATIONS OF THE FIFTEENTH CENTURY

(a) **Doubts:** One answer, of course, was to try to consolidate and improve upon all the prototypes by then on offer; and this in large measure was the response actually supplied by playmakers and actors of the fifteenth century. Another was to press on with fresh innovations; yet two awkward questions had already arisen from all this varied and energetic activity which served in the event to inhibit this alternative: both related to matters of propriety. First, to what extent was it proper for ordained priests to devote their time and energy to writing plays, let alone to making public spectacles of themselves in sensual or militaristic romances and scurrilous farces? Secondly, how far was it appropriate for the Church to enforce its own control through monopoly over the provision of play-scripts and thus over both content and performance? Equipped with power to excommunicate actors and audiences alike, how should the cardinal-archbishops and bishops respond? Most of them had hitherto behaved responsibly, each answering such questions as they arose within his diocese

with a discreet commingling of tolerance and mild restraint. Only on rare occasions do we learn of this ultimate weapon being used. It was frequently threatened in Italy, France, England and Poland in the context of the Feast of Fools from 1199 onwards, while in 1352 Bishop Grandisson of Exeter employed it to prevent performance of a satirical play about alleged extortionate trading by the city's leatherworkers which he feared, if allowed to proceed, would lead to riots, injuries and deaths: but no records survive to indicate that writers or actors were frequently brought before ecclesiastical courts and summarily punished for unbecoming conduct. In the latter half of the fourteenth century, however, this gentle approach appeared to many of the poorer clergy—especially the more evangelically minded of them—to be hypocritical, hedonistic, not to say outrightly pagan; in short, to be advancing the Devil's cause, not Christ's. This puritan streak in European consciousness found a voice in England in John Wycliffe and on the continent in his devoted admirer John Hus in Prague. Both men impugned the Church's own leaders from the Pope in Rome downwards for their hypocrisy, greed, wealth, extravagance and failure to honour their vows to serve God and the poor as exemplified by their actual conduct and in flat contradiction of holy writ. A prime case in point was the clergy's supportive attachment to the theatre. Wycliffe denounced them on this account in 'A Treatise against Miracles' (c.1380) in forthright terms. Hus and his followers were branded as heretics, and burned at the stake. Wycliffe's followers, known as Lollards, were required to recant or meet the same fate. What few could have recognized at the time was that a far greater threat to the future of both Christianity and the theatre was developing in the south-eastern corner of Europe where the erstwhile protective bastion of Byzantium against the periodic onslaughts of Islam was crumbling so fast that it would collapse by 1453; but, in 1400, only in Spain did this threat assume a greater importance than that of internal protest against corruption and abuse. Clamour for reform elsewhere was thus effectively silenced, at least for the next hundred years; but the embers of this revolt smouldered unseen only to erupt again throughout Northern and Western Europe with much greater violence in the early years of the sixteenth century, Spain alone excepted.

(b) **Innovations:** As the fifteenth century dawned, the way was thus clear for the Roman Catholic Church, in the cause of establishing faith and promoting good works, to continue to promote dramatic art as a major means of celebrating its own feast days throughout the year. These objectives served to advance three important new initiatives. The knowledge that the Church had opted to support the apologists for drama within its own ranks and to brand its opponents as heretics (and thus as outcasts fit only to be burned to death) gave actors a substantial incentive to band themselves together and move forward to a more professional way of life and so acquire, simultaneously, economic independence from their titular overlords and a more respected social status. Hence the appearance during the fifteenth century of an ever-increasing number of small troupes describing themselves as 'players of interludes', each numbering about four men, travelling widely and using the livery and letters patent (written authority) of a high ranking member of the nobility both to protect themselves against charges of begging and vagabondage and to gain entry to other noble households in town and country. The second major development was the steadily increasing importance attached by the Church, with popular support, to finding ways in which to celebrate the relatively new festival of Corpus Christi (see pp. 76–7). This midsummer festival grew in scale, attracting during the fourteenth century not only plays and players but guilds especially constituted to fund and organize production: and it is to this development that we owe in the fifteenth century the passion plays in France, Switzerland, Italy and Germany and the so-called miracle or mystery cycles in England. The third was the rapid growth of civic pageantry.

(i) Passion Plays, Miracle Cycles and Saint Plays: No one can claim with certainty just where or when vernacular passion plays started, but all the elements from which they were compounded were available—at least in Latin at Cividale, in Italy, as we have seen—by the start of the fourteenth century: dramatic representation of Christ's Crucifixion and Harrowing of Hell as the centrepiece, flanked by treatments of the Fall of Lucifer and the Fall of Adam at one end and of Christ's Ascension and the Day of Judgement at the other. Vernacular texts followed shortly after, together with scenic conventions for the representation of heaven and hell on the stage as well as every kind of mortal habitation; realistic low-life comedy and farce; high-flown rhetoric; and perhaps most important of all, an insistence on the timelessness of all the events re-enacted and of the characters involved in them. Historical events they were known to have been; but they were regarded simultaneously as re-enactments in the most literal sense, thereby at once dismissing any self-conscious objection to contemporary rather than historical costume, language and location. Anachronism was not seen to pose a problem, for whether in Bourges, Mons, Lucerne, Frankfurt, Seville, or Chester, the Bible simply sprang to life in everyday attire to be recognized as a recurring reality throughout eternity.

King Herod had already been transformed into a Turkish or Moorish tyrant; Pilate followed in the guise of a justice of the peace; scribes and Pharisees became cardinals and bishops; and the same treatment was accorded to merchants, lawyers, shepherds, prostitutes and beggars (see Fig. 71). In this way the passion plays and Corpus Christi cycles of the fifteenth century came to hold a mirror up to contemporary life and then to ask searching questions about the differences and similarities in human behaviour discernible between life in Roman-occupied Judaea in Christ's lifetime and life in any city in medieval Christendom. However depressing the picture that emerged from this comparison, the message of Corpus Christi was still one of hope and joy, and it was that message which the plays existed to celebrate; for since the new feast had come into being to give thanks for Christ's sacrifice of himself to redeem mankind from the bondage of original sin and to offer everyone the chance of salvation through repentance and the Eucharist, so these plays existed to figure these same abstract, theological ideas in concrete, theatrical metaphors intelligible to anyone equipped with ears to hear and eyes to see. As this message was addressed to everyone regardless of social rank or occupation, it applied with equal force to the entire community of the local area surrounding major market towns. Most of them thus became possessed of their own plays, commissioning local authors to provide the texts, equipping them with actors, artists and craftsmen talented enough to set them in action before an audience; and competing to outshine their neighbours with their own achievement.

From a single day's celebration the plays grew in number and length to occupy three whole days (as at Chester and in Cornwall), four days (as in Paris), and seven days (as in London); by the early decades of the sixteenth century performances could sometimes extend over a fortnight or, as in Flanders at Valenciennes, nearly a whole month. The consequences in terms of the preparatory organization and ultimate cost are obvious. The fortunes of the guilds either formed to fund and oversee production or entrusted with these responsibilities varied with the fashions of the market-place, thus obliging one guild to forfeit its rights in these respects to another from time to time, and in some places taxing corporate resources so severely as to raise the question of whether or not yet another revival could be justified. This factor was destined to play a major role in the rapid disappearance of Corpus Christi plays in the south of England and East Anglia, and throughout Germany and France following the Reformation.

74. *Reconstruction of the earthwork 'round' at St Piran, near Perranporth, Cornwall, as used for the revival of the entire 3-day Cornish Ordinalia in 1969. Hell (top left) faces the entry to the arena. The audience was seated on the tiered terraces between the seven scaffolds. University of Bristol Theatre Collection.*

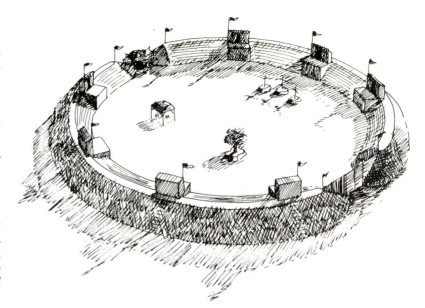

75. *Pageant-car of the Nativity used during the triumphal entry of the Archduchess Isabella into Brussels, 1615. (Compare Plate 7.) Detail from the painting by Denis van Alsloot. London, Victoria and Albert Museum.*

However, despite the vicissitudes of local wars, famines, plagues and other disruptions to normal social life, performances throughout the fifteenth century became increasingly popular and spectacular. Entire communities were involved either directly or indirectly as in ancient Athens. Prizes were not awarded, but fines were levied on inefficiency and indiscipline, and spectators were sometimes promised substantial periods of remission from purgatory as a reward for attendance and orderly behaviour. Courtyards, market-places, even the wider streets were pressed into service to accommodate performances. These frequently began with a Mass and ended with a *Te Deum*. Sometimes a large, raised stage was built of planks placed on barrels on which all the scenic units were set out facing a tiered auditorium of wooden scaffolds with boxes (or private rooms) at the back (see Fig. 65); sometimes an arena was preferred (Fig. 74); and sometimes wagons transformed into floats were used to carry a play scene by scene to audiences in several separate locations, thus involving the actors in repeating each scene three or four times (Fig. 75). Local convenience and practicality was invariably the deciding factor; on the Continent, however, a marked preference was shown for courtyards and market-places whereas in England pageant wagons and earthwork arenas enjoyed greater favour. Pageant wagons also appear to have enjoyed favour in at least some Spanish cities, notably Barcelona, Valencia, and Seville (see Fig. 110).

Musicians had to be hired and rehearsed as well as actors (Fig. 76). Technicians had to be found to supply the elaborate machinery needed to simulate miraculous events and unusual natural phenomena like rain for Noah's flood, or thunder and lightning to accompany the Crucifixion, and ascensions into Heaven. Costumes had to be made or borrowed. Admission tickets had to be issued and sold. Space had to be found for rehearsals and compensation paid for time devoted to them. Meals had to be provided, precautions taken against excessive supplies of drink, and ushers found to police the traffic and man the auditorium. Costume parades had to be mounted and proclamations read by the town crier to publicize the dates and times of performances, the price of admission and other necessaries. And as at all festivals, accommodation had to be provided for visitors. For weeks beforehand the Corpus Christi play became the major talking-point for miles around, generating a degree of anticipation and excitement hard to imagine today. Some vestiges of both, however, may still be grasped by visitors to the annual Palio in Sienna or the Calcio in Florence where similar conditions still pertain in modified form and on a much reduced scale.

76. *Manuscript music for the Passion Play staged in the Wine Market Square in Lucerne, 1583. (Compare Fig. 53.) Lucerne, Bürgerbibliothek.*

In terms of dramatic art, these majestic passion plays, saint plays, and miracle cycles may be regarded as the architectural equivalent of medieval cathedrals: size and cost combined to make both the prerogative of the larger towns. Yet just as beautiful churches existed in all smaller towns and villages, so by the close of the fifteenth century did theatrical entertainments, scaled down in length and scope to fit the physical and financial resources of the local community (see Plate 7). In other words participation as performer, stage assistant or spectator had virtually become the democratic right on calendar holidays of any Christian. Even inhabitants of remote villages in mountain or marshland districts could travel to fairs and festivals elsewhere to share what was offered there with others. The small town of Bassingbourne in Cambridgeshire, for instance, possessed a play 'of the holy martyr St George' which was performed in a field to which no less than twenty-seven neighbouring villages and hamlets made contributions in cash or kind to cover the costs. Nor must it be forgotten

77. A booth stage in the Netherlands. While two actors address the audience, two more peep out from behind the curtain separating the stage from the dressing-room; above, a fifth holds a horn. Note also the provision made for singers and instrumentalists in an adjoining tent. Detail from Temperantia, *a pen and ink drawing by Pieter Brueghel the Elder. Rotterdam, Museum Boymans-van Beuningen.*

that even in country districts it was not unusual for the Church to have established a large monastic house which was ready to offer help with text, music, and funds: although now in ruins, Tintern in Gwent, Fountains in Yorkshire, and many Continental abbeys and priories survive to give us some idea of the likely scale of that help.

(ii) Farces and Interludes: The rapid increase in the number of quasi-professional groups of players of interludes from 1425 onwards likewise increased the number of shorter plays on offer. As most of these were morality plays or farces, their subject matter was not tied to a particular holy day in the calendar; so they could be performed as appropriately on one public holiday as on another and in one place as in another. This applies forcefully to such English plays as *Mankind*, *Wisdom*, or Henry Medwall's *Nature* and *Fulgens and Lucres*; to the Dutch *Everyman*; to such French farces as *Maître Pierre Pathelin* and *La Condamnacion de Bancquet*; and, in the sixteenth century, to the many German *Fastenachtspiele* (Carnival Plays), the best known and most skilful author of which was Hans Sachs of Nuremberg. All such plays could be toured easily by small companies of actors whose sense of professionalism declared itself in their readiness to double or treble parts in one play and to enliven pedestrian verse with physical agility interspersed with robust peasant humour. Scenic and costume requirements were minimal so that even if a small portable stage and changing tent or booth were included, the whole company could expect to travel with its equipment in a single cart (Figs. 77 and 105).

(iii) Civic Pageantry: The diversity of dramatic entertainment, both religious and secular, which was thus becoming available all over Europe during the fifteenth century was further augmented by civic interest in pageantry. Devised specifically to welcome distinguished and powerful visitors into the city—the sovereign, a bride or bridegroom for the heir apparent, or the ruler of an allied country—speeches of welcome were prepared, carefully enveloping messages of the expectancies entertained by the city fathers in return for the time, trouble and money expended on the welcome. City landmarks, like gateways and market-crosses, were transformed into temporary stages. Fine silks and carpets were hung from windows and balconies, and wine was substituted for water in the fountains; actors and choristers were hired, trained and costumed; and the citizens paraded in their liveries to hail the visitors and shower them with flowers and sweets. Allegorical texts and emblematic spectacle reinforced each other, thus ensuring that the messages projected were never delivered as bald statements, but left discreetly for those present to interpret in the manner of a riddle: copies of the speeches were then normally presented to the visitors. To this end the characters employed to deliver the speeches were drawn from legends, scripture, more modern history, and from the whole catalogue of virtues and vices. Echoing in some respects a Roman 'triumph', these pageant theatres (superbly illustrated in Italy by Mantegna, Petrarch and others) became a commonplace from the Atlantic seaboard to the Baltic, expressing in a way that no other form of entertainment served to do the degree of wealth and power now wielded by the merchant and professional classes (Figs. 72, 75 and 78; see also Figs. 103, 104 and 136).

Nowhere did the techniques of presentation receive closer attention than in the Low Countries where chambers of rhetoric were set up in all the cities that had grown rich on the wool and cloth trade and from their banking houses. Like the English guilds, the French *Confrèries*, or the Spanish *Confradías*, these companies had come into existence both to advance and to protect their own professional interests: by the fifteenth century they were stable and rich enough to vie with one another in annual contests for the best speeches and the most artistic style of representation. This initiative was destined to have important repercussions in the sixteenth century on the subsequent development of princely entertainments in Italy and other continental countries from Spain to Hungary, and on the development of the Lord Mayor's Show in England.

9 CORRUPTION, SIN AND DEATH

Despite all these manifestations of joy released in festive celebrations and accompanying revelry in palaces, market-squares and village greens, it must not be forgotten that, like the proverbial worm in the bud of the rose, in fifteenth-century consciousness lay an acute awareness of death. This spectral figure with his hour glass and scythe was poised in the shadows, ready to strike down young and old alike, kings along with beggars, and priests along with merchants and their journeymen, to sweep them to their graves, there to await the fearful summons of the trumpet on Judgement Day. And it was from that quarter that all the suppressed fears and terrors of the innermost psyche released themselves in imaginative pictures of everlasting torment at the hands of ghastly fiends in hell. Fear of the hereafter—of retribution for every thought, word and deed committed throughout mortal existence—was both real and close (see Plate 6). It was pictured in its most grisly aspects in countless depictions of the *Danse Macabre* (Dance of Death) and of Doomsday itself. Self-flagellation, penances, indulgences, prayers to saintly intercessors, and dangerous and costly pilgrimages acquired a relevance and popularity all their own born of attempts at self-protection from these nightmares (Fig. 79). In the theatre Death and the Devil took pride of place as villains—horrific, sinister, yet because it was their job to deceive mankind, charming, amusing, jovial and seductive. The result of compounding all these characteristics was the creation of *The Vice*—villain, enemy and principal comedian at once.

With vice as self-evident as it was in the conduct of the clergy as the fifteenth century drew to its close, it is scarcely surprising that the still-smouldering embers of Hussite and Lollard efforts to obtain reform by recourse to a return to

78. *Double street-pageant stage erected in Paris to welcome Mary Tudor on the occasion of her marriage to Louis XII, 1514. The rosebud in the centre of the lower stage grew visibly upwards and then opened to reveal a young girl (signifying the bride). The lily on the upper stage opened to reveal a young man (the bride-groom). Bride and groom then stood in the centre of the upper stage, flanked by the Cardinal Virtues. In the garden below, God is presented as the machinist. The wall and turrets represent the City of Paris where Peace sits in triumph over Discord. London, British Library.*

the simplicity of scriptural precept and abolition of the entire superstructure of ecclesiastical materialism should have again erupted into flame (see Fig. 52). When it did so, as the fifteenth century gave place to the sixteenth, first

79. *A scene from the Dance of Death which decorates the whole of the roofed bridge over the river at Lucerne. Painted in the sixteenth century by Jakob von Wyl, it was heavily restored in the nineteenth century.*

in Germany and Switzerland under the leadership of Martin Luther and then in England at the instigation of Henry VIII, Thomas Cranmer and Thomas Cromwell, the theatre's long years of consolidation and refinement of earlier dramatic forms were abruptly terminated. Religious conviction and political posture had become inseparable; and since the theatre at the time that this occurred was inescapably rooted in Roman Catholic belief and practice, all its artists found themselves precipitated into the ideological crisis that had arisen with no option but to take sides themselves. In other words, if the theatre was to have

any future and not itself become a sacrificial lamb on the altar of 'World Politics', it would perforce have to renew itself as an organ of propaganda in the service of its own patrons in the century of religious wars that was about to follow and take the consequences.

The story of theatre in Europe over the next two hundred years is thus largely one of gradual, if often violent, attempts to find a *rapprochement*, with suppression or survival as the direct consequence of failure or success. Not unnaturally, the *rapprochement* actually reached differed sharply in those countries which opted to espouse the new religion in its several forms and in those countries which chose to remain faithful to the old one. Either way, nothing about the theatre could ever be quite the same again: the Reformation, every bit as much as the Renaissance, would see to that.

*Plate 1. Ritual dancers
at a Mexican fiesta.*

Plate 2. Actors in a pantomimic dance drama on a mythological theme known as Kathakali, developed in the South Indian province of Kerala. These performances are given at night in temple courtyards or in large town squares, under a canopy 16 feet square. The make-up is symbolic and takes many hours to complete.

Plate 3. *Chinese miniature 'painted-face' make-up models for actors' use. Each model is smaller than a clenched fist. The actor simply selects the appropriate mask for the character he is about to play and copies it. University of Bristol Theatre Collection.*

Plate 4. The theatre at Epidaurus, fourth century BC, *showing the ruins of the skēnē (right); the entrance gate (left); the circular orchestra with its altar space (centre); and the tiered ranks of stone seating above.*

Plate 5. Roman mosaic of gladiatorial combat in the circus, a spectacle which thrilled most Roman citizens but gave great offence to Christians. Rome, Borghese Gallery.

Plate 6. The Dying Man and his Judge. Manuscript illumination from the Rohan Book of Hours. c.1418. Paris, Bibliothèque Nationale.

Plate 7. Pageant-car of the Resurrection. This magnificent Hungarian fifteenth-century 'Pageant' is better described as a tabernacle on wheels than as a pageant stage, since it carries a recumbent effigy of Christ and is surmounted by a catafalque guarded by the Disciples. Esztergom, Christian Museum.

Plate 8. A scene from a dramatized adaptation of the popular chivalric Romance, The Conquest of Jerusalem, presented at a banquet given by Charles V of France (in black and gold, centre) for the Emperor Charles VI (in scarlet, left), in Paris, 1378. From the Chroniques de Charles V. Paris, Bibliothèque Nationale.

PART III

PRINCES AND THEIR SERVANTS: REFORMATION AND RENAISSANCE, 1530–1715

Introduction

It has been possible to discuss the art of the theatre during the Christian Middle Ages as a coherent entity—first in the Romanesque style and then in the Gothic—because it was directed throughout by a single, undivided Church with, throughout Europe, only minor variants separating the stage practice of one country from that of another. During the sixteenth and seventeenth centuries, however, differences of climate, topography and temperament, exaggerated by those of vernacular languages and by deep divisions in religious belief combined to promote a rapidly expanding awareness of nationhood which expressed itself forcefully in the theatre. Foreign clothes, speech and manners become a frequent subject of ridicule for the amusement of native audiences in comedy: villainy, correspondingly, becomes a characteristic in tragedy that playwrights can heighten and ascribe most convincingly to foreigners—thus Italians were the villains *par excellence* of Jacobean England, where both the Pope and Machiavelli became inextricably linked with subterfuge, treachery and cruelty in the popular imagination. Speech, likewise, offered in its sounds and patterns ever more obvious comic targets as national differences in European languages became more distinct.

Nationalism, moreover, was everywhere fuelled by a shift towards absolutism in government which, arming itself with the powers of censorship, secret agents and death warrants, became increasingly despotic as time passed. As a result the prince, or head of State, was transfigured into a god-like being, supported by a court of sycophantic, if jealous, household servants and functionaries whose status, below the prince, was hierarchically organized like the biblical orders of angels. It was in this manner of a god-like ruler over quarrelsome subjects that Charles I of England during the seventeenth century presented himself on the stage to an admiring court in Stuart masques; Louis XIV of France chose similarly to appear as *Le Roi Soleil* (the Sun King) in the *Ballet de Nuit* at Versailles in 1653 (see Fig. 126).

Given this transformation of the political and aesthetic climate in Europe which accompanied the religious Reformation and Counter-Reformation and the artistic Renaissance, those reflections of it by dramatists, actors, painters and musicians on European stages (and catered for by architects in theatres intended only to accommodate privileged and sophisticated patrons) can best be understood if followed country by country—in Italy, England, Spain and France—at least to the end of the seventeenth century. Each is, therefore, treated separately in the four chapters that follow.

As will become apparent, under aristocratic patronage Italy took the lead both in refinement of language and in the revival of interest in the plays of ancient Roman and Greek dramatists. It was also under the patronage of the dukes of Italian city states (and of the popes in Rome itself) that funds were forthcoming to encourage a group of brilliant architects, painters, and musicians to concern themselves with amateur experiment in the theatre. Not surprisingly, therefore, it was in Italy that theatre buildings and opera-houses of the kind familiar to us today first made their appearance in Europe, complete with changeable scenery behind a proscenium arch (Figs. 80–7 and Fig. 92). At popular level, professional actors emerged simultaneously in the form of *Commedia dell'Arte* companies who elected to dismiss both the dramatist and the scenographer as irrelevant, and to concentrate instead on an actor's ability to entertain the public with improvised comic satire.

In England, the slow but remorseless build-up to a civil war, occasioned by the Reformation as administered by increasingly despotic central government in London, disallowed this degree of inventive experimentation. It did, however, lead to the establishment of a professional theatre, nominally maintained by the aristocracy, but effectively serving the public in the capital and in the provinces. This, in turn, encouraged actors, business speculators and young authors to enter into a loosely knit partnership to fulfil the public's rapidly growing appetite for regular theatrical entertainment. It was these conditions which, late in the sixteenth century, produced a spate of theatre building and which accounts for the emergence of a galaxy of actors and dramatists (including Marlowe, Shakespeare and Jonson) which has seldom been rivalled (see Figs. 97–102).

Spain, as the unification of the peninsula became both a geographical and a political fact, remained strictly loyal to Roman Catholicism. Nevertheless, the Church allowed a professional theatre to establish itself in all the larger cities as industry encouraged population growth in the wake of the colonization of the New World. Spanish addiction to song and dance paved the way for the admission of actresses to the professional theatre earlier than anywhere else in Europe. In Spain, it was the princes of religion—the cardinal-archbishops—rather than the kings in Madrid and Lisbon, who controlled the development of the drama of the Golden Age until, in 1621, Philip IV of Spain, assisted by his Master of the Revels, Pedro Calderón de la Barca, began to take control into his own hands.

The last of the four chapters in Part III traces this same story in France; but there, its development did not begin until the start of the seventeenth century—a consequence of the disastrous religious wars which divided the country throughout the later half of the sixteenth century. Only with the accession of Henry IV did central government begin to re-establish its authority over the nation as a whole. Once this had been accomplished, drama and theatre began to develop rapidly along lines virtually prescribed by the governments of Louis XIII and Louis XIV in Paris, producing, in Corneille, Molière, Racine and Lully, a trio of dramatists and a composer of operas and ballets whose example would be copied throughout Europe from Madrid to St Petersburg (now Leningrad) for the next hundred years.

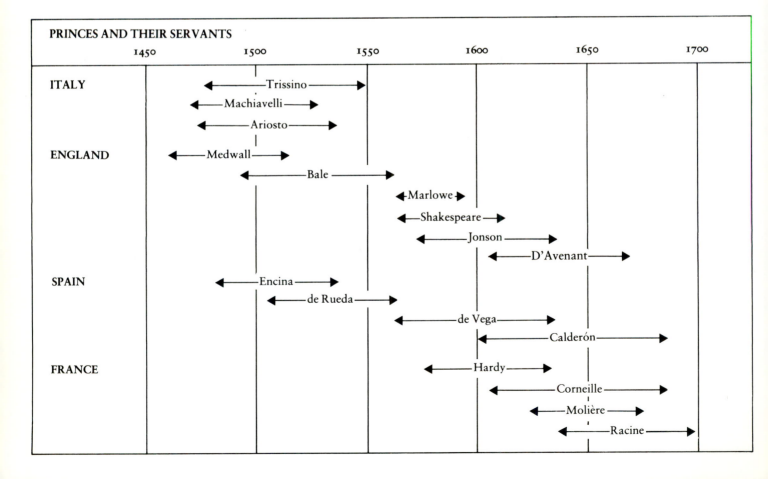

7
Italy

1 PURIFICATION OF THE ITALIAN LANGUAGE

(a) Return to Latin Roots: While Latin remained the international language of the Church, diplomatic circles and the lawcourts throughout the Middle Ages, the local vernacular languages used in daily life for other purposes grew up haphazardly with differences in local dialects often hindering communication and comprehension rather than extending it; and nowhere was this characteristic of vernacular speech more marked in the sixteenth century than in those large areas of Europe which we now refer to as Germany (including Austria) and Italy. Yet it was in Italy in the course of the fifteenth century that a movement (based on earlier 'pressure groups' starting with Dante) began among academics in all the larger city states to purify vernacular Italian by recourse to a disciplined return to classical Latin.

This academic initiative quickly won the patronage of the local ducal families and their courts—the Estes in Ferrara, the Medicis in Florence, the Gonzagas in Mantua and others including the Vatican. Moreover, it was to these palaces and their libraries that the wealthy Genoese, Neapolitan and Venetian merchants shipped the Greek and Latin manuscripts rescued from monastic libraries in the larger cities of the crumbling Byzantine Empire. Among them were texts of Aristotle's writings on the theatre as he had known it in the fourth century BC and the texts of plays by the major Greek dramatists, many of which were literally rediscovered (see p. 42).

(b) Printed Editions of Roman and Greek Plays: Refinement of the Italian language therefore proceeded within the several 'Academies' established to achieve this end through a study not only of classical Latin but also of its Greek antecedents. This was to have revolutionary consequences for the rest of Europe, since the newly invented printing presses guaranteed swifter and wider circulation of edited texts, commentaries and translations than had ever been possible before. In this context the spoken language of oratory was just as important as the written language of history, philosophy or poetry (see pp. 49 and 57). In consequence the plays of Plautus, Terence and Seneca (never wholly forgotten), together with Horace's *Art of Poetry* and Vitruvius' treatise on Imperial Roman architecture, reemerged as works for systematic study and as models for direct imitation. The first printed editions of Terence's plays became available in 1471, and by 1495–7 an edition appeared in England. Between 1480 and 1490 Seneca's tragedies were published.

Greek texts took longer to master, since proficiency in the language itself had first to be acquired; but this had also become possible by the start of the sixteenth century. The plays of Sophocles, Euripides and Aeschylus were published respectively in 1502, 1503 and 1518; some of those by Aristophanes appeared in Venice in 1498, others (but not all) in 1516.

Once access to these texts became relatively easy, it soon became obvious that if the plays were to be used as a firm base for works of commentary they must be acted. But how? Where? If the dialogue was lucid and explicit, the stage-directions were not: thus as much time and thought had to be devoted to experimenting with the visual as with the verbal aspects of theatrical representation. And this could only mean turning for advice first to the practising architects and painters of the day and subsequently—more especially in the case of Greek drama—to the musicians for help in resolving the enigma presented by the choruses, since no musical or choreographic notation appeared in any of the rescued texts. Thus, during the sixteenth century,

ITALY

The Years of Revivalism 1470–1550

1471	First printed edition of Terence's comedies
c.1480	First printed edition of Seneca's tragedies
1486	First printed edition of Vitruvius's *De Architectura* First performance of Plautus' *Menaechmi* (Ferrara)
1502	First printed edition of Pollux's *Onomasticon*
1508	Ariosto's comedy *La Cassaria* (*The Chest*) performed in Florence
1509	First performance of Seneca's *Hippolytus* in Rome
1515	Trissino's tragedy *Sophonisba* written in Italian (published 1518) but not performed
c.1515	Machiavelli writes *La Mandragola* (*The Mandrake*)
1502–18	First printed editions of plays by Aeschylus, Sophocles, Euripides and Aristophanes
1541	Giraldi's tragedy *Orbecche* performed in Ferrara
1545	Serlio publishes his *Architettura*

The Era of Innovation 1550–1640

1560–70	Formation of the first Commedia dell'Arte companies Scaliger's and Castelvetro's commentaries on Aristotle's *Poetics*
1562	Trissino's *Sophonisba* produced in Vicenza by the Olympic Academy
1580	Palladio starts to build the Teatro Olimpico at Vicenza
1585	The Teatro Olimpico at Vicenza (completed by Scamozzi) opens with a production of Giustiniani's *Oedipo Tiranno* (translated from Sophocles' *Oedipus the King*) with music by Andrea Gabrielli Scamozzi builds the Teatro Olimpico at Sabbioneta, near Mantua
1597	Ottario Rinuccini's *opera seria*, *Daphne*, with music by Jacopo Peri, produced in Florence
1607	Monteverdi's opera *Orfeo* produced in Mantua
1618	Aleotti completes the Teatro Farnese in Parma
1637	The first opera house (Teatro San Cassiano) opens in Venice
1638	Nicola Sabbattini publishes his *Pratica di fabricar scene e machine ne'teatri*

Italian academic philologists and critics, whose interest in the theatre as an art form was in general casual and fortuitous rather than deliberate and professional, found that their power to control the pace and direction of the practical implications of their own researches was, with few exceptions, rapidly usurped by such architects and painters of genius as Brunelleschi, Alberti, Bramante, Leonardo da Vinci and Raphael. Once, therefore, respectably accurate, original texts had been established by the scholars, along with some imitations in modern Latin, and duplicated for wider circulation by the printers, the story of theatre in Renaissance Italy became primarily the story of scenography, although this was accompanied, towards the end of the century, by a resurgence of popular entertainment on the one hand and by tentative essays into opera on the other.

(c) **Translations and Experimental Revivals:** Revivals of Roman plays began under the auspices of the Roman Academy headed by Pomponius Laetus in the 1460s, an example followed by other academies as far apart as Naples and Venice during the next thirty years. Following the pattern set by the progress made in editing the texts, comedy led the way. Plautus' *Menaechmi* was staged in Ferrara in 1486, and again in 1491, decked out with scenery; but it was another twenty years before anyone was ready to tackle Seneca. The first choice was *Hippolytus*, presented in Rome in 1509 and again in Ferrara. By this time Latin comedies were being performed in Italian translations together with the first excursions into contemporary vernacular imitations; and major artists were being commissioned to plan and supervise all visual aspects of these productions.

2 COMMEDIA ERUDITA

(a) **Comedy:** The essentially intellectual and aristocratic theatrical concerns of the academics acquired the generic title of *Commedia Erudita* (learned, or serious drama). Constrained to develop along imitative rather than creative lines and within an environment of constant theoretical and interpretative debate, the scholars and the young noblemen who assisted them by producing and acting the plays failed to produce much dramatic literature, comic or tragic, of lasting quality. Some blame for this must attach to their decision to cut all ties with the Gothic past and the popular audiences who had supported the old religious plays (*sacre rappresentazioni*). Although these had been quickly purged by the Catholic bishops of their cruder accretions in an attempt to forestall Protestant attack, they were rejected as being of no further interest to anyone other than peasants and artisans on public holidays and were then ignored until resuscitated by Jesuit colleges following the Council of Trent (1545–63).

Ariosto was the first of the *avant-gardists* to achieve personal notoriety with *La Cassaria* (*The Chest*) in 1508, followed a year later by *I Suppositi* (*The Counterfeits*) which, more than half a century later, George Gascoigne admired enough to translate and adapt into English as *The Supposes*. Then, c.1513–20, Niccolò Machiavelli wrote *Mandragola* (*The Mandrake*), the single Italian comedy of the whole century which posterity has thought worthy of frequent translation and revival. The reason for this would seem to lie in the deliberate departure which Machiavelli made from past precedent by breaking through the single level of meaning habitual in academic comedy, to offer each member of his Florentine audience several layers of meaning and the freedom to choose an ultimate interpretation for himself—or herself. This last distinction is important since the play treats of a young girl married to an impotent old man who is duped into persuading her to take a young lover to bed with her, believing that if his wife is given a drink beforehand containing mandrake root (a known inducer of fertility) the effect will be to kill her partner immediately after intercourse has taken place, yet provide her husband with an heir. With so many ambiguities thus built into his plot and so much variety of motivation for each character's complicity in the action, Machiavelli offers his actors and their director an unaccustomed freedom of interpretation.

The promise, however, declared by this one author within this one play of a new age of brilliant comedy of manners was not realized. In Pietro Aretino (1492–1556) there appeared a writer whose own intelligence and wit enabled him to overcome the obstacle of humble birth; but as the construction of his plays was hasty and uncontrolled, their virtue rested in their vivid depiction of character (taken to the point of caricature) and in the satiric quality of their dialogue: such plays, however, have a habit of becoming quickly dated. What undoubtedly was achieved collectively through all the research and experiment in Italian court circles devoted to Roman comedy was a clear statement of a formula that could be used and embroidered upon by later generations. Fortune *is* fickle; her wheel *does* turn: disaster *does* strike, but it is within man's own nature and capacity to outwit Fortune, to find a remedy, and thus to survive. Romantic love and 'happy-ever-after' endings lie far outside the scope of this type of comedy which is wholly dependent on a chosen situation and the relationships of the characters within it. It exists to expose folly, credulity and pretension in as amusing a manner as possible. Here vice becomes equatable with folly; virtue with the wit to avoid becoming its victim. It can be stretched in the direction of farce; alternatively in that of satire and even of cruelty. Such was the comic legacy of *Commedia Erudita* both to Italians and to the rest of Europe.

(b) Theory and Criticism: That it did not produce many masterpieces must be attributed in part to the stifling effects of conscientious imitation, but also in part to the passionate concern of Renaissance intellectuals to theorize and thereby reduce an unruly art form to timeless laws of order and decorum. In this quest, Horace's *Art of Poetry* was their loadstone (see pp. 48–9); the study of Aristotle augmented it. It is thus theorists and critics, not dramatists, who stand out as landmarks in Italian theatrical landscapes of the sixteenth century. Julius Caesar Scaliger (1484–1558) and Lodovico Castelvetro (?1505–1571) both produced important commentaries on Aristotle's *Poetics*; and it was they who persuaded educated society to accept the unities of time, place and action as *rules* deduced from classical authority to be regarded as binding by dramatists, present and future, and whether composing comedies or tragedies. The tighter these rules became and the more widely they came to be accepted in literary and court circles, the less room dramatists found for poetic imagination and personal freedom of expression.

Classical antiquity, however, had also fostered and legitimized the existence of a third dramatic genre, the satyr play, about which next to nothing was known and around which, therefore, speculation could still roam freely. Loosely attached to the poetic genre of pastoral in Italy in the latter half of the sixteenth century, embellished with music, song and dance, and decorated with scenery, it was this third alternative which offered the best escape route from the tyranny of the theoreticians to poets and other practising artists in the theatre of that time. The decision to take it, and to embark upon what has since become known as opera, was precipitated in the late 1560s by the problems of trying to revive Greek tragedies. A second escape route was found, at least by actors if not by poets, in a sharp, popular reaction against *Commedia Erudita*— itself a reversion to the traditional forms and standards of

80. *The Teatro Olimpico at Vicenza, designed by Palladio and Scamozzi and opened in 1585. Built theoretically as a reconstruction of a classical Roman theatre, it is constructed to a much smaller scale, with the orchestra more nearly resembling a nineteenth-century orchestra pit, and with its ceiling painted to look like the sky. (Compare Figs. 37 and 38.)*

medieval secular drama, *Commedia dell'Arte* (professional, as opposed to amateur, entertainment).

(c) **Tragedy**: Before turning to this or to opera, however, something must first be said about the fortunes of tragedy within the academies and the ducal courts which funded their activities.

Interest in the revival of classical tragedy, as already remarked, followed the same route as that of comedy, but some two decades later. The first original tragedy in Italian

in imitation of Senecan and Greek precedent was Gian Giorgio Trissino's *Sophonisba* completed in 1515, six years after the production of Seneca's *Hippolytus* in Rome: but it had to wait another nine years before it was published and nearly another forty years before it was eventually performed in Vicenza in 1562, twelve years after Trissino's death.

It must remain an open question whether these academicians, whose interests in drama were focused on the tragedies of Seneca, were hesitant about attempting to revive his plays when suddenly confronted with printed copies of Greek tragedies; or whether they became inhibited as pronouncements derived from Aristotle on the true form and content of tragedy proliferated; or whether dukes, cardinals and their entourages were too excited by the swiftly expanding horizons of contemporary life and entertainment to care much about so esoteric a dramatic form as tragedies salvaged from classical antiquity. What is certain is that historians now have to account for the thirty-year delay between the first recorded performance of a play by Seneca (1509) and the first production of a tragedy written in Italian: this was Giraldi Cinzio's *Orbecche*, which was given at Ferrara in 1541. Cinzio himself declared that Seneca was more deserving of imitation than the Greeks, at least for audiences of his own day; but the general trend of academic opinion on dramatic theory and practice was gradually moving in the opposite direction.

(d) Satyr Plays and the Origins of Opera: In Florence during the 1560s a group of poets, musicians and noblemen established a society known as the 'Camerata', which made the study of the practicability of reviving Greek tragedy one of its principle objectives in the conviction that the surviving plays had originally been recited or chanted, and in part danced, to music. This idea and the practical experiments which resulted from it spread elsewhere, notably to Venice where it attracted the attention of the organist at St Marks, Andrea Gabrielli (*c.*1510–86), a leading composer of madrigals where song and instrumental music were linked and called *musica concertata*. It was Gabrielli whom the academicians at Vicenza employed to assist Orsatto Giustiniani with the preparation of the text and score for their production of Giustiniani's translation of Sophocles' *Oedipus Tyrannus* (*Oedipo Tiranno*) to open their theatre in 1585. *Succès d'estime* as this production was, it attracted no imitators outside strictly academic and musical circles. What did stir imaginations (and far beyond the Veneto) was the music (only the choruses survive today) and the building at Vicenza. Designed and started by Andrea Palladio in 1580, it was carried to completion following his death in 1581 by his pupil Vincenzo Scamozzi (Fig. 80). Not only does the theatre itself survive, but on its walls there is a picture in fresco of that momentous performance.

3 THEATRES

(a) Architecture: Within three years Scamozzi had been commissioned to provide Vespasiano Gonzaga, Duke of Sabbioneta, with a similar theatre within his own palace. What Scamozzi gave him by 1590 was a building on a much reduced scale, but with the central arch of the *frons scenae* at Vicenza widened, and with the two flanking doors placed closer to it (Figs. 81 and 82). These openings allowed a single, continuous landscape to be seen through them instead of the separate rows of house fronts depicted in bas-relief and in receding perspective visible through the five doors of the theatre in Vicenza. By 1618, when Giam-

battista Aleotti completed his theatre in the Farnese Palace in Parma, these three doors had been merged into a single, wide opening called the proscenium arch with ample space behind it not only to display a single, painted landscape, but to change one scene for another (Fig. 83). This achievement marks the start of a new era in theatrical representation which reached fulfilment in what Victorians labelled graphically as 'the picture-frame stage' (see Fig. 183).

To understand how and why this should have happened we need first to appreciate that Euclid's treatise on geometry had been translated from Greek into Latin and published in Venice in 1482, four years prior to the publication of Vitruvius' *De Architectura*. This provided the necessary mathematical basis for the mastery of perspective drawing which was itself the *sine qua non* for offering audiences landscape scenery in the theatre. By 1525 Albrecht Dürer had invented the instruments that an artist needed if the theoretical principles underpinning such visual illusions were to be translated into practice; and as Leonardo da Vinci observed in his *Treatise on Painting*, 'Those who become enamoured of the practice of the art [of landscape painting] without having previously applied themselves to the diligent study of the scientific part of it, may be compared to mariners, who put to sea in a ship without rudder or compass, and therefore cannot be certain of arriving at the wished-for port' (Trans. J. F. Rigaud, 1892, p. 37).

(b) Scenery: Although Italian artists of the Renaissance were uncertain how to interpret Vitruvius' observations on the use of scenery in Roman theatres, they at least possessed the certainty of his authority for its use; and that sufficed of itself to allow them to oblige their patrons with commentaries derived from their own speculative studies and with creative, three-dimensional reconstructions realized on stages in the halls, granaries and barns allotted to them for these experiments. In 1545 Sebastiano Serlio published the second book of his *Architettura*: it was printed in Paris and dealt with the art of painting in perspective, especially scene-painting or 'scenography'. Here theatre architecture (including both stage and auditorium), the construction of scenery and the painting of its component parts are all discussed as a single interrelated science and craft. The insistence upon this interrelationship derived as much from the social circumstances in which his research was pursued as from the geometrical and optical precepts of painting in perspective, since it is in the very nature of the latter to dictate that the illusion offered can only be viewed to perfection from a point set at a fixed distance from the stage; and in an aristocratically ordered society the seat in the auditorium commanding this particular view was

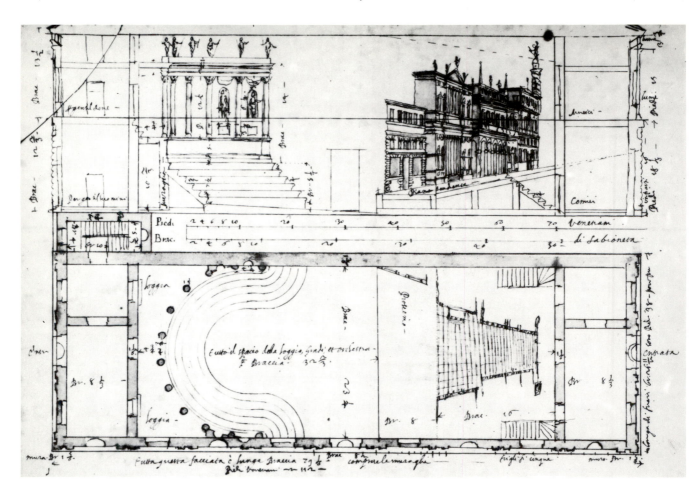

81. *Ground-plan and cross-section of the interior (stage and auditorium) elevation of the Teatro Olimpico at Sabbioneta, near Mantua, designed and built in the ducal palace by Scamozzi, 1590. Note the sharply raked stage and the placement of the vanishing-point of the scenic perspective well behind the back wall. (Compare Fig. 84.) Florence, Uffizi Gallery.*

82. *The auditorium of the Teatro Olimpico in the ducal palace at Sabbioneta, near Mantua, designed and built by Scamozzi in 1590, as viewed from the stage. (Compare Figs. 80 and 92.)*

automatically reserved for that god among men, the Prince. As the quality of the illusion provided deteriorated in proportion to the distance any other seating was situated to left or right of that central seat, so the seating or standing room allotted to others entitled to attend was arranged in strict order of social precedence.

These arrangements derive ultimately from Serlio's belief that theatres should be regarded as a microcosm of the world of man, just as St Augustine and his followers in earlier generations had viewed them as an emblem of God's universe (see pp. 57–8). The horizon in his scenic

83. *The stage and proscenium frontage of the Teatro Farnese, designed and built within the ducal palace at Parma by Aleotti in 1618. Here the five doorways in the* frons scenae *of the Teatro Olimpico at Vicenza have been reduced to a single but much wider arched opening. The proscenium is constructed wholly of wood, painted to resemble marble. (Compare Figs. 80, 92 and 100.)*

perspectives is thus placed at actor's eye-level as seen by the actor when standing at the front of the stage and looking back towards it. To avoid excessive foreshortening in the scenery, Serlio insisted that the horizon be placed behind the back wall of the theatre and at a distance from it equal to the depth of the stage (Fig. 84).

As well as explaining how to construct 'houses' (scenic units), and what we call 'wings', 'legs' and 'flats' by making

84. *Diagram in Serlio's* Architettura, *1545, of the cross-section of a stage and auditorium built of wood. The fore-stage (C) is flat. The area (A–B) between the* frons scenae *or proscenium and the back wall is steeply raked. (Compare Fig. 81.)*

wooden frames, covering them with canvas and then painting them in receding perspective, Serlio offered his readers three engravings representing scenery appropriate for classical tragedy, comedy and satyr plays (Fig. 85). Serlio's work is throughout classical in spirit, but this is combined with a constant rationalizing of Vitruvius which results in a far stronger emphasis on verisimilitude as the ultimate goal.

His book was widely read and exercised immense influence, but it was never taken as definitive since no *permanent* theatres existed when he wrote it (1545). Some modifications to his rules thus became obligatory every time anyone attempted to present a play in a temporary auditorium of different proportions to those which he had envisaged.

Where theatre buildings are concerned, therefore, the years between the opening of the Teatro Olimpico in Vicenza in 1585 and that of the Teatro Farnese in Parma in 1618 represent the transition from this state of affairs in Italy to a new scale of social and cultural values in which it would be assumed from the outset that any building described as a theatre or playhouse would be equipped with scenery painted in perspective. It was during this period of transition that the attention of architects, painters and engineers moved forward to seeking and finding solutions to the problem of changing scenery during the action of a play: this necessitated the use of concealed machinery.

(c) **Machinery and Stage-Lighting:** Interest in machinery for stage use began early, since Vitruvius had authenticated its existence in Roman theatres. The nature of this interest is attested in some of Leonardo da Vinci's drawings. The greatest stimulant, however, behind its early development was the publication in 1502 in Venice of the Greek grammarian Pollux's *Onomasticon* (written in the second century AD): the individual who applied most energy to the practical aspects of its use was the Florentine Bastiano da San Gallo (1481–1551): it was he who first resuscitated the triangular prisms known under the Greek name of *periak-*

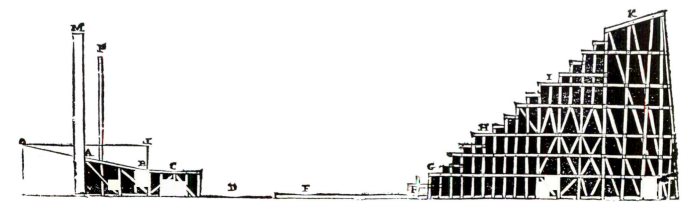

85. *Serlio's imaginary perspective landscape stage-setting for a Greek satyr play. This, together with two other drawings of settings for comedy and tragedy interpreting Vitruvius' and Horace's precepts relating to Roman theatre practice, first appeared in 1545 in the first printed edition of his* Architettura *(Book 2).*

toi and put them to new uses on Italian stages. When Scaliger published his *Poetics* in 1561, he was able to incorporate a translation of the section of the *Onomasticon* on machinery.

Against this evidence we must not forget to set our knowledge that stage machinery of a fairly elaborate and costly order had been used, at least as early as the fifteenth century, in the production of passion plays and saint plays to produce thunder, lightning, rain, the destruction of buildings, conflagrations and such miraculous events as the apparent execution and resurrection of Christian martyrs. What classical authority served to do was to reinforce and rationalize its use, while serving at the same time to provide yet another escape route from the oppressive limitations imposed by the demand from dramatic theorists for unity of time and place in stage plays. The first systematically organized textbook on the construction and use of these machines appeared in 1638, Nicola Sabbattini's *Pratica di fabricar scene e machine ne' teatri*, complete with illustrations; and with that available for consultation, an era in

which the provision of changeable scenery was regarded by dramatists, actors and audiences alike as an essential component of theatrical representation had begun.

4 COURT FESTIVALS, *INTERMEZZI* AND *OPERA SERIA*

(a) *Intermezzi*: A double incentive was provided to this end by the spectacular court festivals of the period and by the growing influence of musicians in the theatre—pressures which, in conjunction, resulted in the provision of *intermedia* or *intermezzi*, lavishly decorated with scenic ornament, and embellished with instrumental music, song and dance (Plate 10 and Fig. 89). Reciprocally, the fascination and sense of wonder which machines provoked in audiences' minds (and which Italians assumed Aristotle to have encouraged) hastened the further advance of *intermezzi* into a single sequence of incidents pertaining to some particular myth or legend, especially those of a pastoral character. The credit for this extension of the *intermezzi* rests with the Camerata in Florence. Originally devised as light *divertissements* for court guests between courses at a banquet, these entertainments could as easily be interpolated between the acts of a *commedia erudita*. Within the limits of these extended *intermezzi*, the pageant-cars of the daytime tilts and triumphs could be simply wheeled into the banquet hall, preceded by torch-bearers and musicians (see Figs. 128 and 129); the ranks of the original mythological or legendary group of disguised noblemen could be supplemented if necessary with more orators, singers and dancers and thus enable the incident presented earlier as a static *tableau-vivant* to be translated into an artistically well-organized re-enactment of the complete scene. Freed in these circumstances from all the irksome restrictions stemming from respect for a prescribed text, the scenic artists found in these *intermezzi* the most stimulating challenge to their personal powers of imaginative invention and technical expertise. They swiftly embraced the challenge to equip these short pastoral interludes with perspective landscape scenery in which clouds, waves, trees and fountains all warranted inclusion; and this, in its turn, challenged them to discover machinery that could both animate them and replace one with another (Figs. 86–9). Slowly such machinery came to be imported into theatres above the stage, below it and in the wing spaces on either side of it, as did large numbers of small oil lamps in coloured glass containers to replace the torch-bearers of the original masquerades or 'disguisings'. Lamps of this sort can still be seen *in situ* in the Teatro Olimpico at Vicenza.

86. *Stage-machinery required for the presentation of a 'Glory' or celestial vision at the San Salvatore opera house, Venice, 1675. The dotted lines on the lower half of the drawing indicate how the machinery slots in between the painted wing-flats on the stage. The whole machine has wheels enabling it to move forward carrying the actors as the backcloth opens (or is raised) to reveal it. (Compare Fig. 132.) Paris, Bibliothèque de l'Opéra.*

87. *A 'Glory' or celestial vision on the stage of the San Salvatore opera house, Venice, 1675. The large archway painted on the sliding shutters parts to allow the four horses to draw forward the huge cloud-machine (see Fig. 86 and Fig. 132). The central circle of the cloudscape is then lowered into place from a capstan winch operated from the fly-gallery while the shutters at the back are closed again, replacing the archway and the vista glimpsed through it. Paris, Bibliothèque de l'Opéra.*

Court festivals had been commended by Machiavelli in his *Discourses* for their ability both to exalt and defend the person of the prince by compelling respect and awe for such munificence. Brought to perfection by the Medici in Florence, they did not themselves break much new ground but they did serve to transform the Gothic appearance of traditional models—tournaments, disguisings, pageants and so on—into a new and elegant style, heavily reliant on a revival of interest in Roman Imperial triumphs and other *ludi*, but richly textured with imaginative originality particular to the nature of the occasion, the locations chosen, and the talent of the individual artists employed (see Plate 10).

Given the Italian climate, most of these festivities were organized by the prince and his officials in open-air settings with city streets, market squares, rivers, lakes, parks, gardens and courtyards all harnessed to the service of spectacular masquerades; many carried on at night, simply being transferred indoors, and extended over several consecutive days. The classical authors were ransacked for

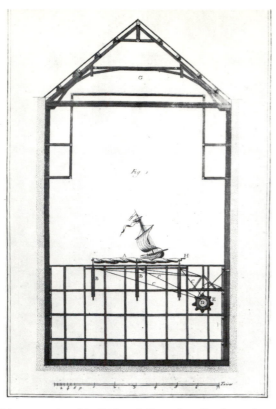

88. *Diagram printed in Diderot's* Encyclopedia, *but taken from Sabbatini's* Design and Construction of Stage Machinery *of 1637, illustrating the method to be used to create the illusion of ships sailing before the wind. (Compare Figs. 119 and 135.)*

opening allowing horsemen and triumphal cars to pass through it, and with two smaller flanking arches for pedestrians, came to eclipse other monuments for use as stages from which to address bystanders (Fig. 103). Rivers, lakes and islands became stages for water pageants, and these natural settings were supplemented by courtyards sealed off and equipped with special machinery to pump water into them for mock sea-battles in the manner of the Roman *naumachia* (Figs. 90 and 91); jousts on horseback and on foot were likewise supplemented by horse-ballets and other entertainments requiring a combination of courage and artistry in the manner of the Roman *ludi circenses* described in Chapter 3 (Figs. 92 and 130). These princely entertainments carried the theatrical enthusiasms of the academicians and their artist friends out of doors, from the make-believe world of the playhouses into the gardens and parks of the real world, endowing life itself with an unwonted, if temporary, theatricality. Obelisks, colonnades, and the classical orders of architecture replaced the turrets and pinnacles of Gothic fantasy; strenuous efforts were also made, regardless of cost, to reduce the vagaries of natural landscape in parkland into vistas obeying the orderly rules of receding perspective, with fountains and statuary to adorn them (Fig. 133).

(b) *Opera Seria:* Reciprocally, many scenic features originally devised to decorate open-air entertainments were

89. *Cloud-machine for the entrance of (left to right) Mercury, Apollo, Jupiter and Astrea, designed by Bernardo Buontalenti for* La Pellegrina, *Florence, 1589. Florence, Biblioteca Nazionale.*

short incidents—comic, lyrical or melodramatic—from mythology and legend which allowed the promoters of the festival to dress up for the amusement of their friends and to impress the local population as Neptune, Venus, Juno, Diana, Mars or Pluto, or as Dido and Aeneas; or as Hector, Achilles, Ulysses or Circe (Fig. 89). Equipped with an appropriate retinue of supporting characters—tritons, wood nymphs, muses, warriors, cherubs, or devils—they appeared before spectators, raised up on carriages ornately decorated with all the emblems needed to identify themselves and their locations; and in all of this they were frequently supported by instrumentalists, singers and orators. A ship, beautifully rigged, sailing on wheels was taken for granted, as were devils issuing from caves with smoke rising above and fireworks exploding to left and right, just as their predecessors in religious drama had been: the difference lay in the fact that this ship was more likely to carry Jason than Noah, and that this cave was more likely to be referred to as Etna or Avernus than hell-mouth or hell-castle.

In city streets the triumphal arch with its ample, central

90. Naumachia, *or water pageant, prepared for the wedding festivities of Catherine of Lorraine and the Grand Duke of Tuscany, 1589. The courtyard of the Pitti Palace in Florence was flooded for the occasion and roofed over with an awning of red satin. Engraving by O. Scarabelli. Florence, Uffizi. (Compare Figs. 107 and 133.)*

carried indoors to embellish the new pastoral *intermezzi*; and it was in these circumstances that the poet Ottario Rinuccini and the composer Jacopo Peri set the story of Daphne to music for performance at the Tuscan court to celebrate Carnival in 1597. This was highly enough acclaimed to spur them to provide in 1600 a second *opera in musica* (i.e. a play accompanied by music for voices and instruments allowing for spoken dialogue and recitative between fully scored arias and choruses)—the story of Orpheus and Eurydice, for which Rinuccini's text but not Peri's score has been preserved. This was so successful that it provoked two rival versions, the second of which was performed in 1607, set by Claudio Monteverdi.

There is no room in this book to discuss the story of opera at any length, but before leaving its genesis in Italian attempts both to revive Greek tragedy and to expand the *intermezzi*, two further aspects of its early history deserve recall since both had consequences for the future of theatre. The first is the alternative art form which it opened up to poets interested in tragedy as a dramatic genre who found slavish imitation of Greek and Roman precedent in this genre uninspiring and unrewarding; for what *opera in musica* allowed above all else was a heightening of the emotions, condensed and expressed through poetry by recourse to the additional melodic, harmonic and rhythmical resources offered by the sister art of music, supplemented by those of the scenographer. This style of drama came to be known as *opera seria*.

The second aspect to warrant mention is the erection in the 1630s and 1640s of opera houses making special provision for the accommodation of musicians, who were placed immediately below the stage in the area described in Greek and Roman times as the orchestra. The first of these houses opened to the public in Venice in 1637. Its leading scenic artist was Giacomo Torelli (1608–78) who was summoned to Paris by Louis XIV in 1645, and of whom more must be said when theatrical events in France are considered (see pp. 155–6). Venetian opera during the rest of the century set standards which not only spread rapidly throughout the rest of Europe, but made it appear essential to all self-respecting kings and princes who aspired to possess a private theatre to employ Italian architects and painters to build and equip it (see Figs. 86, 87, 132, 147). Thus it was 'the opera house' and not 'the playhouse' which determined the shape and appearance of all theatres built in continental Europe, even in Scandinavia and Russia. In this respect England stood isolated and alone in possessing an alternative style of theatre building which it exported via the West Indies to the eastern seaboard cities of North America. (More will be said about that in Chapter 11.)

91. Naumachia, *or water pageant, in the Hippodrome, Rome, c.1650. Aquatic spectacles were popular also in England in the early nineteenth and twentieth centuries (see p. 186). Engraving by C. Coriolanus in* Hieronymi Mercurialis foroliriensis de Arte Gymnastica, Libri Sex, *ed. Amsterdam, 1672 (original treatise, 1569).*

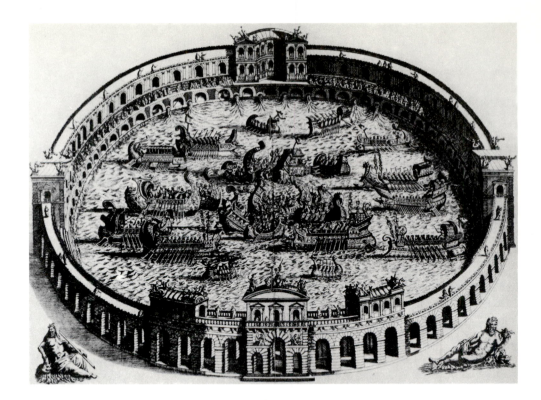

5 *COMMEDIA DELL'ARTE*

Opera seria, being a lineal descendant of tragedy, allowed no room for comedy until, during the eighteenth century, it entered the opera house in the form of *opera buffa* (see Chapter 11). Thus if neo-classical comedy was to have a future in the theatre it had to turn elsewhere. Like tragedy, its early promise proved in some respects to be abortive. After Machiavelli and Pietro Aretino, a few individuals— Giordano Bruno, Giambattista della Porta—are still regarded by Italian critics as representative authors of comedy in the latter half of the sixteenth century who deserve some respect, but their plays lie forgotten north of the Alps. What comedy, as revived and remodelled by the academicians, needed and luckily received was an infusion of a new dynamic to make audiences laugh: and this had to come from some exterior and less doctrinaire source. Some historians claim it came from Bergamo; some that it originated in Naples. Either way, it was popular, with its roots

92. *Aerial view of a* Carrousel *(or horse-ballet) of the kind still offered at the Spanish Riding School in Vienna. Engraving of the Teatro Farnese at Parma, built by Aleotti in 1618. Note the greatly enlarged orchestra extending as an ellipse deep into the auditorium, thereby facilitating its use for elaborate* intermezzi *and* opera seria. *(Compare Figs. 34, 43, 83 and Plate 10.)*

in folk culture rather than in the schools or the court. Being actor-centred instead of text- or author-centred, *Commedia dell'Arte* (i.e. 'of professional artists' as opposed to 'learned' or academic amateurs) needed neither a special building nor subsidy from wealthy patrons: a market square, a public holiday and a crowd with nothing better to do than watch, listen and express their appreciation by putting a coin into a collection-box sufficed. They were not interested in scenery and did not require it: a platform stage to raise them above the heads of a standing crowd, and a booth or tent in which to dress and store their properties, met all their theatrical needs. Human nature as revealed in the daily life of the market-place supplied them with their texts.

Each actor in these small professional troupes, which began to attract attention in the 1560s, specialized in impersonating a single character-type (see Plate 12). The most famous is Harlequin (*Arlecchino*), seemingly a character of peasant origin in the Bergamo region of the foothills to the Alps, but endowed with qualities shared by the parasite, or clever slave, of Roman comedy and also by the god Mercury. He was thus invariably a servant, faithful if naïve, yet astonishingly resourceful. Constantly landing himself in embarrassing situations, he is for ever able to rescue himself by means which are as amusing as they are remarkable. It follows that the actor of this role must be athletic and something of a contortionist. Women, especially young ones, are to him objects of adoration and approachable only with respect and often with diffidence. To him, money is always a means to an end, the lack of which spells trouble, but the use of which is always to buy one's way out of or, on occasion, into worse trouble. His costume mirrors his character. Being two-faced in his nature, he invariably wore a mask; though why it should have been a black one has never been satisfactorily explained. Above it was a peasant's hat with a fox's tail trailing down behind, or sometimes a rabbit's. Being mercurial in temperament, he wore a coat and trousers of patchwork, multicoloured. A purse and a sword were the obligatory accoutrements demanded of him by his role. Onto this basic figure several distinctive variants were grafted as time passed.

Another figure from the Bergamo region was Brighella who, like Harlequin, was an opportunist and also wore a mask and hat; but his principal characteristics were developed in the south around Naples. His mask was brown and green, not black, and was further distinguished by his invariable moustache and beard. His character also differs in lacking any element of faithfulness or altruism: self-interest alone directs his opportunism. He is too lazy to work but knows instinctively where food can be filched and the rich fleeced; and whenever, metaphorically, he recognizes that a ship is likely to sink, he quits. Women exist as commodities for use. In short Brighella differs from Harlequin as sharply as does a rat from a teddy-bear in the affections of a child. In today's society Brighella would be found in amusement arcades pushing drugs, or soliciting tourists in murky side-streets. His principal talents are disguise, his ability to sing and dance, and his accomplishments as a liar and thief. His direct descendant in Italy is Scapino, distinguished by his cowardice, and in France Sganarelle, who excels as a clown (see Fig. 125).

As parasites on society Harlequin, Brighella and their several descendants live off two other groups of characters, inexperienced youth (usually lovers) and older professional people (often rich)—army officers, merchants and bookmen: and in doing this they enlist the help of courtesans. The bookmen include lawyers, teachers, doctors and politicians under the generic title *Il Dottore*, Doctor, signifying a university training and graduate status. All of them were regarded as pompous and more ready to consult books than people: all of them were motivated in their actions by a desire to keep what they had got—children, position, property, money. In order to make them into figures of ridicule, it was thus necessary only to find situations which contrasted their desire to protect their status and possessions with their gullibility in the ways of the world; and this usually meant exposing them as egoists, hypocrites or fools. As a type, this character derived his appearance from that of the teachers at the oldest university city, Bologna. He was thus distinguished by his black hat and gown, and his armful of books and papers. He could be young or old, rich or poor, to suit the story, but did not wear a mask.

The other two professional worlds, commerce and military life, were sketched in similarly sharp outline, but with obvious differences of detail. The archetypal businessman was taken to reside on the Rialto in Venice: hence his stage name Pantalone (a corruption of *pianta leone*, literally 'lion planter'). The lion was St Mark's emblem and thus that of the city: the phrase therefore signified an economic imperialist. His appearance was unmistakably Semitic. Originally he wore a red gaberdine cloak, red Turkish trousers, slippers and skull-cap, but c.1650 the red cloak was exchanged for a black one. He wore a mask with a long hooked nose and straggling grey or white beard. If married, his wife was much younger than he was; any children were good looking and, as the most likely inheritors of his wealth in the near future, attractive to all social predators.

Military life was represented by *Il Capitano*, derived directly from Plautus' *Miles Gloriosus*, but brought up to date in his dress. This consisted of an ornate uniform, hat, and outsize sword or gun (see Fig. 30). A mask with outsize red nose and bristling moustache completed the effect. Most of the comedy in his case developed out of exposing the gap between this costume and the man under it. The more he matched his external appearance by his boasts, oaths, threats and posturing, the more shocking and ludicrous was his discomforture on being revealed to be a coward when forced to fight, and a bungler with women when actually confronted by one. A kinsman to the Braggart Captain was Scaramouche, commissioned from the ranks and much given to drink and loose talk. Another relative was Pulcinella, a deformed simpleton and constant butt of cruel humour: faithful, like Harlequin, he could turn vicious. In Germany under the name of Hanswurst he would later acquire a sausage instead of a baton, and in England he would be translated into that anarchic figure Mr Punch with his shrew of a wife, Judy (see pp. 176 and 192).

The young lovers were in general as conventional as all stage juveniles; but they were given the freedom to adopt names and costumes that accorded with their own personalities. Distinctions, however, were made between peasants and townfolk both in dress and character. Of the servants, one became stereotyped as Columbine to partner Harlequin.

The companies involved in *Commedia dell'Arte* normally took their name from their leader—Ganassa, Gelosi, Confidenti and so forth—during the 1560s, and travelled as far afield as Paris and Madrid (see Plate 12). Plots were constructed around a selection of the typed characters and also round certain carefully rehearsed physical routines of comic incident known as *lazzi*: improvised dialogue was then imposed upon this structure.

During the seventeenth and eighteenth centuries, the *commedia* companies, by offering entertainment that was both varied and amusing—drawing its strength from what was local and topical without being contentious in matters of either religion or politics—delighted aristocratic audiences in court theatres throughout continental Europe as well as in the market-places of its native Italy where it came slowly to replace old-fashioned religious plays. Never did it pose a threat to the State: still less did it ridicule the prince or his entourage. So long as it remained closely in touch with human nature it could be relied upon to provide an ideal *divertissement*—sometimes serious, often frivolous, always harmless. Only in France did the actors let the exuberance of their wit outrun their discretion, an act of folly for which they paid with their expulsion from Paris in 1697. The real enemies of the genre were repetition and stereotyping which, in conjunction, led to a loss of spontaneity (see p. 173).

In retrospect, it has to be admitted that the Italian theatre of the sixteenth and seventeenth centuries did not produce many memorable literary masterpieces; but, notwithstanding this admission, it is to the Italians of that time that the rest of Europe and the Western world owes not only the theoretical basis of its subsequent drama, but the design of theatres, changeable scenery, opera as a new dramatic genre and, in *Commedia dell'Arte*, a style of comedy capable of adaptation to suit the temperament and manners of other nations for nearly two hundred years.

8
England

1 RENAISSANCE AND REFORMATION

(a) **Italian Influences on Drama at the Courts of Henry VII and Henry VIII:** The accession of Henry VII to the English throne in 1485 brought an end to the blood-letting between the rival baronial factions of York and Lancaster known as the Wars of the Roses. It also had an immediate impact on the English theatre.

The new king not only set about surrounding himself with public servants to whom he owed little and who owed their preferment to him—in short to literate representatives of the new middle class—but sought to repair the damage done to national prestige by fortifying relationships with continental Europe in every way open to him.

One way offered itself in dynastic marriages—that of his daughter Margaret to the King of Scotland; his daughter Mary to the King of France (Figs. 72, 78); and his elder son Arthur to Katherine, Princess of Aragon, the daughter of the King and Queen of Spain (see p. 134); when Arthur died, she was remarried to his brother Henry, later Henry VIII.

Another method was to encourage an energetic exchange of English scholars and artists with representative counterparts from Burgundy, Flanders, Holland and Italy. Thus, during Henry VII's reign, the philosopher Erasmus, the historian Polydore Vergil, the architect Pietro Torrigiano and the painter Hans Holbein the elder all came to England while such notable English scholars as Dean Colet, William Grocyn and William Lily studied abroad.

In the theatre the impact of these initiatives was swiftly felt at court, in the universities and in certain major schools and choir-schools, so that by the end of Henry's reign in 1509 it had become as fashionable in court and academic circles to discuss the plays of the Roman and Greek dramatists and the writings of Aristotle and Vitruvius as it already was in Rome, Florence or Amsterdam. In 1497 Henry Medwall, an Eton schoolmaster and chaplain to the Lord Chancellor, Cardinal Morton, wrote the first secular play in English to have survived to us, *Fulgens and Lucres* (Fig. 93). It is a well-constructed, very entertaining play in two parts, centred on a topical question of political and social concern—whether Gaius Flaminius (representing patrician birth and inherited wealth) or Publius Cornelius (representing individual achievement and personal character) will make the better husband for Fulgens' daughter, Lucres. The central debate on this issue is enlivened throughout by two comic servants, A and B, who, in the bawdy sub-plot, court Lucres' maid Joan.

It was in England at this time that Erasmus completed his translation of two plays by Euripides; and with his appointment in 1508 to a new chair of Greek at Cambridge all was set for as rigorous and enlightened a revival of Greek and Latin literature, including stage plays, as that progressing in Italy.

Under Henry VIII performances of Roman plays in Latin began to be given at court by schoolboys. St Paul's school in London had been reorganized by Dean Colet who appointed William Lily as first High Master. Lily had spent five years in Rhodes learning Greek and as long in Rome, where he had become acquainted with early revivals of plays by Plautus and Terence. By 1519 he was ready to present his boys in a play by Plautus to the court, at Greenwich Palace. Shortly afterwards Hans Holbein the younger came to England and was there employed to design settings for plays at court as well as to paint portraits. By 1534/35 Nicholas Udall, as headmaster of Eton, had edited an anthology of extracts from the plays of Terence, which he published under the title of *Floures for Latine spekynge*; and only a year later Aristophanes' *Pax* was presented at St John's College, Cambridge, in Greek.

(b) **Consequences of the Reformation:** *(i) Languages, Loyalties and Polemical Plays:* From this point forward,

Here is cõteyned a godely interlude of Fulgens
Cenatoure of Rome. Lucres his doughter. Gayus
flaminius. & Publi9. Cozneli9. of the difputacyon of
noblenes. & is deuyded in two ptyes/to be played at
ii.tymes. Cõppled by mayfter Henry medwall. late
chapelayne to þ ryght reuerent fader in god Johan
Mozton cardynall & Archebyffhop of Cauterbury.

PD

93. The title-page of the first printed edition of Henry Medwall's Fulgens and Lucres, *written and performed in 1497 (published c.1515). Compare Figs. 108 and 110. San Marino, California, Henry E. Huntington Library and Art Gallery.*

playwriting and performance in England might have been expected to follow the patterns already firmly established in Renaissance Italy, but they did not. This was due to the descent of a sharp frost upon the study of the humanities in England; we call it the Reformation. This followed directly from the fact that Latin was the traditional language of the Roman Catholic Church and Rome, its rock. Before Henry VIII's divorce action against Katherine of Aragon and the severance of ties with the papacy in 1531, many more plays had been written and performed in English than in Latin, most of them short moral interludes like *Mankind* (1497), Skelton's *Magnifycence* (c.1515) and the anonymous *Godly Queen Hester* (1526) as well as the traditional mystery cycles and saint plays: so plays by Roman authors, whether in Latin or in translation, were still something of a novelty and far from firmly established.

The steps taken by Henry VIII after 1531 to amalgamate Church and State in England served to divide men and women in their support for the two ancient languages just as they did in their loyalties to Rome. For Protestant Reformers, Latin was the language of the Pope and thus of Antichrist, idolatory and superstition: Greek, however, as the language in which the gospels had first been written, was the source of truth. Thus under a Protestant monarch—Henry VIII himself (at least during the 1530s), Edward VI and Elizabeth I—to espouse the cause of Latin carried the risk of being accused of heresy, sedition, even treason: under the Catholic regime of Mary I the same applied to championship of Greek. In such circumstances, the active pursuit of the humanities which had characterized the first four decades of Tudor rule was therefore blighted and had to proceed haltingly and piecemeal without attracting too much attention. In the theatre the result was to leave actors and their playmakers with little option but to return to the traditional Gothic patterns of play-construction still popular with public audiences.

(ii) The Origins of Stage-censorship: This reaction against Italian precedent, however, did not debar a playmaker from using the form of the morality play as a vehicle for Protestant propaganda. Indeed, a path had already been prepared before Henry's final break with Rome by authors like John Heywood whose Interludes (written between c.1520 and 1530 and adapted from French farce for choir-boy actors to present to private audiences) exploited the rising tide of anti-clericalism in England (see Fig. 52). The next step, which was to transform this kind of satire into Protestant propaganda, was taken quickly by an ex-Carmelite monk, educated at Cambridge, John Bale (1495–1593). Aided and abetted by Archbishop Cranmer and Lord Chancellor Cromwell, Bale and his followers carried this, in such scabrously anti-Catholic plays as *Three Laws* and *King John*, to such extremes that provincial magistrates became alarmed and even the king took fright. By 1543 Parliament had been persuaded to pass an Act banning 'interpretations of Scripture . . . contrary to the doctrine set forth, or to be set forth, by the King's Majesty'. With this Act the State staked its claim to rival the Church as the ultimate arbiter and censor of plays, but that was not the end of the matter. Bale and many other writers had already fled to Frankfurt or to Geneva. In 1546 the City of London entered the dispute claiming, by virtue of its jurisdiction over all land within the City's boundaries, to possess the right to control players and the places and times

ENGLAND

Early Tudors

1485	Accession of Henry VII
1497	Henry Medwall's *Fulgens and Lucres* performed at Lambeth Palace
1509	Accession of Henry VIII
1519	A play by Plautus performed at court
1531	Henry VIII divorces Catherine of Aragón and abjures the authority of the Pope in England
1536	John Bale's *King Johan* performed
1543	Parliament bans 'interpretations of Scripture' on public stages
1547	Accession of Edward VI; Lutheran and Calvinist exiles return to England
1548	Abolition of the Feast of Corpus Christi
1552	Sir David Lindsay's *Ane Satyre of the Three Estaitis* performed at Cupar, Fife, Scotland
1553	Accession of Mary I restores Roman Catholicism
1556	Cranmer, Ridley and Latimer burnt as heretics at Oxford

Elizabethan

1558	Accession of Elizabeth I
1570	Excommunication of Elizabeth I
1574	Earl of Leicester's players licensed to perform in London on weekdays
1576	James Burbage builds The Theatre; Richard Farrant opens The Blackfriars
1587	Execution of Mary, Queen of Scots
1558	Defeat of the Spanish Armada
1598	Building of the first Globe Playhouse

Jacobean and Caroline

1603	James VI of Scotland accedes as James I of England
1604	Peace Treaty with Spain Ben Jonson and Inigo Jones present *The Masque of Blackness* at court
1616	Shakespeare dies; Ben Jonson publishes his *Works*
1623	Publication of Shakespeare's First Folio
1625	Accession of Charles I and Henrietta Maria
1640	D'Avenant and Inigo Jones present *Salmacida Spolia*, last court masque
1642	Charles I leaves London for Oxford; Parliament closes the theatres
1648	Execution of Charles I

of their performances before public audiences within the City. This battle between Church, Court, Parliament and City, once joined, raged for the rest of the century with the court appearing to emerge as the ultimate victor on the accession of James I in 1603, but having to surrender control to Parliament forty years later on the outbreak of Civil War.

Any critical approach, therefore, to the growth of Italian Renaissance influence on Tudor drama must, at least from the accession of Edward VI in 1547, be viewed in the context of what by then had become an essentially religious and political battle for control of the theatre. It was this battle which, when all is said and done, served to determine the uniquely English qualities of all Elizabethan and Jacobean plays and playhouses.

(iii) Calvinism and English Drama: On Edward's accession, Bale and his fellow exiles returned to England. Some of them, while abroad, had become disciples of John Calvin whose *Institutes of the Christian Religion* was first published in Basle in 1536. Among Calvin's closest friends was the leader of the Huguenot community in Strasbourg,

Martin Bucer. As hostility to his community mounted from the Roman Catholic government in Paris, Cranmer offered him refuge in England and, in 1549, secured his appointment as Regius Professor of Divinity at Cambridge. Bucer, like Calvin, approved of plays and the theatre provided that both advanced the cause of true religion by encouraging Christian zeal. Although very well read in Greek and Roman dramatic literature, he regarded stylistic refinement as a matter of secondary importance, more especially if buffoonery or obscenity was advocated or excused under that cover. These views he presented to the young king as a Christmas gift in 1551 in a chapter of his book *De Regno Christi* entitled 'De Honestis Ludis'. To these views he appended strongly worded advice on the establishment of official censorship as the one sure means of enforcing them. Edward took this advice. His Roman Catholic half-sister, Mary I, endorsed it on her accession in 1553, thereby turning the tables smartly on the Protestant Reformers who once again had to choose between facing the risks of prosecution or exile. With the return of a Protestant government in 1558 on Elizabeth I's accession, censorship of all plays, whether intended for performance or printing, had come to stay: and so, on the return of the Protestant exiles from Calvin's Geneva, had a predominantly Calvinist view of life within the Anglican settlement.

2 ACTORS AND ACTING

(a) **Amateurs and Professionals:** (i) *The Decline of the Religious Stage:* The first major casualty of this religious and political battle for control of the theatre following the Reformation in England was the long tradition of amateur acting. This had evolved over 500 years from a mixture of clerical and secular dramatic experiments tested against the response of a genuine cross-section of society in towns and villages throughout the country—a truly national theatre. Narrative, argument, physical combat, word-games, allegory and dialogue, together with a readily comprehensible code of visual iconography, had all been successfully conflated into the creation of the Tudor stage play—an artifact that was 'made' rather than 'written' and was attributed to a 'playmaker' or 'maker of interludes' rather than to an author or dramatist.

Neither 'dramatist' nor 'drama', as words, existed in English vocabulary at this time, 'drama' being introduced by Ben Jonson and 'dramatist' by John Dryden in the course of the seventeenth century. A 'maker' of medieval plays was invariably a priest; but by the sixteenth century he could often be a schoolmaster, a tendency extended during the reign of Elizabeth I to university graduates, or 'wits', who aspired to be recognized as poets.

Where the amateur actor and maker of plays lost ground to the professionals in Tudor England was in the supply of religious drama once censorship had passed out of local hands into those of central government. With the abolition of the Feast of Corpus Christi in 1548, and the drastic curtailment by Henry VIII of those saints' days which continued to be accepted as public holidays (despite the brief reversal of Mary's reign), the *raison d'être* of all locally organized and locally sponsored theatrical events associated with these religious celebrations virtually disappeared. Prompt-books of Roman Catholic origin and orientation were confiscated and burned; wardrobes were sold and scenic gear turned to other uses or left to decay. The vacuum created by the sudden disappearance of these time-honoured dramatic festivities could only be filled by professional actors with an alternative repertoire of plays which were simple enough to take on tour.

(ii) *The Rise of the Common Player:* The professional companies of actors that had slowly been establishing themselves in Tudor England were not slow to seize this opportunity to make money and, in many cases, were positively encouraged to do so by their aristocratic patrons, who wanted either to be rid of some of the cost of their maintenance, or to gain favour at court—or both. The latter half of the sixteenth century is thus marked by the rapid rise in the economic and social status of the professional or 'common' player and in the growing control exercised by the most successful acting companies over the nature and quality of the plays which they commissioned for inclusion in their repertoire: they retained the exclusive copyright in the performance and in the play for so long as they could prevent the text from being printed. Thus, as the government at Westminster acquired increasing control over their activities, the acting companies responded by acquiring the financial means to fight back by regulating their own affairs.

The first major recognition of this comes with the issue by Elizabeth I of letters patent (a licence or contract) in 1574 to the Earl of Leicester's company—i.e. the twelve household servants whom he maintained as actors and who wore his livery and travelled away from home on his authority—which allowed them to perform regularly on weekdays in London. Two years later, their leader James Burbage, with the financial help of a wealthy grocer, John Brayne, took the unprecedented step of leasing part of a dissolved priory in Shoreditch (in London's north-eastern suburbs) and erecting a public playhouse, the Theater, within its walls. Remarkably, a schoolmaster, Richard Farrant, made a simultaneous decision to do the same thing within the former refectory of the Blackfriars Priory near St Paul's Cathedral: here he presented plays performed by his boys to invited but paying audiences. Both opened their doors to the public in 1576. Within little more than a decade of these momentous events for the future of the theatre in England, Christopher Marlowe was ready to dazzle London audiences in the public playhouses with *Tamburlaine* and *Dr Faustus*, and Thomas Kyd was set to startle them with *The Spanish Tragedy*, while at court John Lyly was delighting the queen and her friends with *Alexander and Campaspe*, *Endimion*, and other plays performed by the Children of the Chapel.

These developments in London bring sharply into focus the differences in the theatrical tastes and preferences between Italians of the Counter-Reformation at the time of the opening of Palladio's Teatro Olimpico in Vicenza in 1585 and Englishmen of the Protestant North. Behind these differences lay a factor of a more sinister character— the association of Catholics with treachery and cruelty, as Marlowe revealed in his *Massacre at Paris* (1593). Beginning with the burning of Protestant heretics at Smithfield

94. '*The manner of burning Anne Askew, John Lacels, John Adams, & Nicolas Beleman, with certane of ye counsell sitting in Smithfield.*' *These Protestant heretics were executed in London by the order of the government of Mary I. Engraving in Foxe's Book of Martyrs (1648 edn.).*

in London and elsewhere (notably at Oxford) in the 1550s which created a roll of English martyrs (Fig. 94), this reputation was sharply aggravated by the activities of the Spanish Inquisition in the 1560s and the attendant *autos-da-fé*, and by the massacre of the French Huguenots in Paris on St Bartholomew's Eve, 1572. In England these fears were exacerbated first by the Catholic rebellion in the north in 1569 and then by the excommunication of Elizabeth I in 1570, a sequence of events which reached their climax with the formation of the Catholic League in 1585, dedicated to an invasion of England, the overthrow of Elizabeth and the enthronement of her Catholic cousin, Mary Queen of Scots, in her place to recover England for Rome.

(b) **Actors and Stage-censorship:** The government in London responded sharply by suppressing all the surviving religious plays which still continued to be performed. Chester lost its cycle of mystery plays in 1574, York and Wakefield theirs in 1576; Coventry held on until 1581, but finally heeded the Privy Council's injunctions and ceased to stage its cycle. Professional actors for their part could only regard these measures as a warning to reform their own repertoires if they wished to be left free to earn a living from acting; and their predicament in this respect was only made the more urgent by the threat posed to their profession by the more extreme Protestant sects who came in droves to England as refugees from Catholic persecution in the Low Countries, France and Germany. In other words, if these actors were to rely on their aristocratic patrons to protect them, they must first ensure that they had heeded government warnings and put their own houses in order. Thus with the staging of Marlowe's *Dr Faustus* (1589) we reach the last overtly religious play to be publicly performed in Shakespeare's England—a play as remarkable for the Calvinist basis of its theology as for its mockery of the Pope in Rome. Indeed, had this not been the case, it is hard to understand how it could have acquired a licence both for performance and printing from the Master of the Revels. This office had been established within the royal household by Henry VIII and had been re-organized in 1572 to administer the censorship of the stage on behalf of the Lord Chamberlain.

All might yet have been well for the players had they not rashly allowed themselves to become involved in a pamphlet war known as the Martin Marprelate controversy which so angered or alarmed the government (possibly both) that it decided to take firmer action to control plays, players and playhouses. To this end, in 1589, it set up a Licensing Commission on which the Privy Council, the Church and the City of London enjoyed equal representation. It was in this nervous and changed climate that the young William Shakespeare and Ben Jonson both had to feel their way as newcomers to the theatrical profession.

The Church and the City then attempted to bribe the Master of the Revels with an annuity to resign from the Commission. On his declining to accept it, they both lost interest and ceased to play an active role: by so doing they left him, as the court's representative, with virtually unfettered powers of control. The force of these powers was demonstrated clearly in 1597 following the unlicensed performance of a play called *The Isle of Dogs* by Ben Jonson and Thomas Nashe presented at the recently opened Swan Playhouse by the Earl of Pembroke's Men. An order was promptly issued for the arrest of the authors and the actors. Nashe escaped to Yarmouth, but Jonson was imprisoned together with the actors. The Swan was never officially relicensed for performances and Pembroke's Men never performed together again. A year later Parliament intervened by amending a statute first introduced by Henry VIII in 1533—'An Act for the Punishment of Rogues Vagabonds and Sturdy Beggars'—with a view to restricting acting in London to performances by three companies each of which served a member of the Privy Council: these were the Lord Chamberlain's (headed by the Burbage family and including Shakespeare), the Lord High Admiral's (owned by Philip Henslowe and the actor Edward Alleyn), and a single company incorporating actors formerly serving the Earls of Derby, Oxford and Worcester. From the court's point of view this legislation went a long way towards meeting the Church's and the City's objections to plays and players by sharply curtailing the number of companies previously exercising a right to perform in London, while ensuring that its own privilege to maintain companies of players for recreational purposes was not surrendered. As a further defence, each of the three licensed companies was allocated its own playhouse–Chamberlain's at the Globe; Admiral's at the Rose; Worcester's at the Boar's Head—and ordered to perform nowhere else in London except at court. Paradoxically, at this very time two companies of boy-actors resumed the practice of playing to private audiences, which had fallen into abeyance since 1584, to offer yet another challenge to the much-buffeted adult companies—the 'little eyases' complained of by Shakespeare in *Hamlet* (II. ii. 325–35). The nature of this challenge must be deferred for later discussion (pp. 127–8).

Throughout Elizabeth's reign London had increasingly become the major magnet of attraction for all ambitious acting companies, not only because of the potential size of the audiences it could offer, but because of the lure of the court. Nevertheless professional actors could not afford totally to ignore the provinces since the London season only ran from the autumn (October) to the early summer (May), and even these eight months were always liable to be interrupted or cancelled by particularly virulent outbreaks of plague. At such times it became habitual, as an elementary health precaution, for the City Council or the Privy Council (usually both in concert) to ban public attendance at plays. It was then that actors needed to use their patron's letters of authority and livery and the prompt-book licence from the Revel's Office to persuade mayors of shire towns to let them use the guildhall, some livery hall, or an inn (hotel) depending on the size of the local population and its interest.

Until Elizabeth's I's death in 1603 these arrangements worked well. The visitors were popular with audiences now denied the former festive plays of their own devising; the plays they brought were seldom contentious in either a political or a religious sense (having already been licensed in London), and such brawls as did take place were normally attributable to drink and quickly resolved. Yet records show that the actors and their audiences contrived to leave an increasing amount of damage to woodwork, broken windows and other repairs for which the local councils or landlords were left to pay the bills, together with a rising number of complaints from the Justices of the Peace about access to these halls while the actors were in occupation. The actors earned a standard fee from their statutory performance before the mayor (normally 6s. 8d.), and charged an admission fee ranging from 1d. to 6d. from all spectators attending subsequent performances; so, if no fortunes were earned on these tours, at least families at home were kept safely housed and fed through difficult months, and sometimes whole years.

Elizabeth I's successor, James I, was confronted on his arrival in London with growing acrimony between White-hall, Guildhall and the Church about actors and acting. He was either advised or decided himself to settle these disputes by taking the three existing licensed companies into his own service and into that of the queen and the heir apparent, Prince Henry. The Derby-Oxford-Worcester Company became the Queen's Men and were licensed to play at the Curtain, the oldest surviving playhouse, and nowhere else. The Henslowe-Alleyn Company, which had abandoned the Rose on the south bank for the newly built, rectangular Fortune Playhouse near Clerkenwell in 1600, was handed to James's eldest son, Prince Henry. The Shakespeare-Burbage Company remained at the Globe and entered the king's own service with the rank of Gentlemen Ushers; they also became known as the King's Men. The two companies of boy-actors were also taken into royal service, those at the Blackfriars being renamed Children of the King's Revels and those at Whitefriars as Children of the Queen's Revels. In short, the City and the Church were asked to settle for these five companies, all licensed under the royal prerogative and confined to their own specified playhouses; in return, they were assured that all other surviving companies were to be banned access to the metropolis.

For the first few years of the new reign a settlement at last seemed to have been reached; but complaints were still voiced, especially by the more extreme Protestant divines, and these were supported by many merchants angered by the absenteeism among their apprentices which they attributed to attending plays on weekday afternoons. Others, recognizing how much money was being made by owners of playhouses, attempted to get round the licensing regulations in the hope of building new theatres. Most of these schemes proved abortive, but the king himself agreed to license two more companies (for Prince Charles and the Princess Elizabeth), and yet another for his cousin, the Duke of Lennox: all three needed London playhouses.

Other companies acquired recognition as provincial branches of the royal companies. York and Bristol, at least for short periods, maintained civic companies of their own. Other companies bravely toured abroad in Protestant countries and found audiences as far north as Sweden and as far east as Poland. For all that, James's original settlement broadly held, and it succeeded in giving posterity not only most of Shakespeare's finest tragedies and the Romances, but also Ben Jonson's best comedies and the whole canon of dramatic masterpieces written during the reigns of James I and Charles I. In the provinces the status quo was successfully maintained until shortly before James's death in 1625: yet an indication of the troubles ahead had already been provided in Norwich in 1623, when the Mayor, in offering the King's Men their normal fee, did so with the crucial difference that, instead of giving it as a reward for a performance, awarded it in exchange for their agreement *not to play*. The actors challenged this decision by performing at an inn without licence and were promptly imprisoned for their pains. Vowing that the king would ensure that the mayor and his brethren would regret this insult, they left the city; but the king took no disciplinary action. Other mayors began to do likewise, usually on the grounds that, as the actors had recently been in contact with the plague in London, they would be likely to spread it in the town if allowed to perform.

The royal cause was not helped in this dispute by the queen's (Anne of Denmark) addiction to participating as a performer in court masques: the costumes, moreover, which were designed for her and her ladies by Inigo Jones—cut low in the bodice and short in the skirt—only added to the reputation for frivolity and extravagance which these performances engendered outside court circles (see Plate 11). This was compounded with positive outrage among the more puritanically minded subjects when her successor, Queen Henrietta Maria, the wife of Charles I, imported a company of French actors *and actresses* whom she authorized to perform publicly in London in 1635 at M. Le Fevre's Riding Academy in Drury Lane.

As Charles I's government became more unpopular, and as Puritan hostility to the stage gained ground, so the actors had gradually to acclimatize themselves to acknowledging, however wounding the admission was to their own self-respect, that they were no longer wanted by many provincial communities who had formerly greeted them enthusiastically and had accorded them their affection and respect. A blight had started to attack the roots of dramatic art on English soil from which it would never wholly recover. Sooner rather than later, the message would get back to London that 'those who want no play also want

95. *Edward Alleyn, leading actor of the Lord Admiral's (later Prince Henry's) Company and founder of the College of God's Gift at Dulwich. The portrait more nearly represents a prosperous Elizabethan City Father of Puritan leanings than the popular image of an actor. London, Dulwich Picture Gallery.*

no king'. When Civil War broke out only one actor, Elliard Swanston, is known to have joined the Parliament army and to have taken up arms against the king.

(c) **Company Organization and Finance:** Whether based in the provinces or in London, most English acting companies under James I and Charles I remained tightly knit family concerns still organized along the lines of medieval guilds, with a master at the head of them—Edward Alleyn, Richard Burbage and Christopher Beeston are the oustanding examples—who took most of the critical business decisions relating to finance, choice of repertoire, apprentices and wardrobe and to relationships with the Revels Office (Fig. 95). Under him were the journeymen, most of whom had invested capital in the company and shared the profits

on a pro rata basis; they also played the major supporting roles. These in turn were supported by the boy-apprentices, who played the female roles. When need arose, supernumerary actors known as 'hirelings' could be added to the pay-roll on a temporary basis. This sharing system, while ideal for the original group, became steadily more cumbersome and awkward to administer as actors died (or joined another company) and either passed on their shares to widows and other relatives, or split them with friends, none of whom necessarily had any active interest in the original company, but all of whom could sue the company at law if they felt they had been cheated. Indeed, much of the detailed evidence describing the playhouses and playhouse-practice of this period descends to us directly from such lawsuits.

Acting as a profession came of age in the Tudor and early Stuart eras. Notwithstanding the frequent alarms and setbacks occasioned by religious and political censorship, by outbreaks of plague that caused playhouses to be closed and by the hazards of having to undertake regular provincial tours, companies expanded, and the profession became more secure and more lucrative for those actors with talent and personality enough to claim the attention and retain the respect of a paying public. Where Henry VII had employed a company of four actors (led by John English) Henry VIII had increased his to six and then to eight. Elizabeth added four more and James I another four making a total of sixteen. In the early days, sharing offered many advantages. Above all it kept profits 'in the family', thus enabling the most successful Elizabethan companies to acquire capital and invest it either in their own playhouses and equipment, or in leasing both from other owners. William Shakespeare was uniquely fortunate among dramatists of the period in being an actor-sharer in the company for whom he wrote his plays. As a result he died a rich man (see pp. 132–3).

Philip Henslowe and his son-in-law Edward Alleyn represent an alternative style of management which resembles more closely the modern business entrepreneur driven by the profit motive to add speculative investment in theatrical affairs to his other concerns. In such companies most of the actors were glorified hirelings, well paid but lacking any democratic voice in the company's affairs or any control over their own career prospects. The major disadvantage of this system was that of instability unless the investment stretched to ownership of a playhouse: and even that could prove an expensive mistake, as Francis Langley discovered to his cost when the Swan was closed within two years of its completion, or as Alleyn learned when the Fortune burned to the ground in 1621, destroying his entire stock of playbooks, wardrobe and scenic properties. Alleyn was fortunate in that at least he had his income as Master of the King's Bears to fall back on, as well as the capital with which between 1614 and 1616 he had endowed the College of God's Gift at Dulwich (which was also his home and where his portrait now hangs); but this itself is indicative of just how lucrative a profession acting had become within Shakespeare's lifetime, at least for its most successful practitioners.

(d) Acting Style: Performance and Rehearsal: There can be little doubt that the style of acting expected by audiences also changed during this period; but as no dramatic criticism of the kind we take for granted existed, it is impossible to do more than guess what that style was like. Shakespeare makes Hamlet, that prince of amateur actors, insist on a 'natural' delivery of lines (III. ii. 1–38), and it must be assumed that sophisticated opinion—at least at court and in academic circles—encouraged this. Yet the conspicuous absence of *descriptions* of actors' performances in particular roles suggests just as strongly that popular audiences at least were content with the broad, rhetorical style inherited from the medieval theatre—a style designed for an open-air environment, or echoing halls, where the intelligibility of the text was all important, and where a code of specific, instantly recognizable postures and gestures was used to express the emotion informing the spoken words.

Thus audiences are said to go to 'hear' a play rather than to 'see' it: and granted a company's need to carry up to forty plays or more in its repertoire each year, it is evident that in rehearsal actors could not hope to accomplish much in the time available beyond memorizing their lines, their cues, their entrances and exits. All of these requirements were vital to the maintenance of discipline in a rowdy auditorium with more spectators standing than sitting. Thereafter, conventions, for long accepted by actors and audiences alike, must necessarily have governed an actor's actual performance. In such circumstances, excesses of bombast or buffoonery would be more likely to be remarked upon and admonished as 'unnatural' than any subtle refinement of delivery or gesture, since the latter was unlikely to be noticed, let alone to be distinguishable for what it was. What is certain is that some actors came to be preferred to others. Audiences were thus learning to become critics, while playmakers of the Jacobean era, like Webster, Middleton, Fletcher and Ford, could increasingly rely upon the actors' virtuosity to sustain an illusion of credibility when devising their more sensational theatrical effects.

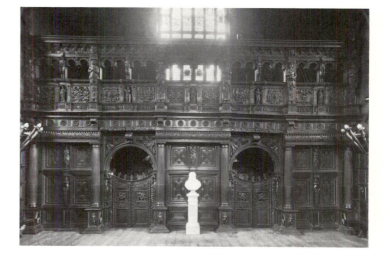

96. *The screen and musicians' gallery of Middle Temple Hall, London. There is a strong tradition that Shakespeare's* Twelfth Night *was first performed before the law students and their tutors in this hall on Twelfth Night, 1601. (Compare Figs. 101a, b and 102.)*

3 PLAYHOUSES

(a) Architectural Features and their Functions: When the Theater and the first Blackfriars Playhouse opened their doors to the public in 1576 the appearance of the stage and surrounding galleries which greeted audiences on entry cannot have been wholly unfamiliar. Most spectators had seen a raised stage backed by a screen with two doors in it, and a gallery above it, in banquet halls and guildhalls for some thirty years or more (Fig. 96). They were also likely to have seen a raised stage backed by a booth or tent at fairgrounds or on village greens for considerably longer. What may have caused more surprise was the shape and size of the auditorium, but even this is to be doubted. Plays had been performed in banquet halls by day and by night for at least 150 years, as well as in market squares and abbey courtyards. They had been presented in churches and churchyards for much longer. Some plays, like *The Castle of Perseverance* and the Cornish *Life of St Meriaseck*, had been staged in circular arenas (see Figs. 73, 74 and 77); others had been staged in the yards and dining halls of inns (Plate 9; pp. 77–8). Two timber-framed arenas existed on Bankside itself for the baiting of bulls and bears, by 1560 if not earlier (Fig. 97). Lists for tournaments were strictly regulated but could be rectangular or circular depending on the nature of the combat: this had been the case since

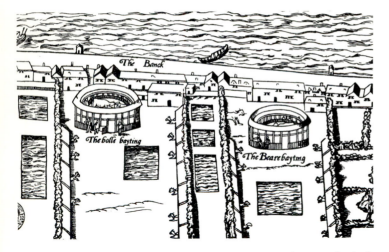

97. *Detail from Agas's map of the Bankside showing the bull-and bear-baiting arenas adjacent to the brothels (known as stews), c.1560. London, British Museum.*

Chaucer's lifetime. There was thus not only precedent but ample variety for any professional builder to discuss with clients who, like James Burbage and Richard Farrant, wished to convert a large, open space whether out of doors or indoors into a game-house or playhouse for 'feats of activity' (martial arts) or stage plays. And it is well-nigh certain that some knowledge existed, at least in academic and diplomatic circles, of Vitruvius' *De Architectura* and the Italian works of commentary based on them: Martin's French translation had been available in print since 1547 and Rivius's German one since 1548 (see Fig. 105 and pp. 102–6). By then some companies were also hiring the courtyards of inns (hotels), which in their appearance resembled the Spanish *corrales* (see pp. 141–2).

What no one knows is whether the Theater, or its immediate neighbour in London's northern suburb of Shoreditch, the Curtain, were octagonal, polygonal or circular—the best guess is polygonal. We do know that 'the frame' (the auditorium) of the former was capable of being dismantled, transported across the Thames and used again in building the first Globe, which Chorus in *Henry V* describes as 'this Wooden O' (Fig. 99). Hollar's drawings of both the second Globe (rebuilt in 1613), and the Hope Playhouse (opened in 1614), which alternated stage plays with bear-baiting, depict circular buildings (Fig. 98). A wooden polygon of some eighteen to twenty-four faces plastered over, and roofed with slates or tiles, when viewed from outside would certainly provide an illusion of a circular building: yet other maps, notably Cornelis Visscher's

(*c*.1616) printed abroad, depicts all playhouses unmistakably as polygons. De Witt's famous sketch of the interior of the Swan (built 1595) suggests a circular rather than a polygonal frame (Fig. 102). Yet the Fortune Playhouse which Henslowe and Alleyn exchanged for the Rose in 1600/1 was unquestionably rectangular: the builder's contract provides, however, for the stage to be a copy of that at the Globe. To confuse matters further we know that the Boar's Head Playhouse, which was in use from 1598 to 1605, consisted of a stage in a yard surrounded by galleries—the stage being moved from the centre of the yard to adjoin the western gallery and the galleries being extended to hold more spectators in 1599. When the Queen's Men moved from there to the Red Bull in 1605 it was to a playhouse converted from 'a square court in

98. *An engraving of Wenzel Hollar's drawing of the Bankside, c.1644, establishing the circular external appearance of both the second Globe (built 1613) and the Bear-Baiting (renamed The Hope, opened in 1614). The engraver in Antwerp in 1647 accidentally switched the labels identifying the two play-houses. London, British Library.*

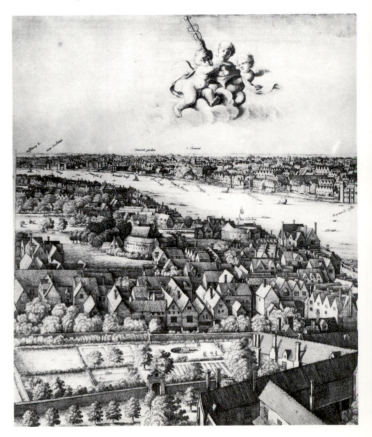

99. John Norden's map of the Bankside in 1600 showing the four playhouses then situated there. Left to right: The Swan, The Beargarden, The Rose (misnamed The Starre), and the first Globe (opened 1598). Stockholm, Royal Library.

an Inn'. We also know that the Cockpit-in-Court at White-hall Palace, which Inigo Jones remodelled for Charles I in 1629/30, was an octagon inside a square, and that Inigo made a drawing of a playhouse with an elliptical auditorium (adapted from his first-hand knowledge of the *Teatro Olimpico* at Vicenza) which may or may not have been built (Figs. 100 and 101a, b): his Banqueting House in Whitehall, which survives for us to inspect today, is rect-angular, but altogether classical in its appearance inside and out.

(b) Pragmatism and Expedience: *(i) Admission and Pro-duction Costs*: The one clear inference that we may draw from all this contradictory evidence is that Elizabethan and Jacobean actors and audiences alike can scarcely be said to have felt any compulsion about a standardized shape or size for a playhouse. In other words pragmatism and expediency were allowed to take precedence over any

100. Inigo Jones's design for the remodelled octagonal Cockpit-in-Court. Unlike the Teatro Olimpico *in Vicenza (Fig. 80) the Cockpit had a trap in the ceiling above the stage with winch machinery above it. Oxford, Worcester College Library.*

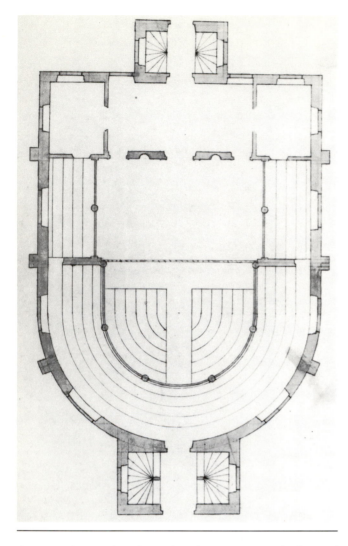

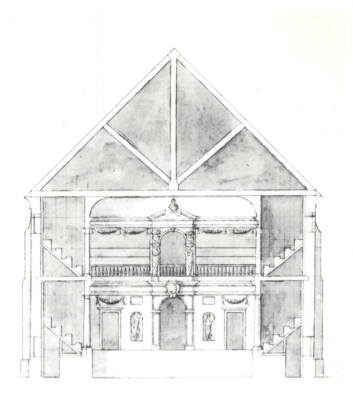

theoretical or archaeological and antiquarian ideology of the kind that inspired Italian experiments in theatre architecture during this same period. If that is true—and only the scantiest fragments of information survive to contradict this view—then we must ask ourselves what factors, if any, controlled this pragmatic and expedient approach to the problem.

The first, from the actors' standpoint, was the need to control admission and thus to ensure payment in advance for the entertainment on offer. Money not only governed the actors' domestic economy, but determined the scope and quality of the productions in their repertoire, the number of which, judged by our standards today, was exceptionally large. The most successful companies expected to rehearse and present at least forty plays a year, some 50 per cent of which were new: the largest items of regular expenditure were wages, costumes and the purchase of

scripts and licences, in that order. Beyond that, to secure the goodwill of the local magistrates, they were expected to contribute up to one tenth of the profits towards the upkeep of the poor and indigent of the parish in which their playhouse was situated. The scale of this largesse played an important role in warding off the frequent demands from hostile citizens for closure and suppression since the only alternative source for equivalent funding was taxation. Some of this local hostility may have been hypocritical; but much of it was clearly inspired by the brothels, called 'stews', (which were also situated outside the City limits in Middlesex and Surrey) whose inmates found it easy to solicit for clients among playgoers.

(ii) The Stage and its Amenities: The next compelling feature for the actors was an acting area and a changing room in the closest possible proximity to the audience. Good

acoustics for all appears to have been accorded precedence over good sight-lines: the latter, together with relative comfort and privacy, was regulated by the price structure of the standing room and seating on offer (Fig. 102). All places were expensive, ranging, in the public playhouses, from one penny for standing room in the yard to sixpence for a stool on the stage and one shilling for a private room. In the private theatres, a multiplication factor of five applied to equivalent seating, a difference due largely to the seating capacity which dropped from the 2,000 places available in public playhouses to three or four hundred in the private ones. It is thus to be doubted whether any of 'the groundlings' in the public playhouses, whom Dekker described as 'rank stinkards', could ever have afforded a place in a private playhouse, even if the repertoire appealed enough for them to wish to pay for entry.

An acting area of some 20 by 20 feet was regarded as the minimum, an objective made the more difficult to realize by virtue of the antics of the rich and leisured gallants who entered through the changing room (the 'tiring house'), chatted up the actors *en route* to the stage, and then set up their stools on either side of the stage, smoking, gossiping and distracting attention from the players towards themselves. By 1595, trapdoors, both on the stage and in the protective 'heavens' above, supported as they were on pillars, had become an essential technical aid to increasing provision for stage spectacle. Among the public playhouses, only at the Hope (which had to alternate bear-baiting with stage plays) was provision made for cantilevering the heavens in order to abolish the need for pillars. Inigo Jones also dispensed with them in his theatres as we know from his drawings (Figs. 100 and 101a, b).

(iii) Music, Dance and Spectacle: The sharpest discrepancy between the priorities of managers of adult and boy companies respectively was that accorded to scenic properties and music. Some provision had to be made for both in public and private playhouses alike. In the latter the close relationship between the type of play written in England by William Hunnis, John Lyly and others for the boys to perform and Italian *commedia erudita* had made both music and spectacle into obligatory requirements from the moment that they opened in 1576: and here the trained singing voices of the boys could be exploited by playwrights as a major attraction. By contrast, the adult companies in the public playhouses, forced as they were to travel widely, had to ensure that production costs were kept as low as possible: accordingly they chose to keep the provision of both music and spectacle to a minimum until early in the 1590s. By then the new wave of university-

102. *Johannes de Witt's sketch of the Swan Playhouse as copied by Arend van Buchel. De Witt visited the Swan in 1596. It was closed by order of the Privy Council in 1597 and never officially allowed to reopen. This is the only depiction of the interior of a playhouse used by actors within Shakespeare's lifetime. Utrecht, Library of the University.*

educated playwrights had started to make radical changes in the style of play-scripts which they submitted to the managers on receiving a commission; and this, when coupled with the evident warmth of audience response, obliged the companies to re-order their priorities.

Musicians were accommodated in a room above the principal dressing room behind the stage (see Figs. 100 and 102). Following James I's appropriation of the major acting companies into the royal household in 1603, the royal consorts of music became available to the managers; and with that development a promise of instrumental music between acts was offered as an additional attraction for the prospective playgoer—especially in the private playhouses. Dances originally choreographed for court masques also found their way into the scripts of stage plays.

Some idea at least of the scenic properties which so tight-fisted a manager as Philip Henslowe felt obliged to provide can be acquired from his inventory, taken at the Rose in 1598—a list that includes trees, arbours, tombs (monuments), a cave and a hell-mouth. The stage directions supplied by playmakers themselves from Greene, Peele and Dekker onwards offer us another source of information. Unfortunately, those scenic properties made for and owned by the Revels Office for performances at court and described in the annual accounts are missing for the reign of Elizabeth I. However, the account books of the major London livery companies offer us a richly detailed alternative source of information—the monies spent on pageants for the annual Lord Mayor's Show on the morning after St Simon and St Jude's Day (29 October) when each new mayor, together with the officers of his company, went ceremonially by river to Whitehall Palace and then, on return, processed through the streets of the city to Guildhall for a banquet. The pageants, both on land and water, were open to competitive tender. Under James I and Charles I Dekker, Heywood, Munday, Middleton and Webster all devised and wrote them. The texts, together with descriptions of the scenic spectacle, were subsequently printed. It is from this source above all others that we learn how the arbours, caves, mountains, orchards, palaces and tombs in use on public and private stages were constructed and what they looked like. In some instances actual drawings survive (Figs. 103 and 104).

In addition to having to provide some scenic properties to identify the location of stage action, managers, actors and playwrights all had to contend with the nuisance of the stools set out on either side of the stage: but with increasing sophistication and a growing awareness of dramatic theory, the nuisance of spectators sitting on the stage was finally grappled with by Charles I who banished them from the stage of the Salisbury Court when it opened in 1630/1. Other changes included the addition of a third door, centre stage. At the Cockpit-in-Court Inigo Jones provided five (see Fig. 100). Notwithstanding the precedent set in court masques, however, changeable scenery was sturdily resisted by the actors, partly because they could not afford it or the legion of technicians needed to handle the machines which operated it, and partly because it was too cumbersome and too costly to take on tour. Broadly

speaking playhouses under Charles I, despite a veneer of neo-classicism apparent in the five-act structure of printed plays, musical intermissions, and an increasing respect for unity of place and time, remained faithful both to the fundamental actor–audience relationships and to the stage conventions habitual in England throughout the late Middle Ages and the Tudor era: the actors saw to that, since they retained the ultimate veto until the theatres were closed in 1642, despite the growing challenge to their authority presented by dramatists who, after 1616, could

103. 'The Garden of Plenty'. One of six engravings of designs by Stephen Harrison for the triumphal arches erected as pageant-stages in the streets of London to welcome James I on his way to his coronation in 1603/4. Texts for the pageants were written by Dekker, Jonson and Middleton. London, British Museum.

104. One of a series of watercolours of pageants for the Lord Mayor's Show, London, 1616: Anthony Munday's Chrysanaleia, the Golden Fishing, *prepared and paid for by the Fishmongers Company. Depicted is a Lemon Tree (a pun on the Lord Mayor's name) surrounded by the Five Senses and guarded by a pelican. London, Society of Antiquaries.*

only as an actor and playmaker, but as a principal sharer in the Burbage family syndicate. No other Elizabethan or Jacobean dramatist enjoyed this privilege. Ben Jonson might have had it extended to him, but chose instead to fight a battle on behalf of all playmakers in his own way. This he conducted on two fronts, by recourse to self-help and noble patronage, a stance directly copied from Roman example. If a playmaker was to be accepted in society as a man of letters (an honour accorded only to poets, philosophers, historians and theologians in Elizabethan England), then he must first avoid the financial temptation to accept collaborative commissions and become his own *exclusive* judge of his script, whether in verse or prose; he must then print it in his own name and acquire the loyalty of a wide reading public—the only sure way to win the approval of the leading academic and aristocratic patrons.

This Jonson set out to do on his release from prison in 1597/8 (two years after Sir Philip Sidney's *Apology for Poetry* was first published) and finally achieved in 1616 (the year that Shakespeare died) with the publication of all his own plays and masques in a single, folio volume entitled *Works* (Fig. 105). James I rewarded him with appointment as poet laureate and a pension of 100 marks a year for life. After his death in 1637 (and a funeral attended by most of the English nobility) he was succeeded in this office by another dramatist, William d'Avenant. It is to Jonson's courage and success in this respect that we owe the publication in 1623 of the First Folio of Shakespeare's plays, more than half of which were printed there for the first time.

(b) English Neo-classicism in the Theatre: This truly revolutionary achievement not only broke the power of the actors, which the young authors of *The Return from Parnassus* had complained of, but ensured that playmakers (dramatists as they would be called after the Restoration of the monarchy) would thenceforward be regarded essentially as writers and that plays would be read (and even studied) as literature. Jonson himself, moreover, came swiftly to eclipse Shakespeare as the writer of plays upon whom any future, self-respecting man of letters should model himself when opting to write for the theatre, and he stayed in the ascendant until the start of the romantic movement at the end of the eighteenth century (see p. 178). Put simply, what Jonson achieved in his lifetime was a crystalization of all the tentative theorizing that had been leavening English thinking about the theatre ever since Sir Thomas More's circle had started discussing it under Henry VIII, and which Sir Philip Sidney and his circle had carried much further following the publication of both Scaliger's and Castelvetro's definitive theoretical works during the latter

claim with reason that it was their plays above all else which would make or break a London company at the box-office.

4 PLAYMAKERS AND DRAMATIC GENRE

Vile world, that lifts them [actors] up to high degree,
And treads us [scholar poets] down in grovelling misery.

(a) Dramatic Poets versus Actors: So wrote two young Cambridge students in *The Return from Parnassus* (1601/2). This difference in both social and financial status of the Elizabethan playmaker and actor largely bypassed Shakespeare since he was fortunate to earn his income not

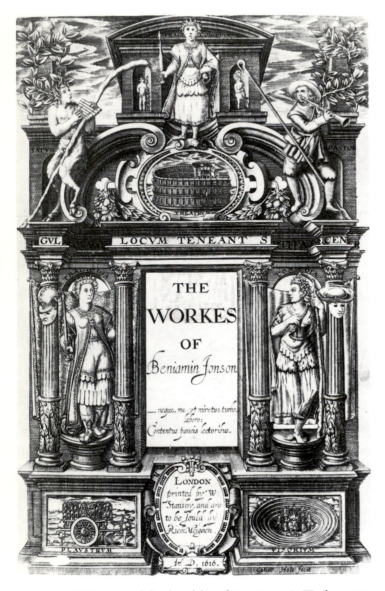

105. *Title-page of the first folio of Ben Jonson's Works, 1616, engraved by Gilbert Hole. Above the standing figures of Tragedy (left) and Comedy (right) is a reconstruction of the Theatre of Marcellus in Rome, flanked by figures representing Pastoral Tragi-comedy. Below is a horse-drawn wagon, carrying actors on tour, and a chorus dancing in an arena.*

even within his dialogue, to spelling out to audiences, whom he took to be ignorant, heedless or both, the precise nature of these 'laws' and 'rules'. *Everyman Out of His Humour*, *Volpone* and *Catiline* offer especially rich examples. Jonson was not therefore a pioneer of these Italianate ideas; but he was the first thoroughgoing, practising propagandist for them in England, and as such failed as frequently as he succeeded in carrying public playhouse audiences with him.

(c) Traditional Dramatic Structure and Reformation Innovations: To appreciate why the battle which Jonson fought on this account was so long delayed in England, it is necessary to recall that virtually all English plays written before the Reformation came into being to celebrate Christian calendar festivals and to teach audiences how to interpret the doctrinal significance of these feasts (see Chapters 5 and 6). A well-nigh indelible pattern of Fall from Grace, Redemption through Repentance and Atonement and return to Grace followed by ultimate Salvation had thus come during the Middle Ages to be imposed upon the structure of all fully scripted plays—in short, a tragicomic form. Of surviving texts only Medwall's *Fulgens and Lucres* and the plays of John Heywood show that wholly secular considerations were uppermost in the minds of their authors. The Reformation served to change this situation in three vital respects while simultaneously serving to reinforce the supremacy of doctrine—'Christian zeal' as Martin Bucer described it—as the principal concern of the playmaker. In each of these respects what confronts us is a change of emphasis rather than a deliberate and radical departure.

First, as already remarked, the spreading influence of censorship and control of the theatre made the Elizabethan triumph of the London-based professional acting companies over their nationwide amateur progenitors and rivals inevitable. Once their hegemony was secured, popular and secular rather than ecclesiastically oriented tastes were likely to dominate the choice of plays commissioned by their managers for performance.

Next, where authors were concerned, acquaintance with Italian *commedia erudita* offered the readiest slip-road out of the danger zone of heretical and seditious dramatic polemic into the quieter area of non-controversial amusement. Revivals of plays by classical authors, and such plays written in imitation of them as *Gammer Gurton's Needle*, *Ralph Roister Doister* and *Gismond of Salerne* (or *Tancred and Gismond*), survive as examples from the middle years of the sixteenth century: and both the comic and tragic examples point a way forward, via Latin plays, to a sharper

half of Elizabeth's reign. This centred on dramatic genre and those 'laws' or 'rules', as Jonson was to call them, which had guided Greek and Roman dramatists in the composition of their plays. It is for this reason that Jonson devoted so much space in his dedications, prologues, and distinction between dramatic genres. Richard Edwards in *Damon and Pithias* (1566) goes so far as to cite Horace as his mentor.

Thirdly, even with Reformation drama of religious polemic, the most radical of doctrinal changes brought with them fresh possibilities for the development of genuinely tragic drama. As early as 1536, John Bale in *King Johan* offered one such possibility in creating as hero and title role a prince who falls, not through error of judgement (tragic flaw) nor through culpability for personal conduct (sin), but through pressures of external circumstances (the machinations of the Pope in collusion with the clergy). John is presented as an innocent, more sinned against than sinning, whose fate—poison administered by a monk—lies in his stars. The play is self-sufficient up to this point, and made explicitly tragic in its outcome by Widow England's long lament over his corpse; but Bale then tacks onto his story a postscript, as it were, designed to illustrate the ultimate triumph of Henry VIII over Pope Clement VII. This he does in order to allegorize English history specifically to equate King John with St John Baptist and Henry (called Imperial Majesty in the cast list and dialogue) with Christ. This coda serves to restore to the play a happy ending, and thus to return it to the realm of tragi-comedy. No less significant as pointers to the future are the anonymous *Jacob and Esau* and Lewis Wager's *The Life and Repentance of Mary Magdalene*, both of which were written during Edward VI's reign and both of which reveal unmistakeable Calvinist influence. The doctrine of predestination is central to both plays. Esau is 'reprobate', Jacob 'elect'; hence Rebecca's conspiracy to rob her first born of his birthright in Jacob's interest. Of this, audiences are baldly forewarned in the Prologue: 'Jacob was chosen and Esau reprobate.' By implication this moral can be extended to all English papists who may be considered to have lost their birthright to rule the country to practising Protestants under a reforming king. Mary Magdalene, too, in Wager's play is 'elect'; despite the depravity of her early life, her subsequent reformation of it into that of a saint is attributed to God's inscrutable Providence. Sooner or later a playmaker would press these new ideas to the point of considering the plight of the reprobate who recognizes that he lacks faith, cannot repent, and must face the prospect of damnation for the rest of his earthly life. This leap forward was made *c.*1580 by Nathaniel Woodes in *The Conflict of Conscience*, a play in which the hero, Philologus, is driven to despair by the knowledge that he recanted, under threat of torture, because he was unwilling to forgo worldly wealth and its attendant pleasures, coupled with the recognition that,

> Christ prayed not, Christ suffered not, my sins to
> recompense
> But only for the Lord's elect, of which sort I am
> none.

It is this same sense of tragic despair that, a decade later, Marlowe's Dr Faustus will face in his final reckoning with Mephistophiles. Significantly, it was during this same decade that Sir Philip Sidney launched his now famous attack on the 'mongrel tragi-comedy' and the pandering to 'laughter' as opposed to the provision of 'delight' offered in London's theatres (*c.*1583). Shakespeare was then nineteen years old and Jonson eleven.

(d) Elizabethan and Jacobean Dramatic Achievements: *(i) Tragedy:* A new dimension was added to tragic possibilities in this same decade by Thomas Kyd who introduced the theme of revenge. Some critics attribute this novelty to acquaintance with Seneca's *Medea*, others to imitation of Spanish precedent, and others again (more remotely) to a reading of the *Oresteia*. Whatever the ultimate source, Kyd's innovation sparked off an immediate response from English audiences which, spurred on by *The Spanish Tragedy* and, possibly, by the first version of *Hamlet*, would remain popular for the next fifty years. Reasons for this are not hard to find. Pursuit of revenge could result in the annihilation of whole families, even of whole dynasties, with wide variations on sensational murders *en route*. Just as important it brought into direct opposition Old and New Testament attitudes to murder, Senecan and Christian philosophies of life, and—not least—a topical note (following the execution of Mary Queen of Scots in 1587) symbolizing the respective stances of Roman Catholic and Protestant subjects towards one another in England under Elizabeth I. Kyd in *The Spanish Tragedy* (*c.*1587) makes his hero, Hieronimo, balance a Latin quotation from the Vulgate, 'Vindicta mihi' (Vengeance is mine saith the Lord) against several from the writings of Seneca which give precedence to a Stoic view of life and the need to preserve the integrity of family honour: he opts for the latter and pays for his decision with his life. Whether or not Kyd wrote the first version of *Hamlet* must remain an open question. Shakespeare certainly re-wrote it.

To this theme of personal revenge Tourneur, Webster, Heywood and Middleton added a recognizably Calvinist element—the doctrine of the total depravity of man. This is articulated at its clearest by Flamineo in *The White Devil* and Bosola in *The Duchess of Malfi*, both of which plays are set in an Italy seen by Jacobeans as the seat of Roman

Catholic cruelty, Machiavellian intrigue, and ultimate corruption seeping from leaders of Church and State downwards to their humblest servants. It permeates Tourneur's
The Revenger's Tragedy, Middleton's *The Changeling* and
Ford's *'Tis Pity She's a Whore*. The horrors and sensations
which all these plays contain, and which appealed from
a theatrical viewpoint to spectators, must not be dismissed
as signs of decadence since, in another sense, they represent
the most stalwart defence of the theatre, from a moral
standpoint, that representatives of Puritan opinion could
muster and could convey to public audiences at least as
large in theatres on weekdays as those assembled in
churches on Sundays.

In this context Beaumont and Fletcher—more particularly Fletcher himself—elected to develop from Kyd's initiative the issue of personal and family honour (the claims
of duty), and in deference to Spanish example (as Corneille
would later do in France) to place it in conflict with those
of love. Production of *The Maid's Tragedy* by the King's
Men in 1610 established this variant as one that would
appeal to aristocratic audiences until the theatres were
closed, and would survive the Civil War to re-emerge in
its most memorable form in Dryden's redaction of *Antony
and Cleopatra* in 1677, renamed *All for Love: or, The
World Well Lost*. Yet within these structural limits, so
opportunely supplied by others, William Shakespeare was
given ample scope to explore in dramatic form his own
objective view of human nature in conflict with the
accepted laws both of God and of his anointed deputy on
earth, the king. Jonson alone attempted to proceed beyond
this towards tragedy written in wholesale imitation of
Graeco-Roman example for performance in public playhouses, with *Sejanus* (1604) and *Catiline* (1609): both met
with so fierce a rebuff as to dissuade him and his 'sons'
from ever repeating this mistake. It was thus left to Milton,
more than half a century later, with *Samson Agonistes*
(1671), to try again (see pp. 163–4).

(ii) History Plays: A curious feature of English Renaissance drama is the uses made of history as source material
for plays. Although public addiction to what we describe
as chronicle plays appears to have been restricted to a relatively brief time-span of some fifteen years between 1585
and 1600, its roots are to be found in medieval saint plays
and its extensions are to be seen in Roman, Scottish and
legendary history as presented to Jacobean audiences in a
line running from Shakespeare's *Julius Caesar* to Ford's
Perkin Warbeck.

A saint play normally recited the life and works of its
title role from youth to martyrdom. Its story line was thus

both extensive and episodic. As the episodes treated
included miracles and particularly savage forms of torture
and death, many were sensationally spectacular and melodramatic (see Fig. 71): the Digby play of *St Mary Magdalene* and the Cornish play of *St Meriasek* offer the best
surviving English examples. The legendary nature of the
source material also made these plays notably romantic in
their style. Saint plays, because of their subject matter,
became the earliest casualties of the Reformation along
with images in sculpture and stained glass; but the form
proved too attractive to abandon and re-emerged with
those secular figures in the title roles who had been made
famous in medieval and Tudor chronicles and romances—
King John, Gorboduc, Palamon and Arcite, Cambyses,
James the Fourth, King Leir. Some of these stories—
especially those replete with tragic incident—came to be
refurbished as historical moralities; others, like those concerning Sir Clyomon and Clamydes or Promos and Cassan-
dra, as tragi-comic romances. Shakespeare at least, taking
the former route, reshaped history in *Richard III* into tragedy, thus paving his own way into the Jacobean era for
the composition of *King Lear*, *Macbeth*, *Coriolanus* and
Antony and Cleopatra.

(iii) Comedy: Despite a similar advance in tragi-comedy,
comedy itself, considered as a self-sufficient dramatic genre,
only succeeded in expanding during Elizabeth's reign upon
neo-classical and farcical precedents already set before her
accession in 1558: Peele's *The Arraignment of Paris*,
Greene's *Friar Bacon and Friar Bungay* and Shakespeare's
The Comedy of Errors supply examples. It was left to
Chapman, Marston and Jonson to do for the comic Muse
what Machiavelli had done with *Mandragola* and to offer
audiences in *A Humorous Day's Mirth*, *Histriomastix* and
Everyman in his Humour respectively a sharply different
and predominantly satirical view of society and its
manners, informed by an underlying, if elementary,
psychological analysis of the characters recruited to provide the initial dramatic situation and its subsequent
development. Each role is provided with its own motivating
and overriding characteristic—the bully, the hypocrite, the
braggart-coward, the ostentatious fool, etc. Once selected,
they are presented by means of sustained exaggeration to
reveal pretension, greed, lust and other vices for what they
are, no matter the vocation or rank of the individual depicted, and to punish them. In general those who are fleeced
of their wealth, cheated of their desires or exposed as
fools—society's 'gulls'—are portrayed more satirically and
brutally than those who gull them: thus Face, the guller
Subtle's prime agent in *The Alchemist*, escapes unpunished

while their victims Sir Epicure Mammon, the Anabaptists Tribulation and Ananias, Dame Pliant and others whom they have gulled all retire badly bruised. Love stories, the foundation stone of romantic comedy, figure scarcely at all in this style; clowning is likewise excluded and characters do not develop: unity of action, place and time, however, are observed with relative care, and battles of wit become matters of major concern. These are the manners of the times, a precept which the principal authors of so-called 'City Comedy' (notably Middleton and Massinger) exploited to the extreme discomfiture of the new-rich, bourgeois, merchant class together with their wives and families. If this earned them friends at court, it lost them far more both in London and in provincial cities who would reap a fierce revenge in the next generation by banning all plays and players from the kingdom.

Shakespeare in *The Merry Wives of Windsor* (1600) revealed that he too could adopt this style if he wished to; but he swiftly demonstrated, by writing *Twelfth Night*, *Much Ado about Nothing* and *As You Like It*, his own preference for romantic comedy complete with clown, a genre which he then proceeded to develop in a highly idio-syncratic and emblematic manner in the sequence of plays running from *Pericles* to *The Tempest* and *Henry VIII* which modern critics describe as the 'Romances'. Here a reversion to the tragi-comic structural pattern of late med-ieval and early Tudor religious drama with a seemingly total disregard for unity of time and place becomes glar-ingly obvious, overlaid as it is with a brilliant display of those striking chiaroscuro effects made fashionable by mannerist painters in Venice, Naples, Madrid and Antwerp, and conjured out of a dazzlingly adroit juxtaposi-tion of legendary narrative, folklore and contemporary political events.

(iv) Tragi-comedy and Court Masques: The vogue for tragi-comedy, which became so marked a feature of English drama after 1607, is attributable in part to the importation from Italy of 'pastoral' as a new dramatic genre supposedly derived from the Greek satyr-play, and in part to the indi-genous development of the traditional disguisings into the court masques devised by Ben Jonson and furnished with changeable scenery by Inigo Jones (Fig. 106). Here gods and goddesses along with naiads, dryads, shepherds and shepherdesses take to the stage alongside mortals in idealized landscapes where danger and death threaten but are not allowed to strike, since reason compels the triumph of order over chaos and since order is the gift of princes (Fig. 107). This is carefully explained by John Fletcher in his 'Preface to the Reader' which he attached to the printed

106. *The wedding masque of Sir Henry Unton. Detail from a nar-rative painting by an unknown artist. The masquers (all ladies) are escorted by children as torch-bearers and introduced by a youth dressed as Mercury as the Presenter. London, National Portrait Gallery.*

edition of *The Faithful Shepherdess* (1609). Those materials for the new genre which were not directly bor-rowed from Italian authors such as Ariosto, Tasso and Guarini had at least been explored in England by the young Spenser in *The Shepherd's Calendar* and by the authors of those entertainments offered to Elizabeth I when on sum-mer progresses to country estates like the Earl of Leicester's home at Kenilworth or Sir Philip Sidney's park at Wan-stead. These start to find their way into the professional theatre with such plays as John Lyly's *Endimion*, Thomas Nashe's *Summer's Last Will and Testament* and Shakespeare's *A Midsummer Night's Dream*; but it is

107. Naumachia, *or water triumph, presented by the Earl of Hertford to Queen Elizabeth I on the Lake at Elvetham, 1591. (Compare Figs. 90, 91 and 133.) London, British Museum.*

within the masque, beginning with Samuel Daniel's *Vision of Twelve Goddesses* and Jonson's *Masque of Blackness* (both presented at court in 1604), where music, song, dance and spectacle could all be fully exploited in the manner of the Italian *intermezzi*, that fusion with dramatic narrative and poetry became possible. Jonson's invention of the anti-masque in response to a suggestion from Queen Anne added the desirable dramatic elements of contrast and reversal; and Prince Henry, by bringing the Elizabethan accession day tilts indoors in a form known as 'Jousts at Barriers' added physical combat and martial arts (see Figs. 128 and 129). With these components included, the genre could only become more spectacular and more costly. The last masque, prepared by William d'Avenant and Inigo Jones, was *Salmacida Spolia* in 1641. In this, the threatening storm clouds of civil rebellion of its anti-masques were dispersed by the appearance on the stage of Charles I and his queen in the roles of Philogenes and Queen of Amazons to tame nature and restore harmony and order to the kingdom in the subsequent masque. Parliament thought differently: within a year the court had fled London for Oxford and masques, like plays and theatres, were doomed.

5 WILLIAM SHAKESPEARE

The single playmaker to prove himself master of *all* the dramatic genres available to what the late Professor F. P. Wilson described as 'Jacobethan' playmakers was William Shakespeare. Our biographical knowledge of his career is as scanty as his own knowledge of humanity and his depiction of it in dramatic art was prodigious.

Born in Stratford-upon-Avon in the heart of the

Warwickshire countryside, yet within easy riding distance of the cathedral town of Coventry, he was educated at the local grammar school. Up to the age of seventeen he could easily have attended the annual performance of Coventry's cycle of mystery plays and thrilled to the sight of King Herod, 'raging in the pageant and in the street also', since the plays were not suppressed until 1581.

While still 'creeping like snail, unwillingly to school', he became acquainted at the hands of such pedantic and provincial schoolmasters as his own Holofernes and Sir Hugh Evans with Latin, and with some at least of the Roman authors—certainly Ovid, Plautus and Seneca; possibly Terence, Cicero, Virgil, and Mantuanus—if not with Greek and the Greeks. Leisure-time pursuits provided him with first-hand knowledge of country sports, wildlife, folklore, and every aspect of the agricultural calendar from winter ploughing to summer sheep-shearing and harvest home in Cotswold villages: they also led him to acquire an intimate knowledge of village wooings and enforced marriage.

Possessed of little beyond this education, some experience in his penurious father's butcher's shop and his own poetic imagination, he left home—possibly apprenticed to James Burbage, the leader of the Earl of Leicester's company of actors based at neighbouring Kenilworth Castle; more probably as a page attendant upon some local young nobleman studying law at the Inns of Court in London. Nothing is known of him during this period. He emerges in the early 1590s as an actor, poet, and playmaker talented enough to attract public notice, and by doing so, to provoke personal attack from his university-educated rival Robert Greene.

Himself a voracious reader of all English writers from Chaucer and Lydgate to his own contemporaries Spenser, Marlowe, Holinshed and North, Shakespeare swiftly earned—both as an actor and as a provider of plays—the privilege of becoming a shareholder in the Lord Chamberlain's company of actors (led by then by James Burbage's sons, Richard and Cuthbert) and, with it, frequent performances at court. By 1600 he was himself a family man, a part-owner of both the Globe and the Blackfriars playhouses and moving freely in the dangerous social and political company of the Earls of Southampton and Essex; he also enjoyed the no less stimulating, if abrasive company of the young Ben Jonson in whose 'humorous' comedy, *Everyman in his Humour*, he had recently acted an important role. He was then on the point of writing *Hamlet*.

The zenith of this remarkable career was reached when, in 1603, he was admitted to membership of the royal household as one of King James I's own company of actors and its leading playwright with the rank of Gentleman Usher. That thereafter, having written all his plays for actors whose characters and capabilities were as well known to him as those of his own family, he should have directed rehearsals of them prior to their first performance can hardly be doubted. By 1613, when the first Globe was destroyed by fire during a performance of his own *King Henry VIII*, he was ready to quit public life and retire to New Place, the great house and garden which his earnings in the theatre had enabled him to buy in his native Stratford-upon-Avon. Small wonder then, as master of all the dramatic genres from comedy to historical morality and from tragical history to tragedy and tragi-comedy, he should be described by Ben Jonson in the memorial poem which prefaces the first folio of all his plays, lovingly assembled and edited from the prompt-copies by his fellow actors in 1623, as 'not of an age, but for all time'. It would take another 150 years, however, for this prophecy to receive the endorsement of the whole world (see pp. 167–72, and 177–9 and 197).

9
Spain

1 GEOGRAPHICAL AND POLITICAL UNIFICATION

It is generally supposed that Spain and Portugal have always been isolated from the rest of Europe by the great physical barrier of the Pyrenees: yet even in the Middle Ages this was not so. The mountains had been outflanked to the west by countless pilgrims from Eastern and Northern Europe *en route* to Santiago de Compostela in Galicia in north-western Spain. An equally well-trodden route existed round the Mediterranean coast between France and Catalonia which, like Valencia, was a province within the Kingdom of Aragón. By the start of the sixteenth century Spain had become more deeply involved in European politics since not only Sicily and Sardinia, but the Kingdom of Naples, had all passed into the possession of the Crown of Aragón, while Castilian eyes, following the recovery of the Kingdom of Granada from the Moors in 1492, were starting to focus on the glittering prospects of a colonial empire in the New World. Since 1479 the two Kingdoms of Aragón and Castile had been loosely linked together (as England and Scotland were to be following the accession of James I in 1603) as a result of the marriage of the respective heirs to both, Ferdinand and Isabella. Portugal alone remained independent—except between 1580 and 1640 when both Portugal and her overseas possessions belonged to the Spanish Crown.

By the end of the fifteenth century, therefore, Spain was poised, despite the heterogeneous character of its political and its social institutions, to play a major role in determining the future of Europe. The break-through came in 1516 when on Ferdinand's death the crown of Spain (which by then included Navarre) was offered to his grandson Charles of Ghent, who in 1519 succeeded in getting himself elected as Holy Roman Emperor on the death of his paternal grandfather Maximilian I. As a Hapsburg and unable at

first to speak Spanish, and as ruler of Spain, Flanders and several German States, Charles V precipitated Spain into the centre of world politics in a hitherto unprecedented manner. No individual had wielded so much power since Charlemagne; and Charlemagne could never have imagined the wealth from the New World that Charles was heir to, backed as it was by the best army in the world and the largest navy. With power and wealth he inherited enemies; the Moors to the south, and the Turks at sea; the Lutherans to the north and in Switzerland; and between them France, resentful, jealous and suspicious.

2 CENTRALIZATION

Surprisingly in these circumstances, Spanish drama held a more consistent course of development from its traditional sources throughout the sixteenth century than any other country in the whole of Europe. Its uniqueness in this respect may fairly be attributed to Spain's undeviating loyalty to Roman Catholicism. This allegiance was reinforced by increasing centralization of government (with Madrid emerging as the capital city of the whole country), to which all external influences, whether of Flemish, German, English, French, Italian or Moorish origin, were made subservient and then absorbed. Ultimately this served to root Spanish drama so firmly in its own soil as to make it exceptionally difficult to transplant elsewhere.

3 THE MEDIEVAL HERITAGE: LITURGICAL DRAMA

(a) **Winter Festivals:** The theatre that had evolved in Spain and Portugal during the late Middle Ages had grown up along lines familiar elsewhere in Europe (see Chapter 6) but with significant differences. The music drama of the Easter and Christmas liturgies had not only survived, but

SPAIN

1479	Ferdinand, King of Aragón, marries Isabella, Queen of Castile
1492	Christopher Columbus discovers the New World
1496	Joanna, third daughter of Ferdinand and Isabella, marries Philip of Flanders, son of the Emperor Maximilian I and Mary of Burgundy
1501	Catherine, eldest daughter of Ferdinand and Isabella, marries Prince Arthur of England; 1507, marries Henry VIII
1504	Ferdinand of Aragón acquires the Kingdom of Naples
1506	Charles, son of Philip and Joanna, becomes Charles V of Spain
1519	Charles elected Emperor
1529	Charles marries Isabella of Portugal
1556	Their son Philip, consort of Mary I of England, becomes Philip II of Spain
1579	Public playhouses established in Madrid
1580	Philip annexes Portugal, Brazil and possessions in Africa and East Indies
1588	Defeat of Spanish Armada
1598	Philip II succeeded by his son, Philip III
1621	Philip III succeeded by his son, Philip IV
1626	Cosme Lotti moves from Florence to Madrid
1635	Death of Lope de Vega
1640	Catalonia revolts and seeks French protection
1640–68	Spain at war with Portugal
1681	Death of Calderón

had attracted aristocratic patrons who encouraged writers to elaborate upon these models in secular environments as well as in ecclesiastical ones. Late in the fifteenth century such plays were being provided in Spain by Juan del Encina (*c.*1468–*c.*1537), Lucas Fernández and Fray Iñigo de Mendoza, and in Portugal by Gil Vicente (1465–*c.*1539), all of them written in the vernacular, usually for performance in private chapels before an invited audience. While still closely related to liturgical practice, these plays are notable for a substantial extension of dialogue and, with it, an increasingly allegorical treatment of the subject matter. This is often allied to lyrical material—especially in the context of the shepherds at Bethlehem–normally associated with the eclogues and pastoral poems of classical literature. Paradoxically this tendency did not exclude the addition of songs, dances and even comic incident. These specifically Iberian developments may explain the erratic application of the words *farsa*, *auto* (literally, a dramatic action, i.e. a play in one act), *égloga*, *representación* and *diálogo* by authors to describe their plays throughout the sixteenth century (Fig. 108). In this respect, at least, time

108. Title-page of a printed copy of an auto sacramental *representing* The Fall of Man, *with woodcuts illustrating the characters and their costumes. Early sixteenth century. Barcelona, Col Sedo.*

Parte primera en la qual se representa la primera edad del mundo que fue desde Adam hasta Noe, contiene cinco autos.

¶ Auto primero, en el qual se representa como Adam comio por la persuasion de Eua del fruto vedado, por cuya culpa fue lançado del parayso terrestre. Y los interlocutores son estos.

**Eua.   Adam.   Dios.   Culpa.
Angel.**

thus appears to have stood still, permitting a dramatic form of recognizably medieval character to survive well into the seventeenth century, even if on a declining scale.

(b) Summer Festivals: In the summer months the Feasts of Corpus Christi and the Assumption likewise attracted playmakers' attention, but the emphasis was here placed on theatrical spectacle rather than literary elaboration. References to processions with banners, pageant tableaux, and musicians begin in the latter half of the fourteenth century in Gerona, Barcelona and Valencia. Of surviving texts, the first were written in Catalan and come from the Balearic Islands, dating from the fifteenth century. In both respects Aragón—possibly because of its connections with France and Italy—appears to have been far ahead of Castile: similar references to Castilian plays only start in the early decades of the sixteenth century.

However, in neither kingdom is there any evidence to suggest that efforts of the kind made in France, England and Germany to dramatize the Feast of Corpus Christi itself were ever attempted or achieved; rather did this Feast, together with that of the Assumption, become occasions which it was considered appropriate to celebrate with the performance of religious plays (Fig. 114). Saint plays, moralities and even dance dramas came thus to be regarded as equally acceptable: floats accompanied by a presenter, or a choir, or sometimes both, continued to co-exist alongside scripted plays. As with the more self-consciously literary Easter and Christmas liturgical plays, however, the tendency to allegorize the subject matter developed rapidly. So did use of the pageant-stages as an extension to pulpits for purposes of theological exposition since the primary purpose of these plays was devotional. These stages were created by the conjunction of three carts (*carros*), that in the middle being used as the principal acting area and those at either end each carrying a scenic tower with doors and an upper level (Fig. 110). The religious character of these floats and of the plays presented on them was thus maintained, notwithstanding the incursions of comic incident, dance and stage machinery. That this balance was preserved must be attributed to the control exercised by senior officials of the Church, both as sponsors and censors of these productions, especially in Castile.

(c) Production Costs: The question of who should pay for the production costs was less easily settled. In Castile it was normal for the rich cathedrals to carry the major burden of these until relatively late in the sixteenth century, but in Aragón costs were met varyingly by public subscription, municipalities, guilds and private individuals. These

109. An emblematic pageant-car for a Corpus Christi festival in Madrid, 1667. In Spain, the medieval floats continued to be used in street theatres long after proscenium-arched stages had replaced open stages in public playhouses (see Figs. 110 and 119).

costs became persistently larger as the taste for spectacle increased and as a competitive element was introduced with the award of prizes. In both Seville and Madrid, where rising costs in the 1550s led to protests, responsibility for meeting them was thrust firmly upon the city, a decision which resulted in a sharp drop in the number of plays presented; but they were not suppressed, nor were they discontinued for lack of popular support. Indeed, the repertoire of such plays was substantially augmented at this time. The establishment of Jesuit colleges in the wake of the founding of the Order by St Ignatius Loyola in 1543 served to enlarge the repertoire of such plays substantially—a course of action that exactly matches (although in the cause of Roman Catholicism) the course of action urged upon Edward VI in England by Martin

Bucer to advance the Reformation (see pp. 115–16). Jesuit students presented their plays before public audiences with notable success; but they complained about the costs of production and the burden of having to compete in this respect with the cathedrals which ought—or so the students argued—to be assisting them. But as cathedrals had by then begun to employ professional actors, it is easy enough to understand why these complaints fell on deaf ears.

Despite this rivalry and despite the continuing resentment from townsfolk of the increasing burden of the taxes levied from them to pay for these plays, Spain never lost faith in its religious drama during the sixteenth century, as happened in Italy, France and England. Thus even in the seventeenth century religious plays continued to co-exist with a secular drama which was wholly controlled by professional actors, as will shortly be explained (see pp. 139–41 and Fig. 109). Professional playmakers were therefore called upon by the public to supply both markets simultaneously.

4 THE MEDIEVAL HERITAGE: SECULAR DRAMA

(a) Iberian Characteristics: As with religious drama, so the sources of Spanish secular drama were broadly European. Its specifically Iberian characteristics derive in part from

111. *Figurine of a* Morisco *dancer, c.1480, by Erasmus Grassner. Dance was an important element in Spanish drama from medieval times to the seventeenth century, which largely accounts for the early arrival of professional actresses on Spanish stages, and for the prominence accorded to dance by professional dramatists of the Golden Age. (Compare Fig. 49.)*

110. *A scene from* La adultera perdonada *by Lope de Vega presented on pageant-carts* (carros), *Madrid, 1608: reconstruction by Richard Southern and Iris Brook.*

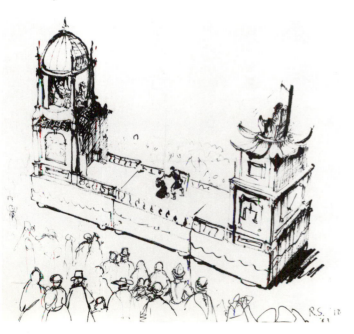

Jewish and Moorish qualities apparent in aspects of folk culture (especially songs and dances), and in part from the geographical proximity of Catalonia to Navarre, whence came the tournaments, *momeries* and *entremeses* of French and English origin. The Jews and Moors who for centuries had occupied Spain's southernmost province of Granada were alike offered a harsh alternative after its reconquest in 1492: accept baptism as Christians or banishment. Many of them opted to stay, paying lip service only to their assumed religion, and became known respectively as *marranos* and *moriscos*. They and their customs became absorbed into the mainstream of Spanish culture, and this goes a long way towards explaining the emphasis placed upon dance in plays written for professional actors late in the sixteenth century, the native style of which is still recognizable today in what we call Spanish dancing (Fig. 111).

(b) Primacy of Dance: This emphasis upon dance, however, is also observable in the *momos* and *momeries* of the
northern court festivals of the late fifteenth century—a
form of entertainment which had close affinities with the
English mummings associated with the Christmas season
and with Carnival (described in Chapters 5 and 6). The
Spanish versions were invariably ornamented with costly
scenic decoration—ships on wheels, arbours, castles and
the like—and were introduced by explanatory allegorical
verses. The giving of gifts, and games with dice, also figure
prominently in these entertainments. In Portugal they
become associated with Gil Vicente, who used them as a
basis for development into loosely structured plays on
chivalric and romantic themes. In Barcelona and Valencia
it was not uncommon to borrow floats made for the Corpus
Christi celebrations for use in banquet halls, and to commission elaborate machinery to make globes turn and open,
to make animals appear to breathe fire, and to facilitate
ascents and descents above and below these portable
stages.

(c) Italian Influences: Early in the sixteenth century these
momeries and *entremeses* began to be affected by the
importation from Italian courts and academies of plays
modelled on Latin originals—*commedia erudita* (see
pp. 100–3). Their arrival coincides with the return to Spain
of Bartolomé de Torres Naharro, to whom the credit must
be given for the publication of six *comedias* in 1517 all of
which had been acted in Italy, but which because of their
anti-clerical satire were at first regarded as unacceptable
in Spain. Most of these plays use a street as the scenic location with a functional upper window. Some of them had
been performed in Rome before being presented in Spain,
and all are divided into five acts. The imitations of Vicente's
and Encina's *églogas* and Naharro's *comedias* which found
favour at court in the early decades of the sixteenth century
all possess a simplicity of structure and setting that amateur
actors, whether adults or children, could be expected to
handle easily. Three acts came to be preferred to five. By
1538, however, a troupe of Italian professional actors was
giving performances in Spain, and within five years of their
arrival a troupe of Spanish actors under the leadership of
Lope de Rueda was presenting plays in Seville to paying
audiences (Fig. 112).

5 PROFESSIONAL THEATRE

(a) Early Beginnings: Little is as yet known about how or
why professional acting should have become popular and
been made legitimate in Spain at this time; but it must

*112. Title-page of an early printed edition of Lope de Rueda's
play* Eufemia. *It was Rueda who, during the 1540s, took the lead
in transforming the acting of plays in Spain from an occasional
festive recreation (whether devotional or secular) into a regular
professional occupation. Barcelona, Col Sedo.*

have been connected with the spectacular growth of the
Spanish colonial empire in the New World, the wealth
represented by huge imports of gold and silver bullion, and
the rapid expansion of Spanish industry to keep the
Emperor's army, navy and colonial settlers supplied with
all their needs. This industrial revolution occurred between
1520 and 1560, drawing peasants off the land into cities,
and in doing so offered professional entertainers a market
for regular performances as large as that already available
in England. By 1565 performances of plays by professional
actors were in sufficient demand for playhouses to become
an attractive investment, not only in Madrid but in all the
major cities. A start was made when leasing agreements
for such performances were reached with the charitable
brotherhood known as the Cofradía de la Pasión, which
maintained a hospital for women, in 1568 and with another

(Cofradía de la Soledad de Nuestra Señora) which maintained a home for foundlings, in 1574. Spanish acting companies were, like their English equivalents, small—normally five or six. From the outset women were employed to sing, and above all to dance: it is thus to Spain that credit should be given for introducing the concept of the professional actress. Boys were not used to play female roles as was the case in England.

(b) Native Characteristics and Isolationist Tendencies: As we approach the Golden Age of Spanish dramatic literature, therefore, we must recognize that at the time James Burbage and Richard Farrant were preparing to establish playhouses in Shoreditch and at Blackfriars, and Palladio and Scamozzi were planning the Teatro Olimpico in Vicenza, Spaniards had already been familiar with such buildings for the better part of a decade, at least in Madrid. We must also recognize that from then on drama and theatre in Spain would develop within three distinct, coexistent, and equally respected forms: court theatre for festive occasions, expensively equipped with lavish spectacle; subsidized religious plays described as *autos sacramentales*; and secular *comedias* presented to a paying public on a commercial basis. As actors and authors of repute expected to receive commissions from all three sources, these distinctions served to govern subsequent Spanish drama with a force that left little room for more than lip-service to be paid to Aristotelian or neo-classical Italian ideas of dramatic genre. Lope de Vega expressed himself forcefully on this point in *The New Art of Writing Plays*, addressed to the Academy of Madrid.

> This subject seems easy, and it should be easy for any of you who have written few plays but know all about the art of writing them. I suffer from the disadvantage of having written them without any art ... When I have to write a play I lock off [viz. up] the [classical] precepts with six keys, and I banish Terence and Plautus from my study ... I know that, though they [my plays] might have been better if written in another manner, they would not have found the favour they have enjoyed.
>
> (Trans. Kenneth Macgowan)

This view was shared by most professional Spanish playwrights as it was in Elizabethan England—though *not* by Ben Jonson (see pp. 127–8 above). Yet so thoroughgoing were Spanish dramatists and audiences in their adherence to this view, even in the seventeenth century, that it was inevitable that Spain would isolate itself from the rest of Europe and follow a theatrical path which, by the eighteenth century, had come to a dead end.

To say this is not to deny the splendour of the theatres which graced Spanish cities in the Golden Age nor to belittle the creative, imaginative and literary genius of the major dramatists, whose plays not only won them the admiration of their own audiences, but evoked responses in other countries, especially in France and England. What modern translators and artistic directors there and elsewhere have found difficult to handle in the printed texts of plays by all the master playwrights of the Golden Age is, in some, the intensity of religious feeling, in others the multiplicity and complexity of intrigues within the storyline, and in yet others a lack of character development, all of which they regard as likely to puzzle, disappoint and even exasperate a modern audience. As a result, revivals are rare and tend to be treated as collector's pieces piously resurrected for specialists, or to win approval from powerful patrons and sponsors. Some blame for this must attach to the authors, many of whom penned more scripts than most dramatists in other countries would have imagined possible. This suggests hasty composition and a keener preoccupation with wealth, social status and popular repute than with art. This view, however, rests on interpreting the word 'art', where drama is concerned, as meaning dramatic *literature* and little else: the eighteenth and nineteenth centuries are both littered with plays now ignored as literature but which were popular enough with audiences to be constantly revived and even translated into other languages for performances in other countries (see pp. 183–4 and 197–8). Lope de Vega was reputed to have written 1,800 scripts, of which over 500 survive; Calderón was not as prolific, but more than 200 survive; Tirso de Molina is credited with at least eighty. To this group must be added Guillén de Castro, the popularizer of a character at least as impressive and influential as Kyd's Hieronimo or Marlowe's Faustus—namely El Cid in *Las Mocedades del Cid* (The Youthful Exploits of the Cid).

6 THE GOLDEN AGE

(a) Dramatists: The first three dramatists represent the Iberian tradition in a fascinating way. Tirso de Molina, as a friar, was a churchman and the principal dramatic spokesman for the continuing dominance of Roman Catholicism in the theatre; yet he happens also to have been the creator of Don Juan in *El burlador de Sevilla*. Pedro Calderón de la Barca (1600–81) became the undisputed controller of court theatre as Master of the Revels to Philip IV; yet it is consistent with the tradition to which he was

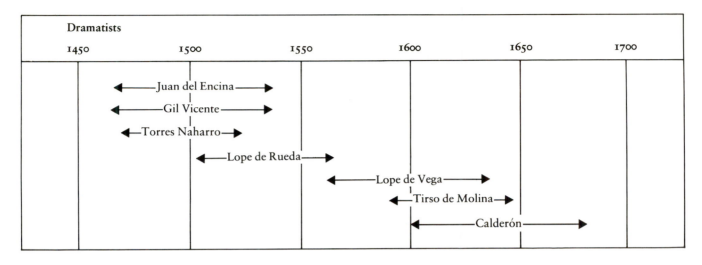

Dramatists

1450	1500	1550	1600	1650	1700

←———Juan del Encina———→

←——Gil Vicente——→

←—Torres Naharro—→

←——Lope de Rueda——→

←———Lope de Vega———→

←—Tirso de Molina—→

←———Calderón———→

heir that he should have chosen, late in life, to be ordained as a priest and accept appointment as a royal chaplain (Fig. 113). He continued, however, by royal command, to write plays and his reputation as a writer rests principally upon their lyrical quality. The best known among those which in translation retain a fitful place in the modern repertoire are: *The Mayor of Zalamea*, which places the familiar theme of honour in a novel context by discussing it equally within both an aristocratic and a peasant environment; *The Surgeon of His Own Honour*, a tragedy of passion which bears some resemblance to *Othello*; and *Life is a Dream* and *The Great Theatre of the World*. In the last pair the exposition of doctrine governs stage action and plot construction (Fig. 114). Lope de Vega (1562–1635), the most prolific, not only of Spanish playwrights, but of all dramatists throughout history, was also the most secular both in his style of life and in his whole-hearted commitment to the theatre (Fig. 115). Educated by Jesuits, he resembles Marlowe in his command of contemporary theology; as a marine who fought through and survived the defeat of the Spanish Armada in 1588, he resembles Ben Jonson, who in the 1590s fought against the Spanish army of occupation in the Netherlands; with his many wives, mistresses and children he eclipsed all Elizabethan and Jacobean dramatists in the notoriety of his private life. Yet he remained steadfastly loyal to his chosen profession of actor-manager-dramatist, and in this respect more nearly resembles Molière in France, or David Garrick and Sir Henry Irving amongst English theatrical personalities of a later era. Like them he also succeeded in attracting powerful aristocratic patronage—notably that of the Duke of Sessa. Somehow, he managed to retain the respect and admiration not only of the nobility but of the Church,

113. Portrait of Pedro Calderón de la Barca, writer of autos, comedias *and librettos for opera-ballets, Master of the Revels to Philip IV, and an ordained priest of the Roman Catholic Church. Museo Lazaro Galdiano, Madrid (artist unknown).*

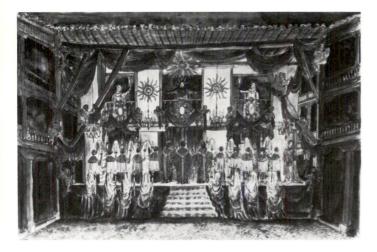

114. *Scene from a performance of* The Great Theatre of the World *by Calderón in the Corral des Comedias, Almagro. Barcelona, Cividad Real.*

115. *Lope de Vega (right): actor, manager and dramatist, and the outstanding leader of the professional theatre in Spain during* The Golden Age. *Portrait by Vicenzo Carducci. Madrid, Prado.*

whose leaders regularly commissioned *autos* from him, notwithstanding the ostentatiously lascivious character of his private life. The *autos*, however, were outnumbered by secular *comedias* in a ratio of at least thirty to one, written strictly for professional actors and actresses, for commercial reward and the adulation of the crowd. In short, it is as difficult—if for different reasons—for the modern critic to arrive at a wholly satisfying appraisal of Lope's personality and achievement as it is of Shakespeare's. Both were geniuses in their own time and within their respective environments, and thus escape all attempts to reduce them to rule, category, classification, or psycho-analytical dissection. Yet, alas, of his surviving 500 or more plays, how many people outside Spain can today name the title of one? What no one can deny is the impact that Lope's commitment to his profession had on the architecture of the Spanish theatre and on acting as a professional career. In these respects his authority carried the same weight as that of Edward Alleyn or Richard Burbage in England in Shakespeare's life-time.

(b) **Public Playhouses:** The story of the construction and development of the public playhouses in Spain (*corrales*, literally 'courtyards') can almost be described in terms of Lope's career. Improving on what he inherited from Lope de Rueda, he was instrumental in confirming the success of the two playhouses first established in Madrid between 1579 and 1582, the Corral de la Cruz and the Corral del Príncipe, and in establishing similar institutions in all large provincial cities—an achievement unique in Europe. By the end of the century *corral* playhouses had even been established in the New World; one existed in Lima, Peru, by 1594 and another in Mexico City by 1597 (Fig. 116). This steady increase of professional play production, however, occurred in conjunction with the rapid centralization of government achieved by Philip II and with it the rise of Madrid as the undisputed capital of the whole country. Thus in the closing decades of the sixteenth century, the theatres in Madrid under the leadership of Lope de Vega were setting standards, both of conduct and performance, which, once approved and endorsed by the government, were adopted elsewhere.

In this Lope de Vega was unquestionably assisted by the timely arrival of *Commedia dell'Arte* companies from Italy, notably that of Alberto Ganassa from 1574 onwards. The popularity of these companies with their largely improvised scenarios must offer a partial explanation for Lope's relative lack of interest in the literary qualities of his own plays, and his corresponding preoccupation with their actability.

116. *Quechua Indian woman celebrating Corpus Christi/Inti Raimi (Festival of the Sun), Cuzco, Peru. Professional actors followed the Spanish and Portuguese armies and merchant settlers to Mexico, Peru and Brazil before the end of the sixteenth century and established* corral *playhouses there. See also Plate 1.*

These playhouses were everywhere established not only with royal approval, but with the active assistance of the religious brotherhoods through the hospitals which they financed and managed on behalf of the poor, the sick and the needy. By leasing their courtyards to the actors, and by entering into contractual agreements with them, the hospitals offered the actors open spaces of the right size for conversion into regular playhouses with controlled admission, which greatly eased their own responsibility for the upkeep of the main buildings and their care of the inmates. If it is asked how professional actors and actresses in Catholic Spain escaped being branded as rogues and vagabonds, then the surest answer is to be found in this intimate association with the hospitals and the charitable good works that their performances helped so greatly to finance (see p. 124 for an English analogy).

(c) **Comparison with Elizabethan Playhouses:** The nearest English equivalent both in size and layout to these *corrales* were the rectangular Boar's Head, Fortune and Red Bull playhouses, all of which were constructed between 1598 and 1605. All Spanish *corrales* contained a large raised platform to serve as a stage, with a gallery at the back and at least two entrances from the dressing room underneath it. To this extent, at least, they bear a close resemblance to De Witt's sketch of the interior of the Swan. 'Heavens' supported on pillars, however, are conspicuous by their absence in such Spanish sketches as survive: instead they show two staircases linking stage and gallery at either end. The area between the gallery and the stage was draped with painted curtains, permitting 'discoveries' as well as entrances, exits, and evident eavesdropping. In Spanish playhouses, unlike English ones, spectators were not normally allowed to sit on the stage.

A large pit at yard level faced the stage with tiered scaffolds running round it which were roofed over to protect spectators from the sun, like those traditionally erected for distinguished guests at tournaments. By the end of the sixteenth century a canvas awning was stretched over the pit (see Fig. 39). Drainage of the pit in bad weather seems to have posed as serious and recurrent a problem as it did in English playhouses. The scaffolds at the back came to be boxed in behind glass for the better segregation of women. This area was known as *la cazuela*—the stew pan. Sale of water and fruit was as carefully provided for as fruit and ale in England. Costumes were likewise lavish, but scenic furnishings, even late in the seventeenth century, were simple and emblematic, unlike those of the Corpus Christi plays (see Fig. 118).

(d) **Court Theatre:** Court theatre developed differently. There, scenic spectacle, having always taken precedence over everything except lyrical poetry and dance, rapidly became susceptible to Italian influence. With money (in terms of box-office receipts) a matter of no concern to any of its promoters or recipients, spectacle progressed on a scale commensurate with imperial wealth. This progress was delayed, however, by the fact that neither Charles V nor Philip II was interested in drama and, unlike Italian princes or the English monarchy, failed to patronize it. Both were constantly exposed to Italian and Flemish plays in the course of their numerous journeys abroad, but this proved to have little influence in Spain beyond encouraging interest at home in the exploitation of classical mythology to embellish arches and pageant cars in the many Roman-style 'triumphs' with which local authorities welcomed visiting royalty into the major cities. Thus only with the accession

117. *A contemporary French impression of Spanish guitarists. Costume designs for the entry of the Spaniards in the* Ballet des fées de la forêt de Saint-Germain, *by Daniel Rabel, Paris, 1625. Paris, Louvre, Cabinet des Dessins.*

of Philip III in 1598 was any serious effort made to provide the court with a style of theatre that was distinctively its own. Special halls began to be built and gardens remodelled along Italian lines to stage court entertainments. These took two forms: plays especially written for performance by courtiers, which bear some structural resemblance to Stuart masques, and plays from the repertoire of professional companies brought to court, as and when required, for the entertainment of the king.

Lope de Vega enjoyed commissions for the provision of both. Lavish expenditure on costumes and settings for the former became habitual; but the spectacle actually offered remained firmly grounded on the simultaneous presentation of all scenic locations and on provision of machines

of the kind familiar in Corpus Christi and Jesuit drama (see Fig. 109). Its principal interest to posterity lies in the wealth of detail surviving in stage directions, descriptions and account books which record its physical appearance and the methods of construction and operation used by the designers, carpenters, engineers and painters paid to provide it.

It was thus left to Philip IV, who succeeded his father in 1621, to exploit this modest start by importing foreigners to implement change of a more radical kind. This he did by commissioning the erection of the new royal palace of Buen Retiro and inviting an Italian engineer, Cosme Lotti, to lay out with his assistants the gardens and fountains and to provide him with a theatre (see Fig. 119). Lotti obliged by constructing a large portable stage in the Serlian style. This could as easily be erected on an island in a lake as in a hall, and could accommodate perspective scenery and the machinery needed to change it, whether on the island or in the hall. The palace was completed in 1632, and three

118. *A performance in the* Corral de la Pacheca, Madrid, c.1660, *as reconstructed by Juan Comba y García in 1888. Madrid, Museo Municipal.*

years later Lotti was asking Calderón to provide him with the text of a play about Ulysses's meeting with Circe, a scenario for which he had devised for presentation on the lake. It included an earthquake (an excuse for transforming the original prospect of a mountain surrounded by woodland trees into the interior of Circe's palace) and made provision for real ships, nymphs who seemed to walk on water, cloud machines, a joust at barriers and a liberal supply of real fish. Calderón responded (as Jonson did when confronted by similar suggestions from Inigo Jones) by insisting that responsibility for the ordering of the scenario must be his. A compromise was reached, and the results survive in the printed edition of *El mayor encanto amor* which Calderón published in 1637. By this time Lotti had begun work on planning a permanent court theatre, to be called

the *Coliseo*, which was finally opened in 1640. Five years later war with Portugal and the Catalan revolts combined, like the Civil War in England, sharply to curtail all court festivities and to so cripple the professional acting companies as to force many of them to disband. Thereafter the sterility of constant repetition of familiar formulas (despite the superficial novelty of baroque ornament) without any new creative initiative after the death of Calderón in 1681 led inexorably to decadence and to the denial to Spain of any significant role in the continuing story of theatre for the next two hundred years.

119. *One of the stage settings for Calderón's* La fiera, el rayo yó la piedre, *as presented in Valencia, 1690, illustrating the use of changeable scenery in plays at court during the latter half of the seventeenth century under the guidance of the Florentine engineer Cosme Lotti. (Compare Figs. 86-8.)*

10
France

1 WARS OF RELIGION, 1545–1610

(a) The Suppression of Religious Drama: If it was the English and the Spanish peoples who, in their different ways, exploited and developed the dramatic and theatrical traditions that had been forged in Europe during the Middle Ages, and brought them to their zenith in the latter half of the sixteenth century and the early decades of the seventeenth, it was left to the French (under Louis XIII and Louis XIV) to do the same for those neo-classical academic and artistic developments which had been grasped, funded and explored by the rulers of Italian city states during the sixteenth century. What French actors, dramatists and critics accomplished between 1630 and 1680 not only lifted French theatre to an unrivalled pre-eminence in Europe, but kept it there throughout the eighteenth century.

In the middle of the sixteenth century France had firmly turned its back on the theatrical past, and very nearly ensured that dramatic art should have no future there at all. In 1548, the Church and the government of Henry II in Paris, alarmed by the success of Lutheran and Calvinist missionary endeavour, persuaded Parliament to pass an edict banning all religious plays in the capital. This action was imitated within a decade by provincial parliaments and succeeded in suppressing the religious stage throughout the country with a speed and finality unparalleled elsewhere in Europe. In the vacuum which this action created, where professionally organized festive and civic theatre was concerned, only isolated academic and amateur productions in Jesuit colleges, universities and at court were left—a situation which was to continue for the rest of the sixteenth century as a result of the social and political turmoil accompanying nearly thirty years of religious civil war (Fig. 120). This proved to be a blow from which the provinces only partially recovered, and then only some two hundred years

120. Ballet Comique de la Royne, *Paris, 1582. The French Ballet of the sixteenth century was a courtly entertainment of song, verses, spectacle and dance corresponding to English Disguisings and Masques. This illustration to the printed text shows 'Circe's Garden' (centre back), a star-spangled bank of clouds (left), and a woodland arbour housing a satyr (right).*

FRANCE

1547	Death of Francis I	1643	Louis XIV becomes King of France
1548	Religious plays banned by Parliament of Paris	1645	Torelli arrives in Paris from Venice
1559	Henry II killed in a tournament	1653	Louis XIV appears as the Sun King in the *Ballet de Nuit*
1562–98	Wars of Religion		
1572	Massacre of Huguenots on St Bartholomew's Eve in Paris	1658	Molière returns from the provinces to Paris
		1660	Corneille publishes his *Discours* and *Examens*
1577	*Commedia dell'Arte* perform in Paris	c.1670	Founding of the Royal Academy of Dancing
1589	Henry of Navarre becomes King Henry IV of France	1671	Founding of the Royal Academy of Opera
1598	Edict of Nantes guarantees freedom of worship to Protestants	1674	Boileau publishes his *Art Poétique*
		1677	First performance of Racine's *Phèdre*
1610	Louis XIII becomes King of France	1680	The Théâtre Français established in Paris
1624	Cardinal Richelieu becomes prime minister	1685	Louis XIV revokes the Edict of Nantes
1635	Founding of the French Academy	1700–13	War of the Spanish Succession
1636/7	Corneille's *Le Cid* produced in Paris	1715	Death of Louis XIV
1642	Cardinal Mazarin succeeds Cardinal Richelieu as prime minister		

later following the French Revolution of 1789. Even in Paris, Frenchmen desirous of seeing professional productions of any calibre had either to travel outside France or await the visits of touring companies from abroad— notably those of the *Commedia dell'Arte* which first appeared there in 1577 (Fig. 121–2). English actors were in Strasbourg in the 1590s but never in Paris, and after the Massacre of St Bartholomew in 1572, which accounted for the death of over 3,000 Protestants, it is to be doubted whether any of them wished to be: Christopher Marlowe's recreation of this atrocity, as presented by the Admiral's Men on the stage of the Rose, sufficed to warn them off.

(b) The Hôtel de Bourgogne: One link with the vanished past, however, survived in the continued existence of the Confrérie de la Passion. This medieval religious guild, which had long possessed the right to organize, finance and present religious plays in the capital, also owned a roofed playhouse within the ruins of the former palace of the Dukes of Burgundy, the Hôtel de Bourgogne. This the guild chose to lease, after 1548, to touring companies offering secular entertainments for profit. This building, despite its antiquated design, was destined after a variety of convolutions to emerge, phoenix-like, refurbished and renamed as the Comédie Française (Fig. 122). In one sense, therefore, the Hôtel de Bourgogne can claim precedence over both

Spanish and English public and private playhouses, as well as over the Teatro Olimpico in Vicenza, as the earliest professional theatre in Europe; but once the quality of the plays presented in all these other theatres is included in the story, this claim becomes difficult to sustain. Not until 1599, when the actor-manager Valleran-Lecomte leased the playhouse from the Confrérie, did Paris acquire a resident professional company complete with a dramatist capable of writing plays for the stage and for a specific company of actors in the manner of Lope de Vega in Spain or William Shakespeare in England. This playwright was Alexandre Hardy (*c.*1569–1632).

Opposite above: 121. A fairground theatre in France in the early seventeenth century. Gille le Niais, the leader of the company, is here seen as a mountebank doctor persuading spectators to buy an elixir of his own concoction. Behind is a painted perspective cloth depicting a bridge. (Compare Fig. 77 and Jonson's Volpone, *II, 2.)*

Opposite below: 122. The stage of the Hôtel de Bourgogne with a farce in progress, c.1630. A Frenchman (extreme left) watches Turlupin rob Gautier Garguille, who is railing at Gros Guillaume, who is too busy pursuing an affair of the heart to take any notice: the cowardly Spaniard, Le Capitaine Fracasse (extreme right), looks on. Paris, Bibliothèque Nationale.

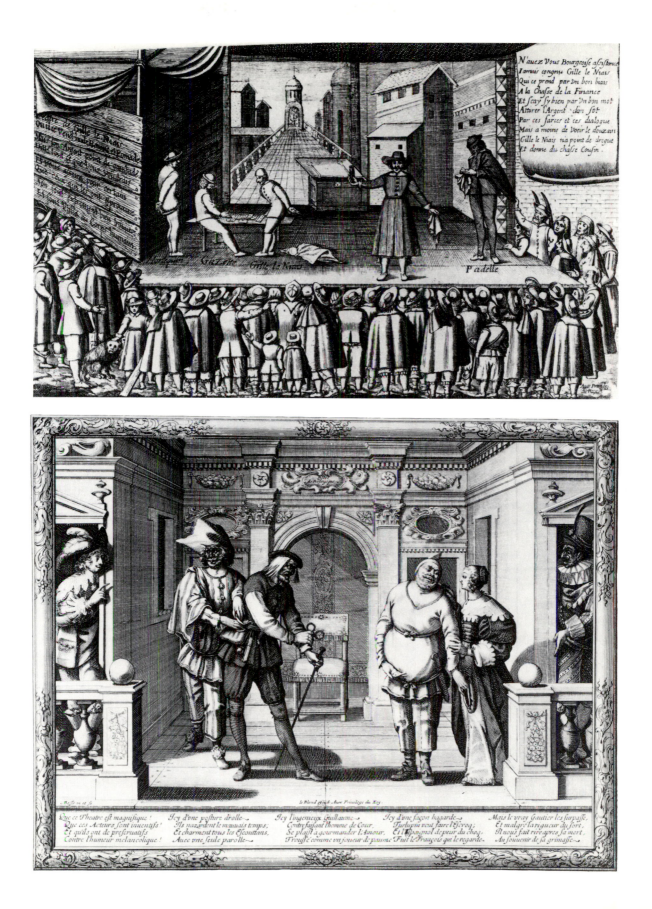

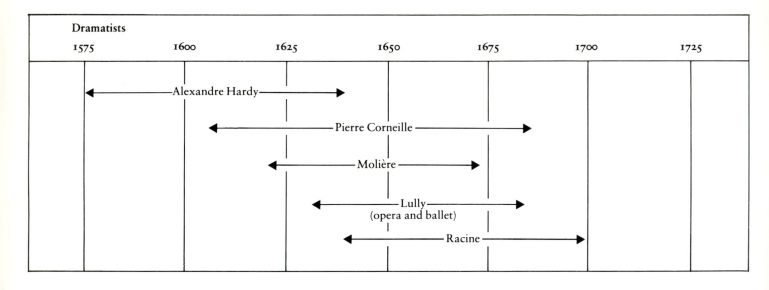

Dramatists

| 1575 | 1600 | 1625 | 1650 | 1675 | 1700 | 1725 |

Alexandre Hardy

Pierre Corneille

Molière

Lully
(opera and ballet)

Racine

2 THE EMERGENCE OF A PROFESSIONAL THEATRE

(a) **Alexandre Hardy:** Hardy was neither a good poet nor a dramatic theorist; nevertheless, by working directly for and with professional actors, he learned to provide audiences with romantic and heroic stage action and rhetoric that gripped the imagination of the French court and its entourage. He is reputed to have written at least 700 plays in the course of forty years, most of which we would describe as melodramas. None were printed before 1624. Those that survive include twenty-two tragi-comedies, eleven tragedies and five pastoral plays.

As a maker of plays, Hardy chose to override the ped-antically imitative neo-classicism of earlier academic writers like Etienne Jodelle and Robert Garnier: he ignored the unities of time and place, banished the chorus, depicted deaths on stage instead of reporting them, and admitted comic, low-life characters and incident to his tragedies. In these respects he resembles Lope de Vega, Calderón and the English Jacobean playwrights; but in one fundamental respect he provided his successors in France with something unique in European dramaturgy: simple and concentrated plots of a kind rarely even attempted elsewhere. His plays are now forgotten, with the possible exception of *Mariamne*; yet by giving Parisians their first experience of French plays professionally acted and offered daily on a regular repertory basis, Hardy and the Lecomte company unquestionably supplied France with the foundations of a contemporary drama that could be improved upon by abler poets and refined though critical debate. All that was

needed to launch it on this path was political stability and patronage.

(b) **The Académie Française:** It so chanced that both were forthcoming in a most timely way. The accession of the young Louis XIII in 1610 was followed by the turbulent regency of his mother, Marie de Médicis; but Cardinal Richelieu, who came to power as prime minister in 1624, gradually succeeded in imposing stability by his absolutist and authoritarian principles. In the cultural domain, a key event was the transforming of the newly created Académie Française from what at first had been a private gathering of friends into the powerful institution it was soon to become. Its establishment was destined to give all liter-ature, including stage plays, a stronger social and political influence in French national and cultural life than in any other country. Its charter was awarded by the King in 1635 and confirmed by Parliament two years later. Where the theatre is concerned, its influence as the ultimate arbiter of good taste and decorum came to be felt as far afield as Vienna, St Petersberg (present day Leningrad) and Stock-holm.

Within a year of the foundation of the Academy, its members were given something to cut their teeth on; for in 1636 Pierre Corneille's *Le Cid* received its first perform-ance in Paris. It was an instant success with the public, so much so that Cardinal Richelieu, in whose private theatre it had also been performed, thrust the script at the Academ-icians for critical appraisal. In 1638 they published *Les Sen-timents de l'Académie sur le Cid*. Nothing in the French theatre could ever be quite the same again.

(c) **Tennis-court Theatres**: To understand why, it is necessary to take account of the state of professional acting at the time, and of the laws regulating the licensing of play-houses. Fundamental to both was the monopoly possessed, and jealously guarded, by the Confrérie de la Passion in Paris. The monopoly was only finally broken in 1634. Until then it had held, despite frequent attempts by provincial or foreign companies to establish themselves both at the annual fairs of St Laurent (summer) and St Germain (winter) and in disused tennis-courts (Fig. 123). Most of these roofed, rectangular buildings with spectators' galleries built along the back wall and down one side, were situated in the Marais district of Paris on the north bank of the Seine and within easy walking distance of the palace of the Louvre. This area contained St Germain's market (the site of the winter fair) and, like the south bank of the Thames at Southwark in Shakespeare's London, the brothels. Acting companies that tried to break the Confrérie's monopoly, however, were either swiftly hounded out of the city under threat of arrest, or permitted to remain on a temporary basis if they paid a fat fee for the privilege. This situation could not but reinforce the claims of the *Comédiens du Roi* (*Troupe Royale*) playing at the Hôtel de Bourgogne to be the only professional company of quality in Paris (see Fig. 122). It was not until 1634 that a second company headed by Guillaume Desgilberts (who, on becoming an actor, called himself Montdory) was permitted, with Richelieu's help, to transform one of these old tennis-courts into a new playhouse for its own, exclusive use—Le Théâtre du Marais.

3 THE GREAT QUARTET

(a) **Corneille**: It was to this company that a promising young writer from Rouen, Pierre Corneille, had presented his first play, *Mélite*, in 1629; and by 1635 he was one of a group of five authors directly commissioned by Richelieu to write plays for him. By the time Corneille came to write *Le Cid* he already had eight plays to his name of which the best were *Médée*, a tragedy, and *L'Illusion comique*, a comedy. *Le Cid*, according to the judgement of the Academicians, was neither: it was a tragi-comedy which, although it seemed outwardly to conform to the classical unities of time, place and action, placed so heavy a strain on the principal requirements of decorum and credibility as to violate both. In other words, Parisians who had received the play with unqualified enthusiasm were told by the Academy that their judgement was at fault. Little could have been better calculated to stir up a hornet's nest of controversy, and thus ensure that dramatists in future

123. *The Royal Game of Tennis, Paris, early seventeenth century. Disused tennis-courts were rented out at this time by the ground-landlords for use by actors, notwithstanding the risk of heavy fines. This was also the case in Flanders and the Netherlands. Paris, Bibliothèque de l'Arsenal.*

would ponder the likely critical reception of a play, as well as the likely popular response, before setting pen to paper. The debate, however, went further than that in its results, for it effectively served to define the classical criteria that would govern the French theatre for the next one hundred years. If the moral justification underpinning the existence of dramatic art (and the toleration of actors) in society lay in its capacity to teach and to please, then audiences must be left in no doubt about the appropriateness of the rewards meted out to characters for their behaviour. It was a lesson Ben Jonson had striven to ram home to English dramatists and audiences some thirty years earlier in the prologues and prefaces to his plays. Comedy should thus ridicule all avoidable conduct and behaviour—for example hypocrisy, pomposity, pretension; tragedy should reveal the disastrous consequences of unbridled passion and criminal deeds.

With this demand that drama, to be allowable, must teach, neo-classical theorists coupled an insistence on verisimilitude, or accuracy in the representation of life on the stage. In other words a sharp distinction must be made between fantasy and reality, not only in the stage action, but in its location and time-span. Norms must be preferred to accident, and this must be stretched to include behaviour as well as incident. Soliloquy came thus to be regarded as unreal: if an individual's private thoughts needed to be revealed to audiences, then that character must be provided with a confidant to whom he could articulate them. Being trusted, these companions must proffer rational advice (thus speaking for the audience) and must not betray that trust. The insistence upon the banishment of irrelevant detail led naturally both to the elimination of sub-plots and to the excision of deviant characteristics in human behaviour that detracted from the desired impression of universal applicability. A five-act structure became obligatory and scenes within acts began and ended with the arrival or departure of a character. Within criteria as clear cut as these, stage characters could scarcely avoid being reduced to types operating in situations that were themselves largely stereotyped, and argument inevitably replaced narrative and romance as a play's *raison d'être*. It thus became likely that only dramatists of genius would be able to transcend these limitations and create plays of more lasting interest than as mere mirrors to contemporary fashions and concerns. France was therefore fortunate to be rewarded with two such dramatists—Molière and Racine—who, within a generation of the founding of the Academy, were ready to succeed Corneille.

Corneille himself, having inadvertently drawn the sting of academic reproof with *Le Cid* (his own highly original adaptation of *Las Mocedades del Cid* (*The Youthful Exploits of the Cid*) by the Spanish playwright Guillén de Castro), and despite his inclination to follow his own instincts, chose to avoid similar attacks in future. His next three plays, *Horace*, *Cinna* and *Polyeucte*, all written and performed between 1639 and 1640, were 'regular' tragedies; a comedy, *The Liar* (*Le Menteur*), followed in 1642. These four plays established him as the undisputed leader of the French theatre and prepared the way for his admission to the Academy in 1647. During the next thirty-seven years he had to witness first Molière, and then Racine,

building on his foundations to eclipse his own achievement as a writer both of comedy and tragedy. Yet Corneille himself wrote another thirteen plays, secured the patronage of Louis XIV, collaborated with Molière, earned the admiration of Racine, and enjoyed through his younger brother, the playwright Thomas Corneille, an active association with the professional theatre until his death in 1684. No wonder then that in a funeral eulogy before the French Academy Racine declared him to have been the principal reformer of the French theatre and the man who above all others had replaced sentiment with reason and irregularity with order.

(b) **Molière and Racine**: Like Marlowe, Jonson, and Milton in England before them, Molière and Racine had acquired a firm grounding in Greek, Latin and Theology before making any contact with the theatre. Molière, whose name was then Jean-Baptiste Poquelin, received his schooling from the Jesuits at the Collège de Clermont and Racine his from the Jesuits' opponents the Jansenists, first at Port-Royal and then at the Collège de Beauvais. Young Poquelin was expected to follow his father into the upholstery business in the service of the king. It was hoped that Jean Racine (who was orphaned when only four and brought up thereafter by his grandmother) would become a lawyer or, perhaps, a priest. Instead, both young men drifted by different routes into the theatre, Poquelin as an actor, Racine as a poet. In 1666 they met and, for three years, became working colleagues.

Twenty years earlier Poquelin had decided that neither upholstery nor the law was for him and had joined an avant-garde 'fringe' theatre group originally calling itself *Les Enfants de Famille* but renamed in 1644 as *L'Illustre Théâtre*. This decision made, he changed his name from Poquelin to Molière, probably to save his family from the shame and disgrace of having their name sullied by his association with actors and actresses. The company was led by Denys Beys, but its moving spirits were the five Béjarts—at first Joseph, Madeleine and Geneviève, and later Louis and Armande. This venture failed, taking Molière to prison as a debtor. Nothing daunted, the young company reformed itself with a view to leaving Paris to experiment in the provinces. With twelve other companies already touring there, competition proved to be stiff; but this helped them to acquire the skills and experience needed to avoid bankruptcy, both as actors and in the provision of their own scripts. Molière proved to be exceptionally talented in both capacities (see Plate 12). By 1655 he had become the leading actor, and in *The Blunderer* (*L'Étourdi*) he gave them a comedy comparable with those of Corneille.

This play was written in the twelve-syllable Alexandrine couplets that by now constituted the established verse form used by all writers of tragedy and by most authors of comedy aspiring to literary as well as theatrical success. Curiously, while Molière's own verse comedies were to enjoy the greatest critical praise with his own and subsequent generations, only a minority of his total output of thirty-three plays are actually written in verse.

Shortly after the production of *L'Étourdi*, the company acquired the patronage of the King's brother, the Duc d'Anjou, in Rouen, which in turn led to their return to Paris and a performance before the King himself at the palace of the Louvre on 24 October 1658. The play chosen was Corneille's *Nicomède*—a mistake on all counts—but this was redeemed by Molière's own *Love-sick Doctor (Le Docteur amoureux)*, presented as an after-piece.

The twelve years of training in the provinces was now over. Money, a playhouse and public support all followed.

LE VRAY PORTRAICT DE Mᴱ DE MOLIERE
en habit de sganarelle

125. *Molière in costume in the role of Sganarelle. Engraving by Simonin. London, British Museum. (See Fig. 111.)*

124. *The Great Hall of the Hôtel du Petit Bourbon, adjacent to the Palace of the Louvre, after conversion into a theatre, c.1614. It was here that Molière installed his company in 1659. Including apse, the stage measured some 45 feet by 45 feet, and was regarded as exceptionally large.*

Accredited as the *Troupe de Monsieur*, licensed to share the Hôtel du Petit-Bourbon (Fig. 124) with Cardinal Mazarin's own company of Italian Comedians (on paying them a hefty rent for each day of use), they could also rely for the first time on a regular income supplied (or at least promised) by their new master, and on the ticket money actually received from a public composed of courtiers and the leisured habitués of the Paris salons eager to see the company at work and to compare its repertoire and skills with those of the rival company at the Hôtel de Bourgogne. These skills, of course, included Molière's own as a comedian which embraced the athleticism of the clown and farceur, the pathos of the wronged, snubbed or misunderstood victim of others' mirth, and the brilliance of timing in word and gesture (combined with perfect taste) required of high comedy, to an unrivalled degree (Fig. 125). It was this combination of skills that endeared him to his friends and admirers and got him out of difficult and dangerous situations at court brought about when his wit gave serious offence.

The year 1659 saw the production in Paris of Molière's first satire on contemporary manners, *Les Précieuses Ridicules* (only roughly translatable as 'Female Affectations') which was an instant, if scandalous, success. Next came a farce, *Sganarelle; or the Imaginary Cuckold* (1660), and then a serious, or heroic, comedy, *Don Garcie de Navarre* (1661) which failed to please: this, however, was offset by the welcome given that same year to *The School for Husbands* (*L'École des Maris*). By then Molière had safely established himself in the eyes of both Louis XIV and the fashionable world of Paris as the leading comic writer in France. What was still needed was an equally prestigious successor to Corneille as a writer of tragedy; so it was fitting that in 1662, through the good offices of the poet La Fontaine, Molière should meet Racine, who only two years earlier had attracted the King's attention with an ode on his marriage which earned him a royal annuity. Racine then tried his hand at playwriting with *Amasie*, a tragedy which was bought by the *Troupe Royale* but never staged; it was then lost or destroyed. His next attempt was *La Thébaïde, ou les Frères Ennemis*. This he showed to Molière, who helped him to get it professionally staged in Paris in 1644 at the Palais Royal, a sumptuously equipped theatre built by Richelieu for his own use, and after 1661, as a mark of royal favour, allocated to Molière and his company. Although *La Thébaïde* enjoyed only a *succès d'estime*, its reception was favourable enough to warrant the commissioning of another, *Alexandre le Grand* (1665). Racine then behaved disgracefully towards his friend and benefactor by letting himself be persuaded to allow the Troupe Royal to produce the play simultaneously at the Hôtel de Bourgogne. Excelling in tragedy, they did it better. Molière, understandably, never spoke to him again. However, Racine was now launched as the most promising tragic dramatist in Paris, an impression confirmed a year later with the production of *Andromaque*, again at the Hôtel de Bourgogne.

(c) **Lully**: With Molière now at the height of his powers as a comic dramatist (*Le Tartuffe* was already written and *Le Misanthrope* in the course of composition) and with Racine poised to lift tragedy to the same level of distinction, France needed only an exponent of lyric drama of the same calibre, and a latter-day Aristotle to distil and encapsulate these achievements through criticism based on an existing corpus of dramatic theory. Both were almost instantly forthcoming, the latter in the poet and critic Nicolas

126. *Louis XIV as a young man in the role of the Sun King in the* Ballet de Nuit, *1653. Paris, Bibliothèque Nationale.*

Boileau and the former in Louis XIV's dancing master, Jean-Baptiste Lully (1632–87).

Lully had acquired his music training in Florence, but had migrated to France in 1646 where he was placed, some six years later, in the King's own service. There, his new master's passion for dancing assured him of a close and continuous patronage. By 1660 Lully had met Molière and other dramatists such as Philippe Quinault who, like him, needed a composer to provide incidental music for plays, or full scores for the fashionable *Ballets de Cour*. Louis had made his famous appearance on stage as the Sun King in *Le Ballet de Nuit* as early as 1653 (Fig. 126).

Between 1661 and 1672 a Royal Academy of Dancing was established in Paris with its standards set by Louis XIV and Lully, who up till then had often performed together in public. The subject matter for these princely lyric spectacles was normally drawn from classical mythology, but was frequently flavoured with pastoral overtones native to France: yet decorum at court imposed upon them a degree of formality that is self-evident in the costume designs of Jean Bérain (1637–1711) where large head-dresses, high-heeled shoes and heavy, panniered skirts are taken for granted (Fig. 127). Not until the eighteenth century were more diaphanous clothes and dancing slippers admitted to ballet among the innovations pioneered by Marie Salle and Camargo (see Figs. 149 and 163). Nevertheless, the example set by the new Academy sufficed to ensure that where the future of ballet was concerned, France would be the pace-setter and the rest of Europe would obediently follow its lead.

With opera, the case was different; for there the Italians had already established the forms both in Venice and Vienna (as related on pp. 108-9), making it almost impossible for their immediate successors in other countries, like Lully and Jean Philippe Rameau in France or Purcell in England, to do more than adapt them to fit another language, or to accommodate those differences of emphasis which native taste and talent dictated to secure public approval. Following the example of the Medicis in Florence a century earlier, the French court chose to celebrate its own existence with a succession of spectacular entertainments (often including horseback ballets known as *Carousels*) which could be staged in parks, gardens and

128. *Combat at Barriers, Nancy, 1627. Here the chivalric tournaments of the Middle Ages have been reduced to 'soft and silken wars'. The combatants enter the hall in elaborate scenic cars, dressed emblematically as mythological characters, escorted by costumed torchbearers, attendants and musicians. (Compare Fig. 129 and Plate 8.) Contemporary engraving by Jacques Callot.*

courtyards as well as indoors and all of which were elaborately decorated by Torelli, Bérain and others (Figs. 92 and 130). It was on some of these entertainments that Lully first began to collaborate with Molière. Together they became responsible in 1664 for *Le Mariage forcé* and *La Princesse d'Élide*; *Le Sicilien* followed in 1667, and

127. *The Clockmaker. A costume design by Jean Bérain for a character in a ballet at the court of Louis XIV. The formal and stately character of the dancing may be judged by the stiffness of the shoes as much as by the nature of the costume itself. Monumenta Scenica.*

129. *Combat at Barriers, Nancy, 1627. The entry of the Lord Chamberlain, Le Comte de Brionne, disguised as Jason. He is depicted standing on the poop of his ship surrounded by an orchestra of Tritons. Below are two other 'entries': the Island of Colchis, with the Golden Fleece tied to a tree, and Mercury in front of his palace. Contemporary engraving by Jacques Callot.*

130. *Costume designs by Jean Bérain for a* Carousel *(ballet on horseback) in the park at Versailles, 1662. Each participant made a spectacular 'entry' in an exotic costume appropriate to the theme of the occasion. This* Carousel *consisted of five Quadrilles: Romans (the King's own), Persians, Indians, Turks and Americans. This design is one of those for the Turks. Monumenta Scenica.*

By then the great creative era was over. Molière had died in 1673, while playing the title-role in his own *Le Malade imaginaire* (Fig. 131). Corneille had followed him in 1684. Racine was to write two more plays, *Esther* (1689) and *Athalie* (1691), both of them for a girls' school with music by J.-B. Moreau. Between them this great quartet of artists had changed the face of dramatic art in Europe. They could not have done it without the loyal and enthusiastic patronage of the royal master whom they all served with such zeal; nor could their respective achievements have been as durable as they were without the existence of the French Academy and the subsequent Academies of Dance and Opera; for between them these institutions served to ensure that the pioneers who had subjugated their own idiosyncrasies to the cause of order, self-discipline and excellence in artistic expression in the theatre would become the exemplars to which their successors must conform if they were to win public recognition and approval. Corneille did publish his *Discours* and *Examens* in 1660; but it is to be doubted whether Molière or Racine had the time or inclination to conduct a retrospective review of their achievement. Posterity has made up for that since by never tiring of undertaking such reviews: indeed, as with Shakespeare criticism, it has become an industry. Happily, in both cases, this essentially literary and historical process has been tempered by constant revivals of their plays by actors; and this has served to offer new insights, generation by generation, into the nature and quality of the achievement, while frequent translation into other languages has continued to add others. Both processes have served to confirm the timelessness of their plays by revealing that their

Georges Dandin in 1668; and then, in 1671, came the comic *Le Bourgeois Gentilhomme* and the tragic *Psyché*, both written specifically at the King's request, the former to supply him with a vision of Turks on the stage, the latter to provide pictorial illusions of hell and dancing devils. It was in this same year that a Royal Academy of Opera was founded with Lully at its head, a move which secured for him the monopoly of presenting opera in the capital. A year later he produced his first complete opera, *Les Fêtes de l'Amour et de Bacchus*; and from then on, having found in Philippe Quinault an ideal librettist, he devoted himself primarily to this genre. In *Armide* (1686) they were to provide Glück with a model compelling enough to be still capable of adaptation to suit Viennese taste a century later. Despite composing twenty operas in fourteen years, Lully found time to help Racine by composing the music for *L'Idylle sur la Paix* (1685) before his death.

131. *A scene from* Le Malade imaginaire *as presented before Louis XIV and his court in 1674, in a theatre created in the park at Versailles. Engraving by Le Paultre. Paris, Bibliothèque Nationale.*

observations of human nature and behaviour were so accurate as to continue to be relevant as one generation of audiences followed another.

4 THEATRICAL REFORM

(a) **Actors and Acting:** The forty years spanning the first performance of Corneille's *Le Cid* in 1636 and that of Racine's most famous tragedy, *Phèdre* (1677), inevitably brought great changes in the style of presentation. The hit-or-miss improvisatory acting techniques of Molière's *Illustre Théâtre* during its provincial exile were steadily replaced on its return to Paris with more restrained and subtle skills. These were largely governed by the refinement of the dialogue, coupled with the logical progression of the arguments advanced, and the quality of the wit required by sophisticated audiences. The rivalry between Molière's own company of actors and the troupe at the Hôtel de Bourgogne served also to sharpen these skills and to give a keener edge to the mundane processes of recruiting talented players and training them to live up to, or to excel, audience expectancies. No better example of the importance of this exists than that of the respective receptions given to the simultaneous presentations of Racine's *Alexandre le Grand* in 1665 which destroyed Molière's and his mutual respect and friendship.

It is difficult for us now to understand how actors could still have been regarded as social outcasts undeserving of Christian burial: yet this stigma still applied in France to artists as highly regarded, indeed revered in Paris, as Bellerose, Montdory, Jodelet, Floridor, Montfleury, La Grange and even Molière himself—together with such actresses as Mlle Desoeillets, or Madeleine Béjart. Even the Protestant opponents of the stage in seventeenth-century England, where they had succeeded in closing all theatres between 1642 and 1660, never treated actors quite as shamefully as was the case in Catholic France: only in Catholic states of Germany and in far-off India and Japan can parallels be cited at so late a date (see also p. 57).

(b) **Stage-settings: Mahelot and Torelli:** The reforms which these actors and their companions effected in respect of acting itself were also carried into the wider aspects of actor-audience relationships by stage-settings, costumes and lighting, all of which were to a large extent dependent on the design and physical resources of the theatres in which these actors performed their plays. At the start of the seventeenth century traditional medieval methods of identifying the locality of stage-action continued to be acceptable both to the public and the court, as we know from the sketch books of Laurent Mahelot, principal stage-manager and scenic artist at the Hôtel de Bourgogne before 1636. The earliest sketches show a few 'mansions' coexisting with some use of perspective, and some attempt to integrate the former with the latter. Serious efforts to achieve integration began with the production of Cardinal Richelieu's *Mirame* in 1641; but it was not until Cardinal Mazarin (impressed by the new scenic techniques invented in Italy and already exploited in England by Inigo Jones) invited Giacomo Torelli (1608-78) to leave the Teatro Novissimo in Venice and come to Paris in 1645 to redesign and re-equip Richelieu's private theatre for him in the Palais Royal that serious attention began to be devoted to neo-classical methods of theatrical representation. Torelli's presence in Paris, coupled with the French Academy's insistence that dramatists must respect the unity of place as well as of action, ensured a rapid general extension of the principles governing both the architectural structure and the machinery needed for swift changes of scenery to other theatres: and this served, in turn, to make 'appropriateness'

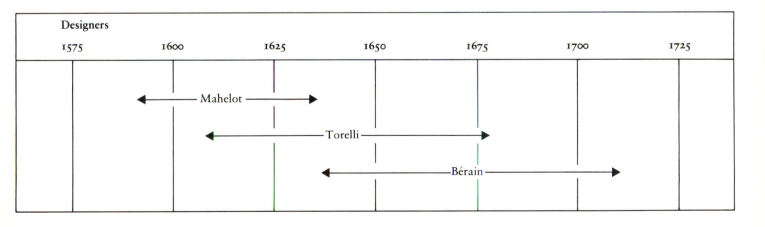

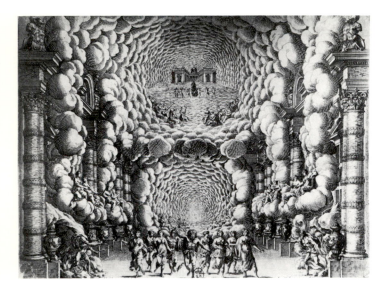

132. *One of Torelli's stage-settings for the opera-ballet* Noces de Tétis, *1654. (For the stage-machinery, see Figs. 86 and 87.) Yale University Library.*

the new yardstick for critical appraisal of both settings and costume (Figs. 127, 130 and 132).

It was Torelli who made it possible in 1650 for Corneille to oblige Cardinal Mazarin by providing him with a spectacle-opera, *Andromède*, in five acts, each with a separate set. He also assisted Molière to remodel the Petit-Bourbon for his own company in 1658/9 (see Fig. 124).

133. Naumachia *at Versailles, 7 May 1674. In this scene, Louis XIV (centre), seated beneath a canopy, watches an aquatic ballet. The palace at the end of the vista represented the enchanted Island of Alcina and vanished within a spectacular firework display at the end of the performance. (Compare Figs. 90, 91 and 107.)* Monumenta Scenica.

Moreover, it was Torelli's imaginative skills and authority that permitted Louis XIV to carry theatre out of doors just as another Italian, Cosme Lotti, had done for Philip IV of Spain, and as yet another, Giovanni Burnacini (and his son Lodovico) were doing for the Emperor Leopold I in Vienna (Fig. 133; see also Plate 13). All these artists thus came to incorporate real trees, arbours, lakes and fountains into the stage-settings for ballets and carrousels, thereby giving literal expression to the growing philosophical demand to subject nature itself to the demands of human reason and ideas of order.

5 THEORY AND CRITICISM

Even so, the triumph of French example in the theatre might not have been so assured and complete as it became throughout Europe had it not been for the timely arrival in Paris of critic and theorist Nicolas Boileau (1636–1711). Boileau at first contented himself with demolishing all earlier and contemporary writers other than the pioneers of neo-classicism; but he then proceeded to offer the world in *L'Art Poétique* (1674) a definitive treatise on what ought to be the objectives and methods of any self-respecting poet. Nature, he proclaimed, which it was the theatre's business to reflect, must be approached with the eyes of reason, stripped of all irrelevant detail and then held up to view within forms copied from classical antiquity. By 'nature' he meant human nature—not abnormally distinguished, heroic or passionate individuals, nor exceptionally foolish, depraved, or bestial persons, but rather what reason proclaims to be the norm, since reason is a constant, unvarying from one generation to the next (or from one individual to another), and the factor above all others distinguishing men from animals. In Boileau's vocabulary nature and reason are virtually inseparable, and both are used almost as synonyms for truth; and truth, to be truth, must be universal. Others had argued this case before Boileau in relation to the stage. His confirmation of it thus made it the more difficult for dramatists, designers and actors to persist with graphic localization of stage-action and the depiction of idiosyncratic, grotesque or incredible behaviour. By these criteria, deaths on stage are incredible; so are rapes, battles and journeys known to occupy days or weeks presented as being accomplished within minutes. Unnatural rhetorical speeches, extreme changes of mood or attitude in characters, and unmotivated behaviour should similarly be disallowed. So too should extraneous frivolity. In all these respects, in Boileau's view, classical literature offered the best examples—beauty distilled from truth and thus worthy of imitation.

It was a cold, hard creed, but one that had found its justification in the mature comedies and tragedies of Corneille, Molière and Racine, and one which, a little later, would extend to the operas of Lully. No one could reasonably complain therefore that what Boileau preached was impossible for dramatists and actors to practise. If Boileau's doctrine has been judged in the nineteenth century and in our own as too restrictive and inhibiting, and his scholarship dismissed as faulty, he himself lived long enough to watch French opinions regarding genre, decorum and *vraisemblance* winning international approval. Yet within two decades of his death, practising dramatists and designers, preferring to trust their own judgement of audiences' sensibilities, rebelled, as will be seen in Chapter 11 (see pp. 169–171). Before the end of the seventeenth century, however, some aspects of the critical stance articulated in Boileau's *Art Poétique* had become deeply enough implanted in French minds for them to colour the conduct of what was to be the first 'National Theatre' in Europe, Le Théâtre Français. This company, which either to distinguish itself, or to be distinguishable from the Italian players, was also known as La Comédie Française, came into being as a child of necessity. When Molière died, his company faced bankruptcy unless his theatre could remain open to his public and actors could be found to replace him in his own most notable roles.

6 THE COMÉDIE FRANÇAISE

It was the actor La Grange who, like John Hemming in England following the deaths of both William Shakespeare and Richard Burbage within three years of each other, held the company together. The first calamity to be overcome was the loss of the Palais Royal to Lully and his opera. This was met by an agreement with the company at the old Théâtre du Marais to amalgamate and to take over the playhouse in the Rue Guénégaud as a joint venture. By 1680 the company at the Hôtel de Bourgogne found itself in a similar situation when ordered by the King to hand over its playhouse to the Italian Comedians. They too met this crisis with a merger, but this time with La Grange. As a result Parisians found themselves obliged to accept a single company licensed to present plays in French in the capital. This company called itself Le Théâtre Français. Its monopoly was reinforced by the company's right to lay claim to any actors or actresses in a provincial company that it wished to recruit. Its constitution was closely mod-

elled on that inherited from the Hôtel de Bourgogne, which itself reached back to the late Middle Ages when it had been the home of the actors employed by the Confrérie de la Passion. This constitution provided for a co-operative society in which all members were guaranteed a share of the profits and, ultimately, a pension. For these advantages members were expected to abide by a strict code of discipline. After several changes of location during the first hundred years of its existence, the company settled in its present home in the Rue de Richelieu (1799). It is now officially described as Le Théâtre Français (Salle Richelieu).

No precise date can be provided for the first choice of name. All that is certain is that it had occurred some time before the Italians were banished from the capital by the King himself in 1697. Impetuous and trivial though this action may have been, it is symptomatic of a more serious disease—censorship—which is so often a corollary of autocracy, and which was rigorously used in France to stifle any public utterance thought be be critical of the monarchy or suspect to the Church. Molière had collided with it twice when presenting *Tartuffe* and *Don Juan* to the public in the 1660s. Censorship, coupled with the monopoly which the Comédie Française had acquired by the start of the eighteenth century, goes far towards explaining the decline in the quality of both comedy and tragedy written during the closing years of the Sun King's reign. Nevertheless, despite the humiliations of military defeats abroad at the hands of English and Austrian generals, and the growing discontent of an oppressed peasantry at home, when Louis XIV died in 1715 the glamour of his personal despotism and the brilliance of the cultural life at his court sufficed to dazzle and intrigue the rest of Europe from Madrid to St Petersburg, making imitation seem as reasonable as it was irresistible. In *Lectures on the History of France*, first published in 1851, Sir James Stephens observed: 'During fifty successive years Louis continued to be the greatest actor on the noblest stage, and in the presence of the most enthusiastic audience in the world' (vol. II, p. 433). This metaphor is more than apt, since never before or after has the theatre's normal role of reflecting contemporary life been so nearly reversed as it was in seventeenth-century France where it was elevated to provide the standards of conduct by which life itself should be both lived and judged. Indeed, it is hard at times, judging by contemporary descriptions, to distinguish which was the more theatrical, court life at Versailles or the plays presented at the Théâtre du Marais and the Hôtel de Bourgogne.

PART IV

Expanding Frontiers

Introduction

Despite the ebb and flow of sectarian religious controversy, frequently pressed to the extremities of civil war during the sixteenth and seventeenth centuries, only a tiny minority of Europeans then doubted the existence of God.

In the theatre, stage censorship and strict control of playhouses and players (operated in Roman Catholic countries largely by the Church and in Protestant ones wholly by the State) ensured that such doubts, where they existed, should not be publicly expressed on the stage. Nevertheless, during these same two centuries Renaissance preoccupation with man's individuality and freedom of action had informed tragedy, comedy and the new arts of opera and ballet to such an extent that it had effectively removed God from the centre-stage position He had occupied in all European theatres of the Middle Ages to a less conspicuous position back stage—except, that is, in Spain.

During the eighteenth and nineteenth centuries, however, while the gods and goddesses of Greek and Roman mythology were ever more frequently to be observed at play on the stages of all well-regulated court theatres (distinguishable by their emblematic costumes), the Pantocrator of the Christian universe was distanced there, and in the public playhouses patronized by bankers, merchants and well-to-do tradesmen and their families, to a point where His mysterious ways could only be recognized in the rewards meted out to virtuous characters in plays and in the punishments that overtook the wicked.

The Renaissance idea that dramatic entertainment should be the prerogative of princes, extended by *their* grace and favour to others residing near their courts who could afford to pay for admission, also came under attack. Until the end of the eighteenth century this attack was confined to the form and content of plays and to the size and number of playhouses in which they could be seen; but even this was sufficient, given the rapid growth of cities and in the wealth and power exercised by the new class of mer-

chant princes who resided in them, to oblige theatre managers, and the dramatists and actors who worked for them, to make radical changes in their repertoires.

A cardinal assumption in this changed world of the new-rich burgher princes of the Protestant North was that man was born naturally good and could thrive on earth by recourse to his own wits and industry. If he did not, then that was unfortunate but the price to be paid for idleness, willful disobedience or both : it was among God's functions to make the difference clear in the rewards accorded to men and women during their earthly lives. In the theatre, therefore, dramatists were required to show that virtue was properly rewarded and vice duly punished. Questions of dramatic genre, decorum and verisimilitude had accordingly to be revised to fit, or to be relegated to the outer circumferences of a dramatist's priorities.

This romantic, or 'sentimental', view of life was diametrically opposed to the more pessimistic and reflective outlook of European courts and their attendant academicians. There, tragedy had been required to express a combination of destiny—or fate—and the consequences of uncontrolled passion, and comedy had been regarded as a means of exposing fools and folly and of rewarding both with ridicule. Within this strictly rational and objective theatrical code, few concessions, if any, could be made to pathos, whether in terms of lovers' emotions, hardship and distress or other mitigating circumstances.

In the course of the eighteenth century, however, first in England and her North American colonies, and then in continental Europe, merchant princes in major trading cities acquired the financial power to enforce a more flexible and romantic approach to dramatic composition and performance which reflected their own more pragmatic approach to life. Managers quickly took note; and, in so far as royal monopolies and government censorship permitted, radically reformed their repertoires; actors likewise adopted a more 'natural' approach to their art. It is the progress of this revolt that informs Chapter 11, starting with the Glorious Revolution of 1688 in England (itself modelled on Dutch example) and culminating in the movement known as *Sturm und Drang* (Storm and Stress) in Germany, in the American War of Independence and in the French Revolution of 1789.

Chapter 12 examines the extension of this revolt, following these events, to include the recreational interests and demands of manual labourers—neglected by the theatre for nearly three hundred years—who by then were flooding into manufacturing towns and cities to service the industrial revolution. In the theatre, this involved not only

the collapse of traditional managerial monopolies derived from the authority of princes, but also the radical revision of many irksome restrictions placed by the Church and the court on the repertoires of acting companies and over the mobility of actors, especially in the provinces. All of these changes were accompanied by a rapid extension of entertainment of a dramatic character, previously held to be illegitimate, including circuses, song, dance, the slap-stick comic sketches of the fairs and taverns and, above all, the spectacle of melodrama embellished with all the realistic devices with which the new technology of the princes of industry in this new era of liberty, fraternity and equality could endow it.

11

Merchant Princes and the Theatre of the Eighteenth Century

1 REPUBLICAN HOLLAND

Late in the seventeenth century the smallest of Europe's Protestant States, Holland, emerged like a young David to challenge the Goliath of French imperial ambition. Founded as a federation of tiny republics liberated from the tyranny of Catholic Spain in 1581, this democratic union of prosperous burghers, farmers and seafarers under the leadership of the house of Orange provided in its cities (most notably in Amsterdam) homes for free-thinking refugees from war and persecution.

This new society, dominated by an urban middle class, had the courage to allow the known will of its own people to take precedence over the more remote and questionable will of God. In doing so, it created in the course of the seventeenth century a world where tolerance and tranquillity could be taken for granted by every citizen. Jews lived side by side with Christians; French Huguenots with German Lutherans; Italian bankers with English merchants. Irrefutable signs of this remarkable achievement leap forcefully from the paintings of Frans Hals, Pieter de Hooch, Vermeer and Rembrandt. Life as depicted there was neither luxurious nor ostentatious; but it was comfortable, leisured and harmonious (Fig. 134).

Within this new culture the theatre steadily absorbed the pragmatic philosophy of corporate responsibility in government. This the Dutch substituted in their drama for the authoritarian doctrines which, elsewhere in Europe, kings and princes employed actors and designers to promote. In the first place there was no court theatre. The Dutch simply adapted their own lively theatrical traditions, pioneered in the sixteenth century both by the popular touring comedians and by the more intellectually disposed chambers of rhetoric, to meet their own needs. The former

had established themselves in country districts during the sixteenth century, as may be seen in several paintings by the Bruegels and by Hieronymus Bosch (Figs. 77 and 135). The latter (organized like guilds) existed in every town and took responsibility for the celebration of all civic festivals. For them, the art of rhetoric (or public oratory) was of supreme importance since it was regarded as a powerful instrument of persuasion in society, and allowed topical issues—whether religious, political or social—to be discussed objectively in a public forum. The repertoire of the chambers included morality plays and poetical disputations, which were frequently conducted on a competitive basis. Both could be farcical, serious, even tragic, and were always illustrated by elaborate tableaux of an emblematic

---

134. Rembrandt van Rijn, The Sampling-Officials of the Cloth-Makers' Guild. *Oil. 1662. Amsterdam, Rijksmuseum.*

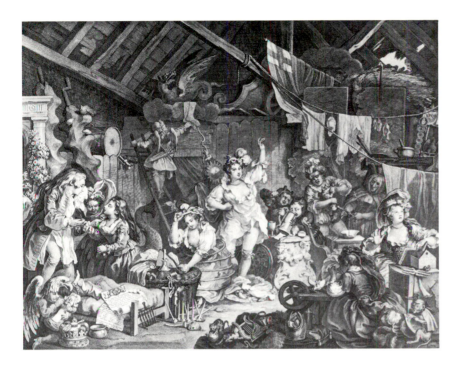

135. *'Barn Stormers' in Holland, 1635. In this makeshift dressing-room, the juvenile lead (left) talks to an actress dressed as a mermaid. Behind her are the waves on their rollers (see Figs. 88 and 146). The leading lady (right) rehearses her lines while a hole in her stocking is stitched up. Cupid climbs a ladder to retrieve a pair of stockings, while a dancer rehearses a routine. Engraving. London, Victoria and Albert Museum.*

character—the persons, settings and costumes being symbolic or allegorical rather than representational (Fig. 136).

It was on these firm popular foundations that full-length plays following English and French models were built during the early years of the seventeenth century. The establishment of a Dutch Academy in Amsterdam in 1617 gave further impetus to these literary and dramatic developments and led directly to the building of a permanent theatre. This was called the Schouburg. Designed by Jacob van Campen, it opened its doors to the public in 1638 with a performance of Joost van den Vondel's *Gysbrecht* (Fig. 137).

The theatre itself represented a compromise between the traditional scenic arrangements of the chambers of rhetoric and the novel picture-stages created by Palladio and Scamozzi in Italy and by Inigo Jones in England (see Figs. 80, 81, 100, 101a, b). By 1665, however, this theatre had been remodelled to contain changeable scenery: it re-

136. *A typical street theatre erected by the Chambers of Rhetoric in the Low Countries during the sixteenth and seventeenth centuries. This contemporary engraving shows one prepared by the Antwerp Chambers to welcome Francis, Duke of Brabant, in 1582. On the main stage, Abraham's sacrifice of Isaac; in the prison below, a fury or a devil. (Compare Figs. 103 and 137.) London, Victoria and Albert Museum: Oskar Fischell Collection.*

LE LIEU DE LA COMMEDIE.
DE SCHOUBURGH van binnen
op 't Tooneel aen te sien.

137. The stage of Jacob van Campen's Schouburg Theatre, Amsterdam, opened in 1638. The frons scenae, while bearing some resemblance to that of the Teatro Olimpico in Vicenza of 1585 (see Fig. 80), retains many of the characteristics of the settings for the Passion Play at Valenciennes of 1547 (see Fig. 65). The fore-stage with its proscenium and doors and barred windows above can clearly be cut off from the rear portion of the setting by the striped curtain suspended from a wire. Engraving by S. Sarry. University of Bristol Theatre Collection.

opened with Jan Vos's *Medea*. The auditorium, significantly, remained structured by the price paid for a seat.

2 RESTORATION ENGLAND

(a) **A Fresh Start:** With the restoration of the monarchy in England in 1660, a court which in exile had resided for more than a decade in Paris attempted on its return to London to re-establish its former control over theatres, actors and plays. As before the Civil War and Com-

monwealth, the Revels Office under the Lord Chamberlain again became the principal instrument for enforcing it.

Charles II authorized two dramatists, Thomas Killigrew and Sir William D'Avenant, to form acting companies to serve, respectively, himself and his brother James, Duke of York. D'Avenant established his company (The Duke's Men) first in Lincoln's Inn Fields and later in a sumptuous new playhouse in Dorset Gardens (1671) designed by Christopher Wren. (This theatre lasted until 1731 when the company moved to a new one, again especially built for it, in Covent Garden.) Killigrew established his company (The King's Men) first in Vere Street, then Bridge Street and finally, in 1663, in Drury Lane. Although housed some distance away from Whitehall Palace, both playhouses were designed to cater for a small audience of leisured courtiers, and not for the public at large. Once securely housed, and protected by royal charters, these two companies exercised as tight a monopoly as that prevailing in Louis XIV's Paris. In 1682 they merged to become a single company, an arrangement which lasted until 1695, when they again went their separate ways.

As in France, the first theatres of the Restoration era were small, built in the Italian style to incorporate machinery for changing scenes and adequate space for musicians, and with a seating plan designed to reflect the social priorities of the court. Unlike continental playhouses, however, they retained a large apron-style stage, and flanked this with doors cut into the proscenium-arch. French influence extended to include the employment of actresses in female roles, since no boys had been trained in the intervening years to be capable of playing them well (see Fig. 138). Dramatists likewise found themselves obliged to choose between traditional English Jacobean principles of play-construction and those dictated by the French Academy. Fashion insisted that the more orderly and polite French models should be preferred—at least in theory. But building a repertoire of scripts takes time, and in practice the acting companies found themselves forced to rely heavily on revivals of English plays written before the Civil War; in consequence, the staging of such revivals persuaded audiences that yesterday's models still possessed enough vitality to commend them. Retention of proscenium doors in English playhouses, moreover, provided English dramatists with the means to achieve comic chases and surprises of a visual kind not available to continental playwrights (Figs. 158 and 182). The nature of the theoretical argument that ensued is brilliantly expounded by John Dryden (1631–1700) in his *Essay of Dramatick Poesie* (1668), which he cast in dialogue form as a neo-Socratic debate. Slowly a compromise evolved which, while in many respects 'incorrect' if judged by the standards set by Boileau in his *Art Poétique*, at least satisfied the court and its entourage—the only audience— that it was an accurate reflection of its own beliefs, tastes and manners.

(b) Caroline Court Drama: The principal effect of this compromise was to impress upon audiences the idea that plays exist to present arguments and not to tell stories. Expressed in Tudor or even Jacobean terms, this meant preferring the form of the morality play to that of miracle cycles, saints' plays and chronicles (all of which were built on romantic or epic narrative) and adapting its theatrical components to conform to neo-classical precepts and contemporary manners. What this shift of emphasis implied, however, was that henceforth the words 'tragedy' and 'comedy', when used to describe dramatic genre, should be confined respectively to 'serious' and to 'witty' arguments: 'tragi-comedy' should be removed to the lyric theatre now called 'opera'.

Tragedy was to involve persons of high rank placed in extreme situations and faced with agonizing emotional choices. Low-life characters and comic incident were to be shunned unless their inclusion served to throw the argument into higher relief. With civil war and exile all-too-recent facts of life—brother against sister, lover and beloved in opposing camps, death as the alternative to treachery—conflict between love and honour, between self-sacrifice and betrayal, or between patriotism and cowardice became favoured subjects, more especially when distanced to some far-off, exotic land such as India or Mexico, since this offered opportunities for designers and composers to supply glamorous settings, costumes and music to delight both eye and ear (Fig. 138). Written in rhymed couplets—an English answer to French Alexandrines—these 'heroic' tragedies—D'Avenant's *The*

---

138. *One of England's first actresses: Mrs Bracegirdle as Semerina in one of the earliest plays to be written by a woman, Mrs Aphra Behn's* The Widow Ranter, *which was first performed at Drury Lane Theatre, November 1688. Engraving by M. Vincent from a painting by J. Smith. London, British Museum.*

139. David Garrick as Jaffier and Mrs Cibber as Belvidera in Thomas Otway's Venice Preserv'd. *Oil painting by John Zoffany, c.1760. London, The Garrick Club.*

Siege of Rhodes (1656); Dryden's *The Conquest of Granada* (1669/70) and *Aureng Zebe* (1675)—were at first well received. The artificiality of the form, however, together with a marked straining after effect, served quickly to expose both the sentiments of the characters and the language in which they were expressed as pretentious and absurd. Ridiculed in *The Rehearsal* by George Villiers, Duke of Buckingham, on the stage of Drury Lane in 1671, the genre died a swift and natural death. Only John Milton's *Samson Agonistes* (1671), John Dryden's *All for Love* (1678) and Thomas Otway's *Venice Preserv'd* (1681) stand out as achievements which later actors and directors have considered worthy of occasional revival (Fig. 139).

Comedy fared better. Its arguments were to be confined to the sentiments of 'people of quality' and to reflecting their humours, manners and intrigues. Verbal wit was to be used to expose their follies, but more especially to satirize the morality of the despised bourgeois merchant class (not least those who had condoned regicide). Another target was the tedium and boorishness of country life. These sentiments are faithfully mirrored in such play titles as Sir George Etheredge's *The Man of Mode* (1676), William Wycherley's *The Country Wife* (1674/5), Mrs Aphra Behn's *The Rover: or the Banished Cavalier* (1677) and William Congreve's *The Way of the World* (1700). Wealthy merchants and their families, however, began to protest at

the constant railing in such plays against the industrious pursuit of wealth and social status and at the no less constant pursuit by the principal characters of marital infidelity and gambling. At their best, writers of comedy brought a cold, bright intellect ruthlessly to bear upon the conduct of their own society, in a style copied in part from contemporary French examples and in part from earlier English plays by Jonson, Fletcher and Shirley. As Swinburne observed:

> In Congreve all is plain and clear if hard and limited; he makes no effort to escape into the region of moral sentiment; if his world is not healthy neither is it hollow; and whatever he had of noble humour and feeling was genuine and accurate vigour, and his verbal wit the most brilliant and forcible in English literature.

(c) The Glorious Revolution: Sentiment versus Satire: Nevertheless, the fact that Congreve's wit and that of all other writers under Charles II and James II should have given such deep and constant offence to middle-class city dwellers provoked so strong a reaction both against the theatre and against court manners that after the Glorious Revolution of 1688, which brought the Dutch William of Orange, following the abdication of the Roman Catholic James II, to the throne without another war, managers and actors became obliged to reconsider the relationship between their repertoires and their box-office receipts.

It was the actor-manager-playwright Colley Cibber (1671–1757) who first recognized this change of moral climate and took practical steps to woo the patronage of the rich burghers, into whose hands, with Dutch (and later Hanoverian) help, political power was rapidly passing. This became evident in his first play, *Love's Last Shift* (1696), which was presented at Drury Lane two years before Jeremy Collier published his notorious *Short View of the Immorality and Profaneness of the English Stage*. Acting as self-appointed spokesman for non-conformist bourgeois opinion, Collier attacked in the six chapters of this pamphlet what he claimed to be the 'Exaltation of Vice and the mockery of Virtue' on the stage, immodesty of character and incident, profanity of language and abuse of the clergy. Ill-considered and inaccurate as some of his arguments were, this pamphlet and its retaliatory sequels had disproportionately wide-ranging and long-lasting consequences for the English theatre.

The most serious of these was the revival of that deep-seated distrust of plays and players which had led to the closing of the playhouses in 1642. This hostility was destined to infiltrate not only every nonconformist religious institution—Quakers, Baptists, and later on the Methodists—but also academic life at every level, and to cause the theatre to be regarded by half the population throughout the eighteenth and nineteenth centuries as at best frivolous and at worst subversive, and thus to be shunned if it could not be banned.

The theatre itself, however, responded to the pamphlet-war with only minor changes initially; yet these involved further departures from the French neo-classical doctrine relating to decorum and verisimilitude as well as modest concessions towards bourgeois sensibility. By 1722, when Sir Richard Steele (1672–1729) (Joseph Addison's school-friend and partner in the founding of the *Tatler* and the *Spectator*) gave Cibber his play *The Conscious Lovers* (a reworking of Terence's *Andria*, now set in Hanoverian London) for production at Drury Lane, these changes had assumed proportions that amounted to a complete reversal of Restoration moral values. No matter how far credulity had to be stretched in the auditorium, on the stage virtue *must* triumph and be appropriately rewarded: vice, by the same token, must not go unpunished. Characters were no longer to swear. Accidents—for example letters which miscarry, long-lost relatives unexpectedly returning from foreign parts, industrious but indigent sons or daughters rewarded with a fortune overnight by the timely discovery of a missing will—came back to the stage, together with repentance, tears and forgiveness, as essential mechanisms to resolve tangled plots in need of a happy ending. Pathos also recovered legitimacy in comedy. Indeed, at times it becomes difficult to distinguish a play from a sermon or a tract—a notable case in point being Mrs Centlivre's *The Gamester* (1705), which aimed to reform addicts to London's gaming tables as much as to entertain the public. (This is not to be confused with Edward Moore's bourgeois tragedy of the same name produced, with a prologue by Garrick, in 1753.)

Ten years after the astonishing success of Steele's *The Conscious Lovers*, George Lillo (1693–1739) won public acclaim for bourgeois tragedy with *The London Merchant* (better known, perhaps, as *George Barnwell*) which was first produced at Drury Lane in 1731. By elevating a virtuous but weak-willed London apprentice to the title role, and by proceeding to tell a tale of crime and punishment ending with Barnwell's execution, Lillo did no more than return to plays like the anonymous *Arden of Faversham*, or Thomas Heywood's *A Woman Killed with Kindness*, from the mainstream of Elizabethan and Jacobean domestic, or homiletic, tragedy; yet in another respect he deliberately flouted prevailing neo-classical theory. Seduced by a *femme fatale*, young George (otherwise a pattern of moral rectitude) succumbs to avarice which leads him to rob his employer (whose daughter he might have married) and to murder his uncle; both he and his seductress are discovered, tried and hanged. The play's instant success prompted Lillo to follow it up with another in the same vein, *The Fatal Curiosity* (1736), this time set in Cornwall. Although a relatively unimportant dramatist himself, Lillo's influence through these two plays on the future development of the theatre in both France and Germany was as disproportionately great as it is astonishing to us.

Just as influential, if less flamboyantly so, was another minor dramatist of the time, Nicholas Rowe (1674–1718), who in deciding to edit Shakespeare's plays paved the way for another counter-attack on the supremacy of French dramatic theory throughout continental Europe. Effectively he reversed the Restoration belief that if Shakespeare was to be tolerated on the stage in polite society, his plays must either be transferred to the opera house (where fantasy was allowable), or else rewritten. Rowe tried to restore the original texts. He published his edition in 1709, printed in six volumes. He equipped each with an engraved frontispiece of characters in a stage-setting, and divided the text of each play into acts and scenes, all of which were supplied with stage-directions. Most of these were Rowe's, but they came to be regarded as Shakespeare's own. Many of them have continued to be thus used by some editors until recently. What Rowe began, Pope, Dr Johnson, Stevens and Malone completed by the end of the eighteenth century. Thus when Voltaire came to England in 1726, he was able to acquire Rowe's edition; and by the time that Garrick embarked on his two-year tour of the Continent in 1763 (appearing in scenes from many of his most famous Shakespearean roles), his admirers could obtain one of several reputable editions of all the plays to study and to translate at their leisure.

Despite the warm response accorded by the wealthy middle class to the romantic and morally reformative plays of Cibber and his followers, the school of satirists which survived from the Restoration era was by no means destroyed by Collier's attack. Congreve, assisted by the architect and dramatist Sir John Vanbrugh (1664–1726), retaliated in kind both with pamphlets and by writing *The Way of the World* (1700). (Vanbrugh is principally remembered as the architect of Blenheim Palace; but three of his plays—*The Relapse* (1696), *The Provoked Wife* (1697) and *The Confederacy* (1705)—have been frequently revived.) The retaliation of Congreve and Vanbrugh was supported by the young Irish playwright George Farquhar (1678–1707), whose two best plays, *The Recruiting Officer* and *The Beaux' Stratagem*, were presented at Drury Lane shortly before his death; they reveal, in the good humour which tempers the mockery of his verbal wit, a gentler attitude to human frailty and a warmer appreciation of provincial life than is evident in earlier comedy.

Even so, a rapidly changing political and social scene such as that which marks the reigns of Queen Anne (1702–14) and George I (1714–27) brought with it other targets for satirists' pens; and among those who sought fame and fortune by this means in the theatre were John Gay (1685–1732) and Henry Fielding (1707–54). The shift from monarchical rule to government by cabinet and parliament brought with it its own abuses, most obviously in the bribery and corruption which accompanied elections and which also prevailed in the lawcourts and prisons, as well as in the sleepy cloisters of the established Church and universities. In choosing to expose corruption, therefore, Gay and Fielding could scarcely avoid creating powerful enemies. It was one thing within this apparently harmonious and complacent society to lampoon the absurdities of the fashionable craze for Italian opera (notwithstanding the arrival in England of George Frideric Handel in 1710), or to ridicule fustian imitations of Shakespeare and Racine, or even to suggest that priests and physicians could be hypocrites and charlatans; it was quite another to lampoon the Whig aristocracy, the Prime Minis-

ter and even the German King—a lesson that Gay and Fielding would soon learn to their cost.

London's shortage of playhouses adequate to serve the needs of a rapidly increasing leisured population had led to the establishment of several new ones, built and opened without royal licence. Two of these were opened in the Haymarket, one for Italian opera in 1705 and the other for plays in 1720; a third opened in Goodman's Fields in Whitechapel in 1729. All three were tolerated by the government on the understanding that if ever what was presented in them should give serious offence, they could immediately be closed; and very great offence is exactly what Gay's ballad operas and Fielding's burlesques supplied. Their popularity with the public only served to make them seem more dangerous.

(d) The Licensing Act of 1737 and its Consequences: The *Beggar's Opera* started its career in Lincoln's Inn Fields in 1728. Two years later Fielding imitated its burlesque treatment of Italian opera in *Tom Thumb* and *The Author's Farce* in order to attack the pretensions of the managers of the licensed theatres, their leading actors and the unreality of 'sentimental' drama (Fig. 140). He followed these two plays in 1731 with his first foray into political

---

140. *Lucy Lockett and Polly Peachum plead in prison for Captain MacHeath in John Gay's* The Beggar's Opera, *as first staged by John Rich at Lincoln's Inn Fields, 1728 (see Fig. 192). Oil painting by William Hogarth. Private collection.*

141. *English strolling players performing* Hamlet *before the Squire, his wife and their servants, 1772. The raised stage and painted backcloth show little advance on the booth stages of sixteenth-century fairgrounds (see Figs. 77 and 135). Engraving by Robert Saint George Mamoh. London, Victoria and Albert Museum.*

satire, *The Welsh Opera*, which was later revised and retitled *The Grub Street Opera*. The topicality, refreshing realism and irreverence of all these pieces quickly won them a *succès de scandale* among an admiring public and opened up a rich vein for adventurous (or greedy) managers to exploit. Thus encouraged, Fielding acquired the lease of the Little Theatre in the Haymarket and, with his judgement clouded by his early success, advanced further into this political minefield, first with *Pasquin* (1736) and then with *The Historical Register for 1736*. These proved too much for the Prime Minister, Sir Robert Walpole, and his cabinet, who promptly ordered Parliament to equip the Lord Chamberlain with statutory powers to ban all acting and all plays other than those expressly authorized by his office.

This Licensing Act of 1737 had far-reaching repercussions. Not only was it applied to London theatres, but it was used to meet the swelling tide of official opposition in the provinces to the activities of companies of strolling players, who had by then become numerous and successful enough to have started to acquire theatres of their own, again built and opened without a licence. This was already true in Bath, Bristol, Ipswich and York. The new act required these to be closed and gave magistrates power to imprison and fine any offender.

A reading of Euripides' *The Bacchae* might have warned Walpole and his colleagues that although this legislative action might scotch the snake, it would not kill it (see pp. 36–7 and Fig. 141). In the event, more than a hundred years would elapse before this act was replaced by the more liberal Victorian Licensing Laws of 1843, but by then the provinces at least had won their case and had secured royal charters for the building of theatres royal wherever a genuine demand could be proved to exist (see p. 195).

More enduring was the damage done to the nature and quality of subsequent dramatic literature. Fielding quit the theatre. Gay had died before the Licensing Act was on the Statute Book; only Oliver Goldsmith and Richard Brinsley Sheridan, with less than ten plays between them, kept the banner of satiric as opposed to sentimental comedy flying during the rest of the eighteenth century. Goldsmith's *She Stoops to Conquer* (1773) is particularly notable in this respect since it borrows all the techniques of sentimental comedy only to turn them inside out, a device that befitted the author of a brilliant essay on 'Laughing and Sentimental Comedy'. Sheridan's plays all received their first performance between 1775 and 1780 (Fig. 142). A full century thus separates the production of *The Rivals*, *The School for Scandal* and *The Critic* from the return of effective satire

142. *The screen scene from R. B. Sheridan's* The School for Scandal *as presented at Drury Lane Theatre, 1777. Left to right: Mr King as Sir Peter Teazle, Mrs Abington as Lady Teazle, Mr Smith as Charles Surface, and Mr Palmer as Joseph Surface. Oil painting by James Roberts. London, The Garrick Club.*

to the London stage in the comedies of Oscar Wilde. If posterity can thank Walpole for obliging Fielding to turn his talents to the writing of novels it can also lay at his door the responsibility for that rapid decline in the literary quality of English drama which was only finally rescued from near total eclipse by Tom Robertson, W. S. Gilbert and Bernard Shaw during the latter half of the nineteenth century.

With Lillo's death in 1739, tragedy sank with all hands. What saved the English theatre from collapse during the latter half of the eighteenth century was its actors and actresses, led by Charles Macklin and David Garrick. Macklin was Irish by birth and regarded as little better than a wild strolling player until, at the age of forty, he startled and delighted audiences at Drury Lane by restoring tragic dignity to the role of Shylock in *The Merchant of Venice* in 1741, thus starting the wholesale reform of English acting (especially in Shakespeare) which Fielding had demanded and Garrick completed (see pp. 170–171). Both of these actors won as much acclaim abroad for the naturalness of their delivery and deportment as they did at home, and not only on the European continent (most notably in France and Germany) but also across the Atlantic Ocean.

3 THE THEATRE IN THE NORTH AMERICAN COLONIES

Many actors, finding themselves forced to abandon their habitual provincial circuits as a result of the Licensing Act of 1737, took courage from the prospects which the West Indian and North American colonies offered to anyone willing to bring a repertoire of English plays to present to English-speaking audiences. A primitive playhouse had been established in Williamsburg, Virginia, as early as 1716, and another at Charleston, South Carolina, in 1736. By the middle of the century the bravery and industry of the early pioneers had been rewarded with the establishment of a number of towns along the whole eastern seaboard, each wealthy enough to sustain a leisured minority anxious, despite the denunciations of Puritan preachers, to proclaim their ability to support a stable cultural life. It was to these communities (which by 1750 included Philadelphia and New York) that Lewis Hallam Senior, his wife, three children and seven other actors brought the professional experience they had acquired in his father William's unlicensed theatre at Sadlers Wells, in London's northern suburbs. They brought a repertoire of plays by Shakespeare, Rowe, Steele and Garrick, together with the necessary resolve and guile, to create a touring circuit of the kind familiar in the English provinces. The company

chose *The Merchant of Venice* to open their first season at Williamsburg on 5 September 1751. A year later Steele's *The Conscious Lovers* was selected to open the new playhouse in Nassau Street, New York. During the rest of this decade the French lost to the English all their colonial possessions to the west and north of the eastern seaboard in Ohio and Canada, an event that was to determine the future of the theatre in North America by making English the lingua franca of the subsequent United States.

When Hallam died, his widow married the leader of another company, resident in Jamaica, David Douglass, and her son Lewis took over the leading juvenile roles. Together they returned to the mainland determined to consolidate their earlier successes and then press on northwards into New England. The first part of this plan was rewarded with profits large enough to permit capital investment in new playhouses. First came the South Street Theatre (or Southwark) in Philadelphia in 1766; this was followed a year later by the John Street Theatre in New York, with an auditorium equipped with a pit encircled by boxes and a gallery, and a stage with proscenium doors in the manner of Georgian provincial playhouses in England. However, the company's resolve to repeat these successes in Boston and Providence, Rhode Island, met with determined opposition, and ultimately their hopes proved abortive. This failure was due as much to growing anti-British feeling at the time as to the more deep-rooted, nonconformist opposition to plays and players in the New England colonies. Prudence thus suggested retreat to the friendly South where, shortly before the outbreak of the War of Independence in 1775, they adopted the new name of The American Company.

This simple change of name was as shrewd as it was expedient; for it enabled the company, after riding out the storm of the war years back in Jamaica, to return to its old circuit in 1784 as an acceptably indigenous professional company. It thus soon recovered its former popularity and within three years was secure enough to be able to present the first successful play written by an American for an American audience, Royall Tyler's *The Contrast*, which was subsequently printed in Philadelphia in 1790 (Fig. 143).

4 THE FRENCH CONNECTION

(a) **Refugees**: Meanwhile, back in England, in the aftermath of a bloodless revolution which had brought first a Dutch and then a German king to the throne with powers controlled by Parliament, English social and cultural life was attracting as much attention from continental philosophers, scientists, artists and craftsmen as it was from their

Plate 9. Entry of the Knight-Challengers and Knight-Defenders accompanied by their Esquires, Heralds and Trumpeters into the Lists at the start of a Tournament, with the ladies supporting them respectively segregated into private boxes at either end. The Judges and their Marshal stand in the central scaffold while a King-at-Arms (centre) acts as umpire in the Lists below. French, fifteenth century. From Le Livre des Tournois du Roi René. *Paris, Bibliothèque Nationale.*

Plate 10. Night festivities in honour of Christina of Sweden in the courtyard of the Barberini Palace, Rome. Oil painting by F. Lauro and F. Gagliardi. 1656. Rome, Museo di Roma

Plate 11. Costume design by Inigo
Jones for a Daughter of Niger in The
Masque of Blackness by Ben Jonson,
with costumes and settings by Inigo
Jones, presented by the Queen to James
I, 1604/5. Chatsworth, Devonshire
Collections.

Plate 12. Commedia dell'Arte *in France in the mid-seventeenth century. A Serlian comic setting in sharply receding perspective including virtually all the important* commedia *characters: the Braggart Captain (see Figs. 30 and 122), Harlequin, the Doctor, Brighella, Pantalone and Pulchinella. Molière himself is at the extreme left. Paris, Musée Carnavalet.*

Plate 13. *Costume designs by L. O. Burnacini (1636-1707) for a grotesque ballet performed at the end of an opera. Burnacini was the principal designer at the court theatre of the Emperor Leopold I of Austria. Grotesque ballets have something in common with English anti-masques and the* commedia dell'arte, *and also anticipate, to some extent, eighteenth-century* opera buffa. Monumenta Scenica.

Plate 14. This poster (London, 1885) illustrates vividly the shift of emphasis from verbal to visual techniques of stage narrative and plot construction developed by writers of melodrama during the first half of the nineteenth century. University of Bristol Theatre Collection.

Plate 15. Costume design by Leon Bakst for Diaghilev's Ballets Russes. *Private collection.*

Plate 16. Nathalie Goncharova's backcloth for the ballet Tirana, 1920. Private collection.

THE

CONTRAST,

A

COMEDY;

IN FIVE ACTS:

WRITTEN BY A

CITIZEN of the *UNITED STATES;*

Performed with Applause at the Theatres in NEW-YORK,
PHILADELPHIA, and MARYLAND;

AND PUBLISHED *(under an Affignment of the Copy-Right)* BY

THOMAS WIGNELL.

Primus ego in patriam
Aonio———deduxi vertice Mufas.
                                          VIRGIL.
      (Imitated.)

Firft on our fhores I try THALIA's powers,
And bid the *laughing, ufeful* Maid be ours,

PHILADELPHIA:

FROM THE PRESS OF *PRICHARD & HALL,* IN MARKET STREET,
BETWEEN SECOND AND FRONT STREETS.

M. DEC. XC.

143. Title-page of the first edition of Royall Tyler's The Contrast,
published in Philadelphia, 1790.

American counterparts. The first arrivals had been the French Protestant refugees who, following the revocation of the Edict of Nantes in 1685, had settled in London and had there established a colony of their own. Many of its members met regularly at the Rainbow Tavern in Marylebone, where they discussed English institutions and busied themselves with translating journals and in trying to create similar centres for the propagation of English ideas in France itself. By 1724 these initiatives had resulted in the founding of the Club de l'Entresol in Paris, which survived unmolested by government officials for seven years. When it was finally shut down, its members took its ideals to an ever-widening number of coffee-houses and salons where the exchange of ideas in general conversation avoided the rigorously enforced official censorship of books and plays.

At first French interest in things English was centred on that combination of political stability and freedom of thought, whose uniqueness appealed so strongly to the wealthy yet despised professional classes on the Continent. Their ranks included those merchant adventurers who, in partnership with army and naval officers, had begun to build colonial empires overseas just as the English were doing. Gradually this interest began to extend beyond religion, politics and trade into cultural life, bringing to London many continental artists including Handel, Johann Christoph Bach (the cousin of Johann Sebastian), Gluck, Philippe Destouches, Voltaire, the Danish playwright Holberg, and Hayden.

Destouches (1680–1754) had started to write comedies imitative of Molière before being sent as a diplomat to London in 1716. There he became acquainted with Shakespeare's plays and the new vogue for 'sentimentalism' in the English theatre. Six years later, having acquired an English wife, he returned to France to resume writing for the stage and to give Parisians their first taste of moralistic, romantic comedy. The most contentious of his plays, *Le Glorieux*, in which he went so far as to contrast the aspirations of the middle-class *habitués* of the Club Entresol and other coffee-houses with those of the impoverished and discredited nobility, was produced in 1732 shortly after the suppression of the club.

(b) **Voltaire:** Voltaire (1694–1778), who had written his first tragedy, *Oedipe*, in 1718, found himself imprisoned for a second time for alleged outspokenness in 1726, and was banished on his release. Arriving in London as a refugee, he stayed for three years, acquiring a glittering circle of friends in high places, many of whom reciprocated this friendship by frequenting French coffee-houses and salons when visiting Paris. These visitors included Burke, Lord Chesterfield, Gibbon, Garrick and Hume.

On his return to France Voltaire published his highly influential *Lettres Anglaises*, or *Lettres philosophiques*, which served both to satisfy and to extend his countrymen's curiosity about English institutions and manners. As Montesquieu remarked on return from his three-year visit in 1731, 'l'Angleterre est à présent le plus libre pays qui soit au monde'. While resident in London Voltaire had made

a superficial study of Shakespeare and had become a frequent visitor to the theatres at a time when Steele, Gay and
Fielding were its most celebrated and controversial playwrights. By the time he left, English actors and audiences
had persuaded him that dramatic art should be regarded
as primarily a vehicle for the propagation of moral and
philosophical ideas. Two plays written on his return to
France, *La Mort de César* and *Zaïre* (1732), reveal an
indebtedness to Shakespeare, with *Julius Caesar* and
Othello respectively providing the principal inspiration.
While still convinced of the validity of French neo-classical
forms, he conceded to English example the need for spectacle as an accompaniment to tragedy; this he provided in
many of his subsequent plays by setting the action in exotic
Eastern or South American countries, by supplying crowd
scenes, and by enriching them with authenticity through
the detail of local colour. *Alzire* (1736), *Mahomet* (1741),
Sémiramis (1748) and *L'Orphelin de la Chine* (1755) all
offer striking tableaux of foreign figures dressed in picturesque national costume set in unfamiliar landscapes
(Fig. 144). This interest in countries of North Africa and
in the Middle and Far East grew steadily for playgoers who
by then were becoming aware of the riches brought back
to France by their own early colonists.

It was thus through Destouches and Voltaire that the
English theatre began to repay to France some of the debt
incurred during the Restoration era by Dryden, Shadwell,
Cibber, Addison and others through their extensive use of
plays by Molière and Racine and of Boileau's *Art Poétique*.
The rest of this debt was discharged during the next thirty
years by French translators and an English actor of genius.
Shakespeare's plays became available to French readers
first in Laplace's partial translation of 1745–8 and then in
Letourneur's complete edition of 1776–82. (Ducis's Galli-
cized stage adaptations of Shakespeare appeared between
1769 and 1792.) Lillo's *London Merchant* and Moore's *The
Gamester* were adapted respectively by Mercier and Saurin
for French audiences in 1768 under the new titles of *Jen-
neval* and *Béverlei*.

(c) **David Garrick**: Central to the whole process of conversion was the impact made by David Garrick on the theatrically minded public in France and on Diderot in particular,
by his informal portrayals of Shakespearean roles and by
his advocacy of theatrical reform during his two-year visit
to France, Italy and Germany which he began shortly after
the long naval and trading wars in India, Canada and the
West Indies had been concluded by the Peace of Paris in
1763.

Garrick's theatrical career was by any standards a

144. *A performance of Voltaire's* La Princesse de Navarre, *a
comedy-ballet, before Louis XV and the French Court at Versailles, 1745. London, Victoria and Albert Museum.*

phenomenon (Fig. 139). From the moment he made his
London debut in *Richard III* at the playhouse in Goodman's Fields in 1741, until his funeral in Westminster
Abbey in 1779 which was attended by dukes, earls and
members of the House of Commons, he was idolized by
rich and poor alike. Acknowledged as a competent dramatist, as well as as an actor of extraordinary promise, he
was ready by 1747 to move into management with the purchase of a half share in the lease of Drury Lane; on his
partner's death he became its sole manager. While there,
he put into effect most of the reforms that Fielding had
clamoured for in his earlier theatrical satires, not the least
being an insistence on an observance and imitation of

human nature at first hand instead of a simple copying of the mannered posturings of other actors. He shared this belief in imitating nature rather than stale and lifeless stage-conventions with his near-contemporary Charles Macklin. A contemporary attributed Garrick's success as an actor to his 'easy and familiar yet forcible style in speaking and acting' and to his 'mobile features and flashing expressive eyes'.

5 THEATRICAL REFORM

(a) In England: The principle of trusting nature was one, moreover, which he sought to instil into all young actors and actresses recruited into his company by training them himself, and one which he then extended to stage-scenery and lighting. Painted as he had been by Gainsborough, Hogarth, Reynolds and Zoffany, Garrick took the pictorial representation of landscape very seriously. Having succeeded in banishing spectators from the stage by 1765, he commissioned Philip de Loutherbourg in 1771 to direct all aspects of scenic design including directional lighting. The importance of this change may be gauged as much by the fact that de Loutherbourg's salary was twice as high as that of any of the leading actors as by looking at those models of his astonishingly realistic, romantic, yet atmospheric stage-settings, which are still preserved at the Victoria and Albert Museum.

Garrick visited Paris three times; as a tourist in 1751 and at the beginning and end of his Grand Tour of Europe between 1763 and 1765. On his first visit he went to the theatre thirteen times, catching performances of Voltaire's *Zaïre* and Rameau's *Indes galantes*; for all that, he formed a very low opinion of French acting, singing and dancing. On his second and third visits, while supposedly resting, he was prevailed upon immediately, as a guest at a lavish party in the Embassy, to perform scenes from *Hamlet*, *Macbeth*, *The Provoked Wife* and *King Lear*. His fellow guests, who included Baron de Grimm and Diderot, were astounded. Tears were said to have streamed from all eyes. Garrick, for his part, found himself just as fascinated by the French tragedienne, Mlle Clairon; he was no less impressed by the comedian Préville (with whom he could converse in English and who felt disposed to call him *Maître*) and there was even talk of an exchange of companies, but nothing came of this. Nor did it prove possible for Garrick to accept Voltaire's pressing invitation to meet him, much to the regret of both men.

(b) Reforms in France: *(i) Actors and Acting:* However, Garrick's zeal for theatrical reform was shared by his

French friends. By the time he arrived in Paris in 1763, Mlle Clairon, together with the actor Lekain, had already begun to follow his example at Drury Lane in abandoning rhetorical delivery of lines in favour of a more natural style of speech, gesture and deportment, and in instituting more systematic rehearsal procedures (Fig. 145). They were also trying to rationalize stage-costume, settings and lighting and, in 1759, had finally banished spectators off the stage. Fortuitously, it was the need for more acting space for crowd scenes in Shakespeare's plays that gave them their excuse to effect the last of these reforms. Garrick's visits

145. Mlle Clairon as Idame in Voltaire's L'Orphelin de la Chine, *1755. Her costume was designed and made by the royal dressmaker, Sarrazin. Engraving by Dupin from an original by Le Clerc, 1779. Paris, Bibliothèque de l'Arsenal.*

helped greatly to reinforce the validity of all these reforms
and led them, after his return to England, to found an École
royale d'Art dramatique in 1774.

(ii) Theory and Criticism: By the time Garrick concluded
his tour in 1765, a journey which had taken him to Turin,
Florence, Rome, Naples, Venice, Innsbruck and Munich,
his views on the need for theatrical reform had acquired
as much notoriety throughout Italy and Germany as had
his reputation as an actor. These views would shortly be
enshrined for all to read by Grimm in his cultural newslet-
ter, *Correspondance littéraire*, and by Diderot in *Observations sur Garrick* (c.1770) and *Paradoxe sur le comédien*
written between 1770 and 1778; for by then a clear correla-
tion was emerging between bourgeois philosophical and
moral attitudes to drama on the one hand and the aesthetic
tenets of the leading theatrical artists of the day both in
England and in France on the other. And since French views
on all aspects of cultural life still commanded the respect
of all rulers of Eastern and Northern European States, those
of the English merchant princes relating to plays, acting
and theatres were certain to be transmitted at second hand
through French sources to Vienna, Stockholm and St
Petersburg. As Diderot remarked in a letter to Catherine
the Great in Russia in 1775: 'It is clear for everyone with
eyes to see that without the English both reason and philosophy in France would still be in a despicably infantile
condition.'

What Destouches, Voltaire, Montesquieu and ultimately
Grimm and Diderot had all come to recognize was that
the nouveau-riche upper-middle class, in France as in England, wished to see itself represented on the stage as serious,
responsible and interesting human beings, possessed of
their own ideals and excitements and capable both of
experiencing their own sorrows and of responding compassionately to those of others, instead of being constantly
caricatured by actors as boorish monsters or as avaricious
and hypocritical fools fit only to be ridiculed. It is to be
doubted whether any of them, however, imagined that
within another fifty years the largely illiterate and oppressed labouring classes would be harbouring the same ambitions for themselves and making similar demands upon
managers, writers and actors (see p. 182). What is truly
remarkable is that notwithstanding the efforts of the *ancien
régime* to suppress radical opinion by recourse to censorship, fines and imprisonment, the frequency of coffee-house
debates and the politer conversations in the many Paris
salons as the eighteenth century advanced should have succeeded in countering them, and in allowing the swelling
tide of translations of English plays, novels and journals

to force even the French Academy both into adjusting its
stance on neo-classical principles of dramaturgy and into
accommodating contemporary bourgeois ideals. This had
to include acceptance of a new dramatic genre, described
as *drame*, to provide a home for *comédie larmoyante*
(weeping comedy, or comedy of pathos) and *tragédie
bourgeoise* (cautionary tales relating to the merchant and
professional classes).

(iii) Dramatic Genre: None of these innovations reached
France as ready-made imports; rather were all of them grafted individually onto firmly established French roots.
Crébillon (1674–1762), Voltaire's principal rival as a writer
of tragedy, began the process by aiming to excite horror
and terror rather than pity and fear, and by electing to treat
of unnatural crimes mixed with love intrigues. Audiences
responded warmly, welcoming him as another Racine, a
second Aeschylus; but his methods earned him a stinging
reproof from Boileau who described him as 'a Visigoth in
an age of good taste'. Voltaire deliberately challenged
Crébillon on his own terms, impudently borrowing some
of his subjects for his own plays and moving nearer to
English example in respect of melodramatic situations and
stage-spectacle; but he never capitulated wholly, as did
Nivelle de la Chaussée (1692–1754), to bourgeois demands
for tragi-comedies designed to invite sympathy for anyone
whom the circumstances of life tempt into straying off the
strictest paths of virtue, and to arouse hostility towards
those who abuse positions of power and wealth by oppres-
sing or corrupting the weak and distressed. Yet de la Chaussée had the satisfaction of seeing most of his plays
translated into Dutch, English, German and Italian.

Comedy, no less sentimental in essence but far more
refined both in subject matter and in style, was provided
simultaneously by Marivaux (1688–1763). No English
equivalent exists. The crude, farcical mimes and dances
introduced as harlequinades, or pantomimes, to London
audiences by John Rich at Lincoln's Inn Fields (at Covent
Garden after 1732) and which were then copied at Drury
Lane, were certainly derived from *commedia dell'arte* performances in Parisian street-theatres; but they bear no
resemblance to the finely textured plays which Marivaux
fashioned from the same raw materials. These early
London offerings were indeed destined to develop into the
far more impressive Victorian pantomimes, but that forms
a later part of this story (see pp. 192–3). To understand
Marivaux's unique achievement it has to be remembered
that at the death of Louis XIV the banished Italian Comedians were invited back to Paris and were encouraged to
integrate themselves wholly into French life. This they did,

and it was for them that Marivaux chose to write. Exploiting the delicacy of their pantomimic acting style, he concentrated on portraying the joys and pangs of young love (particularly in young women) as may be judged by the titles of his plays—*Arlequin poli par l'amour* (1720); *La Surprise de l'amour* (1722); *Les Fausses Confidences* (1737), and so on—all of which are informed with a degree of sheltered elegance and refinement far removed from the thrusting vulgarity of city life. Set and costumed by Claude Gillot, many of whose designs survive in the Louvre, Marivaux's plays provided a theatrical style which was later to inspire the paintings of Watteau.

(c) Reforms in Italy: Goldoni and Gozzi: Two years before Marivaux died, a successful Venetian playwright, Carlo Goldoni (1707–93), was invited to become director of the Comédie Italienne and took up residence in Paris. Disenchanted with the improvisatory techniques of the Italian *commedia* troupes which, by the time Goldoni started writing for the stage in 1734, had become stale and stereotyped, he approached the task of reform by offering to supply them with fully scripted plays of character and intrigue provided that they would abandon their masks. His offer was accepted by the San Samuele Theatre Company in Venice; but they were opposed in this venture by Count Carlo Gozzi (1720–1806), a reactionary traditionalist who viewed the advancing bourgeois philosophical and literary trends of the time with alarm. Believing Goldoni to be using 'reform' as a smoke-screen to conceal his more radical intentions, and dismissing his plays as 'deluges of ink', he set about revitalizing existing *commedia* stage-conventions himself, arguing that masks must be retained and that all that was needed was a stronger story-line. This he proceeded to supply in what he called *fiabe*, fairy-tales, part scripted, part improvised: the most successful of them was *Turandot*, which Puccini would borrow later as the basis for the libretto of his much more famous and familiar opera.

Although, like Addison and Steele in England, Gozzi was primarily a journalist and critic, when it came to writing about the theatre, it was Goldoni in his *Mémoires*, written in French, who provided a far better guide to the aims and methods of playwrights and actors working for and with the last of the *commedia* companies. Of the 250 to 300 plays he is reputed to have written, the most popular continue to be *La Locandiera* (1753, *Mine Hostess*) and *Il Servitore di due padroni* (1745, *The Servant of Two Masters*). Some of his best plays were written in Venetian dialect and on that account are singularly difficult to translate successfully. By 1770 he could even trust himself to write plays

in French and to provide libretti for the newly accepted *opéra bouffe*, or comic opera. The paintings of Guardi supply as good a visual equivalent to his style as those of Watteau do for Marivaux. In the domain of theatrical scenery, Philip Juvarra and the Bibiena family led the way forward to more natural effects (Figs. 87, 146 and 147; see also pp. 181–2).

A French disciple of Goldoni's, at least where revitalizing old comic forms was concerned, was Beaumarchais (1732–99) who provided in *The Barber of Seville* (1775) and *The Marriage of Figaro* (1784) two of the most brilliant comedies of the old, satirical kind in the language; but as both bring us close to the French Revolution, discussion of them is best left over to the next chapter. Suffice it here to say that Beaumarchais, like Fielding before him, succeeded in arousing the wrath of the king and his ministers, and the performance of both plays was banned until so many private readings of them had been held that it had become pointless to forbid it.

6 A SCANDINAVIAN PIONEER: HOLBERG

A European whose plays bear comparison with Marivaux's in their particularity was the Danish polymath, Ludwig Holberg (1684–1754). Born in Norway, and having lived in England, France and Italy as a student, he returned to Denmark to take up his appointment to a professorship in metaphysics at Copenhagen. From 1721 to 1728, while serving also as Director of the Danish Theatre, he set about freeing it from its reliance on French and German plays by composing his own in Danish. The first fifteen of them were comedies of character, and the next eleven comedies of manners. While openly acknowledging that he owed much to Plautus, Molière and English Restoration playwrights as well as to the *commedia dell'arte* in the structure of his plays, he had the courage to add many features, both in his characterizations and in his choice of comic incidents, that were drawn directly from town and country life in Scandinavia. Thus, like Marivaux, he created a style of play that was uniquely his own. His gentle, mocking humour, however, appealed greatly to neighbouring Dutchmen and Germans as well as to his own countrymen, all of whom came to regard him as the true founder of Scandinavian drama and theatre (Fig. 148).

7 OPERA AND BALLET

(a) Opera: The French court, not unnaturally, much preferred the less controversial fantasy worlds of opera and ballet, just as in Stuart England Charles I and his French

146. Set design for a harbour scene by Filippo Juvarra illustrating the principle of perspettivo all'angolo *as applied to landscape painting for the stage, c.1720 (compare Fig. 168). London, Victoria and Albert Museum.*

147. An unknown theatre in the Rococo style of the late eighteenth century, best ascribed to a mid-European court (possibly Vienna, Prague or Dresden) where a member of the Galli-Bibiena family was responsible for stage-settings for opera and ballet. (Compare Figs. 83 and 148.) Oil painting. London, National Gallery.

148. One of the stage settings designed and built for the Swedish Court Theatre at Drottningholm during the latter half of the eighteenth century. Many have survived intact and continue to be used for special performances today.

wife had preferred court masques to stage plays in the years leading up to the Civil War. French opera, as represented by Jean-Philippe Rameau (1683-1764), remained broadly within the forms imposed upon it by Lully until the middle of the eighteenth century when Pergolesi's *opera buffa*, or comic opera, *La Serva Padrona (The Servant as Mistress)* of 1733 was brought to Paris. Presented successfully in London in 1750, where Gay's ballad operas had already set a precedent for it, its production in Paris in 1752 created a storm of controversy known as *La Guerre des Bouffons* concerning the legitimacy of spoken dialogue in opera. This battle raged for two years, with Rameau leading the defence of the old forms in a manner not unlike Gozzi's championship of traditional *commedia dell'arte* in Italy. Traditionalist though he was, Rameau's popularity had actually been earned by his own inventive musicality which had imbued French opera with greater technical flexibility (most notably in the treatment of recitative) and with greater subtlety of characterization. It was left, however, to a Viennese composer of Bohemian (Czech) descent—Christoph Willibald Gluck who, after visiting Italy and England, became Rameau's friend and admirer when in Paris—to revolutionize opera. This he achieved with *Alceste* (1767) and with the manifesto attached in its preface (much as Garrick had done for the theatre, by his insistence on a return to nature) by creating *recitativo*

accompagnato and demanding that the music '*must*, by means of its expression, follow the situations of the story simply and clearly' rather than serve the vanity and idiosyncrasies of particular singers. With that triumph, the way was cleared for Mozart to employ his own genius with a freedom of expression that would otherwise have been inadmissible.

(b) Ballet: Innovation was also the hallmark of eighteenth-century dance, but there the initiatives were exclusively French. The traditional *Ballet de Cour* effectively died with Louis XIV: thereafter change was as rapid as it was radical. It is hard to exaggerate the repercussions throughout Europe (c.1730) of Marie Camargo's decision to raise her skirt above her ankles and to wear slippers instead of shoes when dancing; perhaps only the arrival of Diaghilev's *Ballets Russes* in Paris at the start of this century can be claimed to have had a comparable influence on fashion since (see pp. 221,229 and 242). Born in 1710 and starting her public career in 1726, La Camargo travelled extensively during her long career as the first *prima ballerina assoluta* (Fig. 149). Her place as the driving force of ballet at the Paris Opéra was then taken by Philippe Noverre (1727–1810), the founder of the Ballet d'Action, a friend of Garrick and author of *Lettre sur la Danse et sur les Ballets* (1760). With Noverre, ballet that tells its own story in mime

149. Marie Camargo, the prima ballerina of Louis XV's Court, in an idealized Watteauesque pastoral setting, c.1730. Engraving by Garnier from a painting by Lancret. London, Victoria and Albert Museum.

was born—a creative initiative that led directly to his partnerships with both Gluck and Mozart, and indirectly to the establishment of the full-length romantic ballets of the nineteenth century (see pp. 191–2).

8 GERMANY

(a) The Aftermath of Religious and Dynastic Wars: Both opera and ballet, whether French or Italian, enjoyed a particular advantage during the early eighteenth century in the court theatres of the many princes of German-speaking and Scandinavian countries. As ready-made imports complete with performers and supporting staff, they could be hired at will, thus making it possible to overcome all the obstacles that impeded the natural growth both of an indigenous repertoire of plays and of professional acting companies. The havoc and devastation of religious and dynastic wars during most of the sixteenth and seventeenth centuries had precluded growth of towns large enough to sustain regular performances of plays by resident native-speaking companies; furthermore spoken dialects, so numerous and divergent as frequently to be unintelligible from one principality to the next, militated just as strongly against the establishment of circuits capable of providing a reliable income for touring companies such as existed in France, England and even in North America by 1750. Circuits had been created in northern (and largely Protestant) German States by English actors late in the sixteenth century, who

toured as far east as Catholic Poland, until the outbreak of the Thirty Years War. Similar circuits had been established by Italian *commedia dell'arte* companies in the southern (and largely Catholic) states travelling as far east as Hungary. Such native drama as existed at a popular level evolved around a character derived from the medieval German *Narr* (fool) called Hanswurst, onto the root-stock of which had been grafted characteristics particular to both the English fool and to the Italian *Arlecchino*—a jovial, crude, inebriate bully of a clown whose boorish, obtrusive antics caused him to be scorned by the aristocracy. Efforts to provide serious plays could only be made on an occasional basis in Jesuit colleges (frequently written and performed in Latin) and also in Lutheran schools where, consequently, they were regarded as a component of the curriculum rather than as entertainments for the public; yet these amateur productions did at least serve to preserve some concept of Renaissance dramatic and theatrical ideals.

One German author, Andreas Gryphius (1616–64), succeeded in overcoming these restrictive circumstances and provided several plays of merit for Lutheran schools which, as much in their language as their settings, represent the baroque style in German drama; but the extreme artifice of this style, as was the case with heroic tragedy in Restoration England, invited a reaction just as extreme from rationalist-minded courtiers and mercantile audiences, thus denying it a future. One way out of this dead-end was simply to translate French plays fashionable in Paris; another was to imitate Dutch, English and French example by improving the living standard of the strolling players and educating the bourgeois public simultaneously. Perhaps the greatest incentive to experiment with both possibilities was the growing determination of the aristocracy and the upper-middle class to recover a pride in their own language and literature by eliminating this dependence on foreign example. Early in the eighteenth century vigorous steps began to be taken to this end.

(b) Gottsched and Neuber: Following the precedent set by the regular publication in London of such journals as the *Tatler*, the *Spectator* and the *Westminster Gazette*, Johann Christoph Gottsched (1700–66) set about providing his own critical journals between the years 1725 and 1729. Fortune smiled on his endeavours by bringing him into contact with an acting company based on Leipzig and led by a woman, Caroline Neuber (1697–1760), who was admired as much for her charm as for the emotional power of her acting. It was she who, in 1727, was appointed director of a company with the grandiloquent title of the Royal Polish and Electoral Saxon Court Comedians (see Fig. 147). Gottsched, having already committed himself to the Herculean task of educating the public, decided, on meeting her, to improve her repertoire by supplying her with translations and adaptations of outstanding French plays, a venture in which he was assisted by his wife and a few close associates. This partnership lasted for more than ten years and greatly enhanced the prestige of the company, enabling it to travel as far west as Hamburg and as far east as Russia. By 1740, when bitter quarrels destroyed this friendship, Gottsched's example was being applied by others to the translation of English plays, including some by Shakespeare, while Neuber's own success was prompting other actors (notably Heinrich Koch and J. E. Schonemann, who succeeded her in Leipzig when she moved to Hamburg) to adapt her ideas about curtailing improvisation, introducing disciplined rehearsals and providing appropriate, if simple, scenery. In 1748 Koch set up a company of his own and moved to Vienna. Neuber herself died sadly impoverished and discredited in 1760, near Dresden, where, like Molière nearly a century earlier, she was denied Christian burial (Fig. 150).

(c) Lessing: By then, however, her own and Gottsched's insistence that little of lasting value could be accomplished without adequate theatres and without better financial security for actors had begun to awaken a modest public response—a change which coincided with a dawning sense

150. Caroline Neuber, the co-founder with J. C. Gottsched of the modern German-speaking theatre. Lithograph by Carl Loedel from a painting by Elias Gottlob Hausmann.

of nationhood and an increasing irritation with the despotism of petty princelings. Critical opinion too, voiced by Johann Elias Schlegel (1719–49) and Gottfried Ephraim Lessing (1729–81) was slowly turning against the constraints of French classical plays and acting styles, and was struggling to create a genuinely German form of theatre capable of reflecting national temperament and life. With Neuber's death the centre of activity thus shifted from Leipzig to other cities. The first was Hamburg, port of entry from England and, by 1760, the new centre of intellectual life, where English romantic novels, Shakespeare's plays and those of Steele and Lillo had become the talk of the town. There, one of Neuber's admirers from Leipzig days, Lessing, and one of the actors from her company, Konrad Ackermann, joined forces in 1765 to launch a grandiose new enterprise—the Hamburg National Theatre.

Merchants were persuaded to subscribe towards the demolition of the old opera house and the building of a new theatre. This was to be non-profit-making and run by a business-manager on a regular salary. Actors were to be recruited, trained, salaried and promised pensions. The city itself was to underwrite the entire venture with subventions drawn from local taxes. When it opened on 22 April 1767, Johann Friedrich Loewen had been appointed as manager and Lessing as the *Dramaturg*, or adviser on the choice of plays, with responsibility for editing a critical in-house magazine, *Hamburgische Dramaturgie*. The constitution of the new theatre clearly owed much to that of the Comédie Française, but for Germany it was as revolutionary as it was idealistic. On both counts it was vulnerable to the vagaries of its actors' (and actresses') temperaments and to the fickleness of public taste. It is not surprising, therefore, that within two years the enterprise crashed because of the inability of the actors (suddenly granted such unaccustomed security) to accept any discipline other than that of their own emotions, and because the public wanted to be treated to a more familiar and refreshing repertoire of plays than that imposed upon it by the management for its edification and enlightenment. All, however, was not lost. Some of the actors moved on to other cities. One of the best, Konrad Ekhof, who had founded the first acting school in Germany in 1757, moved first to Weimar and then in 1774 to Gotha where, in the following year, the Duke decided to authorize him to repeat the Hamburg experiment in his own theatre; but that too ended in failure and the actors once more took to the road. Ekhof died in 1778, but one of the most outstanding actors in his company at Gotha, August Wilhelm Iffland (1759–1814), carried the torch of the 'National Theatre' movement on to Mannheim in 1779.

Meantime, in Austria, the Emperor Joseph II had also been inspired by the Hamburg experiment to open his own theatre in the Hofburg Palace to the public; this he did in 1776, marking the inauguration of the famous Burgtheater in Vienna. Just as important for the future was the spread of these liberating theatrical ideals into Scandinavian countries and more especially, via Prussia and Saxony, across Poland to Russia; but discussion of these developments can be more conveniently dealt with in the next chapter.

In Germany itself, where a large number of talented and well-trained actors and actresses were now available, and with the idea of public theatres widely enough established to make regular performances by professional acting companies viable financially, what was most urgently needed was a regular supply of good German plays. No one recognized this sooner or more clearly than Lessing, who had not only attempted to fill this gap himself but had urged others to assist. In his dramatic criticism Lessing followed

Diderot and Garrick in his insistence that dramatic art, to be worth the name, must reflect nature, and that rule books which cramped or inhibited an accurate portrayal of it—no matter who had written them—should be ignored. Shakespeare, as a writer of stage-plays, enjoyed his unqualified approval in this respect: he, therefore, rather than the familiar French idols of the aristocracy, should supply the model for aspiring young writers in German.

As a dramatist, Lessing still cast his plays in the classical mould and never quite lived up to the standards that he set; but, like Christopher Marlowe in England and Alexandre Hardy in France, his best plays sufficed to reveal what could be done in German, and this challenged others to follow his example. His first play, a bourgeois tragedy entitled *Miss Sara Sampson*, written while he was still deeply influenced by the plays of Lillo and the novels of Samuel Richardson, was first produced in Berlin in 1755, two years after Voltaire's stormy departure from the court of Frederick the Great. His best play is *Minna von Barnhelm*, a comedy, first produced in 1767 at Hamburg, which avoids sentimentalism. Its dialogue is conversational and its characterization is lively, humorous and unmistakably German.

Like the *Hamburgische Dramaturgie*, Lessing's efforts to encourage the young to write for the theatre also bore fruit. By proving that there was a public eager to see plays in German by Germans, he prepared audiences for a more general *Aufklärung* (awakening). It was thus against this background that two writers of genius emerged— Johann Wolfgang von Goethe (1749–1832) and Johann Christoph Friedrich von Schiller (1759–1805). Their appearance was as sudden and startling as that of Shakespeare and Jonson had been in England or that of Molière and Racine in France: happily, however, as had also been the case in both England and France, professionally organized acting companies, adequate playhouses and an interested public by then existed to greet them.

(d) Goethe: Goethe was a highly educated intellectual and thus comparable with Racine, but not with either Shakespeare or Molière, both of whom, however widely read, were actors first and foremost. Neither by temperament nor by training could Goethe lay claim to know much about acting as a profession, such practical experience of the theatre as he came to possess being acquired after 1790 as manager and director of the court theatre in Weimar. Yet genius is no respecter of formal training and rule books. Goethe's first play, *Goetz von Berlichingen* (1773) followed the pattern of a Shakespearean chronicle play disregarding all the sacred 'unities' and mixing comic characters and incident with serious subject matter in the manner of a chivalric romance. (It was adapted into English by John Arden in 1963 as *Ironhand*.) Its hero is a sixteenth-century Imperial Knight with Robin Hood characteristics. This character (considered as a torch-bearer of revolt) served as a prototype for less talented young writers to imitate throughout the decade. Yet Goetz was substantially more than just a romantic outlaw, since his swashbuckling individualism offered German audiences a theatrical metaphor of Jean-Jacques Rousseau's much discussed concept of 'natural man' *in action*. Moreover, the play taken as a whole sufficed almost of itself to destroy the sanctity of French neo-classical dramatic forms and thus to make Shakespeare as acceptable in future as Molière, Racine and Voltaire had been in the past. This was put quickly to the test by the young actor Friedrich Schroeder (1744–1816) who presented eleven of Shakespeare's plays in Hamburg within eight years: these included *Hamlet, Macbeth, The Merchant of Venice, Much Ado About Nothing, Richard II, Henry IV* and *King Lear* (Fig. 152). Collectively these productions served both to enhance the growing attraction of the picturesque in stage-costumes and settings for German audiences and to confirm Goethe's liberating discovery of the chronicle play as an acceptable dramatic genre. Both of these revelations encouraged younger playwrights to tackle historical dramas themselves, since this

152. Friedrich Ludwig Schroeder as Falstaff, 1780. Schroeder assisted Lessing at the National Theatre in Hamburg, and as its manager staged Goethe's Goetz von Berlichingen *in 1774 and eleven plays by Shakespeare. He then moved to the Burgtheater in Vienna, where he is reputed to have played 700 roles. Like Garrick he insisted on disciplined rehearsals and natural characterization. Engraving by von Pippo.*

---

151. James Quinn as Falstaff in Shakespeare's Henry IV *(Part I), pictured here being questioned by Prince Hal at the Boar's Head Tavern on their return from the ambush at Gadshill. Engraving by C. Grignon from a painting by Francis Hayman, 1743.*

form possessed the double virtue of romanticizing the past (from which they were striving to escape) and providing them with the same distancing devices to circumvent censorship that Elizabethan and Jacobean dramatists had used in England.

Among the minor playwrights who attracted attention at this time was Friedrich von Klinger (1752–1831), who wrote a poorly constructed and exclamatory play of no great intrinsic importance but one which, nevertheless, set fire to the imagination of German youth in every German-speaking state. Its name was *Sturm und Drang*. Produced in 1776, the year of the American Revolution, this play became the centre-piece of a movement gathered around

153. *A melodramatic scene—Act 4 Scene 5—from Friedrich von Klinger's* Die Zwillinge (The Twins), *a play about fratricide. Engraving by I. Albrecht, Vienna, 1791.*

the young Goethe: that movement, in turn, adopted the name of the play (Fig. 153). Similarly critical plays presented before and after *Sturm und Drang* were J. M. R. Lenz's *Der Hofmeister* (*The Headmaster*, 1774), which exposed the harsh conditions under which tutors had to work, and *Die Soldaten* (*The Soldiers*, 1776), a daringly outspoken attack on Prussian militarism.

(e) **Schiller:** At this point the movement gained added impetus from its second poet of genius, Schiller. Like Goethe, he was well educated, but had received a medical

rather than a legal training. Schiller burst onto the German theatrical scene at Mannheim in 1782 with *Die Räuber (The Robbers)*. Being primarily a poet, and lacking any formal training in theatrical crafts, he relied on verse and emotion to make up for what was lacking in plot-construction and three-dimensional characterization. *The Robbers*, and its successors *Fiesco* (1783) and *Kabale und Liebe* (*Love and Intrigue* 1784), if less philosophically subversive than Goethe's *Goetz von Berlichingen*, were politically more overt and dangerous since they challenged all the important social conventions of the time. To this extent the early plays of Goethe and Schiller complement each other, Schiller providing the patriots, the protesters and the avengers, and Goethe providing the thought processes and verbal soliloquies motivating and informing their actions. To a nation ready to consume as much of either as these playwrights cared to offer, it did not greatly matter *at that time* that neither dramatist seemed able to fuse all these qualities into a single play. It has mattered since, because actors, directors and designers alike have found it difficult to revive these early plays without substantial editing and adaptation: and if this has proved a problem in Germany, it is magnified in translation. Outside Germany revivals have therefore been rare, thus obliging critical assessment to arise from private study rather than stage performance.

It is ironic that the revolution which these early German playwrights seemed to herald should have taken place in America in 1776 and then in France in 1789, but failed to materialize in Germany until 1848. With the head of steam built up through *Sturm und Drang* thus fruitlessly spent, German dramatists (including Goethe and Schiller) had to rethink their own positions both philosophically and aesthetically. What neither they themselves nor other playwrights and actors elsewhere had yet recognized was that across the North Sea, in England, signs of an economic and social change as great as that which followed Martin Luther's attack on the Roman Catholic Church nearly three centuries earlier were beginning to alter the landscape. There another revolution, industrial rather than political, was starting to change the balance between country and urban life irrevocably—a process that would spread, like some infectious disease, swiftly into Europe and America. Its principal consequence for the theatre would be to oblige managers and artists to listen to the claims for theatrical recreation of the labouring classes working in the newly built factories, a factor largely ignored since the Middle Ages. And to these claims would be added another, altogether new demand—for a voice in *the choice* of the entertainments on offer.

12

Princes of Industry and the
Theatre of the Nineteenth Century

1 SPECTACLE AND MELODRAMA

The motto of enlightenment is therefore: *Sapere aude!* Have courage to use your own understanding.
(Kant, *An Answer to the Question: 'What is Enlightenment?'*)

(a) **Industrial Revolution**: *(i) Playhouse Lighting:* It can be argued that most of the major changes that overtook the theatre during the nineteenth century owed more to engineers—civil, mechanical and optical—than to actors or dramatists. If such a claim is thought to be perverse, it has to be remembered that the candles and oil-lamps, which had provided the sole form of lighting in every theatre until the end of the eighteenth century, were banished first in favour of gas and limelight and then in favour of electricity. Furthermore, by the start of the twentieth century the invention of photography, and more especially of motion pictures, was obliging the theatre to consider whether it had a future at all. It is thus worth taking the role of industrial engineering in the theatre of the nineteenth century seriously enough to examine at least its salient features (see p. 159).

The illumination of indoor playhouses pioneered in Italian proscenium-arched theatres of the Italian Renaissance (see Chapter 7) had been adopted during the seventeenth century throughout Europe virtually unaltered. Filippo Juvarra (1676–1736), the Galli-Bibiena family, Philippe de Loutherbourg and others attempted during the eighteenth century to provide audiences with more natural and atmospheric pictorial effects (Fig. 146). Their efforts, however, applied solely to angular perspective and to the illumination of the stage: the auditorium was not darkened and the spectators, therefore, continued to attend theatres as much to be seen as to see the actors or hear the play (Fig. 164). It was only with F. A. Winsor's invention of illumination by coal-gas in 1803 that it became possible for a stage-manager to *control* both the quantity and direction of light used. The first theatres to risk installing gas (together with the literally miles of rubber piping which supplied the jets) were Drury Lane and the Lyceum opera-house in London, both of which advertised its use as a special attraction to open their autumn seasons in 1817. Thereafter, both in England and abroad, the practice became general. Within the context of imitating nature, the ability to control *all* sources of illumination in a theatre from a single 'gas table' in the prompter's corner of the stage made it imperative to consider whether actors should continue to stand out on a fore-stage, or whether they should be required to retreat into the landscape (or interior setting) within which their actions were supposed to be taking place (Fig. 154). With the auditorium darkened, the attention of an entire audience could automatically be focused on the stage; and with the addition of lime (or calcium) light, introduced shortly afterwards by Thomas Drummond, that focus could be sharpened and narrowed to particular acting areas. Thus as managers found themselves called upon to provide ever more realistic pictorial effects, so it became inevitable that actors would be forced to subject their own predilections to the will of the scenic designers, painters and illuminators, and that fore-stages and proscenium doors would gradually disappear.

Gas lighting was not immediately hailed by the theatre critics as an unqualified improvement on the subtlety of candle and lamplight, and its installation caused the number of theatres destroyed by fire within the next fifty years to double; but its use in theatres that were rapidly growing in size to meet public demand was vital if the actors and scenery were to be seen at all! (Figs. 158 and 182). Electric lighting, when it replaced gas in the 1880s, was similarly criticized for its comparative harshness and glare; but as

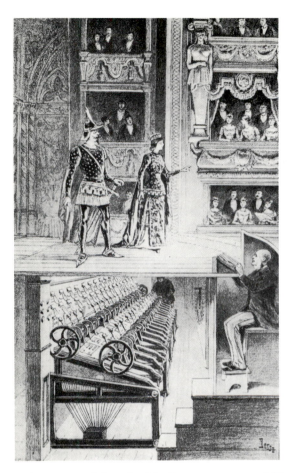

154. Lighting control board with the operator seated like an organist at the manual control table. Paris, Opéra, 1893.

it served substantially to decrease the fire risk, insurance companies and the police came to exert financial pressures on managers that soon became irresistible.

(ii) Scenic Spectacle: Second only to lighting among theatrical innovations was the growing demand for more lavishly realistic scenic spectacle, which was occasioned as much by the needs of barely literate communities of factory workers migrating from the country to the new manufacturing towns as it was by romantically minded middle-class theatre-goers with antiquarian interests. Habitual patrons were already bored with the stock stage-settings that had been trotted out time and again to service new plays along with revivals through most of the eighteenth century; newcomers without the schooling needed to listen to lengthy arguments wanted sights to amaze them and to remember

afterwards. Charles Kenney, commenting on the scenic splendours of the Drury Lane production of *Antony and Cleopatra*, remarked:

> There are in a miscellaneous public . . . many whose imaginations are not to be kindled by merely verbal delineations, and are best pleased when the eye is made interpreter to the sense. What may be called the childish part of the public, and it is a large one, must be conciliated if success on a large scale is to be aimed at . . .'
>
> (*Poets and Profits at Drury Lane Theatre*
> (1875), p. 43).

To meet this demand, theatre architects and their engineering consultants translated the floor area of their stages during the nineteenth century into a kind of jig-saw puzzle, fretsawed into long, narrow strips running down the sides of stages from front to back, and laterally across the whole width of the proscenium arch, to permit scenic walls and painted profiles to be raised from, or lowered to, cavernous basement storage areas. To match this, tall towers came to be built above stages to accommodate an elaborate system of grid and fly-gallery and bridges controlling counter-weighted rope lines from which both painted scenic cloths and large batteries first of gas lamps and then of electric ones could be suspended; these are still called fly-towers, much of the related machinery now being electrically operated. German and American engineers provided mechanically operated double stages (Fig. 155); an earlier British innovation was the provision of aquatic facilities for the representation of naval battles, river crossings, and other heroic incidents reminiscent of the Renaissance and Roman *naumachia* (see p. 51 and p. 108, and Fig. 90). Without the aid of such technological advances Wagner could hardly have required the Rhine to overflow its banks, or the Palace of Valhalla to come crashing to the ground when *Der Ring des Nibelungen* was given its first complete performance in the purpose-built Festspielhaus at Bayreuth in 1876. By the end of the century, revolving stages carrying three different stage-settings could replace one with another within a few seconds at the touch of a button or switch.

(iii) The Steam Engines and Printing Presses: No less important from a manager's viewpoint was the rapid growth of railways and of the size and number of trans-Atlantic steamers, which made it possible to consider taking on tour these ever more lavish productions not only in their country of origin, but abroad, and to an extent never imagined before. A third industrial innovation which

served to expedite change in the theatre affected play-scripts rather than theatrical representation; this was the mass production of cheap newspapers, magazines and books which, combined with the untrained, essentially visual, taste of the new audiences, compelled dramatists to give priority to pictorial techniques of story-telling. Novels began to be serialized in magazines. By 1835 colour printing had been invented, and by 1850 Applegarth's rotary press had made mass production of newspapers possible. Plays, in marked contrast, ceased to be economically attractive to printers, booksellers or publishers. Playwrights, partly on this account and partly because of the demand for novels and stage-spectacle, rapidly lost their former status in society and failed to recover it until near to the end of the century. Coleridge, Keats, Shelley and Wordsworth all wrote for the stage, but failed to convince theatre-managers that their plays would fill an auditorium. Byron actually joined the management committee of the rebuilt Drury Lane, but *Marino Falieri* (1821) was the only one of his five plays to be produced before his death in 1824, and then without success. Perhaps most significantly of all, Charles Dickens—amateur actor, writer of burlettas and owner of a private theatre—deliberately chose not to write professionally for the theatre, leaving it to other authors to adapt his novels for the stage.

(iv) The Status and Economy of Dramatists: It would be wrong to ascribe this state of affairs to one cause only. Undoubtedly the low market-value of plays was a principal one, exaggerated in England and America by the inadequate copyright laws of the time. In France dramatists were far better protected: after the Revolution, no play could be performed without the author's written permission, and he could then insist on payment of a royalty for every performance given. By contrast, English playwrights had to content themselves with selling a play outright for a fee or serving as a 'house dramatist' on a miserable retaining salary. By 1820 fees paid by English managers for plays were so low that, to survive, a dramatist might have to write between twenty and thirty plays a year, which clearly could only be done by abandoning genuine creativity and having recourse to writing to a formula or to adapting for the stage novels, foreign plays and journalists' descriptions of criminal court proceedings. Reporting to *The Select Committee on Dramatic Literature* in 1832, W. T. Moncrieff complained: 'it is impossible for any man, whose misfortunes may oblige him to resort to that species of writing, to obtain a fair remuneration for his labour and talent.' In marked contrast, novelists like Sir Walter Scott could obtain upwards of £4,000 for a single novel. It should occa-

155. *Two pre-set stage settings operated by large counterweights to facilitate swift changes of scenery, as installed by Steele MacKaye at the Madison Square Theatre, New York. Diagrammatic drawing in* The Scientific American, *5 April 1884.*

sion little surprise, therefore, that something approaching a new Dark Age should have overtaken English dramatic literature until late in the nineteenth century. On the Continent the situation was not as extreme, and the reasons for that will be considered later. In other words, forces other than poetry and literature moved into the ascendant late in the eighteenth century, overthrowing the dominance of the writer and the architect in the theatre, which had characterized the classical, baroque and rococo styles in Europe, and elevating a new partnership between landscape painters, engineers, journalists and showmen. This new partnership launched a new era of spectacular (but highly moralistic) sensationalism—realistic demolition of castles, conflagrations, floating ghosts that passed through seemingly solid scenery, drownings, train crashes and, ultimately, the ability through the motion-picture camera to present the hero rushing from the shipwreck, through the forest-fire to the earthquake to rescue the heroine before she disappeared down some newly opened chasm in the road outside her collapsing home, or on an ice-floe drifting towards a waterfall (see Figs. 161 and 162).

(v) New Audiences: One other factor was needed to launch this new chapter in the story of theatre on its course—a clamour from the labouring masses to be admitted to the temples of dramatic art as a matter of democratic right. The final push required to sweep away the aristocratically organized theatres established in the sixteenth and seventeenth centuries by princes and their servants for the entertainment of their courtiers was delivered in France with the storming of the Bastille prison in 1789. In the subsequent 'reign of terror', the literal blood and thunder of the guillotines served to endow Jean-Jacques Rousseau's 'noble savage' with that same moral virtue and sentimental piety in a political sense that had been so ardently propagated by bourgeois playwrights and so fervently applauded by their audiences down the eighteenth century. Liberty, equality, fraternity: these were to become the catchwords informing the drama of the new era—an era best known today as that of melodrama.

(b) The Origins of Melodrama: The origins of melodrama are to be found in Germany and France where the same word was adopted to describe two newly coined but sharply contrasted dramatic forms. In France the idea that music might be interpolated between passages of speech to indicate what characters were feeling and representing pantomimically was borrowed by Jean-Jacques Rousseau during the *Guerre des Buffons* from opera (see pp. 173–5), where this device had been first used to avoid the harshness of recitative, and then applied to his own monologue *Pygmalion* (1771). Brecht, in our own century, revived this device in the use he made of songs within his plays (see pp. 232–3). In Germany the librettist Jean Brandes and the composer Georg Benda applied the term to their *Ariadne auf Naxos* (first presented at Gotha in 1775), where speech was backed by music to heighten the emotional quality of the scene. This technique was carried over into the twentieth century, and is still used constantly in the cinema and on television, all too often to conceal the banality of trite scripts.

In normal circumstances both of these experiments, being devised to serve a limited function, might be expected to have warranted only a brief life; but the circumstances were not normal. Both in France and England the number of licensed theatres was tightly controlled and plays were severely censored. Melodrama therefore offered an ideal way of getting round the law. By this means the illegal boulevard theatres in pre-revolutionary France and the pleasure gardens and tavern annexes (later known as music halls) in England were able to link songs, dances and spectacular tableaux into sequences illustrating some popular theme with a well-defined beginning, middle and end. These shows came to be called 'burlettas'. All that was required to give this embryonic type of popular entertainment a shape and quality of its own was a suitable injection of moral, philosophic and literary animation.

(c) The Lifeblood of Melodrama: *(i) Morality:* Long before the American and French Revolutions, the authors of sentimental comedies and bourgeois tragedies had succeeded in establishing the idea that divine providence took a special interest in virtue (see pp. 165). To be possessed of virtue sufficed as a talisman against all dangers, while steadfast preservation of it ensured a rich reward on earth as well as in heaven. Vice, by contrast, while it could flourish temporarily, could not pass undetected indefinitely, and would be punished by loss of health, wealth, strength and even life itself.

In taking hold upon society as a whole during the closing years of the eighteenth century—more especially in Britain and America—this greatly simplified code of moral conduct was strongly influenced by the religious revival led by John Wesley, the founder of the Methodist Society. The Society was aimed at the agricultural workers who were leaving the land and moving into the expanding industrial towns. Methodists and other nonconformist Churches held no brief for the theatre, but they did believe in virtue as the highway to happiness, and in social equality before the law. A philosophy, therefore, which extolled the potential virtue of the common man and saw in the New World a never-ending landscape in which that potential could express itself, came to be imprinted on plebeian minds from countless pulpits in Britain and America. The ground was thus prepared for the ready acceptance of such ideas in the new 'democratic' theatres that took shape during the early decades of the nineteenth century. In these, the agents of divine justice, instead of playing a physical role in the stage action (as the good and evil angels of medieval morality plays had done), hovered above and beyond the visible world of the stage ready to intervene in the last act by bringing the vicious characters to justice and by rewarding the righteous.

(ii) Philosophy and Revolution: A second source of energy for the emerging popular theatre came from two philosophers, Rousseau and Kant. Rousseau offered ideas relating to the noble savage, the natural goodness of man and

156. *Jolly Jack Tar, the folk-hero of British nautical melodrama. This hand-coloured engraving by R. Lloyd, c.1840, from a drawing by W. Cocking depicts Andrew Ducrow, a circus entertainer whose specialization was miming typical incidents from life at sea—scaling the rigging, reefing the sails, firing a gun in battle and tending a wounded comrade—while standing on the back of his horse as it galloped round the circus ring. London, Victoria and Albert Museum, Enthoven Collection.*

(iii) Romantic Novels: In seeking means to implant these highly emotive abstract and political values on the popular imagination, managers and dramatists still had to discover a method of transforming these new theatrical metaphors into an illusion of reality for largely illiterate audiences. The answer emerged in stage-spectacle: and here they were fortunate to find that most of the preparatory work had been done for them by novelists who, during the latter half of the eighteenth century, had created a pseudo-medieval Gothic world of castles, dungeons, and mountain strongholds as a setting for the extravagant actions of the rapacious tyrants and pitiful victims of their romances. Credit for this is usually given to Horace Walpole, whose *Castle of Otranto*, published in 1764, took the literary world by storm. The haunted castle is peopled with portraits of ancestors who walk out of their frames and with statues that drip blood; a century later the subject was still topical enough to offer W. S. Gilbert and Arthur Sullivan an object for parody in *Ruddigore*. Castles proliferated, and with them dungeons and torture chambers; and it was in the dungeons of such castles as those of Boutet de Monvel's *Victimes cloîtrées* (1791) and Mrs William Radcliffe's *The Mysteries of Udolpho* (1794) that virtue became identified with incarcerated prisoners and vice with the owners, whose cruelty eventually drove them to mad-

the equation of evil with inequality; Kant emphasized the individual's right to freedom. Rousseau's views were quickly received into the theatre by Beaumarchais in *The Barber of Seville* and *The Marriage of Figaro*, in which a servant was portrayed as fully capable of outclassing his master in everything except his privileged social status, and by the young Schiller urging audiences, in his early plays, to escape from the restrictive bonds of petty despotism and stifling social conventions (see pp.173 and 180). Outside the theatre, Rousseau's ideas were harnessed in Germany to moral and political ends by Kant during the 1780s; and in North America and France the noble savage became endowed with revolutionary fervour. From that point, it was only a short step towards the equation on the stage of revolutionaries with the existing, idealized concepts of virtue and of the discredited establishment with vice, a process that gave the world of burletta in the unlicensed theatres of the early nineteenth century its new popular heroes—Figaro, Jack Tar, Davy Crockett and, ultimately, the cowboy (Figs. 156 and 157). The genuine 'noble savage', as represented by American Indians and by the Aborigines in Australia, fared very differently at the hands of their white 'democratic' masters (see pp. 261-2).

157. *The saddle-mending scene in Frank Murdock's* Davy Crockett, or Be Sure You're Right, The Go Ahead, *1872, set in Tennessee. Frank Mayo became identified with the role (like certain television actors today) and played it continuously until 1896. Harvard Theatre Collection.*

ness or death. Monvel offered audiences a hero and a heroine (a nun at that) imprisoned in adjoining cells; Mrs Radcliffe, in a novel heavily indebted to Goethe's *Goetz von Berlichingen* and Schiller's *The Robbers*, provided in her hero, Montoni, a Wordsworthian figure who rejoices in forest sanctuaries and lakeland caves and makes daring forays on behalf of wronged prisoners into stubbornly guarded fortresses. Three years later, Mathew Gregory ('Monk') Lewis, a young English diplomat, by collating all his gleanings from English, French and German romantic novels and plays, offered what he claimed to be his own original work, *The Castle Spectre*, to Sheridan for production at Drury Lane. Sheridan accepted it, wisely, for it proved to be a box-office success. This play introduced audiences to ghosts, negroes, mysterious singers at dead of night and entombed prisoners tapping feebly at dungeon walls. Here then in books was all the spectacle that scene-painters could ask for, and visual effects enough to supply literate and illiterate audiences alike all over Europe with fearsome and horrific sights to remember for years to come (Plate 14).

(iv) Circuses: In real life, events, at least in Paris, improved on fiction. The Revolution swept away overnight two centuries of theatrical monopoly and forced the managers of the street-theatres and circuses to dramatize and depict the fall of the Bastille. Their success was such as to prompt immediate transfer to London, and there, despite the efforts of the licensing authorities to stop it by banning performances and imprisoning actors, it was played in an amphitheatre called the Royal Circus to great applause.

The name 'Circus', although reminiscent of the Roman *ludi circenses* (see pp. 49–51), had by then come to describe a novel form of entertainment which owed its birth to an English ex-sergeant-major and trick-rider, Philip Astley, who, as Hippisley Coxe has explained, discovered that if he galloped in a circle while standing upright on horseback, 'centrifugal force helped him to keep his balance'. In 1768 he roped off a ring on a piece of waste ground in Lambeth and invited spectators to pay to watch him: there he was joined by the strolling acrobats, jugglers and other entertainers who had previously earned a living at fairgrounds and racecourses. By 1780 he was able to build an impressive auditorium containing a pit, boxes and a gallery, and was highly enough regarded to receive an invitation to Paris to perform for Louis XVI which resulted in the establishment there of the 'French Circus'. From then on he occupied himself at home by adding pantomime and burlettas to his repertoire, and abroad by helping to start other circuses in Italy and Eastern Europe until his death

in 1814. It was at Astley's Circus, and the rival Royal Circus (later the Surrey Theatre) built in 1782, that equestrian spectacles came to be translated into epic battles and seiges presented in dumb-show but as colourful and stirring to the eye as any medieval tournament or any entertainment offered in Roman Amphitheatres (see Plates 5 and 9, and Figs. 34, 39 and 43). The titles of these entertainments include *The Death of General Wolfe at Quebec, Slaves of Barbary, The Blood-red Knight* (a crude adaptation of Schiller's *The Robbers*), *The Fatal Prediction, Monkish Cruelty, The Crusaders, The Fall of the Bastille, The Battle of Waterloo* and *The Burning of Moscow:* (Fig. 159). No wonder they proved irresistible, for it was there that the morality of sentimental drama, the political philosophy of revolution and the scenic images of romance met; and in a form, moreover, as acceptable to raffish Regency beaux as to tradesmen and artisans since horsemanship was still a skill demanded in every walk of life. Circuses enjoyed the advantage of having enough space to accommodate collapsible castles and whole squadrons of horsemen or, alternatively, of ships: battles, moreover, could be fought there, with the discharge of guns and cannons on a scale undreamt of by the writers of Elizabethan history plays or by the directors of the Carrousels at Louis XIV's Versailles. And amid all the noise and pageantry, what need of words so

---

158. Astley's Amphitheatre, 1808. Note the proscenium arch behind the orchestra-pit and circus ring, the two proscenium doors, and the size of the audience accommodated in the four galleries. Drawn and engraved by Pugin and Rowlandson.

159. *Astley's Amphitheatre in 1855/6, showing a performance of a military spectacular. Note the use made of the stage space behind the proscenium arch. (Compare Fig. 158.) Poster. London, Victoria and Albert Museum.*

long as the hero rescued the prisoners or the heroine, virtue triumphed and the wicked met with their just deserts? This formula could be varied infinitely, with different décors and costumes, and in different countries and periods. Interestingly enough, this same formula, when stripped of the horsemen but set throughout to music, supplies a firm base for Beethoven's *Fidelio*, produced in its first version in 1805, its second in 1806, and its final form in 1814.

(d) The Forging of Melodrama: *(i) Pixérécourt:* With all the ingredients of the new form to hand by the start of the nineteenth century, melodrama was fortunate enough to find a genius capable of fusing them into a single entertainment of extraordinary emotive power. This was Gilbert de Pixérécourt. Born in France in 1773, he survived the Revolution (changing sides several times) and, with Napoleon as ruler of France, started his theatrical career by adapting two novels—F. G. Ducray-Diminil's *Victor, ou L'Enfant de la Forêt* and Mrs Radcliffe's *Mysteries of Udolpho*—for the stage. His success secured for him the management of the Théâtre de l'Ambigu in Paris, where he set about adapting the building to contain the scenic marvels of the circuses. Using a large orchestra to arouse the emotions of his audiences, Pixérécourt swiftly added many variations to the stereotyped situations and characterizations of the circus tableaux. Disguise, and with it blackmail, bigamy and other quasi-criminal characteristics, supplied surprise as well as variety, thereby expanding the narrative content within the conventional stage-settings of Gothic claustrophobia. Moving from the Théâtre de l'Ambigu to the larger Gaîté, he added explosions and volcanoes to the stock of scenic marvels and finally, in *Le Chien de Montargis* (1814), a play with a dog as its leading actor. It was the sensational popularity of this piece which finally drove Goethe to quit the theatre in disgust when his patron insisted on its being performed in Weimar in 1817. No less sensational were the riots in Dublin when the dog went missing and could neither be found nor replaced for two whole weeks (Fig. 160). Here we may see the progenitor of *Lassie, Son of Lassie, Daktari* and 'The wonderful world of Disney', which have so delighted audiences on cinema and television screens in our own times. Pixérécourt, however, took his art seriously enough to write about it before he died in 1844; he produced in *Le Mélodrame* and *Dernières réflexions sur le mélodrame* a justification and a textbook for imitators to turn to their own use. While modestly claiming himself to have written primarily for those who could not read, his plays were good enough to attract the serious attention of better writers like Alexandre Dumas (the elder) and Victor Hugo, and so were responsible for influencing, at least in France, the development of later dramatic literature.

(ii) English writers: In England and America Pixérécourt's plays were shamelessly pillaged by adapters such as Thomas Dibden (1771–1841), who simply changed the names of characters and introduced a few incidents to provide local and topical interest; he also turned his pen to the adaptation of the novels of Sir Walter Scott. Novelty again reared its head with the adaptation of novels by two female writers, Mrs Amelia Opie's *Father and Daughter* (1801) and Mary Shelley's *Frankenstein* (1818). From the former sprang a progeny of domestic dramas which had unmarried mothers as their heroines (usually pathetically

160. Poster advertising a peformance of Poor Dog Tray, Ever Faithful, *a melodrama with a dog as its hero. Note the inset representations of the dog hero saving the heroine from the assaults of the villain. c.1840. London, Victoria and Albert Museum.*

accompanied by a baby), starving and seeking work, or abandoned in the snow. From Mary Shelley's novel there developed an even more prodigious tribe of demonic and horrific melodramas set in mountain fastnesses, laboratories and charnel-houses in which women as well as men became the victims of vampires, witches and devils. Again, however, with the production in Berlin of Weber's *Der Freischütz* in 1821, little time was lost in transferring much of this Gothic fantasy to the still aristocratically controlled operatic stage (see pp. 187, 192).

The next thematic landmark was provided in 1828 by Douglas Jerrold with an amalgamation of the traditional

'Rake's Progress' and contemporary temperance tracts into *Fifteen Years of a Drunkard's Life* which brought crime into the foreground as a major element of later melodrama. A year later he wrote his highly successful *Black-Ey'd Susan* with 'the jovial sailor, William' as its sorely tried hero. The fully realized prototype of this genre followed in 1831 with a production of the anonymous *Maria Marten: or the Murder in the Red Barn*. With this play was launched that never-ending stream of detective fiction which has provided the staple diet not only of many boulevard theatres in the twentieth century, but also of our own film and television industries.

The suave, good-looking and seemingly well-heeled villains of criminal melodrama from Maria Marten's murderer to Sweeny Todd, the demon-barber of Fleet Street, swaggered from theatre to theatre, but always had to accept a punishment fitting their crimes. Alongside them in one spectacular melodrama after another marched the patriotic heroes of military and nautical campaigns, and the pathetic victims of marital infidelity. From the outset melodrama had been anti-aristocratic. Its villains thus frequently bear titles, while its heroes—especially the Figaro and Jack Tar figures—are as often of humble origin. By the 1840s, however, melodrama could scarcely proceed further within the constricting form of burletta where the uneasy balance between music, spectacle, dumb-show and dialogue was serving to impede character development and to forbid anything but the crudest social criticism. Already it had broken its own seams in spilling over from the minor theatres into the surviving preserves of the aristocracy and wealthy merchants—opera, ballet and legitimate drama—sweeping all before it by transforming both the subject matter and the traditional forms of these types of theatre into reflections of itself, while retaining its own firm grip over the uneducated and industrious labouring class and advancing inexorably in its own pictorial techniques of theatrical story-telling towards the magic, but as yet unimagined, world of cinema. How then was it to advance? To this question different answers emerged in several countries. These will be discussed in Section 4 of this chapter, 'Serious Drama'.

(iii) American Contributors: Melodrama itself, however, still had a final but very important contribution to make to its own future which was distinctively American. In 1848 gold was discovered in California. This event supplied a goldmine of its own in terms of new narrative and plot material for the contrivers of these entertainments for the rest of the century. Chief among them was the gold-rush itself with its races and chases across the continent, and

161. Poster advertising the 'sensation scene' in Augustin Daly's Under the Gaslight, *first performed in New York, 1867, and presented at the Pavilion Theatre, Whitechapel Road, London, a year later. University of Bristol Theatre Collection.*

its encounters with terrible natural obstacles—rivers, mountains and deserts—all peopled by an exotic new enemy, Red Indians. To the story of the race to the west coast was added the romance of the early railroads. Greedy capitalist employers here came face to face with the hard-pressed labourers whose lives they were placing in constant danger and whom they were paying to build both the railroads and their own fortunes. Rivalry between railroad speculators also admitted dramatic conflicts involving fascinating new variants on the routine sensations of melodramatic spectacle—ambushes, dynamite, collapsing viaducts, explosions in tunnels, head-on collisions and, best of all, virtuous hero or heroine strapped to the track a few miles ahead of the approaching train (Fig. 161). The new technology ensured that the train would arrive on cue. As the frontier itself moved west, so the stories of hardship and endurance drawn directly from the experiences of the pioneers supplied American dramatists with subject matter that struck audiences as being more relevant and realistic than that of European novels.

Another aspect of the gold-rush, important to play structure, was the spectacular reversals of fortune which acquisition, or loss, of this precious metal could itself effect, coupled with the part that women could play in precipitating such reversals. Thus the gold-rush gave not only American but European drama a quasi-religious moral framework that it had hitherto lacked.

Slowly, 'Western' narrative and moral possibilities began to be grafted onto the root-stock of melodrama by an Irish emigré American, Dion Boucicault (1822–90), and

were brought to their full maturity by a native-born Californian, David Belasco (1859–1931), in *The Girl of the Golden West*, first produced in 1905, which Puccini saw and used as the libretto for his opera *La Fanciulla del West* (see pp. 208–9).

Boucicault and his actress wife, Agnes Robertson, shot to international fame in 1857 with the production of *The Poor of New York* and *Jessie Brown: or The Relief of Lucknow*, followed two years later by *The Octoroon*. What distinguishes all three plays from most of their predecessors is the relative depth of characterization and degree of social criticism with which they are informed. *The Octoroon*, while avoiding firm commitment to one side or the other, dared to make slavery its central issue. *The Poor of New York* (which when presented elsewhere could be billed as *The Poor of London* or *The Poor of Paris*) exploited the banking panics of 1837 and 1857 to contrast the ability of the rich to withstand such catastrophes with the misery inflicted by them on the poor. *The Relief of Lucknow* replaced the simple exoticism of earlier Eastern melodrama with a more realistic portrayal of army life in India and provided, in the Reverend David Blount, the first of many stage-priests whose duty to his country is at odds with his duty to God. All three plays were also so constructed as to allow the narrative to be conveyed pictorially while taking full account of the technical skills needed to ensure pictorial continuity. These skills, being essentially those which we have come to regard as cinematic, are best described in the language of the camera—panorama, close-up, cross-cutting, flashback, and so on: and it was here that the great

162. *Dion Boucicault's* The Colleen Bawn, or The Brides of Garryowen. *Myles rescues Eily from the lake in which Danny has just tried to drown her. The play was staged in Boston and New York in 1860, and at the Adelphi Theatre, London, in the same year with Boucicault as Myles and Agnes Robertson as Eily. Harvard Theatre Collection.*

improvements in mechanized stage-equipment in the service of realism began to play an active role in the art of dramatization: the villain in *The Octoroon* is caught by use of the recently invented camera.

Boucicault, however, like most Irish dramatists before and since, was a master of spoken dialogue, a lesson learned from the French and applied to the speech rhythms of Irish dialect. This he proved during the next decade in *The Colleen Bawn* (Fig. 162), *Arrah-na-Pogue* and *The Shaughraun*, all of which drew to some extent on Irish patriotism and revolutionary fervour at a time when Irish Catholic immigrants were invading the United States as refugees from famine and persecution. From then on there was no need to apologize for melodrama as a genre for

serious dramatic composition, as will become apparent in Section 4 of this chapter, 'Serious Drama'.

2 OPERA, BALLET AND PANTOMIME

As already remarked with respect to Mozart's *The Marriage of Figaro*, Beethoven's *Fidelio* and Weber's *Freischütz*, the new democratic spirit released by Beaumarchais, Rousseau and the leaders of *Sturm und Drang* had infiltrated that last theatrical bastion of aristocratic privilege, the opera-house, at a surprisingly early date. This in turn obliged the employment of the best landscape painters and machinists, and recourse to a style of acting, singing and dancing that was flamboyantly rhetorical and romantic—'Penny plain: twopence coloured'—and the construction of larger theatres to contain it.

(a) 'Grand' and Comic Opera: In opera the pioneers of these changes, as might be expected, were German and French: English opera had died with Handel and survived only in the debased forms of ballad-opera and pantomime. In Paris, the Italian and French styles of the eighteenth century were replaced by the lavishly spectacular operas of Auber (1782–1871) and the German Meyerbeer (1791–1864), who between them introduced audiences to what we call Grand Opera. It was in Germany, however, that the past was most emphatically rejected and replaced by romantic opera, *in German* instead of in Italian, bringing with it the prisons, Alpine storms, ghosts, and woodland glades of melodrama. The moving spirit was Carl Maria von Weber, who was born in 1786 and died in London in 1826 shortly after conducting the première of his opera, *Oberon*, at Covent Garden. By then Italians were ready to respond to the new mood, and in Rossini, Donizetti and Bellini found musicians who were able between them to create a new school of composers and librettists capable of fusing traditional *opera buffa*, or comic opera (see pp. 173–5), with pantomime and farce, and *opera seria*, or tragic opera, with melodrama. Rossini's *La Cenerentola* (1817) and Donizetti's *Don Pasquale* (1843) offer outstanding examples of the former: Bellini's *Norma* (1831) and *I Puritani* (1835) and Donizetti's *Lucia di Lammermoor* (1835), adapted from Sir Walter Scott's *The Bride of Lammermoor* (1819), illustrate the latter. As Weber in Germany prepared the way for Wagner's music-dramas, so these Italians laid the melodic, orchestral and scenic foundations for Verdi.

Folklore and folk tune, allied with the romantic poetry of the age, operated no less powerfully on the emergent national drama of Slavonic countries to produce indigenous schools of operatic composition. Even in St Petersburg, where French and Italian influences had been predominant until late in the eighteenth century, forces of change were also at work. The arrival of German actors, the defeat of Napoleon and the first stirrings of national pride brought into being a brilliant school of composers, led by Mikhail Glinka (1804–57) and culminating in Peter Tchaikovsky (1840–93), who all wrote for the theatre. Glinka's *A Life for the Czar* was produced in St Petersburg in 1836, followed by *Russlan and Ludmilla* in 1842. From then on opera developed on national lines, assimilating what was spectacular in Western melodrama together with pantomime and Russian folk dance. Other Slavonic countries, borrowing as much from German example as from Russian initiatives, struck out on their own, especially Bohemia (now Czechoslovakia) where Smetana (1824–84) and Dvořák (1841–1904) produced operas which quickly won international acclaim.

Comic opera also acquired a new life of its own activated (at least in part) by the pretentious claims of Wagnerian music-drama. Following the precedent established in the eighteenth century by the Opéra-Comique in Paris which, during the nineteenth, accommodated the operettas of Offenbach (1819–80), the Theater an der Wien (and later the Volksoper) in Vienna made room for those of Johann Strauss (1825–99), and delighted their audiences with the cancan and waltzes. In England, Richard D'Oyly Carte (1844–1901) built the Savoy Theatre in 1881 (equipping it with electric lighting) to house the light operas of Gilbert and Sullivan, who excelled in parody of *opera seria*.

(b) Romantic Ballet: In ballet the transition from the classical to the romantic style was effected primarily by a single dancer, Marie Taglioni (1804–84), whose father Filippo (himself an Italian ballet-master resident at the Royal Dramatic Theatre, Stockholm) composed *La Sylphide* in 1832 especially for her. In a costume that was derived from eighteenth-century interest in the diaphanous *chiton* of Greek classical drama, but which had been adapted to meet Napoleonic ideas of decency while revealing the body in motion, Taglioni confronted her audiences with the skin-coloured tights, plimsols equipped with 'points' (wooden toe blocks) and *tutu* that have since become the standard costume of the ballerina (Fig. 163). Classical though the derivation of Taglioni's costume and those of the *corps de ballet* may have been, the plot was Scottish and as romantic as any Gothic novel. These innovations were reinforced in 1841 by a production of Adolphe Adam's more famous ballet, *Giselle*, at La Scala, Milan, complete with graveyard and madness, in which the title

163. *A. E. Chalon's portrait of Marie Taglioni in her most prestigious role in* La Sylphide, *especially choreographed for her in 1832 by her father Filippo Taglioni. Lithograph by R. J. Lane from a drawing by A. E. Chalon, 1845. London, Victoria and Albert Museum.*

role was danced by Carlotta Grisi and which is still popular in the modern classical repertoire. Having thus acquired firm foundations of its own within the new romantic era, ballet was just as able as opera to take from melodrama such pantomimic and spectacular elements as it needed to surprise and delight its audiences; and by the end of the century in the choreography of Marius Petipa (1822–1900), and with music by Tchaikovsky, such full-length three-act ballets as *Swan Lake* and *The Sleeping Beauty* could provide a complete evening's entertainment.

In Western Europe the relative undress of ballerinas served to advance their command over audiences at the expense of male dancers, who gradually found they had little more to do than lift or support their partners while miming their own emotional responses, if any. Since ballet, however, normally shared the same stages as opera, it became habitual in Western Europe to include a short ballet within an opera. Gounod's *Faust* (1859) and Verdi's *Aida* (1871) provide good examples. In Russian ballet, however, thanks as much to the addition of one *divertissement* after another to provide variety in a long evening's entertainment as to any other reason, such spirited native folk-dances as Mazurkas, Gopaks and Czardases continued to give men a chance to present themselves to audiences in genuinely masculine roles.

In England, by contrast, the legacy of ridicule attached during the eighteenth century to Italian opera singers (especially *castrati*) and to French male dancers served, in the nineteenth century, to stamp both opera and ballet as absurd, effete, effeminate occupations, tolerable in foreigners but unacceptable among Britons (Fig. 164). Lacking any encouragement, such talent as may have existed either never emerged or was deflected into other channels; outstandingly the most important of these were pantomime and the diversions of the tavern annexes and pleasure gardens.

(c) **Pantomime:** The music-halls of the late nineteenth century were originally little more than annexes to taverns, like skittles or bowling alleys. In the course of the eighteenth century, these halls and gardens acquired a sudden surge of popularity as a consequence of the Licensing Act of 1737. By styling his theatre a refreshment room, a manager could legitimately present singing, dancing, gymnastics and pantomime as an alternative to the 'legitimate' spoken drama offered in the licensed patent theatres. One such was Sadler's Wells, where the medicinal spa waters of Islington had for long attracted a fashionable clientele. By 1765 this had become a stone-built theatre. Being consistently well regulated, it made money for its managers and, by the start of the nineteenth century, it had added aquatic melodramas to its repertoire, the first being *The Siege of Gibraltar* (1804). The fashion spread rapidly, providing inspiration for most of the unlicensed 'minor' theatres of the time. Next to aquatic and equestrian spectacle in popularity were the comic or pathetic popular songs, dances and burlesques which enjoyed as great a following then as modern pop groups and folk singers do now.

Alongside of both was pantomime, already developing rapidly into those dramatized versions of fairy-stories by Nicholas and Pierre Perrault, Jacob and Wilhelm Grimm, and Carlo Gozzi, which J. R. Planché and others transformed into the typical Victorian Christmas entertainments, supposedly intended for children, but relished

IOHN BULL AT THE ITALIAN OPERA.

164. *This caricature by Thomas Rowlandson, published as an engraving in 1811, not only captures British mercantile responses to opera and ballet of the late eighteenth century but sets the tone of those that were to prevail throughout the nineteenth century. London, Victoria and Albert Museum, Enthoven Collection.*

equally by their parents. The topical element was a legacy from the harlequinades of the eighteenth century, as was the playing of the male juvenile lead by an actress *en travestie*. The frequent introduction of topical subject matter through jokes, songs and even whole scenes—so typical of the anarchic Punch and Judy puppet-shows—into the fabric of these short fairy-tales, combined with the sexual ambiguity of the characterizations (compounded later by the playing of older women's comic roles by men) served to create a degree of unrivalled confusion in respect of dramatic genre which has habitually baffled foreigners, yet which continues to bemuse and delight English audiences who never go to a theatre on any other occasion. If melodrama elaborated the magical transformation scenes,

MR. FLEXMORE

165. Owing something to seventeenth-century Commedia dell' Arte, *something to the eighteenth-century Harlequinade, and something to nineteenth-century circuses, this charming Victorian pantomime dancer (Mr Flexmore) illustrates the theatre's abiding conservatism while adapting itself to the public's changing demands. Lithograph by G. Giles from a drawing by J. T. Desvignes, 1850. London, Victoria and Albert Museum.*

and contributed the fairy godmothers, demon kings, and wicked barons and stepmothers to Victorian pantomime, and if opera and ballet added the chorus girls and dancers, the core of the original harlequinade survived in the treatment still accorded to the roles of the principal boy and girl in pantomimes today (Fig. 165).

Such was the dearth of skilled serious dramatists in England at the start of the nineteenth century, and such was the competition offered by the minor theatres to the patent theatres, that their managers eagerly offered pantomime the hospitality of their own stages to stave off the threat of bankruptcy. Their other routine solution to this prob-lem, there being no indigenous opera or ballet companies to help out, was to fall back on revivals of those plays by Shakespeare which continued to offer leading actors and actresses their most challenging roles. However, the texts in which these theatrical luminaries appeared were still far removed from those that Shakespeare wrote.

3 SHAKESPEARE PRODUCTION AND THE LEGITIMATE DRAMA

'Legitimate' as applied to drama meant 'spoken drama'; and in England that meant licensed by the Lord Chamberlain for performance in the patent theatres over which their managers held a jealously guarded monopoly in the early decades of the nineteenth century. Shakespeare fell firmly within this category—despite the fact that most revivals continued to be presented in texts severely altered by other playwrights like Dryden, Cibber and Garrick. While Garrick had won international fame through his interpretations of Shakespearean title roles, he had approached the actual play-texts with as much opportunism (some might say hypocrisy) as any of his predecessors among managers and actors, omitting scenes in some plays and adding scenes of his own contrivance to others. In an age that still received *Macbeth* in D'Avenant's version, with its ballet of flying and dancing witches, and *King Lear* in Nahum Tate's with its happy ending, this is at least understandable. His principal successors—John Philip Kemble (1757—1823), Sarah Siddons (1755—1831) and Edmund Kean (1787—1833)—did not fare much better, although Kean did restore the original ending to *King Lear* in 1824, and William Macready restored the Fool.

(a) **The Texts:** The theatre is a superstitiously conservative profession, stage-business being faithfully handed on by one performer to his or her successor, and an artist's personal, imaginative flair always has to be contained within the limits that a paying public will permit. Thus, as the eighteenth century gave place to the nineteenth, no sooner had Edward Capell established a near definitive text and the first three 'Variorum' editions been published (1803, 1813, 1821), than Thomas Bowdler (1754–1825) set about emending or expurgating the plays of all passages which he regarded as offensive. His ten-volume *Family Shakespeare* was published in 1818 with everything 'unfit to be read by a gentleman to a company of ladies' removed: hence the word 'bowdlerized'. For similar reasons, Kemble created in his Hamlet a Prince whose sweet, philosophic and gentlemanly nature—a wholly 'romantic' Prince—became the prototype for all actors from then onwards to aspire to until the Second World War encouraged experiment with more controversial interpretations. Mrs Siddons, likewise, declined to tackle Cleopatra on the grounds that any natural interpretation must embarrass her audiences. Edmund Kean, by contrast, exploited the public's taste for melodrama by excelling in villainous roles like Othello, Iago, Macbeth, and Sir Giles Overreach in Massinger's *A New Way to Pay Old Debts* (Fig. 166). *Troilus and Cressida* failed to find actor-managers willing to take the risk of reviving it, and *Measure for Measure* fared almost as badly. Respect for nature, however, where stage-costume was concerned, was translated into a concern for historical authenticity. It was Charles Macklin, who had been the first to restore Shylock, in what was then called *The Jew of Venice*, to something resembling the stature of Shakespeare's original portrait (1741), who in 1773 played Macbeth in Scottish Highland dress. Kemble likewise, while content to play Othello in a British general's uniform, adopted a costume approaching Roman dress for Coriolanus.

(b) **Critical Approaches:** As actors and audiences wrestled with the problems of what was and what was not acceptable regarding text, costumes and scenery, Samuel Taylor Coleridge, Charles Lamb and William Hazlitt ushered in the new Romantic criticism—aesthetic, personal and subjective. This had its principal theatrical repercussions in new approaches to stage-design. More significant in the long-term view was the impact of Lamb's essay, 'On the Tragedies of Shakespeare, considered with reference to their fitness for Stage Representation' (1811), for this marks the release of the scholar and the gentleman who, on religious or other grounds, found the theatre distasteful, from any further obligation to consider Shakespeare's plays as texts created for actors to project to assemblies of people— that is, in terms of a distinct artistic medium with a visual and an aural dimension as well as a poetic one. From this time forward, it became possible to regard all Shakespeare's plays (and thus those of other Elizabethan and Jacobean playwrights) as if they, like poems or novels, could be more fully appreciated through private reading than by seeing them acted. An inevitable consequence of the acceptance of this approach was to prepare the ground for speculation about Shakespeare's life, character, and purpose as a writer divorced from the practical realities of his career as actor, director of plays and theatrical shareholder. The sowing of these dragon's teeth, which germinated in Victorian libraries and drawing-rooms and reached maturity in the school and college classrooms of the twentieth century, transformed Shakespeare criticism the world

166. *Edmund Kean as Othello about to murder Desdemona. Lithograph by Dean and Munday from a painting by E. F. Lambert. London, Victoria and Albert Museum.*

over into a battle-ground between scholars and actors which, sadly, is still fought over today.

(c) **Illustrated Editions:** A no less potent force on the popular imagination of the early nineteenth century was the spate of 'illustrations' of scenes from Shakespeare which rolled off the printing presses to adorn Victorian homes: starting with those of Henry Fuseli (1741–1825), drawn in the romantic vein of William Blake, they came to include others flavoured with neo-Gothic sentiment, pedantic antiquarianism and Pre-Raphaelite piety as fitted the taste of the time.

(d) **Scenic Representation:** In the theatre itself the trend towards restoring historically appropriate costume was pursued into recovering architectural authenticity for stage-scenery—a move which in itself served to distort the texts by shifting attention away from spoken poetry towards pictorial glamour. It is easy to be scornful about this development; but it must be remembered that this was one of the few means by which the public of the early nineteenth century, in Britain or anywhere else, could acquire an understanding of what a medieval banqueting hall filled with guests (as in *Macbeth*) or the pageantry of Tudor processions (as in *Henry VIII*) actually looked like; and the more realistically such scenic artists as Clarkson Stanfield, William Telbin or Sir Lawrence Alma-Tadema presented them on the stage, the more they were admired and discussed (Fig. 176). In short, the early exuberance and extravagance of melodramatic spectacle came thus to be refined into a form of stage realism that was historically informative.

The pioneer was Philip Kemble's brother Charles who, in his production of *King John* at Covent Garden in 1823, employed J. R. Planché—Somerset Herald, no less, and author of a *History of Costume*—to design his sets and costumes. This quest for historical verisimilitude was carried on by William Macready and Samuel Phelps. Macready became manager of Covent Garden in 1837 and moved to Drury Lane in 1841. When Parliament revised the old Licensing Act of 1737 to legalize the reality of the existing theatrical situation by abolishing the patent theatres' theoretical monopoly of spoken drama in 1843, Phelps, who had been trained by Macready, instantly took advantage of this change by acquiring control of Sadler's Wells where he proceeded to present serious drama for the

168. *Stage setting representing the Hall of Nimrod from Lord Byron's tragedy* Sardanapalus, *at the Princess's Theatre, London, 1853: a spectacular use of angular perspective (see Fig. 146) and archaeological exoticism.*

next twenty years. When he retired in 1862, he had presented thirty-four plays by Shakespeare, his own best parts being Bottom in *A Midsummer Night's Dream*, Lear and Othello. His productions were much admired for their scenery, which aimed to be realistic but which was also restrained. This cannot be said of Edmund Kean's son, Charles, who took over the Princess's Theatre in 1850 and gave free rein during the next nine years to his own obsession with antiquarian detail (Figs. 167 and 168). While this certainly encouraged the respectable middle class to return to the theatre to see his magnificent tableaux, the difficulty of the scene-changes necessitated constant interruptions of the action: yet so warm was the audience response that his successors had little option but to copy his methods. In doing so, first Irving at the Lyceum, and then Beerbohm-Tree at Her Majesty's aroused the wrath of Bernard Shaw who complained in the *Saturday Review* that they had smothered intelligiblity in scenery (Fig. 177).

(e) **Shakespeare in America**: The fact that English remained the language of the United States of America, notwithstanding the Revolution, ensured that Shakespeare's plays would continue to dominate the repertoires of the many new playhouses that were built as the frontier expanded westwards. Slowly, the early amateur dramatic performances given in make-shift playhouses came to be replaced by custom-built theatres acceptable to professional companies. Their history is confused by exceptionally rapid

167. *Henry V's triumphal return to London after the battle of Agincourt, as represented in Charles Kean's production at the Princess's Theatre, 1859.* Illustrated London News, *23 April 1859.*

changes of managerial responsibility, but it is safe to say that both New Orleans and St Louis possessed theatres with a seating capacity for at least 1,500 spectators by 1835, catering for both resident stock companies and touring productions: these were the St Charles and the St Louis. Chicago, although only numbering two thousand inhabitants, was able by 1838 to support a smaller but no less purpose-built theatre, The Rialto: this was replaced in 1847 by a larger one in Randolf Street. In California, religious dramas presented by Roman Catholic missions, and vaudeville devised and presented by groups of soldiers and sailors on the coast, were superseded, immediately after the Gold Rush of 1848, by the Eagle Theatre in Sacramento (1849) and by others in San Francisco (1852) and elsewhere.

As the building of these theatres encouraged professional acting companies to expand their touring horizons, so leading British actors continued to set the standards of performance and production, at least initially. George Frederick Cooke, Edmund Kean and Macready were among those who made the journey, but this, in turn, challenged Americans to emulate them. The first to dare to cross the Atlantic in the reverse direction was John Howard Payne, who appeared successfully both at Drury Lane in 1813 and at the Comédie-Française. He was followed by Edwin Forrest (less successfully) in 1836, who also performed in Edinburgh: the rivalry between Forrest and Macready culminated in a night of riots in New York in 1849 which left thirty people dead (see Fig. 216). All doubts about the abilities of American actors and actresses, however, were

170. *Edwin Booth as Hamlet. Booth created a personal record by playing this role for 100 consecutive performances in New York in 1864. Contemporary photograph. New York, Lincoln Centre, Library of the Performing Arts.*

169. *Charlotte Cushman, the American actress who took London audiences by storm with her performance of Shakespearean roles in 1845, seen here as Romeo saying farewell to Juliet.* Illustrated London News, 16 February 1855.

demolished with the arrival in London in 1845 of Charlotte Cushman (1816-76) whose Lady Macbeth, Portia and Beatrice were all well received. She even dared to play Romeo opposite her sister Susan's Juliet (Fig. 169). Macready was so impressed with her that he invited her to play Queen Katherine to his own Wolsey in *Henry VIII*. Her triumph was followed in 1861 by that of Edwin Booth, who had already visited Australia in 1854. A playhouse had been built in Sydney in 1833, and a touring circuit of the country (including some towns in New Zealand) was slowly being established. His best roles included Richard III, Shylock, and Sir Giles Overreach, but his outstanding success was Hamlet, which he played for a hundred successive performances in New York in 1864. London audiences welcomed him again in 1881 and 1882 (Fig. 170).

This cross-trafficking over the Atlantic and the Pacific ensured that theatrical representation of Shakespeare's plays became as heavily smothered in realistic scenery in America and Australasia as in Europe; but in 1888 the chance discovery of a drawing in the Library of the University of Utrecht sparked off a reaction that arrested this process and set it in reverse. This drawing was Arend van Buchel's copy of Johannes de Witt's sketch of the interior of the Swan Playhouse, made during his visit to London in 1596. One of the most striking features of the sketch was the absence of any scenery other than a single bench (see Fig. 102). Six years later William Poel founded the Elizabethan Stage Society which, from 1895 onwards, began experimenting with productions of Elizabethan and Jacobean plays on a stage resembling De Witt's (see p. 244).

(f) Shakespeare in Europe: In continental Europe, translation of Shakespeare into both French and German during the eighteenth century led quickly to translation into Hungarian, Italian and other languages. By the start of the nineteenth century many of his plays had become as firmly established in the repertoires of German-speaking companies as in England and America, and leading German actors were beginning to rival one another in their interpretations of the major roles, particularly F. L. Schroeder and A. W. Iffland (see p. 178). By the end of the century this development had repeated itself everywhere from Italy to Slavonic and Scandinavian countries: Spain alone remained aloof. The Italian actor Tomaso Salvini (1829–1916) appeared as Macbeth, Lear, and Othello, playing Othello on one visit to America opposite the Iago of Edwin Booth. The Polish actress Helena Modjeska (1844–1909) likewise won herself an international reputation in Shakespearean tragic roles. In France, Shakespeare, having been retranslated by Laroche (with an introduction by Dumas *père*) and by Victor Hugo, continued to inspire many fine actors and actresses from Talma to Mounet-Sullet and from Rachel to Sarah Bernhardt to appear in his plays. Musicians too fell under Shakespeare's spell, providing programme music either as incidental music for productions, like Mendelssohn's for *A Midsummer Night's Dream* (1844) which included his famous Wedding March, or Sullivan's score for Irving's *Macbeth* (1888), or as independent overtures. These musical essays were as potent in their effect as the illustrated editions and led directly to the composition of full-length operas and ballets. Rossini's *Otello* appeared as early as 1816. Berlioz, deriving his inspiration from the English actress Harriet Smithson, whose performances in Paris of Desdemona and Ophelia he deeply admired (as did Rachel), and whom he finally persuaded to marry him, composed his *Béatrice et Bénédict* in 1862. As the century ended, Verdi crowned his own operatic achievement with *Otello* (1887) and *Falstaff* (1893).

4 SERIOUS DRAMA

The apostolic succession from Aeschylus to myself is as serious and as continuously inspired as that younger institution, the apostolic succession of the Christian Church.

(Bernard Shaw, preface to
Our Theatre in the Nineties, I. vi.)

Anyone disposed to try to puncture the imperious impertinence of this claim could scarcely do better than start with the early years of the nineteenth century; for the flag of 'serious' dramatic writing for the stage was then carried almost single-handed by Germans. The plight of British dramatists has already been commented upon; Spain and Italy produced no champions; in France, following the Revolution and the Napoleonic Wars, it was not until late in the 1820s that any playwright of distinction emerged.

The theatre throughout Europe was in a turmoil: this was in part due to the erosion of the old Italian and French rule-books for dramatic composition to a point where only the real die-hards of conservative opinion continued to respect them, and in part to the admission to theatres of tradesmen and manual labourers who knew little about these rule-books and cared less. All men of letters were therefore obliged to rethink their position. Who were they writing for? How should they write? In verse or in prose? Reflectively, or as evangelists? And what about music and spectacle? How were playwrights to acquire an appropriate style to meet this challenge?

(a) German Pre-eminence: In Germany Goethe and Schiller abandoned the *Sturm und Drang* movement and went their separate ways (see pp. 178–80): Goethe, after a two-year sojourn in Italy, chose a more classical manner of expression; Schiller, after three years of enforced living off the charity of friends, chose the study of history. Goethe returned to the theatre in 1787 with *Iphigenia in Tauris* (Fig. 171) then *Egmont*, followed by *Torquato Tasso* in 1790 and finally *Faust*, Part I in 1808, part II (posthumously) in 1832. The episodic character of *Goetz* and the violence of his sentiments, together with the naturalism of his characterization, was modified in these later ones by their opposites: so much so that it may be doubted whether the poetry of the classical plays stands to gain much by being acted. In other words the emotion which actors legitimately bring to a role tends positively to damage, if not destroy, the cool detachment and lucid simplicity of these dramatic poems, so regular in form, so remote from conflict, so idyllic in mood.

171. A drawing by Angelica Kauffmann of a scene from Goethe's Iphigenia in Tauris, *1787. Weimar, Goethe-Haus.*

Schiller's style changed less abruptly. First came *Don Carlos* (1787). His study of history as a teacher at the University of Jena provided him with the subject matter for his next plays, all of which were tragedies. First *Wallenstein* (in three parts, 1799), which is conceived on a vast scale and which contrasts sharply with the tight structure of *Maria Stuart* (1800). *The Maid of Orleans* (1802) differs from both being quasi-operatic, while *The Bride of Messina* (1803, and more invention than history) emulates Goethe's late, tragic style (Fig. 172). His last work for the theatre was *Wilhelm Tell* (1804) which celebrated the liberation of the Swiss cantons. The great difference between these and his earlier plays lies in their sense of stage-craft. In the later plays his character-drawing has become much firmer and his dialogue less rhetorical and more lyrical. Verse has replaced prose.

None of these plays has aged well outside German-speaking countries. It is ironic, therefore, that it should have been a contemporary of theirs, August Friederich von Kotzebue (1761–1819), who, at least from a theatrical standpoint, eclipsed their immeasurably superior poetic and philosophic talents in plays that crossed all frontiers from Russia to America. Most of his working life was spent in St Petersburg, Vienna, Weimar and Königsberg. He was eventually assassinated in Mannheim by a fanatical student. Critical reaction to Kotzebue's plays—all of them rich in melodramatic incident and sensational situations, if in little else—was instantly hostile and has in general remained so. As his success with managements and the

public spread, however, so he was attacked as a selfish, immoral, destructive figure, who in his readiness to supply the new public with what it wanted, accelerated the disintegration of all accepted standards of taste and decorum. 'He turned Parnassus', wrote Wolfgang Menzel in 1836, 'into a brothel and assumed himself the role of procurer . . . with the object of gratifying the weaknesses and evil inclinations of the educated public and of indulging the vanity of the uneducated.' Yet his plays were immediately translated into other languages. In England, Sheridan himself took on *Die Spanier in Peru*, presenting it at Drury Lane in 1799 as *Pizarro* with Kemble as Rolla (Fig. 173), following the success of Benjamin Thompson's *The Stranger* the previous year which had been adapted from *Menschenhass und Reue*. In France, Pixérécourt followed Sheridan's lead with his *Pizarro* in 1802; in America, William Dunlap made a speciality of adapting Kotzebue's plays, the most successful being *Lovers' Vows* translated from *Das Kind der Liebe*. Some idea of his overwhelming popularity may be gained from the fact that, even in Germany, at the theatre in Mannheim, 116 of Kotzebue's plays were performed on 1,728 evenings during the twenty years between 1788 and 1808 while Schiller's played there for only 28.

Things might have been different in Germany if the young Heinrich von Kleist had not been driven to suicide in 1811, and had not a rigorous stage censorship been introduced in the wake of the Napoleonic wars. As it was, Kleist wrote one brilliant comedy, *Der Zerbrochene Krug* (*The Broken Jug*) in 1808 and, among four other plays a sombre

Left: 172. Oil painting of a scene from Friedrich Schiller's The Bride of Messina, *1803. Weimar, Central Library.*

Below: 173. John Philip Kemble as Rollo in Pizarro, *translated and adapted for production at Drury Lane by R. B. Sheridan from Kotzebue's melodrama* The Spaniards in Peru, *1799. Oil painting by Sir Thomas Lawrence. Kansas City, Mary Atkins Museum of Fine Arts.*

drama of military life, *Der Prinz von Homburg*, before his early death: since the latter was regarded as being directed at Napoleon it could neither be performed nor printed while he was alive. Thereafter Goethe's and Schiller's successors flicker like guttering candles through the early decades of the nineteenth century. Nestroy, Raimund and Grillparzer had considerable success in Vienna. Elsewhere, Georg Buechner and Friedrich Hebbel struggled to find a style which would marry their own interests and talents to contemporary theatrical taste; but they lacked the imaginative force and consistency of purpose needed to command instant success. In retrospect, the striking originality of Buechner's naturalistic style has received due recognition; but although *Danton's Death* was written in 1835—*Wozzek* was still incomplete when he died at the age of twenty-four in 1837—it was thought confusing and had to wait until after the First World War for production by Max Reinhardt in Berlin. Hebbel too wrote his best plays—the biblical *Judith* (1840) and the middle-class tragedy *Maria Magdelena* (1844)—in a style that antedates in some respects the psychological dramas of Ibsen, Chekhov and Strindberg by nearly half a century. This struggle for a satisfactory style of expression could only fully be resolved after Duke George II of Saxe-Meiningen had succeeded during the 1870s in imposing the concept of 'ensemble' upon his own troupe of actors, embracing costumes and settings as well as acting, to give audiences a unified realization of a text in performance (see Fig. 178). More will be said of this in Chapter 13.

(b) **English and American Playwrights:** Similar stylistic problems affected British and American writers of serious plays through most of the nineteenth century. As has already been remarked, most men of letters not only found that stage-censorship and the absence of adequate copyright had transformed writing for the theatre into poorly rewarded hackwork; but they also lacked either the patience to master the crafts of the theatre or the time and imagination to write well. Of English romantic poets, Shelley, in turning to the melodramatic horrors of Webster and Ford, managed in *The Cenci* to get near to writing a fine play, but it was not acted until 1886 and then only by amateurs. Among managers, Macready at least thought well enough of Byron's *Werner* (1822) to include it in his own repertoire in 1830, and was sufficiently encouraged by its success to add *Sardanapalus* (written in 1821) in 1834 (Fig. 168). Of English novelists, only Bulwer-Lytton thought it worthwhile to write his own plays: by subjecting himself to the discipline of learning stage-craft from French masters he succeeded in proving that if logical thought and well-written dialogue could be injected into a melodramatic frame, the result could provide a stimulating experience for the mind as well as the senses. By achieving this himself in *The Lady of Lyons* (1838) and *Richelieu* (1839), he provided the theatre with two plays which proved irresistible to actor-managers for years to come. In America, similarly, Dion Boucicault was ready to stiffen native melodrama by recourse to the same means as Bulwer-Lytton (see pp. 189–90 above). Another factor influencing this change in England was the active interest taken by the young Queen Victoria in the theatre, especially the construction of a private theatre at Windsor and the sequence of Command Performances given there by Charles Kean and others in the 1850s. This did much of itself to persuade her wealthier subjects that theatres might once again be visited without risk of public scandal or eternal damnation.

A steady shift thus becomes discernible away from the rhetorical excess of romanticism towards greater realism and more serious social concern in the plays of Tom Taylor (Professor of English at London University), Charles Reade and Tom Robertson, written between 1860 and 1880 in England, and later by Bronson Howard, Augustin Daly and David Belasco in America. And with these advances, stepping-stones at least were laid on both sides of the Atlantic for the return of a lively dramatic literature to the stage at the hands of Oscar Wilde and Bernard Shaw in the 1890s.

(c) **French Playwrights:** In France, where dramatists at least enjoyed the protection of copyright and reasonable remuneration, the post-Revolution breakdown of the old monopolies, in combination with the explosion of popular street and circus entertainments, led at first to the same uncertainties about a suitable manner of dramatic self-expression as already remarked upon elsewhere. The return of censorship in 1804 made matters worse, leaving the way clear for Pixérécourt and other purveyors of melodramatic spectacle to dominate the theatrical scene. Nevertheless, young French literary rebels still had one citadel to storm which in Britain and Germany had long since fallen—the precious 'unities' preserved virtually intact by the Academy and the Comédie-Française for nearly two hundred years. There was also a need to recover a sense of national pride, severely bruised by the defeat of Napoleon. To this challenge there arose a champion, the young Victor Hugo (1802–85), poet and self-proclaimed leader of the Romantic movement. In the theatre it was sparked off by Charles Kemble's productions of Shakespearean tragedies in Paris in 1827. Hugo, in the preface to his unacted play *Cromwell*, raised the banner of defiance to classical precepts: three years later, on 25 February 1830, he replaced words with deeds in the production of his verse drama, *Hernani*. It created an uproar throughout the performance, and nightly thereafter throughout its long run. After that, no French theatre-goer could doubt that the world had changed.

If, today, we wonder what all the fuss was about, we should recall that France had not possessed a *romantic* theatre of its own since medieval religious plays were banned in 1548, and that young artists of all descriptions were determined to force it into being with the same fervour and ruthlessness with which their fathers had disposed of the aristocracy. Hugo's flamboyant gesture, reinforced by Alexandre Dumas *père*'s 'cloak and dagger' prose dramas *Henri III et sa cour* (1829) and *Antony* (1831), swept resistance aside; Hugo himself, fighting the censor at every turn, wrote six more plays, the best being *Ruy Blas* (1838). The movement, however, like *Sturm und Drang* in Germany, was short lived, and ended with *The Count of Monte Cristo* (played in two parts on alternate nights in 1848) and Alexandre Dumas *fils*'s *La Dame aux Camélias* in 1852.

The public, surfeited on romantic excess, then turned instead to the brilliantly contrived but light-weight plays of Eugène Scribe (1791–1861), Eugène Labiche (1815–88) and Victorien Sardou (1831–1908). All three dramatists have since shared some of that same critical disapproval and abuse levelled at Kotzebue; but Labiche's *Un Chapeau de paille d'Italie* (*An Italian Straw Hat*, 1851) is still frequently revived, while Sardou provided many magnificent roles for Sarah Bernhardt, including that of La Tosca (Fig. 188).

It was these plays, in conjunction with operettas at the Opéra Comique and vaudeville at the Folies Bergère (opened in 1869) which gave rise to the legendary 'Gay Paree' that exercised so magnetic a fascination on more puritanically minded countries in Northern Europe, and in England and America, and which lives on in the vividly evocative theatrical drawings and posters of Toulouse-Lautrec. Yet against these images must be set the prevalence in France of plays of political and social polemic (*pièces à thèse*) inaugurated by Émile Augier (1820–89) in a reaction against historical romances. These in their turn came to be attacked by Émile Zola in *Thérèse Raquin* (1873) where he sought to offer audiences a photographic copy of life.

(d) Dramatic Awakenings in Northern and Eastern Europe: In Eastern Europe and Scandinavia as the nineteenth century began, a wholly different situation prevailed. Given what was effectively a two-tier classification of society into landed aristocrats on the one hand and an illiterate peasantry looked upon as serfs on the other, with only a smattering of middle-class functionaries in between, no national drama of consequence had yet been written. Outside of royal palaces, and capital cities, theatres still had to be built: patrons had still to be found to fill them, together with trained native-speaking actors and writers to provide a repertoire of plays (see Fig. 222).

After the defeat of Napoleon, national pride gave artists some encouragement to throw off the yoke of Italian, French and German tutelage in drama as in music, and strike out on their own. Thus in Hungary, Poland, Russia, Sweden and Norway authors began to write in their native tongue for the stage, and actors came forward to perform their plays.

The first to acquire a more than local reputation were the two great romantic poets, Adam Mickiewicz in Poland (1798–1855), and Alexander Pushkin in Russia (1799–1837), whose *Boris Godunov* (1825) and *Eugene Onegin* (1831) later provided libretti for operas by Mussorgsky and Tchaikovsky. Russian comedy was launched shortly after by Nicolai Gogol (1819–52) whose *Revisor* (known both as *The Government Inspector* and as *The Inspector General*) was produced in 1836 and has since been constantly translated and revived.

By the 1850s, with the emergence of Turgeniev and Ostrovski, Russian theatre had come of age. In Balkan countries, escape from more than three centuries of Turkish rule allowed drama to be readmitted as an art form to national life, and by 1852 work had started on the building of a Roumanian National Theatre in Bucharest. At the same time, in the far north, Björnsterne Bjornson and Henrik Ibsen in Norway and August Strindberg in Sweden were preparing to lay the foundations for a revolution in the theatre—as remarkable and far-reaching as that launched from Germany by Goethe and Schiller a century earlier—the effects of which remain with us today.

PART V

THE DISINTEGRATION OF STYLE: HYPER-REALISM AND ANTI-REALISM

Introduction

Anyone who has followed the story of theatre through the preceding twelve chapters will recognize that while dramatic art, as a mirror of society itself, is as capable as any other art of adapting both its forms and its content to reflect changes in public beliefs, taste and manners, it is usually the last of the arts to do so. This apparent conservatism stems, as stated in the Prologue, in part from the public's own reluctance to desert familiar territory for the unfamiliar, and in part from the lack of security which has always plagued acting as a profession. Shocking language, sights and sentiments usually have a disquieting effect on the audience; and if authors from Aristophanes to Henry Fielding, Victor Hugo or Alfred Jarry (Kenneth Tynan's *Oh! Calcutta!* supplies a more recent example) have always hoped that the shock administered will provoke change, most audiences find it hard to reconcile discomfiture with their normal expectancies of an entertainment.

Governments have proved themselves no less prone to take fright if, on religious or political grounds, playwrights and actors appear to threaten the status quo by inciting audiences to rebel: sporadic attempts to muzzle or suppress plays and players through stage-censorship and legislation have been the direct consequences. It is highly ironic, therefore, that during the final decades of the nineteenth century, when both in Europe and in America the theatre itself appeared to be triumphantly self-confident, its future existence should have come under simultaneous threat from erosion of its ethical foundations within and a hitherto unimagined challenge from without.

The threat from without developed swiftly from progress in optical science. In 1840 Fox Talbot invented the first modern camera (Talbotype), and with it opened up a new world to be explored, photography. To start with this only challenged the painters; but with the addition of Thomas Edison's phonograph in 1876, William Friese-Greene's celluloid motion-picture film and Edison's first Kinetoscope (both 1889), followed by the Lumière brothers' Cinématographe and the improved Armat-Edison Vitascope-Kinetoscope in 1895, it proceeded to challenge scenic artists, actors and dramatists (Fig. 174).

The attack from within grew insidiously out of the erosion of those moral values which for 150 years had underpinned first the 'sentimental' drama of the merchant classes in the eighteenth century and then popular, romantic melodrama in the nineteenth. Philosophers and scientists now began to question not only the sharply etched concepts of virtue and vice which still sustained all drama, opera and ballet in the 1850s, but even the very existence of the Christian God who for the past two centuries had been rewarding virtuous characters and punishing the vicious. Charles Darwin's *The Origin of Species* was published in 1859; the first volume of Karl Marx's *Das Kapital* in 1867; and Friedrich Nietzsche's *Die Geburt der Tragödie (The Birth of Tragedy)* in 1872. All three books provoked a violent critical reaction which rumbled on into the twentieth century, spreading outwards among artists to create a civil war within the theatre at the very time that it most needed to preserve its collective strength to combat the emerging challenge from the new medium of cinema. Further fuel was added to these disputes by the publication of Sigmund Freud's *Die Traumdeutung (The Interpretation of Dreams)* in 1900 and his *Drei Abhandlungen zur Sexualtheorie (Three Contributions to Sexual Theory)* in 1905.

For clarity's sake, therefore, the theatre's responses to these explosive issues will be split between the following two chapters in a way that they were not at the time. The

174. Penny-in-the-slot kinetoscopes for the viewing of short motion-picture sequences in a San Francisco arcade, c.1899.

battle for the mass audience that developed between the theatre and the cinema after 1900 was largely fought over the question of which of the two media could supply the most convincing illusion of reality in the most spectacular and entertaining manner. The efforts, therefore, of theatre-managers and the artists whom they employed during the closing decades of the nineteenth century will be considered first, along with 'stars' of variety, vaudeville and cabaret whose charm and virtuosity filled the Coliseums, Empires, Palaces and Hippodromes where the early 'movies' were first shown. So too will the early manifestations of revolt within the theatre itself against the commercialization of dramatic art which accompanied these developments.

The theatre's own responses to this civil war and to the competition of cinema, radio, television and spectator-sports will be discussed in Chapter 14.

13
Theatre and Early Cinema

1 HYPER-REALISM

(a) **Archaeologists and Antiquaries**: During the fifty odd years that elapsed between the invention of the camera in 1840 and that of the first kinetoscope in 1889, theatre-managers laboured continuously to portray stage-action realistically by every method open to them. Those responsible for presenting serious drama continued to unite a narrative conveyed in pictorial sequences with moral dilemmas confronting the principal characters, and thus succeeded in endowing melodrama with a strong sense of humanity and social criticism as well as theatrical excitement. The urgency of the moral dilemmas and the relief from anxiety bestowed on audiences by the eleventh-hour solutions came thus to depend directly on the degree of pictorial realism achieved by this childrens'-picture-book technique of story-telling (see Fig. 11).

The credit for perfecting these techniques rests primarily with three individuals of radically different personality—Sir Henry Irving, in England, Duke George II of Saxe-Meiningen in continental Europe and David Belasco in San Francisco and New York. All three borrowed and assimilated ideas developed simultaneously elsewhere; but it was they who funded and organized the pursuit of stage-realism *in photographic detail* to its ultimate extremes in theatrical *trompe l'oeil* techniques.

Sir Henry Irving (1838-1905) took his cue from Charles Kean's management of the Princess's Theatre from 1850 to 1859 and from Sir Squire Bancroft's productions at the Queen's Theatre (renamed The Prince of Wales Theatre in 1865), of which he became joint manager on marrying its manageress, Marie Wilton, and which he managed on his own after her death. Irving, on moving into management himself at the Lyceum, set about carrying their enthusiasm for archaeological exactness in the reconstruction of

period settings to its limit, and proceeded to specialize in the realistic representation of the supernatural. Duke George II, using the seemingly real walls of the box set (introduced in 1841) and varying the levels of the stage floor, demanded that the same minutely detailed attention be lavished on the furnishings of interiors, on costume and on acting. Belasco, by deploying panoramic scenery in motion behind actors and by exploiting lighting to simulate sunrises, sunsets and other natural phenomena, set standards of perfection that won him praise and admiration on both sides of the Atlantic.

(b) **Sir Henry Irving and his Scenic Artists**: Irving's management of the Lyceum Theatre did not begin until 1878; but as early as 1871 he had appeared there in the role of the Polish Jew, Mathias, in *The Bells* (Fig. 175), and

175. *Caricature of Henry Irving as Mathias in* The Bells *at the Lyceum Theatre, London, 1871. The sketch was made from a box above the stage, and Irving is here seen dragging the stage curtains behind him in his agitation. Pen and ink drawing. Private collection.*

in 1874 played Hamlet. The critic Joseph Knight, commenting on this production, remarked, 'To the majority of the audience, the play is wholly spectacle, and Shakespeare's words might almost be regarded as a species of incidental music.' When he took this production to America in 1883, the critic of the *New York Times* compared it to 'an illustrated lecture'. According to Boucicault, when Irving began his own management of the Lyceum, he engaged no fewer than eighty carpenters, fifty property men and thirty gasmen to handle his stage-effects for each performance. This is easy to believe when reading Press notices of his productions, for whether in contemporary melodramas like his revival of *The Corsican Brothers* (1880), with its special stage-traps for the ghost scene, or *The Lyons Mail* (1877) with its real horses for the ambush scene, it is the thoroughness and ingenuity of Irving's scenic artists that repeatedly secures critical acclaim. Here, for instance, is an abridged extract from the notice in the *London Era* of his *Romeo and Juliet* (1882; Fig. 176).

> When the dialogue in Friar Laurence's cell ended, a darkness fell and grew upon the whole house, until the stage faded from sight. A slender thread of mournful melody from stringed instruments sustained the continuity . . . Presently the obscurity became less oppressive, and then an ashen haze seemed to hang across the proscenium, through which there was first perceived dimly and in distorted form, and afterwards more plainly . . . the barred entrance to the tomb of the Capulets. Anon . . . other and lesser tombs took shape . . . Then, as the illumination of the picture assumed the distinctive characteristics of yews and willows which took their place in a churchyard . . . the ghostly gleam quickened and vibrated all over, and the picture was finished. It had been painted before the very eye.

This critic then proceeds:

> Before there was any movement in the picture the moonlight waned as though a cloud had passed before the silver orb, and the attention was wholly centred upon Juliet's tomb by a pale taper which flickered in the dark and inky entrance behind the iron gate. Then the action proceeded. Paris strewed his garlands at the gates; Romeo appeared and with desperate strength burst open the barriers to the tomb, and by his reluctant sword Paris fell, slain, within the portals of the sepulchre. Seizing his torch and dragging after him the lifeless form of his antagonist, Romeo disappeared, descending into the vault

176. *Hawes Craven's and William Telbin's setting for Act V Scene iv of Henry Irving's* Romeo and Juliet *at the Lyceum Theatre, 1882.*

below. While the flare of his torch still reddened the damp walls of the entrance the picture faded from view. Silently it came; as silently it vanished. Once again the theatre was shrouded in darkness.

To us, accustomed as we now are to seeing such scenes beamed regularly into our living rooms on television screens, pictorial sequences of the kind provided by Irving fail to excite much comment; but to most playgoers in the late nineteenth century they were breathtakingly exciting both in their beauty and in their power to amaze.

Some indication of the effort that lay behind this achievement may be gauged from Bram Stoker's account of Irving's choice of Sir Lawrence Alma-Tadema to design his *Coriolanus*: 'The idea was new of getting specialists in various periods to apply their personal skill as well as their archaeological knowledge to stage effect . . . Alma-Tadema had made a speciality of artistic archaeology of Ancient Rome . . . He had so studied the life of old Rome that he had for his own purposes reconstructed it' (*Personal Reminiscences*, ii. 65–6).

Whatever we may think about this approach to Shakespeare, there can be no question but that Irving and Ellen Terry exactly gauged the sensibilities of late Victorian

THE LATE NINETEENTH CENTURY

1859	Darwin publishes *The Origin of Species*
1861–5	American Civil War
1867	Marx publishes vol. 1 of *Das Kapital*
1870	Saxe-Meiningen Players produce Shakespeare's *Julius Caesar*
1871	Franco-Prussian War
1876	Wagner builds his Festspielhaus in Bayreuth
1878	Henry Irving starts his management of the Lyceum Theatre, London
1879	David Belasco replaces gas with electric lighting in San Francisco
1881	Ibsen writes *Ghosts*; Saxe-Meiningen Players visit London
1887	Antoine founds the Théâtre libre in Paris
1888	Discovery of De Witt's sketch of the Swan Playhouse, London, at the University of Utrecht
1889	Otto Brahm founds the Freie Bühne in Berlin; Indo-Chinese dancers appear in Paris
1891	J. T. Grein founds the Independent Theatre in London
1892	Bernard Shaw's *Widowers' Houses* produced in London
1894	William Poel founds the Elizabethan Stage Society in London
1895	Henry Irving knighted by Queen Victoria; The brothers Lumière show silent films to paying audiences in Paris
1896	Thomas Edison shows silent films to paying audiences in Boston and New York
1897	Founding of the Moscow Arts Theatre
1899	Appia publishes *Music and Stage Scenery*
1900	Freud publishes *The Interpretation of Dreams*
1904	First performance of Chekhov's *The Cherry Orchard* in Moscow; First performance of Strindberg's *The Dream Play* in Paris; Opening of the Abbey Theatre in Dublin
1909	F. T. Marinetti publishes his 'First Futurist Manifesto' in Paris; Diaghilev presents his Ballets Russes in Paris
1910	Max Reinhardt's production of *Oedipus Rex* in Berlin
1914	Outbreak of the First World War
1915	Provincetown Players led by Eugene O'Neill founded in Massachusetts
1916	Tristan Tzara launches 'Dada' from Zurich

audiences since he was the first actor ever to be awarded a knighthood—an honour he at first refused on the grounds that 'an actor, whilst actively pursuing his calling, should not be singled out from his fellows'; but in 1895, when convinced that the whole profession must gain in public esteem from this distinction, he accepted it. The same distinction was conferred on Irving's disciple and successor, Herbert Beerbohm Tree, whose management of Her Majesty's Theatre in London carried stage-realism to its British apogee (Fig. 177).

(c) **Duke George II of Saxe-Meiningen and his Actors**: Across the Channel, in Germany, this same insistence on expertise coupled with care for detail was being pursued beyond scenic representation into the art of acting itself. Sickened by the absurdity of leading actors declaiming spoken dialogue like operatic arias from centre stage, Duke George II of Saxe-Meiningen and his actress wife Helene Franz set themselves the task in 1866 of persuading their company to work collectively as an ensemble. To help

them, the Duke's designers varied the levels of the normally flat stage-floor to effect greater contrast between the height of actors when seen in relation to one another, an idea that was to prove particularly helpful in adding a sense of depth and realism to the behaviour of stage-crowds. Great care, moreover, was given at rehearsals to ensuring that each actor, however small his part, became possessed of a personality within his own role, so that by believing in it himself he could bring it alive before an audience. Since none of these actors had an established reputation to safeguard, each agreed to play smaller roles as well as larger ones (Fig. 178).

A more sensible choice than Shakespeare's *Julius Caesar* as the play with which to launch this ambitious enterprise is hard to think of since the role of the crowd is there as important as that of any of the principals: and since these number four, with Antony, Brutus, and Cassius each having as much to do and say as Caesar, deployment of the play's political arguments and ensemble-acting go hand in hand. This production, directed by the actor Ludwig

177. *Photograph of Act II Scene i from Sir Herbert Beerbohm Tree's production of Shakespeare's* Henry VIII, *New York, 1912. The Duke of Buckingham on his way to execution. University of Bristol Theatre Collection: Beerbohm Tree Collection.*

Chronegk, opened in 1870: in May 1874 the company presented it in Berlin, six months before Irving's *Hamlet*. Such was the interest generated by it that these actors applied the same methods to other plays by Shakespeare and added several by Schiller including his trilogy *Wallenstein*. In the course of the next fifteen years they travelled abroad, visiting no less than nine countries, including England in 1881 and Russia, where bankruptcy brought their endeavours to an abrupt end in 1894. As they travelled, so the quality of their productions persuaded contemporary

writers (including Björnson, Ibsen and Tolstoy) to let them stage some of their plays: one such was Ibsen's *Ghosts*. Their work also led directly to the founding of the Théâtre libre in Paris in 1887, the Freie Bühne in Berlin in 1889, the Independent Theatre in London in 1891 and the Moscow Art Theatre in 1897 (see below pp. 218–20).

178. *A scene from Kleist's* Prinz von Homburg *as presented by the Saxe-Meiningen players, c.1880. Pen and ink drawing. Yale University Theatre Collection.*

(d) **David Belasco and his Technicians:** While the Meiningen Players and Sir Henry Irving's company were, in their different ways, advancing the cause of stage-realism in Europe, 6,000 miles to the west in San Francisco, David Belasco (1859–1931) was pursuing the same ends with equal single-mindedness, but with other methods. In the first place he was not greatly interested in Shakespeare or Schiller: in the second, he abandoned acting for stage-management and playwriting at the age of twenty, determined to make himself a master of all stage-crafts. With hindsight we can recognize that he was aiming to become what we now call an artistic director.

As an apprentice actor in San Francisco he had been hired by Charles Kean when touring the west coast in 1868, and played the young Duke of York in *Richard III*. He thus became acquainted at first hand with archaeological stage-realism as practised by Kean, and was never slow thereafter to apply such lessons as he picked up from others to his own productions and plays. As an American working in stage-management, at first in San Francisco and then in New York, he was among the first to be able to experiment with electric lighting, and this he applied to all his work from 1887 onwards.

Most of his own plays were adapted from the novels and stories of others; but where Irving and the Meiningen Players favoured romantic period epics, his own choice inclined towards those depicting moral dilemmas of domestic life in a recognizably American environment, either recalling from boyhood memories of California or reflecting what he later saw in the city life around him. Into these homely situations Belasco then injected the theatrical tension and excitement he had encountered when acting or stage-managing traditional melodramas, narrating his story by showing it in action pictorially while ensuring that his dialogue remained prosaically conversational. It was on these foundations that his long line of Broadway 'smash hits' was grounded in the decade leading up to the First World War: these included *Madame Butterfly* (1900), *The Music Master* (1904) which ran for four years, *The Girl of the Golden West* (1905), *The Easiest Way* (1909) and *The Return of Peter Grimm* (co-produced with Cecil B. de Mille in 1911; Fig. 179). Puccini was so impressed by his work that he adapted two of these plays to form libretti for two of his best-known *verismo* operas.

In the more conventional world of spectacular melodrama Belasco made himself a special master of the chase sequence depicted in 'Western' terms. He wrote and directed *The Girl I Left Behind Me* (1893) while still in San Francisco. This was not the first stage-representation of frontier life, since it had already been treated in such plays

179. David Warfield in the title role of David Belasco's The Return of Peter Grimm, *with Janet Dunbar, New York, 1911. Belasco's assistant director for this production was Cecil B. de Mille. Harvard Theatre Collection.*

as T. B. Walden's *Kit, the Arkansas Traveller* and Frank Murdoch's more famous *Davy Crockett* (1870; Fig. 157); what Belasco added, however, was the technical skills needed to weave three stories into one on the same stage. This he did by dividing the stage itself into three areas (one for each strand of the story) and then cross-cutting (to use a cinematic anachronism) from one to the other until it became possible to make all three lines of narrative intersect at the climax. Thus Red Indians (stage right) besiege a settlers' stockade (stage left) which only with great difficulty holds out until the cavalry (centre back) arrive to effect a rescue. One first-night critic was so impressed by the illusion of reality achieved in performance that he told his readers: 'The onrush of the dozen mounted cavalry men, covered with alkali dust, is something which will live in the memory. It is an exact copy of many such a scene.'

This impression was confirmed by another critic in Boston. 'The fidelity to the real conditions of army life in the West is noticeable throughout every scene.'

The determination which Belasco shared with Irving to bring the ideal of verisimilitude in stage-scenery as near to living photographs as possible is well illustrated in their respective treatment of snowscapes in *The Corsican Brothers* and *The Girl of the Golden West*. Irving's biographer, Bram Stoker (the author of *Count Dracula*), describes the former, saying that it was,

> as real as anything can be on a stage. Trees stood out separately over a large area so that those entering from side or back could be seen passing behind or amongst them. All over the stage was a deep blanket of snow, white and glistening in the winter sunrise. Snow that lay so thick that when the duellists, stripped and armed, stood face to face, they each secured a firmer footing by kicking it away. Of many wonderful effects the snow was perhaps the strongest and most impressive of reality. It was salt, tons of it.
>
> (*Reminiscences*, I. 159–160)

Motion was here supplied only by the actors; no wind in the trees, no falling snow. In Belasco's play, as William Winter makes clear in his graphic description of the storm scene, it appeared to be supplied by the elements:

> Nothing of the kind which I have ever seen in the theatre has fully equalled in verisimilitude the blizzard on Cloudy Mountain as depicted by Belasco in the Second Act of this fine melodrama—such a bitter and cruel storm of wind-driven snow and ice as he had often suffered under in the strolling days of his nomadic youth. When the scene, the interior of the *Girl's* log-cabin, was disclosed the spectators perceived, dimly, through windows at the back, a far vista of rugged, snow-clad mountains which gradually faded from vision as the fall of snow increased and the casements became obscured by sleet.
>
> Then throughout the progress of the action, intensifying the sense of desolation, dread and terror, the audience heard the wild moaning and shrill whistle of the gale, and at moments, as the tempest rose to a climax of fury, could see the fine-powdered snow driven in tiny sprays and eddies through every crevice of the walls and the very fabric of the cabin quiver and rock beneath the impact of terrific blasts of wind,—long,—shrieking down the mountain sides before they struck,—while in every fitful pause was audible the sharp click-click-click of freezing snow driving on wall and window . . .
>
> The operation of the necessary mechanical contrivances required a force of thirty-two trained artisans,—a sort of mechanical orchestra, directed by a centrally placed conductor who was visible from the special station of every worker . . . the perfectly harmonious *effect* of this remarkable imitation of a storm necessitated that at every performance exactly the same thing should be done on the stage at, to the second, exactly the prearranged instant.
>
> (*Belasco*, II. 205–7)

Stoker's reference to 'tons' of salt, and Winter's to the 'mechanical orchestra' required to initiate the snow storm, are particularly revealing since their descriptions suffice to make it obvious that stage-realism, carried to this pitch, must increase production costs to a dangerous level which only longer runs could cover. Nor could leading actors who were also the managers find the time required to marshal these armies of carpenters, painters, electricians and wardrobe staff, to administer the account books efficiently and to attend to all the exigencies of rehearsing the actors. In short, as melodrama became pictorially more realistic during the last decades of the nineteenth century, responsibility for the management of its theatrical realization became too onerous for one man to handle.

(e) **Managerial Syndicates:** (i) *Show Business:* Greatly extended capital resources were thus needed to finance these productions. Failure to please the public brought with it the risk of proportionately heavier losses. Edwin Booth, when writing to a friend following his own bankruptcy in 1873, advised him, in the light of his experience, to put the money he had spent on realistic scenic effects into finding good actors, and into regaining control of artistic direction—just as the Meiningen Players were about to do. This advice, however, went largely unheeded in Britain and America (and to a lesser extent in France) since bigger theatres, more machinery, and vastly improved travelling facilities had already combined to destroy tight-knit companies and to herald the advent of what became known as the 'star system'.

By taking advantage of railways and fast ocean liners, managers were discovering that instead of waiting for audiences to turn up at their theatres, productions could be transported to other audiences in equally well-equipped theatres at home and abroad with an actor or actress (sometimes both) at the head of the company whose personal reputation was sure to attract crowds wherever they appeared. Journalists and photographers followed them wherever they went, thus embellishing these reputations with all the gossip and attendant publicity stunts of an advertising campaign.

This development attracted businessmen with little or no experience of the theatre, but with a flair for anticipating public taste, to enter into theatre management by acquiring chains of theatre buildings and thus to keep a single production running for a year or more. In this way 'star billing' and 'long runs' came to assume an overriding importance in theatrical production at the expense of artistic considerations respecting choice of play and ensemble acting. Augustin Daly in America (1836–99) followed by Daniel Frohman (1851–1951) and his brother Charles (1860–1915), and Sir Edward Moss in England (1852–1912) followed by Sir Oswald Stoll (1866–1942), pioneered this new style of production organization and amassed huge fortunes from it. Daly came from journalism to the theatre, Moss from the circus. Their successors improved on their example by grouping themselves into syndicates which, because they owned the theatres, could dictate what productions and which actors they would permit the public to see and which they would not. In so doing they brought into being by the end of the century what we have come to call 'commercial theatre' and with it 'show business'—vigorous, glamorous, and ruthlessly efficient. Confined to central districts of major metropolitan cities—Shaftesbury Avenue in London; Broadway in New York, and so on—this approach to theatre had genuinely sought to provide its patrons with a guarantee of value for their money, but it has also proved itself to be relatively indifferent to social and aesthetic aspects of dramatic art. It was this indifference which the pioneers of the Little Theatre Movement set out to challenge at the end of the century, a movement as much inspired (as its name implies) by a determination to break the syndicates' monopoly of theatre buildings as to promote 'plays of social and literary merit' and greater integrity in the art of acting. This civil war was thus fought at the very time that the syndicates and the surviving actor-managers had to face the threat posed by motion-pictures to their hitherto unrivalled control of the mass audience, and more must be said about it shortly.

(ii) Variety and Vaudeville: Ironically, this threat was developing within the other branch of theatrical entertainment which the syndicates had absorbed into their empires—the music halls, where the major elements of melodrama had first secured a grip on the popular mind following the French Revolution. There, singers, dancers and comedians had found that they could demand large fees for their highly individualized performances and dictate the moment within the miscellaneous programmes offered at which they appeared. By the middle of the century this applied to such artists as George Laybourn (nicknamed 'Champagne Charlie' after his most famous song), Sam Cowell and Jenny Hill (the Vital Spark). A more fitting overall title for the programmes in which these artists appeared than 'variety' can scarcely be imagined. The virtuosity of the entertainers, the brevity of their 'acts' or 'turns' and their booking procedures known as 'dates' at once reflected the spirit of the new industrial age and suited the syndicates admirably. Thus syndicates came to control the music hall, variety and vaudeville houses as they were variously known, and to endow them with such grandiloquent names as Alhambra, Coliseum, Palace and Empire. There they offered consistently brash but slick entertainment at low cost to weary working men at the end of a long day, with alcohol and female company available in promenading areas at the back of the auditorium. Sentimental, jingoistic and suggestive as many of these 'turns' became—especially the songs—they owed their enormous popularity to a sense of humour that could translate the harshness of daily, working-class life into the emotional release of laughter, tears and the sort of stoical reconcilement to life so endearingly represented by Shaw's Doolittle in *Pygmalion* (Fig. 180). Patrons were promised fun and a good time, neither more nor less: leading artists toured unceasingly at home and abroad as 'stars' in their own right. In doing so they came to rival leading actors and actresses of legitimate drama to a degree where the latter felt obliged to join them in brief excerpts from their more famous roles, bringing about in the process such improbable couplings as Sarah Bernhardt with the clown Grock, or Sir Herbert Beerbohm Tree with the singer Marie Lloyd on the same stage in the same show.

In America variety was known—at least from the 1850s—as vaudeville (although frequently called burlesque), a name imported from France where it had been associated with street theatres of the Paris fairs, and one which may have originated among the wandering *jongleurs* and *trouvères* of medieval minstrel troupes (see pp. 86–8). This produced during the 1820s and 1830s a unique American variant, the 'Negro Minstrel Show'. The idea that white entertainers should black their faces in imitation of negro slaves was popularized, if not invented, by Thomas D. Rice (1806–60). Starting in Kentucky, it led to the creation of a new theatrical character—Jim Crow. Such was Rice's success, especially in New York, that troupes of black-faced singers, dancers and comic-patter duos were quickly formed throughout the United States as the theatre

In Europe, outside of Britain, this type of entertainment became the prerogative of cafés and cabarets, some of which were replaced during the latter half of the nineteenth century by theatres specializing in vaudeville and operetta like the Folies-Bergère in Paris (Fig. 181) or the Tivoli Gardens in Copenhagen. In Eastern Europe, including Russia, it continued to be associated only with the annual fairs. A decadent variant known as *Grand Guignol* was derived from French marionette shows and specialized in the sado-masochistic pleasures of horror, pain and terror: this appeared in the Montmartre district of Paris during the 1890s, spreading first into German cabaret and later into films (see p. 230). An equivalent debasement of vaudeville occurred shortly after the First World War in America, where burlesque came to mean strip-tease shows for men—a development vividly charted by the late Ethel Merman in her last great musical, *Gipsy* (1959), in which she played the stripper's devoted but hostile mother.

(f) Early Cinema: During the final decade of the nineteenth century, however, just when the syndicates' control over

180. Harry Lauder (1870–1950), the Scottish star of the music halls whose absurdly large glengarry and gnarled walking-stick became as famous as his songs throughout the English-speaking world. He was knighted in 1919.

181. Programme cover for the Folies-Bergère, Paris, c.1923. London, Victoria and Albert Museum.

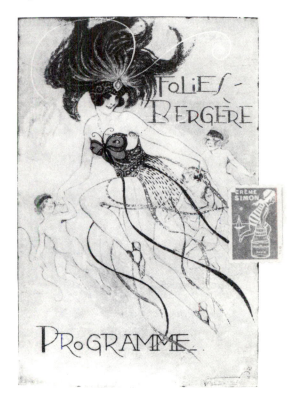

expanded westwards and into Europe: they have proved popular enough to have provided material for television song and dance spectaculars until very recently. Their sudden disappearance in the late 1960s reflects the theatre's belated recognition that such shows would give grave offence with political consequences on both sides of the Atlantic.

182. *The Theatre Royal, Haymarket, London, as rebuilt in 1821. Note the continued presence of a forestage, proscenium doors and boxes above them, with stage and auditorium still illuminated by candles and oil lamps. Engraving by J. Stow from a drawing by Schebbethe. University of Bristol Theatre Collection.*

both variety and the legitimate theatre appeared to be complete, development of photography presented them with an unexpected challenge in the form of motion-picture cameras, projectors and silent films.

Having patented his 'Kinetoscope' in 1889, Thomas Edison was by 1892 allowing his short strips of film (made on kinetographs) to be projected in his penny-in-the-slot kinetoscopes, placed in amusement arcades and fairground booths in the USA (Fig. 174). This novelty was quickly copied by others who evaded his copyright by calling their machines mutascopes, vitascopes and bioscopes. In

Paris, the brothers Louis and Auguste Lumière presented a short film, *The Arrival of the Paris Express*, on their Cinématographe to paying Parisian viewers in 1895: audiences, it was reported, were terrified by the approaching train as it drew into the station at Lyons: in 1896 Edison himself supervised a public exhibition on his own and Thomas Armat's improved kinetoscope of a short excerpt from a play then running on Broadway. The critic of the *Boston Herald* was certain that the laughter from Edison's audience, in response to this short sequence (described as *May Irwin Kiss*), equalled that normally anticipated

183. *The Theatre Royal, Haymarket, London, in 1880. The forestage and proscenium doors have been removed. The proscenium itself has now become a frame for the stage pictures behind it, and the auditorium can be blacked out as a result of the installation of gas lighting.*

when the scene was played on the stage.

When this young cuckoo-in-the-nest was first introduced into vaudeville and variety theatres in the closing years of the century as nothing more than just another 'turn' or 'special attraction', actors were even more contemptuous of it than the managers, believing that since films were silent they could not pose a threat to the stage. And since, for the most part, these early films consisted of little more than short news items and brief travelogues (the fascination of which resided simply in their actuality), stage actors can hardly be blamed for having adopted this attitude. During the first decade of the new century, however, the threat posed to the future of the legitimate theatre by these innocuous-looking innovations in the variety theatres became serious enough to require a more active response than a passive reliance on the advantages of spoken dialogue (see pp.223-5).

The first manager to counter-attack was Belasco. Having already risked everything to challenge the syndicates by acquiring a theatre of his own in which to direct and present his own plays, he was well placed to exploit the other major resource which a theatre still possessed when competing against a film—the controlled lighting of interior scenes. Recognizing that only scenes filmed in full daylight would be sufficiently well defined to be acceptable to a paying public, Belasco wrote and directed plays which offered audiences beautifully lit interiors, deliberately devised and constructed for maximum effect (see Fig. 179). In Britain

it was the Variety Theatres themselves that fought hardest to stave off the challenge. In 1901 Edward Moss opened his Hippodromes, with vast water tanks containing 100,000 gallons of water into which divers could plunge from the dome above, elephants could be slid down a chute, and hounds and horsemen could pursue foxes. Sir Oswald Stoll matched him at the Coliseum with a great revolving stage which he used for chariot races and a mock Derby.

Nevertheless, despite the ridicule heaped upon films by their detractors during these early years, it quickly became clear to managements that theatres had begun to close and to be *replaced* by purpose-built cinemas for the exhibition of films. In Britain, where fourteen new theatres had been built in London alone between 1880 and 1900, there were no less than 5,000 auditoria described as cinemas by 1914: 300 of these were in London. The message was unmistakable: the public now had a choice. By the time the First World War ended in 1918 that choice had been made and the theatre had lost the allegiance of the mass audiences which it had enjoyed throughout the nineteenth century. Ironically the theatre's defeat was due in large measure to the achievement of its own leading playwrights, designers and directors in developing the crafts of pictorial narration into a fine art which the new movie-makers had only to copy to excel. Panoramas, tracking scenes, action tableaux, close-ups, slapstick farce had all been carefully explored and interrelated in stage-plays from the 1860s to 1900. When these techniques were applied to location settings with real waterfalls, real ambushes, real guns, ships and aeroplanes, and real continuity was added with collapsing bridges, charging cavalry, chariot races and rioting crowds, the advantage accruing to directors of four-to-ten-reel epic films like *Napoleon, Man of Destiny* (1909, Vitagraph: J. Stuart Blackton), *The Battle Hymn of the Republic* (1900, Vitagraph: Larry Trimble), *Nero and Britannicus* (1913, Pathé) and *The Last Days of Pompeii* (2nd version 1913, Ambrosio) over their theatre rivals becomes obvious. What was no less obvious to manual labourers and their families was the cheapness of cinema seats and the lack of formality prevailing in the auditorium. All these films, it must be remembered, were silent: but in America this proved to be an overwhelming advantage, since language—a major obstacle in the theatre for recent immigrants— automatically ceased to be one in the cinema. Cinema had become an industry.

What is not so obvious is how or why a theatre capable during this same period of enlisting dramatists of the calibre of Ibsen, Strindberg, Chekhov, Hauptmann, Wilde and Shaw should have lost ground as rapidly and as severely as it did. That must concern us now.

2 REVOLT: ANTI-REALISM

Here the reader must take a deep breath, close his eyes, and try to visualize a theatre with some three thousand seats; then set beside it a mental picture of an auditorium containing a mere three hundred (Figs. 183 and 197). These images give a fair idea of what, numerically, theatres throughout the Western world lost in terms of paying customers to the cinemas between 1900 and 1920—a loss of 90 per cent of their former patrons. In other words, the number of theatre-goers whose loyalty was rewarded with the long list of fine plays by major dramatists during that same period was relatively small, and probably no larger in aggregate than all the theatre-goers of the eighteenth century. It must not be imagined, however, that the patrons who ceased attending theatres in favour of the cinema were confined to the labouring classes who had been newly admitted to theatres in the nineteenth century. The dramatists themselves saw to it that among the deserters would be a substantial proportion of middle-class theatre-goers who found many of the new plays distasteful at best; at worst disgusting or incomprehensible. Gone were the days when a common code of moral and social values informed a common code of stage-conventions understood and accepted by dramatists, actors and playgoers alike. Many patrons found it exciting to be asked to think for themselves, but many more did not.

(a) **French Beginnings:** The revolt against realism started innocuously enough in the middle of the nineteenth century in France as a protest by young dramatists and critics against the theatre's apparent obsession with spectacle and pictorial realism. It took the form of *pièces à thèse*—plays centered upon the serious treatment of social and ethical problems of everyday life, in which such matters as illegitimacy, prostitution, or religious bigotry were dramatized and discussed. Émile Augier's *The Marriage of Olympia* (1855) and Dumas *fils*'s *Le Demi-monde* (1855) offer adequate examples. Even so, public response was muted and confined to the liberal bourgeoisie, as was the case with Tom Robertson's *Caste* (1867) in England. These plays were followed, however, by the more radical 'slice-of-life' naturalism advocated in the 1870s by Émile Zola: but again the public was not impressed and booed his *Thérèse Raquin* off the stage. Nevertheless these tentative efforts to force the theatre into sparing some room for intelligent discussion of recent developments in contemporary thought prepared the ground for playwrights in other countries, less handicapped by the weight of theatrical tradition, to be more adventurous. Slowly this movement spread into Scandinavia and Russia, where there were few theatrical traditions and taboos to respect. As it passed into Germany and England with its undercurrent of new ideas, it could be viewed, from a theatrical standpoint, within the context of the new realistic production techniques so ably demonstrated by the Meiningen Players on their tours abroad. And as this radical movement gained adherents throughout Europe, so it came to be viewed in the far more disquieting context of the published writings of Darwin, Marx and Nietzsche, the aesthetic tenets of Wagner's music-dramas, and the ideas of the German philosopher Schopenhauer. From that point onwards a disintegration of all previously accepted standards of both form and content in dramatic art became an inevitable sequel. The only common factor remaining as a constant among the new generation of rebels was their right to hold all traditional values, moral, social and aesthetic, up to question.

(b) **Scandinavian Perspectives:** The first and certainly the most notable of these young rebels was the Norwegian Henrik Ibsen (1828–1906). Norway had only received independence from Denmark in 1814, and even then only as a condominium with Sweden, a bond not finally severed until 1905. Ibsen's own early plays and those of his contemporary and fellow countryman Björnson were coloured by that same historical romanticism which, half a century earlier, had been so fashionable in Germany and England. Both men gained some practical knowledge of the stage

184. *Gordon Craig's design for a stage-setting for Act V Scene 2 of Ibsen's* The Pretenders. *University of Bristol Theatre Collection.*

from holding administrative posts in Norway's early theatres, but both aimed to become poets. Of the two Björnson was the more fortunate both in his family upbringing and in his career. Blessed by good fortune and success as manager of a theatre in Bergen, and then as newspaper editor, politician and novelist, his plays reflect the technical skills of a fine craftsman and the concerns of a liberal but provincially minded patriot. Rejecting historical dramas in favour of controversial social and moral evils in *The Editor* (1874), *The Bankrupt* (1875) and *A Gauntlet* (1883), his journalistic flair ensured that these plays would advance his reputation, but his outlook and approach to his subjects also ensured happy endings to his plays. As yet, ambiguity of meaning and controversial or depressing conclusions were not thought to be compatible with entertainment.

This success story rankled with the young Ibsen, whose early life had been dogged by poverty and disappointment: yet he was not only the better poet, but able (thanks to travel grants which took him to Denmark, Germany and Italy) to acquire a sense of objectivity which enabled him to question the values and conventions of small-town life more searchingly than Björnson—especially when assessing human character and motivation. These qualities make an early appearance in his romantic, historical drama *Kongsemnerne* (*The Pretenders*) in 1863 (Fig. 184), and in the austere *Brand* (1866), an uncompromising attack on compromise. This theme he develops through rhetorical questions—accusing question piled on accusing question, probing ever deeper as the questions fail to elicit denials or even a response. This technique foreshadows the famous scene in his *Peer Gynt* (1867) where Peer peels an onion layer by layer and asks, 'When am I going to get to the heart?' only to reply,

> God, it hasn't got one! Right to the middle.
> It's layers and layers, each getting smaller.
> Nature is witty! To Hell with thought!

Now self-assured enough to direct this method of character analysis towards contemporary Norwegian life, Ibsen abandoned verse for prose and began that ruthless exposure of hypocrisy, greed, lust and ambition lying close behind the conventional standards of virtue and vice preached both in public and in private in the towns of his youth. Beginning with political corruption in the ironically titled *Pillars of Society* (1877)—a subject to which he later returned in *Rosmersholm* (1886)—he then focused attention on the grim social conventions governing marriage in *A Doll's House* (1879) and *Ghosts* (1881). Experience and success thus equipped him with the masterly command of psychology and dramatic economy and power needed to convey the subtle interaction of human motives and responses which distinguish *The Wild Duck* (1883/4) and *Hedda Gabler* (1890). An expatriate for most of the time between writing *The Pretenders* and *Hedda Gabler*, Ibsen quickly acquired an international reputation sufficiently distinguished to secure early translation of his plays into other languages. William Archer's English translations began appearing in 1890, and his edition of all of Ibsen's plays was published between 1906 and 1908. Some indication of the challenge that they presented to conventional public opinion can be gained from the general hostility of critical response to early performances in both London and New York.

While Ibsen was at the height of his powers another young rebel was undergoing a dramatist's apprenticeship in the theatres of Norway's eastern neighbour, Sweden. This was August Strindberg (1849–1912), whose questioning of the whole fabric of Western inherited culture impressed Ibsen enough as an old man to remark to a friend, 'There is one who will be greater than I.'

Strindberg's career was itself tempestuous, pockmarked by poverty, two disastrous marriages and a mental breakdown, all of which were overridden by a blazing imaginative genius that extended the horizons of dramatic art more radically than any individual had done before or has done since. In his youth he shared Ibsen's earlier struggles against penury and rebuffs but succeeded in acquiring some

notoriety as a journalist. He started to write for the theatre in 1869, with only limited experience as an actor to guide him. Most of his early plays, like those of Björnson and Ibsen, were historical romances strongly coloured by the views of the Danish philosopher Sören Kierkegaard. In 1883 Strindberg left Sweden to travel, and it was during the next six years, while living abroad, that he began to submit all the moral values and social conventions he had grown up with in Sweden to searching examination in a sequence of naturalistic plays beginning with *The Father* (1887) and *Miss Julie* (1888). These, of all his plays, remain those most often revived today. The highly personalized manifesto which he attached as preface to the printed text of *Miss Julie* created an even greater outcry from outraged conservative opinion than the production of the play itself in Paris. Nor could he have expected to please female theatre-goers as one play after another denounced women as destructive predators born to consume men. Much of the source material for these plays—*Comrades* (1886-7) and *Creditors* (1888), *Mother Love* (1892) and the two-part *Dance of Death* (1901)—was drawn from the experiences of his own wretched marriages. By 1895 he was tottering on the brink of a mental breakdown. Although this responded to cure, he remained subject to schizophrenia, thus oscillating in his writing between reversions to pseudo-classical historical dramas (the best of which is *Gustavus Vasa*, 1899) and highly subjective and surrealistic plays like *The Dream Play* (1904) and *Ghost Sonata* (1907), both deeply indebted to the writings of Freud. When he died in 1912, although still regarded as an outlaw by the Swedish Academy, his countrymen accorded him a hero's funeral.

(c) **Russian Awakenings:** Yet further to the east, in Russia, the theatre was also poised to attract attention in the West. Maturity had been rapidly attained once Gogol and Ostrovsky had succeeded in using the stage to draw public attention to the concerns of the emerging middle class (see p. 201). Despite battles against censorship, their plays had found a permanent place in the repertoire by the middle of the century. Ostrovsky, besides being a skilled, professional dramatist, was an able organizer; and after appointment as Director of the Imperial Theatre in Moscow he proceeded, during the 1870s, to copy French example in founding a Royal Academy of Dramatic Art and a Society of Dramatic Authors and Composers.

It was in this same decade that Ivan Turgenev's masterpiece, *A Month in the Country*, was first performed (1872); that Count Leo Tolstoy (1828–1910) published *War and Peace* (1870) and *Anna Karenina* (1875); and that Feodor Dostoevsky published *The Possessed* (1871/2). The last of these novels, together with its companions *Crime and Punishment* (1868) and *The Brothers Karamazov* (1881), were soon dramatized, and by 1887, Tolstoy himself had been persuaded by friends to write for the stage. His acquiescence marks a major change in the fortunes of the Russian theatre since he not only chose to write in a fully realistic idiom but also to espouse the cause of the peasant in Russian society and thus to force upper-class audiences to consider the injustices, squalor and degradation on which their wealth and prosperity had rested. In doing this he made enemies; but this he was ready to accept as the price of discharging what he regarded as simply his Christian duty to his fellow men.

His first play on this daring theme, *The Power of Darkness*, was followed by *The Fruits of Culture* (1889), a satire, realistically conceived and directed against landlords and their relationships with their tenants. The questions raised by Tolstoy in these plays concerning the existing social order had to be answered, either sooner in the manner of England's 'Bloodless Revolution' of 1688, or later in the more agonizing manner of France's 'Reign of Terror': but Russian society was not yet ready for change on this scale. The two major dramatists to follow Tolstoy were, therefore, restrained from doing more than invite others to share their own compassion in looking to the future. Anton Chekhov (1860–1904) died a year before the abortive uprising of 1905: Maxim Gorki (1868–1936), having written his best play by 1902 (*The Lower Depths*), promoted revolution as an exile in Italy until 1913; but he then quit Russia for Germany shortly after the October Revolution, and did not return until 1929.

Gorki enjoyed none of the advantages of his upper-class predecessors. Orphaned at seven and put out to work at nine, he took to the roads as a tramp in his teens. When he first succeeded in publishing a story at the age of twenty-four, he was the first Russian writer who was entirely self-taught. What he lacked in ability to give form to his thought, he made up for with his first-hand experience of life among society's casualties and rejects—the cripples, beggars, prostitutes and alcoholics of city back-streets and the oppressed, peasant farm-labourers in the country, depicted in short stories like *Makow Chudra* (1892). Once established as a writer, he devoted his creative energies consistently to the struggle to offer the proletariat a better future; but of his subsequent plays only *Yegor Bulichev* (1932) has survived translation to be professionally produced in the West.

If Gorki can thus be regarded as the herald of the future in the final years of Tsarist Russia, Chekhov was as definitely the last of the prophets of change. Born into a middle-class family and trained as a doctor, he retained far more of the milk of human kindness than any member of the medical profession depicted by Bernard Shaw in *The Doctor's Dilemma* (1906). No sooner had he qualified than he began to devote most of his time to writing. As an author he chose, like an impressionist painter, to portray the flickering hopes, disappointments, ambitions and frustrations—even despair—of his patients and acquaintances within brilliantly constructed stories and plays, moving between broad farce and tragedy. To some extent this must reflect the temperament not only of a doctor confronted with the ailments of his patients, but of an individual who was himself subject to moods alternating from deep despondency to roguish merriment. *Ivanov* (1887), his first play, reflects the former; but so do *The Seagull* (1896), *Uncle Vanya* (1899, re-worked from the earlier *Wood Demon* of 1889) and *The Three Sisters* (1901). All are irradiated with humour and fitful gleams of hope, but the tedium of life and the futility of the characters' aspirations underscores them all like a musical ground-bass: it is only the grasping, vulgar and insensitive individuals among them who appear to act either decisively or optimistically. It is open to anyone to see in this a resignation on Chekhov's part to the inability of the older generation to accept change, or to abandon personal possessions and prerogatives in the interest of the general good; for nowhere is this view of Russian provincial life at the turn of the century made more explicit than in his last and greatest play, *The Cherry Orchard* (1904; Fig. 185).

The cheerful side of Chekhov's nature emerged in his short farcical comedies—*The Bear* (1888); *The Proposal* (1889); *The Wedding* (1890)—but these he abandoned after writing *The Anniversary* in 1892. Most modern directors discern a lyrical quality in the serious plays which it has proved difficult for translators to capture: and this in turn requires exceptional sensitivity from the actors if the subtlety and nuance of the characters' emotions are to emerge clearly from under the deliberately naturalistic dialogue. This is also true of most translations of plays by Strindberg and Ibsen: yet notwithstanding this obstacle, such is the international esteem now accorded to their plays that it is hard for us to recall that when they were first produced, they were well received only by the intellectual avant-garde, and that these audiences formed only a tiny fraction of habitual theatre-goers. Compared to the melodramas, musical comedies and classical revivals offered by the last actor-managers and the syndicates, their plays were regarded as freaks—corrupting, subversive, depressing, even ludicrous. None of these managements displayed the least interest in translating or producing such plays. How

185. A scene from Act III of Anton Chekhov's The Cherry Orchard *as first presented at the Moscow Art Theatre, 1904 (original photograph).*

could it be otherwise? Short of deliberately seeking to outrage their patrons, with disastrous consequences at their box-offices, they lacked any incentive to do so—or so they thought at the time.

What none of them could foresee was the impact that the ideals and production methods of Richard Wagner's opera-house at Bayreuth and the Meiningen Company's foreign tours were having on that small but vociferous band of opponents to melodramatic stage-spectacle and all that it stood for morally and aesthetically in France, Germany and Russia. Denied theatres for the staging of plays by the rebel writers, they clubbed together to provide their own; denied the services of leading professional actors, they took advantage of the theatre's perennial ability to produce talented amateurs instead; denied space and newsprint in the national papers, they published their own magazines and leaflets. As this opposition gathered energy and recruits, so it began to assume the proportions of a major revolt. Intellectual and aesthetic rather than political in its initial phase, it developed steadily from a protest against stage-spectacle and frivolity into one against social and moral values deemed to be outmoded and altogether removed

from the realities of life itself. In the vanguard of this movement were a Frenchman, a German, a Dutchman and two Russians: Antoine in Paris, Otto Brahm in Berlin, J. T. Grein in London, and Stanislavsky and Nemirovitch-Danchenko in Moscow.

(d) Storm-troopers of the Avant-garde: *(i) Antoine in Paris:* André Antoine (1858–1943) was an amateur actor with a mission. By day he worked as a clerk for the Paris Gas Company; in the evening he devoted his time and energy to an amateur dramatic society in which he was the moving spirit and which he transformed into a private club which rented a small hall in Montmartre with a stage and seats for 342 spectators. He called it Le Théâtre libre since it was his own and his fellow actors' intention to present only modern plays in the naturalist manner espoused by Zola, unfettered by problems of censorship. As the venture was designed to supply young writers, who had failed to persuade managers to produce their plays, with an alternative stage and adequate actors, one-act pieces were as acceptable as longer ones. Antoine financed the club's productions out of his own savings; when these ran short he opened a subscription list. He himself wrote out the invitations—1,300 of them, it is said—and then delivered them himself. No wonder his head of department at the Gas Company, as Antoine noted in his diary in April, 'me fait des yeux terribles et surveille mon travail de beaucoup plus près!' ('Glares at me and keeps a much closer eye on

my work!') The theatre opened on 30 March 1887 (Fig. 186).

Understandably, many of the plays chosen for performance were considered shocking by critical spectators: so was the acting which, in its naturalism, was regarded as a deliberate affront to the Comédie Française. However, after two seasons which had attracted enough curiosity and notoriety to necessitate moving the company to the much larger Théâtre Menus Plaisirs and resulted in the accumulation of debts of 12,000 francs, Antoine's faith began to be rewarded with some critical support. Thus encouraged he launched an appeal for sponsorship in order to establish a permanent professional repertory company committed to the production of new plays in an adequately equipped theatre. The whole programme has a singularly modern ring to it, not least the failure to secure the required funds! Yet the company survived this disappointment and, following the example of the Meiningen Players, took its productions to Belgium, England, Germany and Italy; just as importantly, it gave Parisian audiences their first chance to see plays by Ibsen, Strindberg, Tolstoy and the young German dramatist Gerhart Hauptmann (1862–1946), as well as those by uncompromising young French authors

186. Scene from a production of Menessier's The Earth, *adapted from Zola's novel* La Terre, *as presented at the Théâtre libre, Paris, 1902. The old man second from left is played by Antoine himself.*

like Eugène Brieux, Maurice Donnay and Henri Bataille. Ibsen's *Ghosts* was produced, with Antoine as Oswald, in 1890. After that came *The Wild Duck*, Strindberg's *Miss Julie*, Brieux's *Damaged Goods*, Tolstoy's *The Power of Darkness* and Hauptmann's *The Weavers*. Nevertheless, the enterprise exhausted the company's strength: actors drifted away to better-paid engagements; debts increased to over 100,000 francs; and finally Antoine himself lost heart, leaving the company in 1894 to stagger on as best it could.

(ii) Otto Brahm in Berlin: When Antoine quit, however, his ideal was, like the phoenix, being reborn in other centres, arousing new controversies and begetting more plays and writers. By 1889 a group of Germans in Berlin had prevailed upon the critic Otto Brahm to organize an equivalent of the Théâtre libre. Its objectives were to be

the same—to promote new plays on controversial issues free of censorship—but the methods were different. No money was to be spent on leasing a hall: instead, liberally minded theatre-managers were to be persuaded to lend their buildings on a Sunday for private performances given by professional actors. Their first play was one which had been banned by the police—Ibsen's *Ghosts*. That was followed by the first German portrayal of working-class life, Hauptmann's *Vor Sonnenaufgang* (*Before Sunrise*) and then by Strindberg's *The Father*.

The Freie Bühne (Free Stage), as this loosely federated group of enthusiasts styled itself, gambled on the hope that by producing plays which commercial managers had refused to accept, audience response would convince them of their mistake—a policy which could only succeed if the acting and direction were strong enough to do justice to the plays. Happily, Brahm possessed both the stature needed to recruit good actors and that rare combination of authority and patience required to persuade exceptionally self-willed individualists like Else Lehman and Max Reinhardt to submit themselves to the disciplines of acting within an ensemble. So successful was Brahm's leadership that a year later another Berliner, Bruno Willie, went a step further and launched another company, the Freie Volksbühne (Free People's Stage) for the benefit of working-class patrons. This he financed through discount subscription tickets, a method that sufficed not only to keep the enterprise in being but to raise enough capital by 1914 to build the splendidly equipped Volksbühne.

(iii) J. T. Grein in London:

By 1891 the movement had spread to London where an expatriate Dutch critic, J. T. Grein, in partnership with William Archer and George Moore, founded the Independent Theatre Society which, like Brahm's Freie Bühne, presented its productions 'of plays which have a literary and artistic rather than a commercial value' in existing theatres to privately invited audiences. It too opened with Ibsen's *Ghosts*; but like the Théâtre libre, it too had discovered within a year a major new dramatist—George Bernard Shaw, whose *Widowers' Houses* was performed under its aegis in 1892. Grein's initiative, coupled with William Poel's experimental productions of Elizabethan and Jacobean plays for the Stage Society on a platform stage resembling de Witt's sketch of the Swan Playhouse (Fig. 102), opened the way for J. E. Vedrenne's and Harley Granville-Barker's fully professional seasons at the Royal Court Theatre. These began in 1904 and introduced John Galsworthy's plays to the public as well as those of Barker himself, Bernard Shaw and others.

(iv) Nemirovitch–Danchenko and Stanislavsky in Moscow:

News of the achievements of the Théâtre libre and of its offshoots in Berlin and London between 1887 and 1892 was bound to travel; and with the highly successful touring productions of the Meiningen Players it finally reached Moscow. There, in 1897, three years after the bankruptcy which overtook the Meiningen Players in Odessa and the collapse of Antoine's company in Paris, a well-to-do young amateur actor and director, Constantin Stanislavsky, and the established critic, playwright and teacher Nemirovitch-Danchenko had their notorious fifteen-hour restaurant meeting at Danchenko's request during which they agreed a constitution for an Art Theatre in Moscow. Danchenko was to take charge of all aspects of the literary management of the repertoire while Stanislavsky occupied himself with directing the actors—a mixed group of students and professionals—and the designers. The almost immediate success of this venture owed much to the fact that the founders, unlike Antoine, Brahm and Grein, were assured of ample funds to fulfil their ambitions and to cover large losses. Without the faith and loyal support of their immensely wealthy merchant-benefactor, Savra Morozov, these successes might well have eluded them. This financial backing ceased to be so important after Chekhov was persuaded to allow them to revive *The Seagull* in 1898, and its success sufficed to bring them his next four plays. Chekhov, in turn, secured Gorki for them.

No one can doubt the dramatic change in traditional Russian styles of acting which Stanislavsky's dynamic control of rehearsal methods brought about during the first decade of the Art Theatre's history in sweeping all fustian rhetoric and insincerity out through the stage-door; but posterity is at liberty to ask whether the veneration later accorded to his 'methods' derives from actual responses to performances, or from the fact that Stanislavsky, alone among the pioneers of naturalistic theatre in the 1880s and 1890s, described them in detail in his two books *My Life in Art* and *An Actor Prepares*, published respectively in 1924 and 1926. Certainly the Moscow Art Theatre has survived until now in a way that neither the Meiningen Players nor the Théâtre libre proved capable of doing; but its repertoire after 1914 was undistinguished, whereas in Paris, Berlin, Vienna and London the spirit of these two earlier pioneers with shared ideals has continued to open up vigorous new styles of play and of approaches to their production; a trend matched later in the United States with the founding in 1916 of the Provincetown Players by Eugene O'Neill, Robert Edmond Jones and Kenneth Macgowan at Cape Cod, Massachussetts, followed by the Theatre Guild and the Washington Square Playhouse in New York.

(e) Anti-naturalist Innovations: *(i) Symbolists and Aesthetes:* By far the most important among the many changes which overtook the theatre in the West at this time was the revolt against both pictorial realism and Zola's 'naturalism' that began to appear in several shapes and forms around 1900. This conflict was bound to fragment audience reaction into ever smaller coteries. Those theatre-goers who continued to support naturalism—despite being dismissed by their avant-garde opponents as reactionary traditionalists—sought to strengthen and widen public concern with social evils, in particular the squalid living conditions of manual labourers and their families. Their opponents meanwhile followed the lead of the painters Georges Seurat, Paul Cézanne, and Henri (le douanier) Rousseau towards symbolism, stylization and psycho-analytical exploration of the subconscious mind. Leaders appeared in many countries: in Belgium Maurice Maeterlinck (1862–1918); in Germany Frank Wedekind (1864–1918); in Italy Luigi Pirandello (1867–1936); in Ireland W. B. Yeats (1865–1949); in Austria Arthur Schnitzler (1862–1931) and Hugo von Hofmannsthal (1874–1929); and in France Edmond Rostand (1868–1918) and Paul Claudel (1868–1955). All were of a generation, inspired by Strindberg, that sought in their different ways to probe beneath 'slice of life' naturalism (as Impressionist, Cubist and early Surrealist painters were already doing in response to the progress of photography) in order to rediscover the mysterious and poetic aspects of life which they sensed that the naturalist theatre was threatening to lose. And in this quest the writers were strongly assisted by certain designers and directors—most notably Adolphe Appia in Switzerland (1862–1928), Edward Gordon Craig in England (1872–1966) and in Russia, Vsevolod Meyerhold (who was born in 1874 and disappeared mysteriously some time between 1940 and 1943). No less startling in this respect was the descent on Paris in 1909 of Serge Diaghilev's Ballets Russes which offered the exotic settings and costumes of Leon Bakst and Alexandre Benois, and which was headed by Michel Fokine, Vaslar Nijinsky and Anna Pavlova. The company visited London in the following year and amazed audiences there, as in Paris, with the savagery and sensuality of Borodin's caucasian dances from 'Prince Igor', Rimsky-Korsakov's 'Schéhérazade', and 'Coq d'Or', Debussy's 'L'Après-midi d'un Faune', and Stravinsky's 'Fire Bird', 'Petrouchka' and the cubist 'Rite of Spring' which provoked a riot in the auditorium (see Plates 15 and 16).

The relative ease and speed of travel and communications from 1900 onwards makes it difficult—almost absurd—to try to attribute particular developments to one artist rather than to another, still more so to this country or to that. With Paris by then universally recognized as the artistic capital of the world, it is more profitable, from a critical standpoint, to regard new developments as expressions of an international response to the new philosophical, political and psychological horizons of the twentieth century, with clearly discernible national and cultural stylistic variations.

Thus in Britain, a special concern with Shakespeare led, through William Poel's experiments, towards the ultimate removal of the proscenium arch which had been an obligatory feature of all theatres for nearly three hundred years. By 1913 this idea had spread to France through Jacques Copeau's productions at the Vieux Colombier, whence it would pass into Germany and other countries (Fig. 197). Another development which moved in the same direction was the growth of interest in the open-stage techniques which were still in regular use in the Far East. The appearance of an Indo-Chinese dance company at the Paris Exposition Universelle of 1889 created quite a stir: Antoine saw these performances and expressed himself as 'thrilled'. Increasing commercial and diplomatic contact with China and Japan served to add the remarkable stage-conventions of the Peking Opera and Japanese Noh and Kabuki plays to the melting-pot of European theatre. In play form these found expression in Ireland in Yeats's *Four Plays for Dancers* (1916–17).

Similarly, Appia's ideas for supplying a more atmospheric form of stage-lighting to make the characters in Wagner's operas stand out sharply from their settings were widely copied (Fig. 187). Once they had become available in his *Die Musik und die Inscenierung (Music and Scenography)* in 1899 they were eagerly taken up and expanded by Gordon Craig and Meyerhold who used them in their productions of plays old and new in whatever country in which they were called upon to design and direct. Craig, for instance, directed Ibsen's *The Pretenders* in Copenhagen, *Venice Preserved* in Berlin and *Hamlet* in Moscow before retiring to Italy in 1908 to edit his highly influential journal, *The Mask*, and to run a theatre-school in Florence.

Once a new atmospheric and emblematic approach to stage-settings had replaced the traditional realistic one, symbolist playwrights like Maeterlinck, whose characters exist as extensions of their creator's inner life, found it possible to use the visual aspect of dramatic art to enhance and intensify the poetic quality of their texts. What Maeterlinck achieved through productions of his *Pelléas and Mélisande* (1892), *The Blue Bird* (1908) and other plays thus at once became public property for von Hofmannsthal to use in Vienna, or for Yeats to try out in Dublin.

187. *Adolf Appia's design for a stage-setting for Wagner's* Rhinegold, *1892. University of Bristol Theatre Collection.*

Imaginatively designed and simplified scenery together with stylized costumes and delicate lighting encouraged other writers to experiment again with verse-drama. Here the reversion to 'little theatres' could only help the poets since nuances of vocal delivery and facial gesture were made possible by the intimate actor–audience relationship in these buildings that were unthinkable in the larger commercial theatres.

Among the more influential of these new theatres, many of which began under amateur auspices, was Nugent Monk's reconstructed Elizabethan-style theatre, the Maddermarket, in Norwich where he also experimented with revivals of medieval religious plays. Another was the People's Theatre in Newcastle, a group founded in 1911 which, on acquiring a theatre of its own in the 1920s, became the first in Britain to be organized on the socialist lines of Bruno Willie's Freie Volksbühne in Berlin. Yet another was Lady Gregory's and Miss Horniman's Abbey Theatre in Dublin which opened in 1904 as a home for Irish plays by Irish writers performed by Irish actors. On the Continent, similarly, 'art theatres' began to spring up like mushrooms from the Théâtre des Arts and the Théâtre de l'Oeuvre in Paris to Stanislavsky's and Meyerhold's Studio Theatre in Moscow. More must be said about these in Chapter 14 (see p. 230).

(ii) Anarchists, Futurists and 'Dada': Against these relatively gentle protests aimed primarily at breaking the stranglehold of commercial managers over dramatic art must be set those which were deliberately designed to shock rather than to woo audiences. These are best viewed in the context of the creation of the Salon des Indépendants. This Art Gallery was the successor to the Salon des Refusés (established by Napoleon III in 1864) where pictures which the jury of Academicians at the Salon des Beaux Arts declined to accept for hanging (Cézanne's were invariably rejected) could be seen and judged by the public. These annual exhibitions encountered much critical hostility, but it became evident to artists that critical abuse could be more effective than praise in attracting attention.

In the vanguard of theatrical shock tactics was Frank Wedekind. His *Spring Awakening (Fruehlings Erwachen,* 1891) was the first play to discuss openly the problems of adolescence and puberty. This was followed by the three plays which he built around his character, Lulu—*Earth Spirit (Erdgeist,* 1895), *Pandora's Box* (1904) and *The Dance of Death (Totentanz,* 1906)—whom he presented as a personification of sex as life's most destructive force. In Paris he was matched by Alfred Jary whose Aristophanic and anarchic *Ubu Roi (King Ubu)* provoked riots when it was first produced in 1896. The thrust of these attacks—

and here one must include Strindberg's surrealist plays—was directed towards the dethronement of reason and its replacement by uninhibited natural instinct, especially sexual instinct.

As these attacks proliferated, so they became more outspoken and violent. In 1909 *Le Figaro* printed the Italian playwright F. T. Marinetti's 'First Futurist Manifesto' which, as it reveals more clearly than any play what had happened in the course of the past twenty years and the shape of things to come, is worth quoting here.

A Racing Motor-Car, its frame adorned with great pipes, like snakes with explosive breath ... is more beautiful than the Victory of Samothrace.

The Past is balsam for prisoners, invalids, and men on their death beds who see the future closed to them.

We will none of it. We are young, strong, living—we are FUTURISTS.

Museums are cemeteries, public dormitories ... We are out to combat Moralism, Feminism [i.e. suffragettes and women's rights campaigners] and all Opportunist and Utilitarian meanness ...

We extol aggressive movement, feverish insomnia, the double-quick step, the somersault, the box on the ear ...

Poetry must be a violent onslaught. There is no masterpiece without aggressiveness ...

It is from Italy that we launch this Manifesto of Destructive Incendiary Violence.

Italy has been too long the market place of the Second-Hand Art Trade.

We must free our country from its canker of professors, archaeologists, cicerones, antiquaries and second-hand-dealers ...

Signed: F. T. Marinetti

In retrospect we can see that it was but a short step from this to the destructive violence of the First World War—described by the Futurists in their Manifesto as 'the only health giver of the world'—and from there to the Café de la Terrasse in Zurich, in neutral Switzerland, the headquarters of the Dadaist movement founded in 1916 and led by the Roumanian Tristan Tzara and Hans Arp. Given a world which by then could be seen to be intent on committing genocide with guns, bombs, and poison gas, it is easy to appreciate why this movement should have been as anarchic and nihilistic as it was. Rather than tamely submitting to inherited notions of reverence and respect for order and restraint as a distinguishing characteristic of art, its members dedicated themselves to the destruction of all traditional aesthetic disciplines. It was in pursuit of these ideals that Marcel Duchamp exhibited a china lavatory bowl as a piece of sculpture in 1917 and that Guillaume Apollinaire's one and only play, *The Breasts of Tiresias* (*Les Mamelles de Tirésias*, written in 1903 and described in his Preface as 'un drame surréaliste') was performed in Paris in 1917/18.

During the war-torn years the Dadaists in Zurich and their friends abroad could fairly claim to have been attempting to do for art (including dramatic art) what Nietzsche some twenty years earlier had already done for inherited culture and religion in the West. Arguing in his essays and books the need to reject all cultural and moral values (especially religious ones), Nietzsche had postulated in *Also sprach Zarathustra* (1883–92) the arrival of a new era ordered and controlled by 'supermen'. Yet as the long and hideous nightmare of the war came to its abrupt end in 1918, following political revolutions in Russia and Germany, much of Nietzsche's heroic romanticism had come to ring as hollow in the ears of the war's survivors as the stage rhetoric of the old actor-managers: for if the war had done nothing else for art, it had revealed all too clearly how feeble modern man actually was, and how frail was his continuing hold on civilized life. The way ahead begged questions at every turn; and where dramatic art was concerned only the cinema seemed to know with any certainty where it was going.

(f) **New Cinematic Horizons**: The mini-travelogues of the late 1890s, the principal objective of which had been to photograph motion—trains, horses, crowds, boats on water—were supplemented in the first decade of the twentieth century by two more kinds of short film. The first was fantasy; the second was visual jokes presented, like vaudeville 'turns', in front of a still camera. The pioneer of the former was Georges Méliès, a sometime conjurer and magician. Not surprisingly, therefore, it was to the world of pantomime with its frequent 'transformation scenes'—pumpkin into coach, mice into ponies, woodland glades into castle ballrooms or marine grottos—arranged and directed by fairy godmothers or mad professors, that Méliès went for his subject matter. The response he wished to provoke from viewers was 'How did he do it?' Even today a screening of his *Voyage à la lune* can be relied upon to arouse that response from its audience. More important for the future were the technical advances which resulted from his pursuit of trick-photography—'dissolves', 'cross-fades', 'superimposition' and so on. Thus from simple fairy-stories like *Cinderella* and *Red Riding Hood*, filmed

188. *Oil painting of Sarah Bernhardt by Georges Clairin, 1876. Paris, Musée du Petit-Palais.*

in 1901, Méliès proceeded to early science fiction and so, by 1905, to motor cars and melodrama.

The pioneer of filmed melodrama was E. S. Porter. By adapting Méliès's technique of extending a mere incident into a short story, he perfected the ten-minute, single-reel movie, and then applied it to melodrama. What was different and new in his *Life of an American Fireman* (1902) and his *Great Train Robbery* (1903) was that both were filmed 'on location' with *real* fire engines, *real* trains and *real* guns.

It is thus no coincidence that by 1905 financial speculators and real-estate operators had begun to pour money into separating the showing of films in music halls from other vaudeville attractions by erecting custom-built cinemas from which they would receive all box-office receipts instead of a mere fraction (see page 226). The discovery that films were transportable and could as easily be shown in London as in New York or in Sydney as in Paris only accelerated this process. Since the films themselves were silent, only the scripted captions needed to be changed and spliced back into the film for them to become appropriate to any change in screening location. Pianists could be hired locally to provide a suitably melodramatic score. Between them, these developments forced actors and theatre-managers alike to take notice of what was happening and to try to respond to it or face bankruptcy as their audiences shifted allegiance from theatres to cinemas.

As early as 1912, Sarah Bernhardt had bravely decided to risk her reputation by appearing in the title role of a four-reel feature film *Queen Elizabeth* (Louis Mercanton), declaiming as she did so, 'This is my one chance of immortality' (Fig. 188). By 1915 W. D. Griffiths in America had completed the making of *Birth of a Nation* (Epoch Films) at a cost of $100,000; and Sergei Eisenstein three years later was about to leave the Red Army to start making films in Russia. When the armistice was finally signed on 11 November 1918 even high society had become disposed to take films seriously and to declare itself ready to invest them with the social respectability of gala premières.

In the face of this proudly self-assertive competition, where was the theatre to go, stripped not only of the mass audiences of pre-war years but of any coherent theological and philosophical dynamic acceptable alike to its artists and the remaining theatre-going public? At a time of unexampled privation, misery and confusion, there could be no certainty. Only in Bolshevik Russia and in defeated, socialist Germany had a political dynamic emerged which playwrights and actors could seize upon and try to interpret and promote (or challenge) from the stage. Elsewhere the only alternatives appeared to lie between introspective questioning of the past and overtly hedonistic entertainment. In general, the commercial theatre opted to 'play safe' by providing the latter, and to leave the former to the Little Theatres and the amateurs. Such was the sombre theatrical scene in Europe and America when the peace conference assembled in Paris in January 1919 to try to settle the future of the world with the signing of formal peace treaties.

14
Armageddon and its Aftermath: 1900-1950

1 INTRODUCTION

Two World Wars and their consequences – political, social and cultural – tower over the twentieth century like erupting volcanoes that have buried a once familiar landscape in molten lava, ash and dust. So too, if to a lesser degree, do images of the Bolshevik Revolution in Russia, the Wall Street Crash in the United States, the holocaust in Nazi Germany, atomic bombs on Japan, the Vietnam War and the Berlin Wall.

Within a context as destructive, inhumane and barbarous as this, no one should be surprised that the theatre, in attempting to reflect the rapidly changing problems and aspirations facing its dwindling audiences, disintegrated stylistically in frenetic efforts to find new forms capable of matching the ever more radical, shocking and disturbing subject-matter of contemporary life.

Scarcely less convulsive, at least as viewed in retrospect from the final decade of this turbulent century, were those advances in scientific, medical and technological knowledge that have provided society with psycho-analysis, cinema, radio and television, contraceptive pills and computer memory systems: each of these in turn has confronted playwrights, actors, designers and managers with new challenges, and their audiences with new choices and fresh standards of critical evaluation.

Throughout the first decade of the new century commercially orientated theatre managements both in Europe and in America could still plausibly sustain themselves in the belief that a familiar diet of melodramas, problem plays, musical comedies and farces would attract enough patrons to fill their metropolitan and provincial boulevard theatres and thus provide them and their backers with healthy profits. Yet even then this roseate scenario was being stealthily undermined, as recorded in the previous

chapter, by silent films and the Little Theatre movement (see pp. 210-25). Between the outbreak of the First World War in 1914 and the Armistice which concluded it in 1918, these challenges to the theatrical *status quo* were greatly augmented, where audiences' personal circumstances were concerned, by previously unimaginable catastrophes occasioned by some twenty million deaths from machine-guns, shells, bombs, torpedoes and poison gas followed immediately by an influenza epidemic of unprecedented proportions.

In retrospect it can be seen that despite the signing of formal peace treaties, the Armistice signed in 1918 meant exactly what that word implies: a temporary cessation. The animosities provoked by the Treaty of Versailles festered through the next two decades until, following the patched-up Munich accord of 1938 between the major warring parties, it became obvious that hostilities must shortly be resumed.

During this twenty-one year intermission, scarred as it was by the Wall Street crash of 1929, the ensuing economic depression, the collapse of the Weimar Republic under the Nazi assault of 1933, and the outbreak of the Spanish Civil War in 1936, theatre continued to fight its losing battle with the cinema. The advent of 'talkies' in 1927 finally exploded the idea that the stage alone could supply audiences with actors and actresses capable of handling dialogue; it also persuaded many actors, whatever their native tongue, that Hollywood was a more profitable base on which to centre their careers than London, Paris, Rome, Berlin or Vienna. Stage stars of the magnitude of George Arliss, Boris Karloff, Fred Astaire, Leslie Howard, Bette Davis, Katherine Hepburn and Charles Laughton found it more profitable to quit the theatre and entrust their future careers to the film studios. This decision served to create an almost unbridgeable gap of some 3,000 miles between

THE TWENTIETH CENTURY: 1914–1950

1914	Outbreak of First World War
1916	Meyerhold launches 'Constructivism' from Moscow
	'Expressionist' theatre launched from Berlin
	Tristan Tzara launches 'Dada' from Zurich
1917	Bolshevik Revolution in Russia
1918	Armistice signed: Germany becomes a Republic
1919	First screening of *The Cabinet of Dr Caligari* in Berlin
1921	Pirandello's *Six Characters in Search of an Author* produced in Rome
1922	Eugene O'Neill's *The Great God Brown* produced in New York
1924	André Breton publishes the first Surrealist Manifesto
1925	Yale University admits Drama as a degree course in America
1927	'Talkies' challenge silent films
1928	Brecht's and Weill's *Threepenny Opera* produced in Berlin
1929	The Wall Street Crash
1933	Nazis attain power in German
	García Lorca writes *Blood Wedding*
1934	Establishment of 'Social Realism' as the only legitimate dramatic style by the First Convention of Soviet Writers in Moscow
1935	Federal Theatre launched in the USA
	T.S.Eliot's *Murder in the Cathedral* performed in Canterbury Cathedral
1936	Outbreak of the Spanish Civil War
1938	Publication of Artaud's *The Theatre and its Double*
1939	Outbreak of the Second World War
1941	*Oklahoma*! opens in New York
1942	Anouilh's *Antigone* opens in Paris under German occupation
1943	Sartre's *The Flies* produced in Paris
1945	Atomic bombs dropped on Hiroshima and Nagasaki
	End of the Second World War
1946	Founding of the Arts Council of Great Britain
	Inauguration of first Edinburgh Arts Festival
1947	Tennessee Williams's *A Streetcar Named Desire* produced in New York
	Bristol University admits Drama as a degree course in Britain
1949	Arthur Miller's *Death of a Salesman* produced in New York
	Bertolt Brecht founds the Berliner Ensemble in East Berlin

the respective capitals of the theatrical and film sectors of American show-business in New York and Hollywood. This has made it exceptionally difficult for American actors and actresses ever since either to work simultaneously in both, or to obtain a standard training to equip them to work in both.

On the other hand, notwithstanding the nihilistic manifestos of Futurists, Dadaists, Surrealists and others, the theatre both in America and elsewhere still managed to claim audiences and persuade writers and actors that loyalty to its cause could reap adequate rewards, whether in Moscow, Paris or New York. Stage realism and spectacle still claimed its adherents in 'problem plays' and musicals respectively; verse drama and symbolist plays attracted a wider public than before the war; and, in the creation of new ground, Expressionist and Surrealist playwrights, designers and directors began to claim critical attention. Nevertheless, these successes have to be viewed in the context of managerial bankruptcies, theatres closed and pulled down or converted into cinemas, and a further decline in the number of regular theatre-goers from the remaining 10 per cent to a figure nearer 5 per cent as cinema tickets became cheaper and theatre tickets more expensive. In country districts the collapse of the theatre was everywhere catastrophic, with the possible exception of market-towns in the USSR where the new government had decided to employ and subsidize dramatic art as a major instrument of propaganda, just as the newly established Protestant regimes had done some four hundred years earlier in Luther's Germany and in Tudor England.

When war again broke out in 1939, the theatre in this severely weakened condition was having to face two new competitors for both its artists and its audiences. Broadcasting by radio, and with it the possibility of transmitting plays directly to listeners in their own homes, had begun in 1920. Television followed in 1936. But both of these rivals offered a simultaneous challenge to the film industry. By then film had come to enjoy the hitherto unprecedented advantage of being easily distributable (thanks to foreign-language sub-titles or to dubbing processes) throughout

189. *The stage of the Vieux Colombier, Paris, as renovated by Copeau for the Compagnie des Quinze, 1919.*

the world, thus making a German, French, or American film as acessible to Asian or Latin American audiences as to any resident of the country in which it was made. In short, a world market could be aimed for; production budgets could be calculated accordingly; and, in aspiring to take advantage of this, the major film studios – Pathé, Metro-Goldwyn-Meyer, Warner, Rank, etc. – simply copied the earlier theatrical syndicates in attempting to control the distribution outlets. What none of them could anticipate in 1939 was the inroads radio and television might make into their monopoly of 'packaged' entertainment.

Set adrift and buffeted by winds of philosophical, social and economic change as radical as those outlined above, it is scarcely surprising that no single dynamic of universal application emerged as the determining characteristic of theatrical endeavour and achievement during the central decades of the present century. Shortly before the outbreak of the First World War several candidates for this role appear at first glance to qualify for consideration. These include the unprecedented variety of styles simultaneously on offer; the influence of dramatic critics; the galaxy of actors and actresses of outstanding talent and personal charisma; the plethora of individual dramatists and directors jostling each other with shock tactics to secure attention from a dwindling public for a particular philosophical, political or aesthetic proposition.

These observations alone, however, suggest that what may really distinguish our theatre as its predominant characteristic is the lack of any uniformity, cohesion and coherence in the absence of a strong cultural influence such as that provided by the Christian Church in the Middle Ages; by the Renaissance in Italy or the Reformation in England in the sixteenth century; or by the delight in pictorial realism and in behavioural naturalism that dominated the theatre of the nineteenth century. In other words, the revolt against naturalism shortly before the start of the First World War sounded the death knell for any broadly integrated style of dramatic composition and theatrical representation, and heralded a process of stylistic disintegration that has accelerated throughout the twentieth century and is still with us.

The most obvious of signposts directing us towards this conclusion is to be seen in the proliferation of '-isms' (creeds with attendant manifestos) which were borrowed from the painters and applied to the theatre during the 1920s and 1930s. To the champions of Symbolism, Futurism and early Surrealism who staked out their claims for 'alternative theatre' before the First World War (see pp. 221-3) must be added the advocates of Constructivism (Formalism) and Expressionism on the one hand and of Neo-Surrealism on the other who offered the first positive resistance to the suicidal exhortations of the Dadaists, and whose plays and production techniques aroused international interest sufficient to attract imitators until the outbreak of the Second World War in 1939. Every step taken along these varied roads widened the number of options open to theatre managements to pursue and the number of choices for audiences to support or reject.

2 THE ROAD TO EXPRESSIONISM

(a) **Nineteenth-century Roots:** Among Wagner's literary admirers during the 1880s was a group of French poets led by Mallarmé, Verlaine and Rimbaud who tried to create a new mystical world transcending that of visible and tangible reality: it was a world which they believed to be perceivable through the senses and communicable to others through art. They saw this process as a single one which involved first the absorption of the external world of objects and people into the internal world of the artist's self, and then the re-creation of it through the internal responses of the self in poetry. In this way, they argued, it could become possible to accommodate a response to one art – in their case music – within another. In addition it would allow for response to the reverberances, echoes and half-truths of real life, and still leave room for the recipient to include, through association, responses particular to him- or herself. Taken up by the Belgian playwright Maeterlinck (see p. 221) and by his fellow dramatist Emile Verhaeren in the 1890s, the Symbolist movement spread slowly eastwards into the German theatre through the poetry of Rainer Maria Rilke, the novels of Thomas Mann and the plays of Frank Wedekind (see p. 222) and finally reached the English-speaking world in Ireland through W.B Yeats and through J.M Synge (see p. 235). It touched Ibsen when writing his last play, *When We Dead Awaken* (1899), and Strindberg in the composition of the *Road to Damascus* (begun 1898, completed 1901) and his dream plays written between 1901 and 1907.

By this time the original ideas informing Symbolism were starting to be coloured by Freud's writings on dreams and the subconscious mind; these imposed a correspond-ing pressure on artists to risk abandoning reliance upon external reality, and trust instead to introspection. The term 'Expressionism', describing this ideal, had once again been first used among painters as early as 1901, where it quickly became associated with revolt against the moral and intellectual decadence of a philistine society which was so preoccupied with ostentatious luxury that it condoned frightening inequalites of wealth, archaically hierarchical notions of social order and soulless mechanization of human skills and crafts. These feelings are epitomized in Edvard Munch's famous picture *The Scream* painted in 1893 (see Fig. 190).

(b) Painters, Designers and Directors: In the theatre the Post-Impressionist painters and sculptors became the natural allies of the Symbolist poets since it was they who were called upon to integrate the visual aspects of drama-tic art with the verbal in a harmonious assault upon an audience's emotions. Where stage-scenery was concerned, Gordon Craig started adapting Cubist thinking to the theatre's needs by replacing pictorially realistic scenery with arrangements of shapes so disposed in relation to one another as to *suggest* the character and atmosphere of an environment rather than depict it literally (see Fig. 184). Adolphe Appia's experiments with lighting enhanced these effects by providing dramatic contrasts of light and shade, as well as striking contrasts of level of the stage-floor itself (see Fig. 187). In accord with the Fauve movement among French painters, whose objective was likewise to liberate colour from representational use, the theatre discovered through Bakst and Benois (the principal designers for the Ballets Russes on their arrival in Paris in 1909) the uses to which fantastic and exotic contrasts of colour could be put in stage-costume (see p. 221 and Plate 15). They also awak-

190. The Scream *by Edvard Munch, a picture which, in drama-tizing the painter's subjective phobias into an objective expressive form, started a movement in European art subsequently labelled as Expressionism.*

ened a new sensitivity to the purely decorative aspects of both scenery and costume. It was Diaghilev who recruited Braque and Picasso to design for the theatre (Plate 16). And so a further step was taken, through experiments with abstract art, towards the full realization of Expressionist ideals in the nightmarish plays of the painter-dramatist Oskar Kokoschka (1886-1980) and those of the more polit-ically orientated playwrights Georg Kaiser (1878-1939) and Ernst Toller (1893-1939) (see p. 231). Their names first attracted public attention shortly before and after the armistice of 1918. By then, however, a new dynamic was entering Expressionist philosophy, supplied this time from Russia. It became known as Constructivism (later as Formalism) and had marked affinities with Italian Futurism (see pp. 222-3). This intrusion requires a brief explanation if German Expressionist theatre of the inter-war years is to be properly understood.

During the thirty years since the original revolt against naturalism in the theatre had begun, texts, scenery, lighting and costumes, as we have just seen, had all been freed from the tyranny of attempts to achieve pictorial realism. It remained in the theatre, if not in the cinema, to reconsider how actors and acting should be integrated within the newly fashioned poetic ensemble. Gordon Craig had raised this issue before the First World War by suggesting that the Saxe-Meiningen and Stanislavskian ideals of ensemble acting should be amalgamated with the responsibility for co-ordinated settings, costumes and lighting and placed under the control of an artistic director. Within this context, he had argued, actors should be permitted to work freely and creatively, but within a code of discipline as severe as that imposed upon the inanimate actors of a marionette theatre – *Übermarionetten* (Super Marionettes) – moving and speaking on stage with the precision of chessmen on a chessboard under the controlling hand of the players. It was a theory certain to appeal to power-hungry actors *manqués* (as Craig's unkinder critics described him), but he was never given the chance to put this theory into practice outside his own theatre in Florence. It was left to Meyerhold, working in Moscow with Stanislavsky, and with his rival Alexander Tairov (1885-1950) at the intimate Kamerny Theatre (of which he had become the director in 1914), to try to carry it into action. The two men had come together through an actress at the Moscow Art Theatre, Alice Koonen, whom Tairov married. The need to realign dramatic art to serve the Revolution gave them their opportunity to reform acting along the lines suggested by Craig; and this they did within a wider movement described as Constructivism.

(c) Constructivism and Formalism: The word 'constructivism' had been coined in Russia to describe Cubist-abstract sculptors and architects whose work met with the approval of revolutionary officials since that appeared, in its austerity, to have dispensed with all concessions to decorative luxury. Applied to the theatre, the term 'constructivist' described an artistic director's concept of play production which regarded a stage as 'a machine for actors'. Russian Constructivism, whether wittingly or not, thus assumed political affinities with earlier Italian Futurism (see pp. 222-3). The actors who were to use this 'machine' were urged to study biomechanics, the employment of which, as Meyherhold believed, would make actors as efficient and reliable as machines and would ensure the automatic emotional response from the audience premeditated by the director. As a result, in Meyerhold's productions (later described as Formalist)

acting became as stylized as the sets and costumes (see p. 220). It was on this foundation that his colleague Tairov then built his own aesthetic of a dramatic art-form which reduced *all* texts to the level of a springboard for flights of personal creativity. By this means he at least secured for himself an escape route from uncongenial commitment to any particular social or political creed (without which his choice of plays might not have been approved), and thus acquired the liberty to move around Europe directing plays by Shaw, O'Neill, and other Western dramatists with far greater freedom than was permitted to any other Soviet director. Remarkably, he was able to pursue this pattern of work for some twenty years before the shutters of ideological conformity descended on the Soviet theatre in 1934 and made explicit adherence to the dogmas of Soviet Realism obligatory.

Between them, the Russian Constructivists (or Formalists), the Italian Futurists, and the Belgian and French Symbolists had demolished any residual allegiance among more adventurous dramatists to the time-honoured unities of action, time and place. By the end of the First World War it had become accepted that the logic of the world of dreams and of the subconscious mind rendered these restrictions meaningless; and only those dramatists seeking to turn out 'well-made' plays for commercial managements and supplying 'drawing-room comedies', 'bedroom farces' or 'thrillers' still found it convenient to adhere to the old forms of the realistic theatre which audiences regarded as 'safe', reassuring and entertaining.

(d) Expressionist Drama and Theatre: *(i) Mainstream Artists:* It was in Germany that Russian Constructivism impinged most sharply upon existing Expressionist thinking as the First World War ended. There, a new dimension was added to it as the shame and frustration of military defeat combined with catastrophic inflation, unemployment, penury and starvation to overthrow the Kaiser and bring the Social Democrats to power. Ex-soldiers and sailors became revolutionaries; communism was openly advocated as the best cure for the sufferings of the people; the theatre became politicized. In Berlin, Hamburg and Munich, Expressionsist playwrights absorbed this sense of despair and anger. So did German film-makers. Within a year of the armistice Berliners were exposed to the first fully expressionistic film – *The Cabinet of Dr Caligari* based on a story which owed something to Mary Shelley's *Frankenstein* and something to the sado-masochistic extravagances of French Grand Guignol (see pp. 187-8 and 211); but it is in the manipulation of plot and the macabre pictorial environment that the Expressionists' approach to the subject-matter is manifested. The genre reached its zenith with the making of *Metropolis* in 1926.

In the theatre the seal was set on Expressionism as a dramatic style by two German playwrights, Georg Kaiser and Ernst Toller (see p. 229). Kaiser's *From Morn to Midnight* was published as early as 1916: *Gas* (a trilogy) followed in 1918 and 1920. Toller's *Masses and Men* was also produced in Berlin in 1921 and *The Machine Wreckers* a year later. All these plays attack capitalist values in an industrialized society. Taking over the techniques of the Constructivists, these playwrights and their followers stripped their characters of individuality and reduced them (in the manner of medieval moralities) to abstract person-

191a, b. An early example of multimedia staging in an Expressionist collaboration between playwright and designer. Above: Traugott Müller's realization of Ernst Toller's request for a single, permanent stage-setting to accommodate all locations specified in the text of Hoppla, wir leben! *(dedicated to Piscator and Mehring), 1927, at the Theater am Nollendorfplatz, Berlin. Below: the Polling Station, with a projected image of the winning candidate. New York Public Library.*

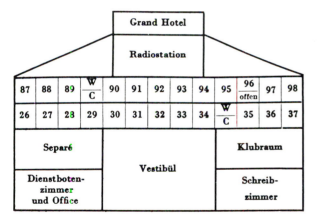

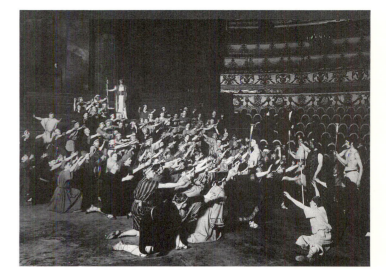

192. Max Reinhardt's production of Sophocles' Oedipus Rex *as presented in St Petersburg, 1912. University of New York at Binghamton, Max Reinhardt Archive.*

ifications embodying a particular viewpoint. They exist, therefore, as symbols rather than people.

In *Gas*, for instance, the cast list includes the Engineer, the Girl, the Gentleman in White, First Gentleman in Black, the Billionaire's Son, and so on. The gas in question is an elemental motive force, invented by the Engineer. The workers who devote their time and energy to making it are blown up in an explosion at the factory, a metaphor to express the idea of a creative force which, used for material ends, leads to spiritual disaster. After the explosion, the Billionaire's Son offers to replace the factory with an environmental paradise; however, the Engineer opposes any changes to the formula; the workers are asked to decide with their votes: they opt for the old formulas. The play is much more richly textured than this synopsis suggests, but subtlety is no more a distinguishing feature of Expressionist plays than it is of medieval moralities.

In this context the playwrights enjoyed the good fortune of assistance from outstandingly imaginative directors and designers like Max Reinhardt, Leopold Jessner and Erwin Piscator who, with their multi-level sets, costumes, crowd-groupings and stage-lighting, were able to enrich the authors' skeletal and didatic plots and characterization with an exciting theatricality (Fig. 192). Given productions of this kind, German audiences began to respond to 'modernism' in the theatre on a scale not encountered before because the subject-matter appeared to be so relevant to

193. Donald Oenslager's setting for the slave-ship scene in Eugene O'Neill's The Emperor Jones *directed by George Pierce Baker at the Yale School of Drama, 1931. Private collection.*

their own lives (Fig. 191a, b). The sheer excitement of the stage spectacle also tempted visitors from abroad, particularly Americans like Robert Edmond Jones and Lee Simonson, to imitate these Expressionist techniques on returning home, or to adapt them to their own use.

In Germany, as one domestic disaster after another turned hope into despair, the cult of Expressionism as a major dramatic force began to decline; but in America it was picked up by Eugene O'Neill (1888-1953), Elmer Rice (1892-1967) and other dramatists in several major plays of which O'Neill's *The Hairy Ape* (1922) and *The Great God Brown* (1926) and Elmer Rice's *The Adding Machine* (1923) were the most successful.

In England Christopher Isherwood (1904-), W. H. Auden (1907-73) and Stephen Spender (1909-) toyed with these techniques respectively in *The Dog Beneath the Skin*, *The Ascent of F6* and *Trial of a Judge* during the 1930s as did Sean O'Casey (1880-1964) in Ireland in his later plays starting with *Within the Gates* (1933) (see p. 235); but by then Expressionism was a spent force. Where it lingered longest was in the provision by stage-designers of permanent settings which could be regarded as three-dimensional works of art in their own right, and in the work of one playwright of genius – Bertolt Brecht (1898-1956).

(ii) Brecht: Although he started writing for the theatre in 1918, Brecht avoided aligning himself either with the Expressionists or with the Surrealists and chose instead to try to create a new style, which he described as Epic

Theatre. He began with an attack on war-profiteers using some realist and some Expressionist techniques in *Drums in the Night* (1922). Shortly after this he became associated with the composer Kurt Weill (1900-50), and in 1928 collaborated with him on the composition of *The Threepenny Opera*, a bitterly satirical transposition of John Gay's *The Beggar's Opera* of 1728 to reflect life in the Weimar Republic, which attracted attention outside Germany as well as in it (Fig. 194). His overt associations with Marxism and the increasingly didactic tone of his plays made it too difficult for him, when the Nazis seized power in 1933, to stay in Germany. Thereafter he became a wanderer in Europe until in 1940 he escaped to the United States. His best plays – *The Life of Galileo*, *Mother Courage*, *The Good Woman of Setzuan*, *The Resistible Rise of Arturo Ui* and *The Caucasian Chalk Circle* – were written during these years of exile between 1937 and 1945.

194. Stage setting for Brecht's and Weill's The Threepenny Opera *at the Kamerny Theatre, Moscow (see Fig.140).*

In all of them the distinction between reality and illusion is a major factor both in his characters and in his dialogue; indeed it was this distinction that led him to define his three theoretical principles for dramatic compostion, namely: *historification* (displacing the subject-matter out of the present into the past); *alienation* (devices designed to switch audience response away from involvement in stage action and towards reflective criticism of it); and epic structure (i.e. a dialectical structure with a narrative punctuated by commentary) in which song, dance, and projected film stills or strips could alternate with speech. With no home base to work from, his major plays remained neglected until his return to East Germany after the war where, with his actress wife Helene Weigel and the designer Caspar Neher, he established the Berliner Ensemble in 1949. It was the work of this company, both in East Berlin and on its tours abroad during the next two decades, that gave Brecht the international reputation which as poet, playwright, theorist and 'man of the theatre' he now holds.

3 SURREALISM

(a) **Nineteenth-century Roots:** Surrealism in the theatre has had a tempestuous and chequered career; yet it has probably had a more enduring and pervasive effect on twentieth-century theatre than any other form of revolt against nineteenth-century naturalism. Its heirs are not only to be found in the contemporary dance groups, and psychedelic 'pop' concerts and 'happenings' of the years since Hiroshima, but in the more rarified intellectual enclaves of the 'Theatre of Cruelty', 'Erotic Theatre' and 'Theatre of the Absurd' (see pp. 254-5).

The first Surrealist manifesto was published in Paris in 1924 under the signature of a trained psychologist, André Breton. There, it is defined as 'pure psychic automatism, by which it is intended to express, verbally, in writing, or by other means the real process of thought. Thought's dictation, in the absence of all control exercised by the reason and outside all aesthetic or moral preoccupations' (trans. David Gascoyne). Although publication of this manifesto conveniently dates the transformation of Surrealism into a formally constituted movement, this is actually misleading since the word *Surnaturel* (Supernatural) was picked upon as early as 1911 by Guillaume Apollinaire to describe the dream-like pictures being offered by Marc Chagall to the Salon des Indépendants that year. Applied to the painter himself, it became *Surréaliste* and was stretched to include the pictures of Giorgio de Chirico and others; but no effort was then made to establish either a definition or a move-ment. In this instance, however, the painters had already been outpaced by at least one writer since the word 'surrealist' was used to describe Alfred Jarry's novel *Le Surmâle (The Superman)* published in 1902; it was also used by Apollinaire himself in 1903, and was applied, more loosely, to some of Strindberg's plays written between 1904 and 1907.

After the outbreak of war in 1914, the ideas which the word 'Surrealism' had come to represent were transferred into Dada by Apollinaire (see p. 223), where they attracted the attention of Louis Aragon, Jean Cocteau and André Breton (see p. 254). When, therefore, Breton quarrelled with Tristan Tzara shortly after the war and set up a breakaway movement of his own, he called it Surrealist. Historically his school is thus better described as Neo-Surrealist.

(b) **Pirandello and After:** The illusory qualities of life which Breton and his followers attributed to chance rather than to design or judgement began to be treated seriously in dramatic form in Italy (the home of Marinetti's Futurism) where, late in life, the poet and novelist Luigi Pirandello (1867-1936) started writing for the theatre in earnest in 1916 to supplement his income as an impoverished teacher with a family to support.

His first major play, *Right You Are – If You Think You Are* (1918), was followed by the better-known and more frequently performed *Six Characters in Search of an Author* (1921; Fig. 195). Both plays in their titles indicate an allegiance to what Sir Herbert Read, in his definition of Surrealism, describes as 'breaking down the barriers, both physical and psychical, between the conscious and the unconscious, between the inner and the outer world'. In Pirandello's view truth was at best relative. Can we ever know our real selves, let alone other people? Is what we pass off as ourselves to our friends and acquaintances real or an illusion? Which is nearer to the truth – the face or the mask? And how much does what we say conceal? These were the questions to which time and again Pirandello returns in his many plays (see pp. 7-8). After the production of his masterpiece, *Enrico Quarto (Henry IV)* in 1922 – a play which rings the changes on madness, sanity and pretended madness with fascinating and shocking dexterity – he created his own company, led by Marta Abba, in Rome, and then took his plays on tour with great success in Europe and America. Although few imitators attempted to copy his techniques, aspects of his approach to the tragi-comedy of human existence can be perceived in some of Jean Cocteau's plays like *La Machine Infernale* (1934) and in T. S. Eliot's *Sweeney Agonistes* (1932) as well

195. *Photograph of Georges Pitoëff's production of Luigi Pirandello's* Six Characters in Search of an Author *at the Comédie des Champs Elysées, Paris, April 1923.*

as in the tricks played with time by J. B. Priestley in *Time and the Conways* and *I Have Been Here Before*, both produced in 1937.

The Neo-Surrealist movement, however, which produced its second manifesto in 1929, proved to be its own worst enemy when it came to recruiting public support. While explicitly seeking to support the cause of Communism, its members became progressively more aggressive and incoherent in their aims and utterances. Its citadel was ballet where Picasso's *Tricorne*, *Train Bleu* and *Parade* won the excited approval of the intellectual élite; but at popular level the movement became an object of derision, with Picasso as the principal target for attack.

It is hardly surprising, therefore, that dramatists and managements whose livelihoods depended on substantial public support should have shied away from Surrealism during the 1930s and 1940s and have preferred to confine their personal interests in psychological approaches to human behaviour within more conventional and acceptable dramatic forms. Surrealism, however, did not die; it simply lay dormant until the problem of handling language in such a way that audiences could comprehend the logic behind seemingly inconsequential events, décor and dialogue had been solved. This major step forward was taken in France by a group of philosopher-playwrights that included Albert Camus and Jean-Paul Sartre during the closing years of the Second World War (see pp. 246-7).

4 POETIC DRAMA

Another innovation, stimulated in part by the Symbolist poets and in part by the Little Theatre movement, was a revival of interest at the turn of the century in the tragedies of both the ancient Greek dramatists and the Elizabethan and Jacobean dramatic poets, a revival which, in England, was led respectively by Gilbert Murray and William Poel. This attracted a varied group of poets and novelists anxious to try their hand at writing for the theatre in London and Paris. Among the ablest English pioneers of this new approach to poetic drama were John Masefied (1878-1967), Oscar Wilde (1854-1900), Gordon Bottomley (1874-1948) and Thomas Hardy (1840-1928).

Wilde's *Salomé* was banned in England, but produced in Paris by Sarah Bernhardt in 1894. Harley Granville Barker thought well enough of Masefield's *Tragedy of Nan* to direct it himself at the Royalty in 1908; Bottomley, with *King Lear's Wife* (1912), *Gruach* (1923) and other plays introduced London audiences, as W. B. Yeats was doing for Irish audiences in Dublin, to those legendary worlds, governed by fear and superstition, of Celtic and Gaelic myth. Thomas Hardy's epic drama, *The Dynasts*, based on the Napoleonic Wars as viewed by a chorus in the Greek style of super-terrestial beings, was first produced by the Oxford University Dramatic Society in 1918.

More successful commercially than any of the English pioneers was Edmond Rostand (1868-1918), whose romantic dramas, *Cyrano de Bergerac* (1898) and *L'Aiglon* (1900), written respectively for the Elder Coquelin and Sarah Bernhardt, have succeeded in retaining a place in the modern repertoire. So too have several plays of Paul Claudel (1868-1955). An avowed Symbolist and uncompromising Christian, he combined a diplomatic career in America, Germany, China and Japan with writing poetic plays that quickly won him an international reputation. His first success, *Partage du Midi* (1905), was followed in 1912 by *L'Annonce fait à Marie*; but his most popular play, *Le Soulier de Satin* had to wait until 1940 for its first production, some twenty years after it was written; however, it then received the accolade of opening at the Comédie Française.

The Italian poet and novelist, Gabriele d'Annunzio (1863-1930) was similarly successful, being fortunate enough to win the support of the great Italian actress, Eleanore Duse (1859-1924), who counted the leading roles in *La Città Morta* and *La Gioconda* (both first performed in 1898), followed by *Francesca da Rimini* (1902), among her many personal triumphs. What D'Annunzio contributed to the theatre of that time was a chilling sense of horror communicated, as Seneca and such Jacobean dramatists as Webster, Middleton and Ford had done before him, in terms of physical experiences.

Eclipsing them all, however, where the judgement of posterity is concerned, was the Irish poet and dramatist, William Butler Yeats (1865-1939) whose eleven plays span nearly forty years of constant experiment and achievement, and his compatriot, John Middleton Synge (1871-1909). If judged by box-office success, Yeats was a far better poet than playwright; but his concern with heroic ideals clothed in poetic myths during an era of assertive Irish nationalism followed by a revolution assured him of a respectful audience both in Ireland itself and abroad. His first plays, *The Countess Kathleen* and *The Land of Heart's Desire*, published respectively in 1892 and 1894, had to wait for several years to be performed. The success of the former, however, in 1899 marks the start of the Irish Dramatic Movement. In 1896 Yeats had met Synge in Paris and persuaded him to return to Ireland to study Irish peasant life. There, together with Augusta, Lady Gregory (1852-1932), they recruited Irish actors and in 1904 acquired the Abbey Theatre. It was during these years that Synge, in writing *In the Shadow of the Glen* (1903), *Riders to the Sea* (1904) and *The Playboy of the Western World* (1907), added a strong strain of domestic realism couched in poetic prose to Irish stage dialogue. Synge then alerted all shades of Irish opinion to the company's existence through the riots occasioned by performances of the first and third of these plays. By 1910 the theatre had become financially independent. It continued to exist as a repertory theatre, but it had actually become a National Theatre dedicated to the production of native and poetic plays and to recruiting amateur actors alongside professionals. A year later it won international fame following a triumphant tour of America. All three founders drew their inspiration from the Irish countryside, the grinding poverty and resilience of its peasants and, above all, from their naturally poetic style of speech. Yeats was also the first playwright in the West to pay serious attention to the simplicity of construction and representation exemplified by the Noh theatre of Japan, an influence most obvious in his *Four Plays for Dancers* (1916-17), and carried to its extremest limits in *Purgatory* (1938).

The firmness of the foundations laid by these European pioneers of verse drama between 1894 and 1918 sufficed to outlast the First World War and thus to encourage a younger generation to follow their example despite the iconoclastic onslaught of the Dadaists. Among the first to attract attention outside his own country was Jean Cocteau (1892-1963) who, in returning to Greek drama for his plots, proceeded to endow them with surrealist overtones of irony and fantasy. *Antigone*, produced at the Atelier in Paris in 1922, was followed in 1924 by *Orphée* at the Théâtre des Arts: a decade later the actor-manager Louis Jouvet set the ultimate seal of approval upon him by presenting Cocteau's version of the Oedipus story, *La Machine Infernale*, at his own theatre.

In London poetic drama finally won the seal of popular approval from Basil Dean's sensational production of James Elroy Flecker's *Hassan*, with its exotic oriental settings and its memorable incidental music commissioned from Frederick Delius, which received three hundred performances at His Majesty's Theatre in 1922. This play was produced posthumously, Flecker having died when only thirty in 1915; but it failed to provoke any immediate successors. These had to wait until the 1930s when a new group of poets led by T.S. Eliot, W.H. Auden and Stephen Spender began to attract the attention of the Bloomsbury intelligentsia.

T.S. Eliot (1888-1965), starting tentatively with *Sweeney Agonistes* (1932) – which he preferred to regard as a poem in dialogue – followed by *The Rock* in 1934 (which he later chose to suppress), achieved in *Murder in the Cathedral* a play that has been regarded as a masterpiece since its original production by E. Martin Browne with Robert Speaight as Thomas à Becket at the Canterbury Festival in 1935. Behind both these plays, as in their sequel, *The Family Reunion* (1939), stand explicit echoes of Sophoclean and Aeschlyean tragedy which are most evident in Eliot's repeated use of a chorus.

His near contemporary, W.H. Auden, collaborated with Christopher Isherwood in the writing of three verse plays – *The Dog Beneath the Skin* (1935), *The Ascent of F6* (1936), and *On the Frontier* (1939). All of them reflect the general malaise, political and social, that accompanied the rise of Nazi and Fascist dictators in Germany and Italy, and the Civil War in Spain, as does Stephen Spender's *Trial of a Judge* (1938).

Three other poet-dramatists of this period whose plays were less seriously flawed from a theatrical viewpoint and have thus proved to be more enduring were André Obey (1892-1975), Frederico Garcia Lorca (murdered in Spain in 1936) and an American, Maxwell Anderson (1888-1959). Obey's highly stylized *Noé* and *Le Viol de Lucrèce* both opened in Paris in 1931, directed by Michel St Denis for his Compagnie de Quinze: shortly afterwards both were translated into English and presented with great success in London – the latter offering Ronald Duncan a text on which to base the libretto of Benjamin Britten's opera *The Rape of Lucretia* in 1946, just as W.H. Auden had provided

Britten with the libretto for *Paul Bunyan* five years earlier.

A preoccupation with fate, dreams and death characterizes Lorca's passionate trilogy of Spanish life drawn partly from folk-lore and partly from the restrictiveness of Spain's cultural inheritence – *Blood Wedding* (1933), *Yerma* (1935), and *The House of Bernarda Alba*, written in 1939 but not produced until it appeared in a French version in London in 1939 and then in English in New York in 1940. Since then, all three plays have quickly established themselves in the international repertoire as modern classics.

Maxwell Anderson's first stage-hit in America was a realistic play, sharply critical of the First World War, *What Price Glory* (1926); but during the 1930s he acquired international respect as a major poet-dramatist. In *Elizabeth the Queen* (1930), *Mary of Scotland* (1933) and finally *Winterset* (1935) – all tragedies in verse – he succeeded in creating a synthesis between strikingly dramatic leading roles for actors and subject-matter of wide appeal without lapsing into rhetorical cliché or sentimentality. Anderson's only serious rival through the 1940s was Brecht, an exile in the United States through the Second World War (see p. 232-3).

A major factor accounting for the successes of all verse-dramatists, Symbolists, Constructivists, Expressionists, Surrealists and other minority groups writing for the theatre through the first half of the twentieth century lay in their being able to promote their respective ideological causes satisfactorily in small theatres in locations outside the central boulevard areas of metropolitan cities. There they could hope to recover production costs and still ensure adequate press coverage to publicize their activities amongst the fashionable and influential intelligentsia in metropolitan cities. Each was thus given firm grounds to believe that it was steadily gaining new recruits, many of whom would become converts. Just as important, each could count among these converts a number of men and women who could be relied upon to discharge debts and to commission new work from young writers, designers and composers. Among such British patrons who helped to make this period so exceptionally creative and diverse were Miss Horniman in Manchester, Lady Gregory in Dublin, Lady Cunard in London and Sir Barry Jackson in Birmingham. In the United States similar, if more organized, support became available from the slow but steady integration of drama and theatre into the teaching curriculum of academic institutions. This began at Harvard University in 1916 and then shifted to Yale in 1925; from there it spread swiftly during the 1930s into other universities and so downwards through the high schools to affect the whole educational system. Thereby it succeeded in supplying the theatre not only with a steadily increasing number of writers and other artists but with more perceptive and appreciative audiences from coast to coast. This process served so to regenerate American theatrical life as to make the United States the undisputed pace-setter of change and innovation in all areas of dramatic art during the years preceding and following the outbreak of the Second World War.

5 SHOW BUSINESS: TRADITION AND THE WINDS OF CHANGE

In the years following the end of the Second World War it became fashionable among the young to dismiss the commercial theatres of the Western world as purveyors of little more than frivolous, bourgeois ephemera. The latter half of the twentieth century, however, has proved them to have been wrong in making so sweeping an assumption. Unquestionably, many of the entertainments offered to the public – plays, musicals and spectacular revues – are best left buried in the oblivion that has subsequently overtaken them; but that is also true of the huge number of forgotten dramatic entertainments from previous eras which have never warranted revival: it is *not* a phenomenon unique to this century. The seasoned moguls of the entertainment industry were not so naive as to be heedless of changing public taste and the prospects for their own survival in a changing social and political environment.

In the first place they had the intelligence to recognize that theatre audiences care as much, if not more, for their favourite actors and actresses as they do for the vehicles in which they display their talents. By retaining the loyalty of trained, classical actors of the highest calibre with large salaries, 'star' billing, and the prospect of a degree of glamour and public adoration otherwise reserved only for royalty, they took the first crucial step towards meeting those challenges that were emerging to threaten their own future (see p. 226). Names that leap to mind in this context include Gerald du Maurier, Sarah Bernhardt, Ethel and John Barrymore, Forbes Robertson and Martin Harvey, Violet and Irene Vanburgh amd Mrs Patrick Campbell; and they in their turn could be relied upon to encourage juveniles (who could be groomed to replace them in due course) to join their ranks; and, not surprisingly, commercial managements quickly began to regard the expanding Little Theatre movement as an ideal training school from which to recruit these newcomers.

Secondly, commercial managements took good care to secure the services of the writers of farce, detective 'thrillers', situation comedies and musical entertainments which they correctly judged would continue to command a wide enough measure of public support to rival both the Music Halls and the new cinemas. Nor were they averse to promoting revivals of those popular classics that appealed as much to leading actors and actresses before and during the First World War as to their audiences. It was a shrewd recipe for success which served, as a bonus, to attract into their orbit many of the writers who had first acquired a reputation as avant-garde tear-aways in the Little Theatres. From their ranks they recruited such notable playwrights as Bernard Shaw, John Galsworthy and Edmond Rostand to endow their cause with respectability, and to encourage others to join them. Among those who chose to do so, following the end of the First World War, were Noël Coward, Jean Giraudoux, Somerset Maugham, George Kaufman, Eugene O'Neill, Clifford Odets and Terence Rattigan; none can be dismissed as frivolous or trivial in either their artistic aims or their dramatic technique. Frequent contemporary revivals of their plays flatly contradict that assumption (see pp. 238-41).

(a) **Farce:** Late in the nineteenth century, farce once again found brilliant exponents in France – Eugène Scribe (1791-1861), Eugène Labiche (1815-1888) and Georges Feydeau (1862-1921) – comparable (at least within this genre) with Molière, Fielding and Garrick. French example was followed in Britain by W.S. Gilbert (1836-1911) and by Sir Arthur Pinero (1855-1934), whose group of plays known as the Court Farces (*The Magistrate*, 1885; *The School-Mistress*, 1886; and *Dandy Dick*, 1887) have all proved resilient enough to warrant frequent revival. Even Bernard Shaw tried his hand at it (successfully) in *Passion, Poison and Petrification* (1909); but the most popular of all these farces has proved to be Brandon Thomas's *Charlie's Aunt* (1892).

The fact is that the twentieth century has since been remarkably fertile both in its loyalty to this genre and in its own achievements, more especially if the cinema is here allowed to share credit with the theatre. In Buster Keaton, Charlie Chaplin, Harold Lloyd, Laurel and Hardy, Abbot and Costello and the Marx Brothers, films found brilliant exponents of the genre who managed to transpose their stage skills to the screen: on Broadway George Kaufman and Moss Hart in *You Can't Take It With You* (1936) kept it alive on the American stage. In Britain, Ben Travers (1886-1980) between the wars (assisted by an oustanding triumvirate of actors, Robertson Hare, Ralph Lynn and Tom Walls) with *Plunder*, *Rookery Nook* and other farces at the Aldwych Theatre, and Brian Rix in the 1950s with

196. *Gertrude Lawrence with Noël Coward in* London Calling, *at the Duke of York's Theatre, 1923.*

the Whitehall farces, became household names, just as Anthony Merriott's *No Sex Please, We're British* has done in recent years.

(b) **Musical Comedy:** This genre had its origins in the hugely popular operettas of Johann Strauss in Vienna, Offenbach in Paris and Gilbert and Sullivan in London which were followed in the present century by such favourites as *The Merry Widow* (1907), *The Chocolate Soldier* (adapted in 1910 from Bernard Shaw's *Arms and the Man*), *Chu Chin Chow* and *The Maid of the Mountains* (both 1916). During the inter-war years the genre was championed in England by Noël Coward with *Bitter Sweet* (1929) but brought into line with the ever-increasing popularity of jazz by a continuous stream of American alternatives of which *No, No, Nanette* (1925), *The Desert Song* (1927) and *Showboat* (1928) supply prime examples. Escapist fantasies as most of these musicals undoubtedly were, their tunes and lyrics continue to bear the imprint of that era as indelibly as nostalgic romance still clings to steam trains, transatlantic liners and the never-never-land of Ruritania engraved on British hearts by Ivor Novello's *Glamorous Night* (1935) and *The Dancing Years* (1939).

Throughout this period commercial managements continued to receive the support of excellent actors and actresses with trained singing voices and fashionable good

197. *Lemuel Ayres's setting for the title-song of* Oklahoma, *New York, 1943. The choreography was by Agnes de Mille.*

looks among whom Gertrude Lawrence, Noël Coward (Fig. 196), Jack Buchanan, Jessie Matthews, Ivor Novello, Dorothy Dickson and Evelyn Laye led the field in securing the loyalty of London audiences. In continental Europe Richard Tauber, Yvonne Printemps, Maurice Chevalier, Lilian Harvey and Lottie Lenya commanded a similar following among French- and German-speaking audiences: but already in America the advent of 'the talkies' in 1927 was beginning to project such formidable singing and dancing stars as Al Jolson, Grace Moore, Nelson Eddy, Jeanette Macdonald, Ginger Rogers and Fred Astaire into cinemas worldwide as alternatives to local stage idols.

After the outbreak of the Second World War the initiative passed almost wholly out of European into American hands, with a seemingly unending flow of freshly minted musicals equipped with much stronger plots from *Oklahoma* (1941, Fig. 197) to *Guys and Dolls* (1950) and beyond, and fortified by infectiously exuberant casts of singers and dancers.

(c) **Comedy of Manners:** Whereas Bernard Shaw's early play, *Mrs Warren's Profession*, was banned by the Lord Chamberlain in 1894 and failed to reach public audiences until the 1920s, his *Pygmalion* was snapped up by that astute actor-manager, Sir Herbert Beerbohm Tree, for production at His Majesty's Theatre in 1912 with Mrs Patrick Campbell as Eliza Doolittle. Its success, preceded by a notable sequence of eleven of his plays staged at the Court

Theatre between 1904 and 1907 (see p. 220), did more than anything else to convince British commercial managements that they could do worse at their box-offices than offer to accommodate new writers who had something serious to say about contemporary social evils, provided that it was said with wit and humour conveyed by engaging characters within a strong story-line – a lesson Broadway managements were later to learn from Eugene O'Neill.

Shaw successfully bridged the First World War with two major commercial hits: *Saint Joan* (1926), with a cast led by Sybil Thorndike (see Fig. 210), and *The Apple Cart* (1929). By then other writers were emerging who preferred to align their careers to the requirements of mainstream commercial managements rather than with those of the avant-garde Little Theatres with their 'special' and thus smaller audiences. The first to appear was William Somerset Maugham (1874-1965) who, as early as 1908, had four plays running in London at once – in itself a theatrical record – one of which, *Lady Frederick*, was still found to be worth reviving in the 1980s. He, like Shaw, successfully bridged the war years with *Our Betters* in 1917 and what is now regarded as his masterpiece, *The Circle*, in 1921. Rivalling Shaw in esteem throughout the 1920s and early 1930s, he then found himself eclipsed by Noël Coward (1899-1973) who, unlike Maugham, was himself an accomplished actor and singer. Coward, likewise, during the 1930s and 1940s had to confront the challenges to his skills as a playwright presented by two newcomers – Osborne Henry Mavor who adopted the pen-name of James Bridie and was the founder of Glasgow's Citizens Theatre (1888-1951) and Terence Rattigan (1911-77), both of whom consistently enjoyed the support of commercial managers and star casts.

Maugham succeeded by speaking for himself. Never aiming to pander to popular taste, he nevertheless won popularity by combining his own sardonic sense of humour and objective detachment with a strong story-line in comedies of situation rather than character-development that managed to surprise and please his audiences. Coward, Bridie, and Rattigan judged the climate of post-war disillusionment and cynicism with similar stylistic accuracy, and succeeded equally well in reflecting the stiff-upper-lip determinaton of the middle and upper strata of society to make the best of life in a world that seemed to be losing its sense of direction. Coward provided in *Hay Fever*, *Private Lives*, *Cavalcade* and *This Happy Breed*, all written and produced between 1925 and 1942, a comedy of manners which in more recent revivals is proving not to have dated but to reveal an accuracy of verbal and visual observation of character that seems likely to place his comedies alongside those of William Congreve and Oscar Wilde (see Fig. 196). He was also one of the first English playwrights to turn his talents to writing songs for cabaret and revues; he provided the film industry, moreover, with two war-time classics – *In Which We Serve* and *Brief Encounter*.

Rattigan's comedies have also survived dismissal in the 1960s as bourgeois frivolities to return to the modern repertoire and to reveal, in such well-crafted plays as *The Winslow Boy* (1946), *Separate Tables* (1948) and *The Deep Blue Sea* (1952), a degree of compassion for human frailty that surpasses anything offered to public audiences by Coward or Maugham.

Bridie has yet to return to favour: yet the range of his plays from *The Anatomist* (first produced in 1930) to *Daphne Laureola* (1949), combined with his mordant wit and his ability to provide star roles for actors and actresses of the calibre of Alistair Sim and Edith Evans, makes it seem certain the best of them will shortly re-enter the modern repertoire as mid-twentieth-century classics. Two other popular dramatists of this period to share this neglect today were the distinguished actor, Emlyn Williams (1905-87), whose *Night Must Fall* (1935) and *The Corn is Green* (1938) both came to be filmed; and the novelist J.B. Priestley (1894-1984), whose special concern with time warps was firmly imprinted on such successful plays as *Time and the Conways* (1937), *Johnson over Jordan* (1939) and *An Inspector Calls* (1946) with Ralph Richardson in the title role (see Fig. 210).

Matching the achievements of these British dramatists were those of two Frenchmen – Jean Giraudoux and Jean Anouilh. Giraudoux (1882-1941), like Claudel before him (see p. 234), was a diplomat by profession; but by 1920 his literary attainments as poet and novelist had attracted the attention of the actor-manager Louis Jouvet who persuaded him to write for the theatre and directed his early play, *Amphitryon '38*, at his own theatre in 1929. Combining a love of mythology and fantasy with a strictly realistic appraisal of Franco-German political animosities, his most popular plays – *Tiger at the Gates* (1938), *Ondine* (1939), *Sodom and Gomorrah* (1943), and *The Mad Woman of Chaillot* (1946) – found a wide public in English translation when produced in London and New York after the war. The first and the last of these provided Michael Redgrave and Martita Hunt respectively with two of their most famous roles.

His rival between 1932 and 1952 was Jean Anouilh (1910-87), who disclaimed any biography other than 'playwright'. He too had been noticed by Jouvet and employed as his secretary: it is hard to conceive of a better appren-

ticeship. Taking a leaf out of Bernard Shaw's book, he classified his long succession of plays as *pièces roses* (meaning pleasant) and *pièces noires* (meaning unpleasant). One success followed another from his first *pièce noire*, *L'Hermine*, and his first *pièce rose*, *Le Bal des Voleurs* (both produced in 1932), a track record which enabled him majestically to override the fall of France and the German occupation of Paris, and to present *Eurydice* and *Antigone* in 1942 and *Roméo et Jeannette* in 1945. The liberation of Paris that same year made no noticeable difference to his creative powers apart from a significant change of classification to *pièces brillantes*: and into that category he placed *La Répétition* (1950), *L'Invitation au Château* (1951) and *La Valse des Toréadors* (1951). Nearly all his plays reveal a concern with innocence betrayed and violated by predators of one sort or another – politicians, sophisticated roués or petty criminals. In retrospect it is now apparent that over and above his quite exceptional command of theatrical technique lies a more radical determination to abolish traditional distinctions between comedy and tragedy than anything that had been attempted by his contemporary British or American boulevard dramatists; and in his effort to portray society as it actually was during and after two world wars, he laid the necessary theatrical foundations on which the young dramatists who have replaced him as the fashionable idols of the latter half of this century have based their own visions of society with its many anxieties, fears and hopes.

The traumas affecting French society from Hitler's occupation of the Rhineland to the German occupation of France itself, which dominated the French theatre through the 1930s and 1940s, were paralleled in the United States by those resulting from the Wall Street Crash of 1929 and the Great Depression which followed it; but there the immediate impact of the economic crisis on the social fabric of the nation deflected playwrights' attention away from comedy of manners towards domestic tragedies. The results in Broadway theatres, however, sufficed to thrust American drama into the forefront of international interest.

With the ground already prepared by the spread of the Little Theatre movement to New York in 1916 (see pp. 220 and 232), by the establishment of drama departments in universities from coast to coast from 1918 onwards (see p. 236), and by the actors' strike in 1919 which won them and their playwrights fairer working conditions and financial contracts from commercial managers, a new generation of actors, actresses and writers was ready to meet the challenges presented to them by a society in a state of shock. While some of them continued to work in the semi-

198. Jo Mielziner's 'street' backcloth for the original Broadway production of Tennessee Williams's A Streetcar Named Desire, *1947. Private collection.*

professional experimental Community Theatres which had sprung up in most of the larger cities during the 1920s, others kept an eye on the more lucrative returns offered by Hollywood and Broadway. Amongst the former, by far the most radical was the nationwide Federal Theater Project founded by Hallie Flanigan in 1935 to cater for unemployed actors and writers but suppressed four years later for political reasons. Those who chose to aim for Broadway production recognized that it was in their interest to write within realistic limits not too far removed from those imposed on American audiences by the film industry.

Those who opted to try to fulfil the requirements of the Broadway managers included Philip Barry (1896-1949), Marc Connelly (1890-1980), George Kaufman (1889-1961) and Moss Hart (1904-1961): between them they provided New York with indigenous comedies of manners that compared favourably with those of Maugham, Coward and Rattigan. Connelly's *Green Pastures*, a humanely perceptive comedy of Negro life (1930); Kaufman's and Hart's

collaborative *Once in a Lifetime* (1930), a satire on the plight of actors and authors from the silent film studios bewilderedly trying to cope with 'talkies', and a dazzling farce *You Can't Take it with You* (1936); and Barry's *The Philadelphia Story* (1939), embrace the best among them. Fortunately, these authors could still rely, like their British and French counterparts, on a regular supply of such outstanding actors and actresses as Helen Hayes, Katherine Hepburn, Henry Fonda, the Lunts and Franchot Tone, and a galaxy of distinguished designers that included Lee Simonson, Donald Oenslager and Jo Mielziner (see Figs. 193, 198 and 208).

Other playwrights of that generation with more serious political and social causes to plead for chose to establish a reputation for themselves under more liberal managements such as those of the Theater Guild Studio or Eva Le Gallienne's Civic Repertory Theatre in New York. With that accomplished, they quickly found themselves courted by Broadway managers. Among those who took this route were Eugene O'Neill, Clifford Odetts, Tennessee Williams and Arthur Miller.

O'Neill (1888-1953) was the son of a distinguished actor, James O'Neill. He first achieved notoriety as a playwright with a sequence of four short plays derived from his experiences in the Merchant Navy which, when performed together, go under the title of *The Long Voyage Home* (1917-18). Two full-length plays followed, again constructed in the realistic vein – *Diff'rent* (1920) and *Anna Christie* (1921). *All God's Chillun Got Wings* (1924) and *Desire Under the Elms* (1925) finally placed him alongside Strindberg, Shaw and Pirandello as one of the twentieth century's most creative and forceful dramatists, an impression confirmed with the appearance of *Mourning Becomes Electra* (1931). *The Iceman Cometh* was completed in 1940 and first staged in New York (1946). *Long Day's Journey into Night* (completed in 1941) had to wait for posthumous production in Stockholm (1956). Both plays are conceived on a Wagnerian scale and take a full four hours to perform.

O'Neill's achievements naturally inspired others to emulate him. Of those who did, the first to taste success were Robert Sherwood (1896-1955) and Clifford Odetts (1906-1963). Sherwood followed up *Idiot's Delight* (1936) with *There Shall be No Night* in 1940, starring Alfred Lunt and Lynn Fontanne in both New York and London. Odett's *Waiting for Lefty* (1935) was likewise followed up later that year with *Awake and Sing*, a study of Jewish life in the Bronx and then, in 1937, with *Golden Boy*, a moving study of a young violinist who, to raise money for his impoverished family, is persuaded to enter the boxing-ring with disastrous results. That year also saw the production of John Steinbeck's (1902-68) powerful and politically emotive drama *Of Mice and Men*, set in a farming community in the Middle West bankrupted by years of drought and soil erosion. This matched Jack Kirkland's adaptation of Erskine Caldwell's novel, *Tobacco Road*, a no less forceful exposure of the poverty and degradation of 'Poor Whites' in the deep South: this opened in 1932 and ran for 3,182 performances reaching London in 1937. Just as quintessentially American was Thornton Wilder's (1897-1975) dramatization of small town family life in *Our Town* (1938) and his subsequent fantasy on mankind's many narrow escapes from annihilation, *The Skin of Our Teeth* (1942), which provided Vivien Leigh in the star role of the maid, Sabina, with one of her most glittering sucesses when it appeared in London (1945; see Fig. 204).

As the war advanced, these playwrights were eclipsed by Tennessee Williams (1911-83), whose sensitive studies of psychological misfits in contemporary American society like the frigid Laura in *The Glass Menagerie* (1944), the alcholic Blanche in *A Streetcar Named Desire* (1947) and the homosexual Brick in *Cat on a Hot Tin Roof* (1955) all reveal an indebtedness to Freud, Jung, Strindberg and O'Neill, but manage to avoid lapsing into clinical casebook histories (see Fig. 198). In *Summer and Smoke* (1948)

and *The Rose Tattoo* (1951; revived in London in 1991 by Peter Hall) he provided audiences with studies of women whose illusions serve first to frustrate and then destroy them.

Four years his junior, Arthur Miller (1915-) adopted a wider approach to the subject of illusion in American society, starting with *All My Sons* (1947), an exposure of wartime profiteering and its consequences. He then turned to American attitudes to success measured in terms of income brackets and status symbols in *Death of a Salesman* (1949) and next – more dangerously – to both religious and political intolerance in *The Crucible* (1953), a play which, while publicly well received, later caused him to be dragged before Senator McCarthy's infamous witch-hunting Committee on Un-American Activities as a crypto-Communist. Surviving that ordeal, he went on to provide another fine play in *A View from the Bridge* (1956).

While Miller dominated the theatrical scene in America through the 1950s, rival claims on international attention were emerging at first in France and then in Germany, Switzerland and Britain (see pp. 246-9).

(d) Shakespeare, Opera and Ballet: In terms of the distinctions hitherto made between experimental and commercial theatre, Shakespeare production in the first half of this century occupied a middle ground. With the days of lavish pictorial settings already numbered by their ever-increasing cost, responsibility for keeping his plays alive for audiences in Britain passed into the hands of three amateur dramatic societies and two professional companies whose leaders – Sir Frank Benson (1858-1939) and Sir Philip Ben Greet (1857-1936) – drew many of their recruits from those societies. It also passed into the care of a theatre founded and built as a memorial to Shakespeare in his own home town of Stratford-upon-Avon.

These innovations all began in the 1880s. Dramatic societies were founded in the universities of Oxford and Cambridge with the express purpose of staging revivals of Greek plays and those of Shakespeare with a view to speaking the verse well and restoring sense to the texts. This ambition was further reinforced, following the discovery of De Witt's sketch of the interior of the Swan Playhouse in 1888, by the founding of the Stage Society in London, dedicated to reviving Elizabethan and Jacobean plays on a platform stage with a minimum of scenery (see p. 220 and Fig. 102). It was within this radical environment that Benson and Ben Greet founded companies of their own (in 1882 and 1886 respectively) which they took on regular and extensive provincial tours. By then the Shakespeare Memorial Theatre at Stratford was presenting annual summer seasons, having opened its doors with a production of *Much Ado About Nothing* in 1879. A national appeal for funds having been greeted with near-total indifference by the British public, the £20,000 required to build it was met by a local citizen, Charles Flower, who died unthanked and unhonoured for his efforts. However, by the start of the new century, both Benson and Ben Greet had allied their companies with the annual Stratford Festivals and thus ensured their continuance.

In London enthusiasm for their example came to be shared by Lilian Baylis (1874-1937), who in 1912 succeeded her aunt, Emma Cons, as directress of the Royal Victoria Hall and Coffee Tavern (formerly the Royal Coburg Theatre). She transformed it from a Temperance Hall dedicated to providing improving entertainment for industrious artisans into a theatre housing its own repertory company and devoted principally to staging Shakespeare's plays, and fondly nicknamed by its loyal audiences 'The Old Vic'. There, under the enlightened direction, first of Ben Greet and then of Robert Atkins followed by Harcourt Williams, it trained a galaxy of young actors and actresses including John Gielgud, Laurence Olivier, Edith Evans, Peggy Ashcroft, Alec Guinness and Ralph Richardson, all of whom were subsequently honoured for their services to the theatre (see Figs. 204, 210 and 217). It was they who, together with Donald Wolfit and Tyrone Guthrie (who were both likewise honoured with a Knighthood), did so much to sustain the morale of London audiences with thrilling sequences of Shakespearean productions during the grim wartime blitzes of which the Old Vic Theatre itself became a casualty in 1941.

Throughout the first two decades of this century Anglo-Saxon audiences persisted in their belief that opera and ballet could only be worth seeing if performed by Germans, Italians or Russians (see pp. 221, 229 and Fig. 164). Thus to succeed in the 1920s, the brilliantly accomplished English dancer, Alice Marks, had to assume the name of Alicia Markova! In the 1930s, however, attitudes began to change. Once again it was Lilian Baylis who was the prime mover in securing and refurbishing the old theatre at Sadlers Wells as a base for British opera and ballet in 1931. The first opera to be staged was *Carmen*. The ballet company under the leadership of Ninette de Valois (Edris Stannus) and Constant Lambert followed shortly after and quickly established a reputation for technical excellence and creative flair. Headed by Frederick Ashton, Robert Helpman, Margot Fonteyn (Margaret Hookham) and Pamela May, this company became known as the Sadlers Wells Ballet, or the English Ballet.

Competitors soon appeared. The first was Ballet Rambert, founded in 1930 and based at the tiny Mercury Theatre which was owned by the husband of its founder, Marie Rambert. The second was a company of German Jewish refugees from Essen led by Kurt Joos which was offered a home by Dorothy Elmhirst at Dartington Hall in Devon. This company achieved notoriety in 1932 with *The Green Table* – a savage indictment of the futile attempts of the League of Nations to deal with Hitler and Mussolini – but failed thereafter to advance its reputation.

Both Ballet Rambert and the Sadlers Wells Company were more fortunate in being able to pick up some of the key members of the Ballets Russes following the death of Diaghilev in 1929 (see pp. 221 and 229). This led immediately to the founding of the Carmargo Society in London with which both Ninette de Valois and Marie Rambert became associated, as did two of Diaghilev's principal designers, Sophie Fedorovitch and Nadia Benois. Two years later Balanchine and Toumanova elected to try their luck in America.

During the decade before the outbreak of the Second World War Ballet Rambert included Antony Tudor's *The Planets* (1934) and Andrée Howard's *Lady into Fox* (1939) in its repertoire; but in 1941 it became homeless and had to be reconstituted in 1943 by C.E.M.A (see p. 224) as a touring company on a more intimate scale, a form it has succeeded in preserving ever since.

The Sadlers Wells Company was both numerically larger and luckier. Having established a reputation for originality before the war with such master-works as *Checkmate* (1937, choreography de Valois; décor E McKnight Kauffer; music Arthur Bliss) and *Horoscope* (1938, choreography Frederick Ashton; décor Sophie Fedorovitch; music Constant Lambert), it moved to the New Theatre in 1943 and there advanced its reputation with at least two striking and controversial ballets, both choreographed by Robert Helpmann – *Comus* and *Hamlet* (see Fig. 199).

In 1946, thanks again to financial assistance from C.E.M.A., both the ballet and the opera company were enabled to move to Covent Garden. There, for the first time since the days of Purcell and Handel, British operas were staged, with works by Benjamin Britten, Vaughan Williams, William Walton and Michael Tippett being performed during the next ten years; and British ballet found itself able to stand comparison with the best in Europe. Almost simultaneously in America there emerged a remarkably creative ballet company under the guidance of Martha Graham devoted to contemporary dance which was able to compete with the New York City Ballet which

199. *Leslie Hurry's setting for Robert Helpmann's Expressionist ballet* Hamlet, New Theatre, London, 1943. *Choreographed to Tchaikovsky's Fantasy Overture for Shakespeare's play, this daring and controversial ballet went far towards confirming the Vic-Wells (later, the Royal Ballet) Company's reputation for creative originality (see Fig.190).*

Balanchine had founded in 1933: both companies have since become the pace-setters for the latter half of this century. With the previously impregnable reputations of the Bolshoi and Kirov companies in Russia seriously tarnished by the repeated defections of such notable dancers as Rudolf Nureyev and Natalia Makarova to the West, the only companies to have matched the Americans as innovators since the 1950s are the Royal Companies in Denmark and the Netherlands and that of Merce Cunningham in the United States itself. Never-theless, audiences' horizons have been widened substantially since then by frequent appearances of exotic and highly talented dance companies from Africa, India and South East Asia (see p. 261 and Fig. 220d) on both American and European stages.

15

From the Fifties to the Nineties

For any author who has spent most of his working life in close contact with the theatre, the past forty years or more present special problems if viewed as 'history'. Personal associations with particular playwrights, actors, actresses, directors, designers, technicians, theatre architects, teachers, theatre critics and historians have inevitably interwoven so much subjective opinion with factual occurrence as frequently to make it difficult to distinguish between memoirs, trends, prejudice and actual events. While no one, therefore, is likely to agree wholly with what they read in the concluding pages of this book, it is still to be hoped that no reader, whether old or young, may find cause altogether to reject the choice of issues singled out as central factors determining what has thus far happened to the theatre between the end of the Second World War and 1990, and what looks likely to happen in the last few years of this century.

1 DEAD ENDS AND NEW HORIZONS

After Hiroshima and the German holocaust, with twenty million dead, the whole world needed a breathing space to repair the damage that the human race had inflicted upon itself in Europe, Asia and North Africa between 1939 and 1945, and also to recover a sense of purpose with which to build a securer future. In that political, social and economic environment, the theatre naturally preferred to stick to proven formulae for box-office success that had enabled it to survive the war battered but unbowed. As Germany, Italy and most of Eastern Europe lay in ruins, little could be expected to emerge from those countries, at least to start with (nevertheless, in Poland, one of the first major buildings to rise above the rubble of shattered Warsaw was a new opera house). Nor could it from either Spain or Russia since both were still controlled by

dictatorships that chose either to suppress the theatre or to license it for use as an instrument of propaganda.

Britain, still faced with the need to ration food, clothes and fuel, and humiliated by its immediate task of finding face-saving ways in which to jettison its former Empire, could provide little beyond what was already on offer: more verse-dramas from T.S. Eliot and some new ones by Christopher Fry and Ronald Duncan interspersed with some realistic plays relating to the war, and yet more classical revivals. All of them were made to seem more durable than they have proved to be by outstanding performances from such excellent actors as John Clements, Kay Hammond, Alec Clunes, Vivien Leigh and the young John Mills, Alan Bates, Claire Bloom, Richard Burton and Paul Schofield. Managements varied this fare with imports borrowed from more lively French and American sources which at least drew the attention of British audiences to new plays by Jean Anouilh, Tennessee Williams and Arthur Miller (see pp. 239 and 241). A signpost, however, to the possibility of a brighter future already existed in terms of two radical decisions taken by governments between 1940 and 1946 relating to the provision of patronage of all the arts in the years ahead. The first of these was the establishment in Britain in 1940 of a Council for the Encouragement of Music and the Arts (C.E.M.A.) that was principally concerned with providing musical and dramatic entertainment for factory workers and home-based members of the armed services. While the principle of government subsidy for the Arts had been taken for granted in continental Europe for more than 150 years, this had not been so in Britain, its Dominions overseas or the United States.

An early consequence of the establishment of the C.E.M.A. was the rescue, after the war had ended, of the Royal Opera House, Covent Garden, from its down-

THE TWENTIETH CENTURY: 1950-1991

1950	Glen Hughes opens the first Arena Theatre in Seattle, Washington
1951	Festival of Britain
1952	Tyrone Guthrie, Alec Guinness and Tanya Moisevitch establish a Shakespeare Festival in a tent at Stratford, Ontario, Canada
1953	Ionesco's *The Chairs* produced in Paris Joan Littlewood's Theatre Workshop housed at the Theatre Royal, Stratford East, London Samuel Beckett's *Waiting for Godot* produced in Paris Death of Stalin
1955	Elizabethan Theatre Trust established in Sydney, Australia
1956	Harold Pinter's *The Room* produced at Bristol University John Osborne's *Look Back in Anger* produced at the Royal Court Theatre, London Judith Melina establishes 'The Living Theatre' off-Broadway Suppression of Hungarian uprising; Suez crisis
1958	Publication of Artaud's *The Theatre and its Double* in English translation First visit of Théâtre Africain to London
1959	Théâtre National Populaire established in France
1961	Arnold Wesker founds Centre Forty-Two in London; Building of the Berlin Wall; Cuban missile crisis
1962	Café La Mama Experimental Theatre Club founded in New York The Beatles and The Rolling Stones win international fame
1963	Assassination of President Kennedy
1964	Peter Weiss writes *Marat/Sade* Opening of a National Theatre in Britain
1965	Edward Bond's *Saved* produced at the Royal Court Theatre Foundation of the National Endowment Fund for the Arts and the Humanities in the USA
1966	Lincoln Center for the Performing Arts opens in New York
1967	Tom Stoppard's *Rosencrantz and Guildenstern are Dead* produced at the National Theatre in London
1968	Productions of *Hair* and *The Connection* bring nudity, drugs, and obscene language into the theatre after the abolition of stage censorship in Britain
	War in Vietnam (1959-75); students man the barriers in Paris streets; American campus riots; suppression of the Czechoslovakian uprising
1969	Publication in Britain of Jerzy Grotowski's *Towards a Poor Theatre*; Publication of Peter Brook's *The Empty Space*; Foundation stone laid in London of Denys Lasdun's National Theatre
1971	Royal Shakespeare Company visits Japan
1972	Richard Nixon resigns as President of the USA
1976	Completion of the National Theatre complex in London
1979	Mrs Thatcher becomes the first woman Prime Minister in Britain
1980	Ronald Reagan elected President of the USA Prosecution of the National Theatre under Britain's obscenity laws for its presentation of Howard Brenton's *The Romans in Britain*
1981	Women's Playhouse Trust founded in London
1982	Falklands War RSC move into the Barbican Centre, London
1984	Ronald Reagan re-elected as President of the USA
1985	Challenger space mission ends in disaster Chenobyl atomic power station explodes in Russia
1986	Andrew Lloyd Webber's *The Phantom of the Opera* opens in London together with RSC's *Les Misérables* Wole Soyinka awarded Nobel Prize for Literature
1987	London revivals of Sondheim's *Follies* and *Pacific Overtures* British Theatre Museum opens in Covent Garden
1988	George Bush replaces Ronald Reagan as President of the USA
1989	Overthrow of the Berlin Wall; reunification of Germany Vàclav Havel elected President of Czechoslovakia Bastille Opera House opens in Paris
1990	Mrs Thatcher dismissed as Prime Minister in Britain £4 million deficit obliges RSC to withdraw from the Barbican Centre in London Lech Walesa elected President of Poland
1991	Gulf War Liverpool Playhouse, Bristol Old Vic and Welsh National Opera face bankruptcy in Britain Sam Shephard's *States of Shock* opens in New York Alan Ayckbourn elected Professor of Drama at Oxford University

graded wartime use as a dance hall (see p. 242) and the saving of the oldest working theatre in Britain – the Theatre Royal in King Street, Bristol, built in 1766 – from the threat of sale for use as an extension to the adjoining vegetable market: after restoration it became the home of the Bristol Old Vic Company and has remained so ever since (see p. 273 and Fig. 200).

In 1946 the C.E.M.A. was reconstituted as the Arts Council of Great Britain and was expressly charged with providing financial blood transfusions to enable managements of many existing provincial theatres to strengthen their companies and augment the funding of productions, and also to encourage others to establish new theatres in areas of the country that had for long been deprived of any local contact with the performing arts. A year later the University of Bristol followed American example in admitting drama and theatre into the ranks of its liberal arts disciplines, a decision that was to be copied by many other universities, and one that automatically translated them into becoming major patrons where the funding of training facilities was concerned, as may be judged by reading the CVs of the actors, directors and designers listed in any theatre programme today.

These changes did much to foster the renaissance of theatre building, theatre architecture, playwriting and acting that was to characterize the next three decades and to restore to the British theatre the international reputation for innovation and excellence that still attracts tourists today. Only in the 1980s did the principle of subsidy re-enter the political arena as an issue in urgent need of questioning and reappraisal (see pp. 252 and 267-70). After the bruising experiences of the Federal Theatre Project in the 1930s (see p. 240), Americans preferred throughout the 1940s and 1950s to rely on private sponsorship and their many universities to promote artistic enterprises: it was not until 1965 that Congress was finally persuaded to establish a National Endowment Fund to assist the many summer festival and regional theatres that were by then in urgent need of support (see p. 252).

In Britain, one of the immediate consequences of the establishment of the Arts Council in 1946 was the inauguration of the Edinburgh International Festival of Music and Drama in 1947, followed in 1951 by the promotion of A Festival of Britain. Among the most notable events of both Festivals was the revival of two medieval plays not seen since the middle of the sixteenth century – Sir David Lyndsay's *Ane Satire of the Three Estates* (annually from 1948 to 1952 directed by Tyrone Guthrie) and the York Cycle of Mystery Plays directed by E. Martin Browne. Both directors employed open stages and reverted (where

theatrical representation was concerned) to the use of emblematic stage conventions originally created to facilitate poetic narrative embracing a multiplicity of scenic locations and, in the case of the York Cycle, a time-span stretching from Creation to Judgement Day. These two productions between them served to overturn all previously held literary and academic critical verdicts on pre-Shakespearean drama in Britain and provoked a wholesale reappraisal of it as community drama which could engage the interest and co-operation of entire townships in the same way as Mardi-Gras carnivals or localized athletic events like football matches and tennis or ice-hockey tournaments do today. This reappraisal has continued ever since, not only in Europe and America but in Japan with results that have served to revolutionize modern attitudes to playwriting, scenic design and amateur dramatics.

Further evidence of new possibilities appeared with the importation to London at first of plays from France and, later, from Germany and Switzerland: the French newcomers were championed by the dramatic critic of *The Sunday Times*, Harold Hobson, and the latter by that of *The Observer*, Kenneth Tynan. British audiences thus came to be exposed to the theatrical expressions of existentialist philosophy on the one hand and to Marxist dialectic on the other. This opened up for young English-speaking writers of the 1950s fresh fields of psychological and political drama that corresponded closely with the hopes and fears of the first generation to have attained maturity after the Second World War had ended, and as the legacies that it had bequeathed to them were becoming fully apparent.

2 SIGNPOSTS TO THE SIXTIES

The German occupation of France, and the attendant humiliation of national pride, awakened the dormant energies of Surrealism as a vehicle through which French writers could vent their feelings about the nightmarish and schizophrenic experiences of the wartime occupation, and justify their own actions to a censorious world. The first to tackle this problem were the playwright Jean Anouilh (see p. 239) and the two philosophers and novelists Albert Camus (1913-60) and Jean-Paul Sartre (1905-80).

In their hands Surrealism acquired a vital dramatic ingredient which had hitherto been lacking, a folk hero as protagonist of the kind that Figaro, Jack Tar and Davy Crockett had given to early melodrama (see p. 185): the Outsider. This character – romantic, alone and self-pitying – had been sketched in poetry and fiction a century earlier by Byron in Manfred and by Dostoevsky in Raskolnikov, and then carried into real life in the twentieth century by the cult of Bohemian café society in Paris, Bloomsbury, Berlin and Greenwich Village. By the start of the Second World War he was thus already classless and internationally recognizable. Anouilh dramatized him as Orpheus in *Eurydice* (1942), Sartre as Orestes in *The Flies* (1943), Camus as Caligula in his play of that name (1945). Audiences found this protagonist not only identifiable but emotionally engaging. The familiarity of the classical story and environment only made the modernity of the protagonists' existential solution to their problems the more striking. These plays and their successors, unlike earlier Surrealist dramas, achieved a genuine measure of success with the public with relatively long runs both in Paris and outside France. These authors, however, left it to their successors, Eugene Ionesco, (1912-), Samuel Beckett (1908-), Arthur Adamov (1908-70), Jean Tardieu (1903-) and others, to dispense with the recognizable logic of plot structure and to substitute situations which appeared neither to have developed out of earlier ones nor to lead on to any other. The surrealistic quality of this topsy-turveydom presented in recognizably realistic settings and dialogue created a new theatrical style distinct enough to warrant description as Theatre of the Absurd.

Such a play is Beckett's *Waiting for Godot* (1953), in which all that the author permits his characters to do is wait: Godot never appears. In Beckett's later plays character development is dealt with just as dismissively, leaving only faintly sketched identities for the actor to fill in with his or her personality, like children filling in an outline drawing with coloured crayons. These characters scratch around seeking a meaning for existence and, finding none, scratch again with the remorselessness of night following day following night, like Krapp and his tape-recorder in *Krapp's Last Tape* (1960). The human condition is reduced in the manner of caricature to a prison, in which actor and spectator occupy the same cell, the theatre itself, unable to escape from each other's company and, maybe, even unable to communicate. Winnie buried up to her neck in a sandpit and her mute husband Willie hovering around it epitomize this situation in *Happy Days* (1961; Fig. 200).

Throughout this period the standard of French acting remained remarkably high. The pre-war generation was still represented by such veterans as Louis Jouvet, Edwige Feuillère, and Charles Dullin; and a new one had joined it which included Jean-Louis Barrault, Madeleine Renault and Gérard Philipe. Between them these writers, actors and actresses did much to restore French self-esteem and self-respect not only in France, but in Britain and America. The Jouvet and Barrault companies were invited to appear at the Edinburgh Festival, the former in 1947 and the latter

200. *Samuel Beckett's* Happy Days, *Bristol Old Vic, 1979, with June Barrie as Winnie, Mark Buffery as Willie. Directed by Michael Joyce and designed by June Jet Harris.*

in 1948 where they were rapturously received: and in 1947 the actor-manager Jean Villar founded an international arts festival in Avignon.

German-speaking countries had to wait longer to attract international attention. Brecht (see pp. 232-3), having chosen to return to East Germany when the war ended, had by 1949 succeeded in establishing with his wife, Helene Weigel, and the designer, Caspar Neher, his own company in East Berlin – the Berliner Ensemble: there he could at last both present his own plays and encourage others to adopt his theories about play construction, production style and ensemble acting. News of these achievements spread to London and New York by the mid-fifties: Joan Littlewood's London production of *Mother Courage*

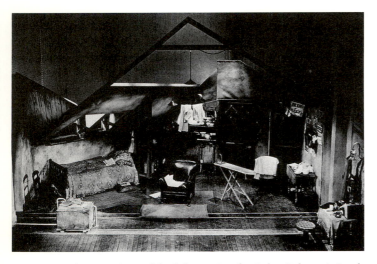

201. Alan Tagg's model of the setting for John Osborne's Look Back in Anger *at the Royal Court Theatre, London, 1956. University of Bristol Theatre Collection.*

in 1955 was followed by productions of *The Good Woman of Setzuan* in 1956, and both *Galileo* and *Baal* in 1963. All of them were seen to represent major changes of approach to subject-matter and theatrical representation.

Critical success at home brought him disciples. Two appeared in Switzerland – Friedrich Dürrenmatt (1921-90) and Max Frisch (1911-91), both of whom disagreed with his philosophical premise that man could change the world but who accepted his manner of representing ideas in theatrical terms. Dürrenmatt, like Sartre, argued that 'for the individual there remains impotence, the feeling of being overlooked and no longer able to take a step and help decide'; chance constantly intervenes in real life to frustrate man's most carefully laid plans. Of his many plays which illustrate this theme, *The Visit* (1955) and *The Physicists* (1961) have been the most highly acclaimed and frequently performed.

Frisch, while regarding man's *potential* as infinite, saw it as subject to curtailment by circumstances (of which chance happened to be one), a view expounded in *The Fire Raisers* (1956) and *Andorra* (1961).

An English disciple of Brecht's was John Arden (1930-), whose early plays – *Seargeant Musgrave's Dance* (1959), *The Happy Haven* (1960) and *The Workhouse Donkey* (1962) which attacked respectively lingering jingoistic values, scientific arrogance and political complacency and duplicity – attracted considerable public attention notwithstanding generally hostile press notices.

Of all British plays produced in the 1950s, however, undoubtedly the most challenging was John Osborne's (1929-) *Look Back in Anger* (1956, see Fig. 201), since this not only provided audiences with an unmistakably English version of 'the Outsider' – the Angry Young Man – but lashed out, as indicated in its title, at all traditional social values still espoused by the British upper classes; it also appeared to advocate radical action to abolish the *status quo* without, as yet, being able to offer any positive alternative. This play, together with Brecht's *Mother Courage* and Beckett's *Waiting for Godot*, set the scene for what was to happen in the theatre during the next decade.

What no playwright (or any other artist) working in the theatre in the 1950s could have anticipated was the impact that television in Europe was likely to have on every aspect of live theatre over the next forty years. It thus seems highly ironic in retrospect that it should have been the televising of one act of *Look Back in Anger*, which had opened to indifferent press notices at The Royal Court and seemed unlikely to run for longer than a few weeks, that transformed it into a *cause célèbre* – a play that everyone had to see! Osborne was equally lucky in finding his next play, *The Entertainer* – a lament for the collapse of the Music Hall – commissioned by Laurence Olivier in 1957; in it Olivier gave one of his most brilliant and moving performances as Archie Rice, the outwardly still chirpy, but inwardly defeated Music Hall comedian of the title (see Fig. 204).

No such good fortune attended another young actor-playwright, Harold Pinter (1930-), whose first one-act play, *The Room*, was produced by the Drama Department of Bristol University in 1956 and whose first full-length play, *The Birthday Party*, when it reached London in 1957 was taken off inside a week. Only in 1960 when it reopened in a new production at the Actor's Workshop in San Francisco (where it ran for two years) and when his next play, *The Caretaker*, opened in London could he claim to have earned a place among the heralds of the next decade. Unlike Arden and Osborne, Pinter avoided overtly political polemic, preferring to borrow poetic and absurdist techniques to explore human paranoia occasioned by external pressures (never explicitly defined) that appear to accompany the intrusion of an outsider into the habitual routines of another couple or small group of people. In these early plays Pinter drew extensively on his first-hand knowledge of working-class life in London's East End and in the theatrical lodging houses of provincial towns for his characters and settings (see p. 265).

Other authors of this decade who chose to expose audiences to the actualities of proletarian existence in town and country were Brendan Behan, Arnold Wesker, Shelagh Delaney and Ann Jellicoe. Behan (1923-64), a self-declared member of the I.R.A., provided in *The Quare Fellow* (1956) and *The Hostage* (1959) two grimly humorous portraits of Dublin slum-life, while Wesker (1932-) offered three equally stark juxtapositions of working-class fatalism and aspiration in his trilogy, *Chicken Soup and Barley* (1958), *Roots* (1959) and *I'm Talking About Jerusalem* (1960). The rough side of life in the Army received similarly realistic treatment from Willis Hall (1929-) in *The Long and the Short and the Tall* (1959); and other windows on the life-style of the under privileged were opened by Shelagh Delaney (1939-) and Ann Jellicoe (1927-) who both achieved West End productions with compassionate but outspoken comedies which flouted the taboo on what was still referred to as 'living in sin' – *A Taste of Honey* (1958) and *The Knack* (1962). The response of most middle-class theatregoers (itself a strange mixture of morbid curiosity and outrage) resulted in the branding of all these plays and others like them under the generic label of 'kitchen sink', an image drawn from the stage action which so frequently took place in a bedsitter incorporating a double bed, an ironing board, some chairs and a kitchen table, stove and sink.

Thus by the end of the 1950s experimental and commercial managements had between them succeeded in opening up their stages for the first time as a forum in all democratically constituted societies for the dramatizing of topical issues that accurately reflected the concerns of all sectors of the population rather than just those of the better-educated and more affluent minorities whose preserve the theatre had largely been up to the outbreak of the Second World War. Two questions still awaiting answers in the decades ahead were: 'How would the public respond?' and 'Would that response match possible defections with a large enough supply of newcomers to preserve live theatre as a financially viable art-form strong enough to beat the growing competition from television to outlast this century?' The answers given to both questions during the 1960s were as varied as they were unconventional.

3 THE EXPLOSIVE SIXTIES AND CALMER SEVENTIES

(a) **A Climate of Revolt:** What distinguished the 1960s from any other decade this century was a cultural revolution throughout the Western World imposed by the young or very young – i.e. those aged between sixteen and thirty – upon their parents, teachers or anyone else in authority over them who presumed to tell them what values they should respect or how they should behave. Teenagers discovered as the 1950s faded into past history that by taking advantage of unprecedentedly full employment they could aspire to obtain financial independence by the time they entered their twenties. Bored by perpetual reminiscences of wartime hardships and heroics, past imperial splendours and soulless suburban environments, they sensed that they had the means and the will to break out of this straight-jacketed existence and to create a new world tailored to fit their own ideals. A powerful incentive to this end was the advent of the contraceptive pill for women which enabled teenagers to enter into casual sexual relationships with the risk of pregnancies so greatly reduced as to permit and even encourage cohabitation; another was the rapid expansion of cheap air travel.

This radical change of stance among the young brought with it a heightened awareness of the authoritarian obstacles and restrictions that still lay between them and their vision of a New Jerusalem. Prime targets among these frustrating limitations included the nuclear arms race between the super-powers; press, film and stage censorship; religious taboos; racial discrimination and all institutions that continued to indoctrinate them with the traditional economic, political and aesthetic values of the ruling establishment. If such targets were to be relentlessly mocked and challenged, surely they could be overthrown.

At first, this revolt took the predictable form of defiant attitudes to conventional clothing, hair-styling, obscene language and other external forms of social behaviour. This was swiftly exploited by young entrepreneurs in the fashion and music industries eager to cash in on the newly acquired spending power of this numerically significant section of the population, and resulted in the emergence of a startlingly fresh 'pop' culture initiated by small groups of young musicians who lacked formal training but who possessed enough natural talent to capture the imaginations of party-goers of their own generation: the pioneers were Elvis Presley in the United States and the Beatles and the Rolling Stones in Britain who between them put jazz in the past tense and launched 'Rock' music on its way, and with it a clandestine cult of hallucinatory drugs. 'Pop' painters, like Andy Warhol in New York, swelled this flowing tide of change; and its young disciples soon found that they had powerful propagandist allies in the theatre to support their cause. John Osborne, Arnold Wesker, Harold Pinter and others had already nailed their colours to the mast (see p. 248). This alliance, in its turn, assisted the dramatists and actors in their own efforts to abolish the archaic powers of an official in the Royal Household – the Lord Chamberlain – to determine what audiences should or should not be allowed to see or hear in a public theatre. It took eight more years of persistent propaganda and protest to accomplish this: but the British Parliament finally decided to yield to this pressure and by passing The Theatres Act, 1968, into law brought four hundred years of Court control over the theatre to an end.

By then, however, protest of a far more threatening kind was setting alarm-bells ringing in Bonn, Rome, Paris and Washington. Anarchist groups, like the Red Brigade in Italy, Bader-Meinhoff in Germany and the Weathermen in America, were abandoning meetings and demonstrations in favour of 'direct action' (by which they meant the adoption of terrorist tactics) in the belief that, with support from young workers and students, they could frighten capitalist governments into submitting to their wishes. In the theatre, the playwright who best represented their views by espousing the cause of those minority groups within society who found themselves harassed and oppressed on account of legal restrictions on their activities or because of race or colour prejudice, criminal records or other abnormalities was Jean Genet (1910-1986). Having himself led a life of crime followed by spells of imprisonment (but having also been encouraged to write by Louis Jouvet and Jean Cocteau), Genet adopted in *The Maids*, *The Screens*, *The Balcony* and *Deathwatch* (all written between 1947 and 1960) the posture of a prisoner viewing the outside world from within his own cell. If this 'through-the-looking-glass' vision of life and society provides ample scope for satire, it is also profoundly pessimistic; but, on account of its compassionate approach to victims of repression, it appealed strongly to the disenchanted students of the 1960s who hailed him as a champion of their own causes. In May 1968, their defiant protests and demonstrations erupted into rioting in the streets of Paris and into the burnings, bombs and shootings which threatened to transform university campuses in Canada and the United States from seats of learning into centres of barbarism by the end of the decade.

The seventies began propitiously in Britain, following the abolition of the Lord Chamberlain's hated powers of censorship, with dramatists and actors eager to exploit the new world of 'anything goes' which promised an era of unprecedented licence, verbal and visual, in all theatres: managements, however, to whom the burden of what constituted breaches of the laws governing obscenity and blasphemy had now shifted, were more sceptical.

Firm action taken by European governments in the early 1970s to control terrorist activity together with a wide range of educational reforms served slowly to anaesthetize the more militant expressions of revolt. In America, likewise, the success of the civil rights campaign and the ending of the Vietnam war restored stability to riot-torn inner cities and campus life from coast to coast. The lesson still to be learned was that the halcyon days of full employment and relative affluence were about to fade into a mirage as the blight of inflation infected national economies and reduced dreams of brave new worlds to shadows of their former selves. The theatre, having chosen in the 1960s to politicize itself and in the 1970s to continue to use many of its new stages for overtly subversive polemical ends, invited confrontation with its business sponsors and the taxpayers whose wage-packets and salaries were being diminished to subsidize so many of the plays produced. That sponsors had a right to withdraw their support and that governments could cut subsidies in order to lower taxes was one lesson which had to be learned the hard way in the 1980s; another was that leading actors might challenge both writers and directors where choice of repertory was concerned (see pp. 262-70).

(b) **New Theatres for Old:** Young British writers, directors and actors of the stormy sixties were fortunate to be the immediate heirs of the Arts Council's far-sighted policy through the previous fourteen years of restoring bomb-damaged playhouses and helping to fund the building of new ones. This had resulted in the commissioning of architects who were willing to substitute what were variously described as 'open', 'thrust', 'apron' and 'arena' stages (or 'theatre-in-the-round') for the traditional proscenium-arched stages and hierarchically ordered auditoria of the pre-war era. By 1950 the need for performance spaces for practical experiment had led to the construction of the first permanent Arena Theatre in the State University of Washington at Seattle and, in 1951, to the building of the first wholly flexible studio theatre (i.e. permitting easy changes of stage and auditorium to match all major period styles of theatre) in the University of Bristol; the latter was followed shortly after by the opening of a similar building for the use of a long-established amateur dramatic society in London, the Questors Theatre at Ealing. It was during the next twenty years that most of the best-known, fully professional open-stage playhouses came to be built, including the Arena Theatres in Paris and in Washington, D.C.; the Festival Theatres at Chichester, at Stratford, Ontario, and in Minneapolis, together with the smaller Octagon Theatre in Bolton, The Crucible Theatre in Sheffield and many others. Architects' drawings of all of them were systematically published in *New Theatre Magazine* between 1959 and 1973 (see Figs. 202 and 221).

Parallel with these developments, the growth of interest

202. Open theatre. The architect Michael Reardon's drawing for
The Other Place, Stratford-upon-Avon, opened in 1991.

in drama festivals at both student and professional levels
encouraged actors, directors and writers to use them as
shop-windows for experimental work to be presented as
fringe events. It was by these means that the plays of
Harold Pinter, Tom Stoppard (1937-) and several other
young dramatists first attracted public notice. So popular
have these festivals now become that at the annual
Edinburgh Festival fringe events outnumber those in the
official professional programme.

Success at these festivals, whether at Edinburgh,
Avignon, Aix-les-Bains, or in many towns in the United
States and European university cities, led several of these
young, amateur student groups during the 1960s to translate themselves into professional companies touring the
small studio theatres that were becoming available to
them, or presenting their work, like medieval minstrel
groups, in market squares, in city streets, shopping

precincts, public bars, river barges and other venues where
rents are cheap or do not have to be paid (see Figs. 218 and
221).

The companies who occupied these new theatres or
other less formally organized performance spaces were
additionally fortunate in Britain in finding their production
budgets expanded by the Arts Council, or the Arts and
Leisure Committees of City and County Councils to enable
them to employ more actors and administrative staff and
to make better provision for costumes and settings than
they could be expected to do from ticket sales alone.
Weekly, and even fortnightly changes of programme vanished into past history to be replaced with longer runs and
longer (and far more costly) rehearsal periods to bring the
ideal of ensemble acting closer to actuality. The primary
beneficiaries of this munificence were the leading repertory
companies in Bristol, Birmingham, Nottingham, Liverpool
and other major cities; but it extended to many newly
established companies like those in Coventry, Hornchurch,
Exeter and Watford. Somehow these claims upon the
resources made available to the Arts Council by successive
Governments had to be balanced against those of the Old

Vic and the English Stage Company, together with the leading opera and ballet companies in London, and the Shakespeare Memorial Theatre at Stratford-upon-Avon. To meet them, the Arts Council strove tirelessly, and with a large measure of success, to jostle local authorities into matching their own annual awards. The ideal aimed at was that already obtaining in the German State Theatres and those in Scandinavia and Eastern Europe. It was never achieved; but in retrospect it is still astonishing how remarkable a change in both availability and standards of performance the acceptance of the principle of subsidized funding of the arts brought with it. Naturally, the degree of funding seen to be available whetted an appetite for more, and incited jealousies not only between London and provincially based managements for fairer distribution, but also from a wide range of semi-amateur groups (with axes of their own to grind) who argued that something they described as 'community theatre' was at least as deserving of subsidy from taxes as professional companies which they dismissed as 'élitist'. However, it was not until late in the 1970s, when the illusion of a fairy godmother with a bottomless purse was punctured by galloping inflation, that these internal bickerings became explicit and made wholesale reappraisal of funding for the arts in Britain imperative.

Americans, still bruised by their experiences of government subsidy for the arts during the 1930s when the Federal Theatre Project came to grief for political reasons, and by its aftermath in the witch-hunt of Senator McCarthy's Un-American Activities Committee (see p. 241), were slow to copy post-war European examples. However, in 1965 Congress agreed to fund a National Endowment Fund for the Arts and Humanities which has since done much to translate the largely amateur standards of regional community theatres into professional companies worthy of substantial local business sponsorship to supplement this assistance. From Louisville, Kentucky, to Denver, Colorado, and from Houston, Texas, to Cleveland, Ohio, the story of regeneration has repeated itself in the building of spacious and attractive theatres and the establishment of resident repertory companies, thus providing American playwrights, actors, designers and directors with the means to rival and even eclipse many of the much longer-established State Theatres in Europe. Similar success stories have accompanied decisions taken by Canadian, Australian and New Zealand governments, also during the 1960s, to subsidize the performing arts from Federal and Provincial government sources.

France, the country which had pioneered the principle of subsidy three hundred years earlier when Louis XIV founded the Comédie Française (see p. 157), followed British example after the war in accepting a modest responsibility for extending state patronage when attempting to decentralize the theatre. To that end funds were made available to create some ten major centres outside Paris, of which the most fruitful have been those at Avignon, Strasbourg, Lyons and Toulouse. Elsewhere in Europe, central and local government support for all major theatres and opera houses continued to be taken for granted.

(c) **New Wave Plays and Playwrights:** Early in the 1960s it became evident that the fashionable addiction to verse drama, drawing-room comedy and American musicals which had dominated the commercial theatres of the 1950s was rapidly losing out to creative experiments in the writing and staging of more democratically orientated representations of contemporary life pioneered by Jean Genet in France, Arthur Miller in America and by John Osborne, Arnold Wesker, Joan Littlewood and others in Britain (see pp. 248-50). This shift in public attitudes was hastened among the young by the advent of 'rock' music whose promoters on both sides of the Atlantic chose to communicate directly with their own generation, and at their own level, ignoring all the taboos respected by their seniors and social superiors. Not the least significant aspect of this change was the elevation of amateurs to professional status without any noticeable previous training. As 'pop' culture came into its own, so its star performers rose rapidly to fame and fortune, encouraging others to follow their example by buying guitars and forming groups of their own distinguished by exotic names like 'The Kinks', 'The Doors' or 'The Who' (see p. 249). Legions of teenagers mobbed them wherever they went, bought their records and adopted the drug-culture and dress which they defiantly promoted.

In the theatre, because drama still depended so much more heavily upon language and dialectic than on simple rhythm and melody, the pace of change was slower. Nevertheless, as texts became more outspoken and provocative, so fringe groups of college students began to imitate the examples set for them by the rock musicians and to seek performance spaces and financial assistance to lift them out of obscurity and into the limelight. In this quest many of them were helped in Britain by the Arts Council and by university drama departments and, more surprisingly, by several professional managements eager to update their public image. Bristol University was enabled by the Independent Television Company for Wales and the West of England to fund a Fellowship in playwriting which, at its inception in 1958, was awarded to John Arden on the strength of the manuscripts of *Live Like Pigs* and *Serjeant Musgrave's Dance*. During the year he held it he wrote (and had produced in the department's recently built Studio Theatre) *The Happy Haven* and *The Business of Good Government*, which received its first performance in the Parish Church of Brent Knoll in Somerset at Christmas. Shortly after this the Arts Council began to add bursaries for aspiring playwrights and directors in several of the provincial repertory theatres which enjoyed its support, a course of action matched on an experimental basis at the Shakespeare Memorial Theatre, Stratford-upon-Avon, and at the Royal Court Theatre in London. New venues like Joan Littlewood's Theatre Workshop, established in London at Stratford East in 1953, and Stephen Joseph's Theatre in the Round at Stoke on Trent (opened in 1962 and managed by his partner Peter Cheeseman after his sudden death in 1971), sought to promote local talent. Seldom can acts of faith have reaped such handsome rewards in so swift a time. The catalogue of plays, authors and actors who led their casts through the 1960s and 1970s is far too long to list in these pages; but fortunately this task has been admirably taken care of by the editors of the annual *Stage Year Books* of the period and Glenn Loney's *Twentieth Century Theatre* (1983). Some of these names, however, were so influential as to demand mention here.

Heading this list is the English Stage Company at the Royal Court, founded by George Devine in 1956 especially to stage plays by young dramatists. This company's success in bringing John Osborne and Arnold Wesker to the attention of commercial managements within the first few years of its existence encouraged a long queue of others to make it their first choice in the 1960s when submitting their typescripts to agents and readers for production. This company thus secured not only Osborne's next three plays – *Luther* (1961), *Inadmissable Evidence* (1964) and *A Patriot for Me* (1965) – but first plays from Ann Jellicoe, David Storey (1933-), Edward Bond (1935-) and Charles Wood (1932-) together with first visits to Britain from such stimulating new American companies as Café La Mama (1969: see Fig. 207) and Bread and Puppet (1970). In different ways most of these productions succeeded in polarizing the generation gap between theatregoers below and above the age of forty. Shocked and outraged by the subject-matter of these new plays, many patrons, whose loyalty to the theatre through the war years had enabled it to regenerate itself in the 1950s, deserted it in droves and have never returned. This reaction, rather than dismaying the young authors, actors and directors of this period, encouraged them to believe that they were succeeding in their prime objective of exposing the public to alternative approaches to moral, political, social and aesthetic standards of behaviour in tune with the realities of modern life, and thus subverting those of 'The Establishment' to a point where they would shortly crumble and collapse. Indeed, they were further encouraged in this belief by the sensational success of the rock-music groups who from early appearances in cellar-bars and other cabaret venues were emerging to attract young audiences of thousands all over the Western world. Many of the lyrics of their songs were at least as subversive as the texts of the new plays; but where rock-music appealed as much to scarcely literate school-leavers as it did to the well-educated among the same age group, theatre was an alien experience to most of the former and made the more daunting by its dependence on language and extended argument. The new companies of actors therefore that began to imitate the example of the rock groups failed to gain new audiences large enough for them to contemplate long runs in well-known London or provincial theatres. In short, although well served by the availability of so many new performance spaces, they found themselves back in the world of 'special' audiences that had characterized the Club and Little Theatres of the 1920s and 1930s (see pp. 218-22).

One escape route from this dilemma was drastically to reduce dependence on words and logical argument in favour of mime, dance, psychedelic lighting effects, multi-media shock-tactics and other techniques borrowed from rock-musicals like *Hair* (1968) or Andrew Lloyd Webber's *Jesus Christ Super Star* (New York, 1971; London 1972), calculated to appeal directly to audiences' emotions.

In France and Germany this course of action was carried to its extremest limits by the virtual dismissal of writers from the theatre. This arose through the elevation of directors, using scripts improvised by their actors on themes of the director's choosing or versions of extant plays free of copyright restrictions re-written, truncated or otherwise adapted to advance particular ideological causes. This situation was made the more acute in the early 1970s when most of the major publishers decided to cease printing new plays.

In Britain the supply of new plays which in the late 1950s had proved attractive enough to warrant the risk of transfer from fringe theatres to the West End did not dry up: Osborne, Pinter, Littlewood, Brecht and Beckett saw to that; and newcomers (whose ranks included Joe Orton, Peter Shaffer, Peter Nichols, Edward Bond, Trevor Griffiths and Tom Stoppard) amply sufficed to replace

*203. A scene from Peter Brook's pro-
duction of Peter Weiss's* Marat/Sade *by
the Royal Shakespeare Company at the
Aldwych, 1964.*

those who like Shelagh Delaney, N.F. Simpson and Arnold Wesker seemed to have little more to say (see p. 265). The new phenomenon particular to the 1960s was the publication of at least six books which all sought to formalize, in terms of new dramatic theories, many of the trends observable in the new plays of the previous decade.

Of these the most influential was Antonin Artaud's *The Theatre and its Double*. Artaud (1896-1948) had been an early disciple of Neo-Surrealism and one of André Breton's most passionate admirers (see p. 233); but he broke with it in 1926 and started writing about the theatre as well as acting in it. These writings were finally collected under this title in 1938 but were not translated into English until 1958. Mentally unstable and addicted to drugs for most of his working life, he died a victim of cancer. It is difficult to be sure whether Artaud objected more to reason or society: what he advocates in his self-styled 'Theatre of Cruelty' is shock tactics. These are to be implemented by such vaguely defined means as 'explosions of passion', the source of which, he claims, is to be the release of primitive instincts which lie deeply submerged within human personality under the irrelevant and corrupt accretions of centuries of civilized thought. This process must involve both self-immolation by the actor in his efforts to slough off this dross, and physical assault on his audience's sensibilities by whatever verbal and visual methods are needed to eradicate all deafening and blinding materialistic detail, in order to reveal cosmic truth. It is to be doubted whether any of his readers in the 1960s fully understood his theo-

ries; but their challenge was instantly recognizable to a generation intoxicated by its own belief in a call to arms that would change the world.

A cause, to become active, needs a leader; and the individual found on this occasion was another of André Breton's disciples, a playwright of the Surrealist school in Germany who had become a Marxist, Peter Weiss (1916-82). His highly didactic and anti-bourgeois *Marat/Sade* (1964; Fig. 203), *Viet Nam* (1968) and *Trotsky in Exile* (1970) fired the imagination of all dissident directors who saw or read these plays and led them to read and experiment with Artaud's theories in the theatre themselves. A leader among them was Peter Brook, who has since gone far towards urging the abandonment of any allegiance to or respect for written texts.

This unleashed a spate of semi-improvised and highly emotive scripts on particular topics of local interest (and some historical importance) or immediate social concern which directors and managers of fringe companies in London and the provinces could offer to audiences under such intriguing labels as 'Theatre of Fact', 'Theatre of Cruelty' and 'Agit-Prop'. Further authentication for this approach to play-writing appeared in Martin Esslin's *Theatre of the Absurd* (1961) and Jan Kott's *Shakespeare Our Contemporary* (1965). Esslin's book legitimized further excursions into Surrealist and transcendental experiment; Kott's book, by taking contemporary relevance as the base-line for interpreting Shakespeare's plays, further undermined established critical views on how to handle all classical revivals. Two other books – John Willet's *The Theatre of Berthold Brecht* (1959) and Robert Brustein's *Theatre of Revolt: An Approach to Modern Drama* (1964) added more fuel to these flames. These five books, together with the English edition of Jerzy Grotowski's *Towards a Poor Theatre* with a Foreword by Peter Brook (see pp. 258-9) and Brook's own *The Empty Space* (both 1969), came to head the list of prescribed reading for all students of the theatre throughout the 1970s.

In the theatre itself the impact of these books was quickly reflected in the increasing use made of shock tactics by the new wave of young playwrights intent upon stirring habitual theatregoers out of their supposed complacency. Among the first was Joe Orton (1933-67), who in *Entertaining Mr Sloane* (1964), *Loot* (1966) and *What the Butler Saw* (production of which was delayed, following his murder, until 1969) employed realistic dialogue and settings to provide a familiar comic frame for the violently disturbing incidents of the stage-action just below its surface. David Mercer (1928-80) and David Storey, who shared a Yorkshire mining background, adopted the same technique to explore, from Freudian and Marxist viewpoints, domestic and ideological situations confronting left-wing intellectuals divorced by their education and subsequent careers from their original working-class lifestyles. Yet it is to be doubted whether these and other young writers like Peter Nichols (1927-) and Edward Bond would have attracted as much attention as they all did had it not been for a coincidental upheaval taking place within the Shakespearian domain as represented at this time by the Memorial Theatre at Stratford-upon-Avon and by the Old Vic in London with its satellite in Bristol.

Plans to establish a National Theatre dating back to 1907 had resurfaced in the wake of the Festival of Britain in 1951 (see p. 246). It had seemed obvious then that the easiest solution would be to elevate the Old Vic to that status and change its name. In the course of the next ten years, however, two factors emerged to subvert this idea, the first being the rapid decline of production and acting standards at the Old Vic itself when compared with those set by Anthony Quayle at Stratford and maintained by his successor, Peter Hall; the second was Hall's decision to challenge the Old Vic by acquiring a shop-window in London.

In 1960 the Governors of the Shakespeare Memorial Theatre at Stratford-upon-Avon leased the Aldwych Theatre in London and allowed Peter Hall to enlarge the company's repertoire by including foreign classics and modern plays, thereby inviting both theatregoers and government funding agencies in the capital to make direct

204. *Laurence Olivier and Vivien Leigh as Titus Andronicus and Lavinia, with Michael Denison as Lucius and Alan Webb as Marcus, in Peter Brook's production of Shakespeare's* Titus Andronicus, *Stratford-upon-Avon, 1955. In this production (the first for several centuries), Brook took recourse to the symbolist techniques of Japanese Noh when presenting the raped Lavinia, shorn of her tongue and her hands, with scarlet ribbons round her neck and wrists in a pure white gown. Spectators fainted frequently and had to be taken out of the auditorium by attendant members of the St John Ambulance Service.*

comparisons between the policies and standards of the two companies. Faced with the invidious task of choosing between them, the government adopted a compromise solution. Laurence Olivier (who was then managing the summer seasons at Chichester's Festival Theatre) was invited in 1961 to take over the management of the Old Vic and install his company there as the National Theatre of Great Britain; Stratford was offered a consolation prize in being re-styled the Royal Shakespeare Company. This solution, far from pouring oil on troubled waters and satisfying personal ambitions, served to ensure a continuance of rivalry and strife. While Olivier battled to recruit a company headed by as many of the legendary classical actors and actresses among his own contemporaries as he could persuade to join him and to find a policy to justify the creation of a National Theatre in Britain (still awkwardly housed at the Old Vic in the murky Waterloo road), Hall used his greatly expanded production facilities not only to recruit new writers and directors but to invite Peter Daubeney to organize and present an annual summer season of World Theatre at the Aldwych to keep it open while the strain of the Shakespeare Festival at Stratford on the company's own resources precluded its presence in London. These World Theatre seasons began in 1964, bringing the Berliner Ensemble, the Moscow Arts Theatre, the Negro Ensemble Company of New York and other distinguished foreign companies to London through the rest of the decade. And in 1965, from his Stratford base, Hall added a small touring company – Theatregoround – created to work in close association with colleges and schools.

Meanwhile, the newly appointed Governors of the National, confronted with this onslaught on their own right to exist in that capacity, finally persuaded the government to fund the replacement of the Old Vic with a tailor-made building containing three theatres, together with well-equipped construction and rehearsal facilities, bars, restaurants, and foyers as spacious as those in continental European opera houses. Denys Lasdun was appointed as its architect and the foundation stone was laid in 1969. By the time it opened in 1976 its cost had escalated to a point where an inevitable consequence of meeting it (and its subsequent maintenance) was a reduction in government funding of provincial companies. Moreover, in the seven years that had elapsed since the foundation stone was laid, Laurence Olivier had become seriously ill and had been replaced as director by Peter Hall in 1973.

Two sharply divergent accounts of these events have since become available to readers in Olivier's autobiog-

raphy and Hall's *Diaries*, the former published in 1982 and the latter in 1983. What is certain is that this unprecedented expansion of prestigious theatrical amenities in Britain during the 1960s and 1970s placed a heavy strain on both the central and local government budgets required to subsidize their continuance. This, combined with the mounting inflationary pressures of the 1970s, would lead to a reckoning in the 1980s (see p. 266–8). It also made it the more certain that both the R.S.C. and the National were unlikely to retain the subsidy they needed to stave off bankruptcy unless they could bolster their claims to it as much by their support of modern plays and new talent as by their ability to preserve the long tradition of an unrivalled classical repertoire. Thus both the R.S.C. and the National began to compete with the English Stage Company at the Royal Court by building Studio Theatres of their own and by offering contracts to the new wave of young writers and directors seeking recognition as practising exponents of the theories of Artaud and Brecht. One such was Edward Bond, whose preoccupation with gratuitous violence and corruption in society was articulated in *Saved* (1965) and *Early Morning* (1968). Both plays were commissioned by the Royal Court, but both were banned by the Lord Chamberlain, a distinction shared by the German playwright, Rolf Hochhuth, whose play, *The Soldiers* (1967), failed to enter the repertoire of the National Theatre for the same reason. These three plays, together with Peter Brook's production of another young German dramatist's quasi-documentary plays – Peter Weiss's *Marat/Sade* (1964) and *Viet Nam* (1968) – for the R.S.C. represent the high-water-mark of the efforts made to challenge and overthrow all previously accepted standards of theatrical decorum and the moral and aesthetic values which had hitherto upheld them. But when the dramatic critic of *The Times* could ask whether these productions deserved to be taken more seriously than the morbid fantasies of decadent Grand Guignol at the turn of the century, and when the critic of *The Sunday Times* could say of *Saved*, 'There comes a point when both life and art are irretrievably debased' and then go on to add, 'Edward Bond's play, in this production, is well past that point', the time was approaching for habitual theatregoers to ask the same questions and answer them by withdrawing their patronage. Leading actors and actresses also began to ask themselves whether these repeated onslaughts on the sensibilities of audiences who, more often than not, had paid for their tickets in order to see *them,* rather than the play or the work of its director, were threatening their own livelihoods.

In the same year that Bond's *Early Morning* was banned

by the Lord Chamberlain only to be swiftly followed by the abolition of his own powers of censorship (1968), nudity entered the theatre for the first time in the American rock-musical *Hair*. Presented on Broadway in 1968, it arrived in European cities a year or two later. The first indigenous British contribution was Kenneth Tynan's erotically decadent *Oh! Calcutta* (1969). After the first shockwave of public protest had passed off uneventfully, nudity played some part in box-office response to early artistic experiments with it (as the many productions of Peter Shaffer's *Equus* demonstrated), but quickly ceased to generate comment. The brave new world of 'anything goes' had finally arrived, as had what was dubbed 'the permissive society'; but, as is the case with all shock tactics, they quickly wear thin with repetition.

As resistance to them from audiences, managements and actors alike hardened, so those dramatists and directors who continued to carry a torch for the methods of Artaud, Beckett and Brecht into the 1970s slowly toned down their attacks on what they most disliked in contemporary society to allow for the rapid return of some semblance of social and political stability to university campuses and urban life in Europe and America. Their reward for this in Britain was to continue to receive commissions from the Royal Court, the R.S.C. and the National Theatre and thus to have their plays presented to an international public by prestigious companies whose casts were headed by such distinguished actors and actresses as Ralph Richardson, John Gielgud, Judi Dench, Peggy Ashcroft, Joan Plowright, Vanessa Redgrave, Paul Schofield, Alan Bates, Anthony Hopkins and others.

Survivors from the stormy sixties to benefit from this munificence – unparalleled anywhere else in the world at this time – were Harold Pinter, Peter Nichols and Charles Wood; newcomers fortunate enough to attract this degree of public attention included Trevor Griffiths (1935-), Howard Brenton (1942-), David Hare (1947-), David Edgar (1948-) and one young woman – Caryl Churchill (1938-). Wood confined his plays to attacking military aspects of the imperial past by subjecting them to theatrical examination stripped of the nostalgically reverential approaches hitherto accorded to them. The first of these targets was the duel that Field Marshall Montgomery and his 'Desert Rats' had fought out with Field Marshall Rommel in North Africa during the Second World War, the received version of which he opened to question in *Dingo* (1967); the second was the Crimean War. Wood had provided the script for the film *The Charge of the Light Brigade* (1968), starring John Gielgud as Lord Raglan, the military heroics of which he then parodied in his stage-

205. *Jonathan Burn and Arlene Philips in the* Pas de deux *from Kenneth Tynan's erotic revue,* Oh! Calcutta!, *Fortune Theatre, London, 1970.*

play *Veterans* (1972) through reminiscences of the shooting of that film in Turkey.

Griffiths chose rather to concentrate on expressing his own disgust with the hypocrisy and corruption implicit in contrasts he saw between the actualities of working-class life and the policies of socialist governments elected to improve them. This he did in *Occupations* (1971), *The Party* (1973) and *The Comedians*, produced at the National in 1975. Nichols, who had first won recognition in 1967 with a compassionate study of a family's struggle to provide a normal life for a spastic child (*A Day in the Death of Joe Egg*), went on to confirm his standing with another sardonic tragi-comedy, *The National Health* (1969), produced by the National Theatre, and *Passion Play*, presented by the R.S.C. (1981).

The most radical of these newcomers was Howard Brenton, who was determined to press to its extremities the licence bestowed on the theatre by the abolition of stage censorship. This he achieved by skilfully persuading provincial managements to produce his plays. *Christie in Love*, about a murderer's masturbatory and necrophiliac fantasies, was quietly slipped into the repertoire of the

Bristol Old Vic in a short season of late-night performances in 1971: *Revenge* (1969), *Magnificence* (1973) and
The Churchill Play (1974) similarly received first performances from provincial companies. A year later his
musical (written in collaboration with David Hare)
Teeth'n Smiles appeared at the Royal Court, and in 1976
he finally arrived at the National with *Weapons of
Happiness*, a play about the workers' revolt in a small
London factory. It was there, however, that his bravado
was challenged when production of his *Romans in Britain*
(1980) resulted in a court case being brought against it
under the obscenity laws (see p. 266).

The only woman to share the critical acclaim accorded
to Wood, Griffiths, Nichols and Brenton during these
years was Caryl Churchill – a protégée of the Royal Court
– whose *Objections to Sex and Violence* (1975) and *Cloud
Nine* (1976) were first staged there. Both highlighted the
changing attitudes of contemporary society to male and
female concepts of their own sexuality and its impact on
their life-styles.

While the new wave of radically-minded polemicists
thus battled successfully through the 1970s to retain the
high profile won for them by their predecessors during the
explosive sixties, it is equally obvious in retrospect that
large numbers of playgoers during this decade were transferring their allegiance to a rising generation of playwrights and composers of musicals, led by Tom Stoppard,
Christopher Hampton, Neil Simon, Alan Ayckbourn,
Stephen Sondheim and Andrew Lloyd Webber, whose
approaches to the theatre were governed neither by politics
nor by special pleading. However, as all of them, and
others like them, only came to dominate the international
theatrical scene during the 1980s, it is logical to postpone
discussion of their achievements to the last section of this
chapter (pp.262-6).

(d) Alternative Theatre: In 1965 a young Polish actor,
Jerzy Grotowski, established a theatre workshop on a
formal basis in the university town of Wroclaw which he
described as the Polish Laboratory Theatre. This had
grown out of informal experiments made with a group of
friends as actors for some five years in the small town of
Opole. There, by improvising upon existing texts, and
with the group itself serving as both actors and audience,
the primary objective had been to explore basic techniques
of communication in dramatic art. In Wroclaw, small
groups of outsiders were admitted to witness demonstrations of more advanced work which acquired the name of
'Poor Theatre' (Fig. 206). By that Grotowski meant a
theatre stripped of all the razzmatazz and glamour of

206. Grotowski's 'Poor Theatre'. Rsyzard Cléslak as the
Simpleton in *Apocalypsis cum Figuris, Wroclaw, 1975. Private
collection.*

theatrical first-nights, and shorn of all the expensive
impedimenta of scenic machinery, battalions of technicians, front-of-house staff and other money-consuming
paraphernalia that surround professional productions of
plays, ancient and modern.

In one sense, and an important one, fulfilment of this
ideal demanded a denial of one of the theatre's most fundamental claims on the respect of society – its function as
a public forum. Yet if, as Grotowski claimed, the theatre
has lost its way in the modern world (and here others
might disagree), then the best means to recover a true sense
of direction must lie with the actor, the performer. In
short, actors must be retrained to regard their instrument –
their bodies and voices – as the *sine qua non* of dramatic
art; and over this instrument they must learn to acquire a
degree of control directly comparable to that of a professional musician over his flute, violin or singing voice. No
costume, no scenery, no machinery must be tolerated that
cannot be justified as an essential extension of the instrument, the actor himself.

Grotowski's 'Poor Theatre' has attracted international
attention during the past twenty years not because of its
achievements to date – very few people have seen any
demonstrations of its work – but because the views
expressed in his book about it, *Towards a Poor Theatre*
(the English edition has a foreword by Peter Brook), have
been seen to correspond with those for long entertained by
many other individuals. It is easy to become so bemused
by the noisy and heavily publicized manifestos of the

Futurists, Dadaists, Constructivists, Expressionists, Surrealists and other axe-grinding theatrical polemicists of the past seventy years as to forget that, outside of the professional theatre, this century has witnessed a steady growth of amateur interest in the theatre which, lacking the funding available to the professionals, has always had to operate in a kind of 'Poor Theatre'. Because it was amateur, it could not concentrate, as Grotowski insists, on the actor's mastery of his own body; but, having always had to make a virtue of necessity, it has enjoyed the advantage of according priority to simplicity.

Starting with William Poel's efforts for the Stage Society at the end of the last century to present Shakespeare's plays on an open stage (see p. 220) and with the simultaneous foundation of university dramatic societies at Oxford and Cambridge, amateur initiatives have proliferated in Britain, the United States, Australia and New Zealand, and in many European and African countries under the patronage of educational institutions and community welfare organizations – not least in Third World countries under UNESCO-funded auspices.

The Oxford University Dramatic Society and the Amateur Dramatic Club at Cambridge began in the 1880s to stage revivals of Greek plays and those of Shakespeare, with a view to speaking the verse well and restoring sense to the texts in performance. Their example began to be followed in other universities from London to Edinburgh and in the United States. It was in America at Yale University that George Pierce Baker translated what had existed as an extra-curricular dramatic society into a formally constituted Department of Drama within the Faculty of Arts, offering courses in theatre history, dramatic theory and criticism, playwriting and stage crafts: there he trained a talented and energetic group of young men and women who, on graduation, moved to other universities and colleges to copy his example. By the end of the Second World War over 500 such departments existed. The first in Britain was set up in the University of Bristol in 1947: there are now sixteen. Within the next twenty years similar departments were constituted in non-European countries, in Australian universities following the creation of the Elizabethan Theatre Trust in Sydney in 1955; in the Victoria University of Wellington, New Zealand, and in Africa at the Universities of Ibadan, Lagos and Amahdo Bello in Nigeria, Accra in Ghana, Dar Es Salaam in Tanzania and Dakar in Senegal. The department at Ibadan was headed for a time by the Nigerian playwright Wole Soyinka; and actors, directors and writers of distinction have recently begun to emerge from the departments in Australia and New Zealand (see Fig. 2).

Between the wars dramatic societies supported and funded by members of staff had begun to play an active role in many continental universities – outstandingly so at the Sorbonne in Paris where two groups dedicated to reviving medieval and Greek and Roman plays (the *Théophiliens* and the *Groupe Antique* respectively) effected a renaissance of interest in long-neglected texts and methods of performance. As both groups toured their productions extensively, they stimulated further research wherever they went. German, Austrian and Swedish universities began to follow their example and went so far as to establish graduate schools of theatre history (Cologne, Berlin, Munich, Vienna and Stockholm) dedicated to research and to providing the state theatres with a *dramaturg*, or literary historical adviser.

The need for theatre space for practical experiment led, by 1950, to the construction of the first permanent arena theatres, drama studios and other experimental workshops (see pp. 250–1). Thus, by the 1960s, Broadway came to be ringed first by small 'Off-Broadway' playhouses and then by even smaller ones 'Off-Off-Broadway', while London's West End Theatreland came likewise to be ringed by new suburban theatres in Greenwich, Richmond, Wimbledon, Hammersmith (Riverside), Islington (King's Head), Hampstead (Bush), Kilburn (Tricycle), and Stepney (Half-Moon). Outside London these were supplemented by the Studio Theatres added to provincial repertory theatres, which led in turn to the addition of similar annexes to the Royal Court, the R.S.C. (both in Stratford and in London) and the National Theatre during the 1970s (see p. 256). 'Poor theatres' mushroomed similarly in San Francisco, Chicago and other large American cities and in European towns both east and west of the Iron Curtain.

It was within these new venues (which extended to buses, barges, parks and pedestrianized streets) that under the general banner of 'Agit-Prop' (a term borrowed from the Constructivists meaning agitation and propaganda) companies dedicated to the writing and production of left-wing political plays hoisted their flags to advertise their playbills under names inspired by rock music groups such as Living Theatre, Portable Theatre, Avon Touring, Hull Truck, Red Ladder, *Café La Mama*, Steppenwolf, Monstrous Regiment, Gay Sweatshop, Bush Telegraph and Shared Experience (Fig. 218). Alongside the better-known writers for these groups from Joan Littlewood and Paddy Chayefsky to Sam Shephard, Snoo Wilson, John McGrath, Ken Campbell, Heathcote Williams and David Mamet (to name only a few of the most prolific) must now be numbered a similarly long list of plays attributed to the performing groups collectively rather than to an

207. *Café La Mama in a scene from* Arden of Faversham *during their season at the Royal Court, London, 1970.*

individual author. Nothing quite like this has been seen since the *commedia dell'arte* and the many anonymous community plays of the Middle Ages.

Everywhere in Europe this story has been repeated, and nowhere more remarkably than in Eastern bloc countries where, despite censorship (often inefficiently administered) lively groups of students have put cellars and cafés to use as theatres in which to present satirical revues and plays which were unacceptable to state-run companies, but which played an important role in preparing public opinion to reject the whole apparatus of Communist government in 1989, and elevated the playwright Václav Havel in Czechoslovakia from the status of a dissident political prisoner to that of President of his country.

In Italy, rather less spectacularly, Dario Fo (1926-), by reverting to the training and improvisational production methods of Commedia dell'Arte, created a style of theatre all his own that succeeds, in his zestful and professional hands, in combining surrealistic techniques with biting anti-clerical, political and social satire to delight huge popular audiences comparable in size to those of rock-concerts – an almost unique achievement. Not surprisingly, at least two of his plays – *Accidental Death of an Anarchist* (1970) and *Can't Pay, Won't Pay* (1974) – have proved to be as readily translatable into other languages as transportable to other countries.

While several other fringe playwrights graduated successfully, like Fo himself, from the confines of 'poor theatres' to the applause of large audiences in commercial theatres – Tom Stoppard, Sam Shephard, David Hare, David Mamet and Caryl Churchill among them – many fell by the wayside together with the companies that launched them. Where in the sixties 'alternative theatre' groups seemed only to have to find a new name and a fashionably revolutionary cause to prosper, in the seventies the restoration of social stability and the end of the Vietnam war served to sap their energy. The first seeds of doubt were sown then about the effectiveness of the theoretical doctrines inherited from Brecht, Artaud and other gurus of the swinging sixties: the citadels of capitalism were plainly not tumbling down like the walls of Jericho before the trumpet blasts of their productions.

By 1973 this malaise was sufficiently serious for Howard Brenton to take it as the central theme of his *Magnificence*, a play about a commune of idealistic hippy-squatters, the grandiloquence of whose rhetoric is matched by their inarticulate inability to formulate their objectives coherently – a fact that renders them incapable of any effectual action. As the truth of this agonized admission slowly began to take root among other fringe writers, directors and actors, so the financial pressures of galloping inflation began to cripple their shoe-string production resources, forcing many companies to disband and others to besiege the Arts Council and local authorities for funds to bail them out. By the end of the decade newly elected governments of right-wing persuasion were in no mood to listen sympathetically to what they regarded as special pleading from habitually subversive and electorally insignificant minority claimants on revenue raised from public taxation. With the inevitability of this change of direction staring them in the face, all fringe companies began to recognize that while there were still enough well-patronized performance spaces in which to keep the flag of 'alternative theatre' flying, they would have to revise and modify their objectives if they were to retain both audiences and adequate funding to survive the decade ahead.

208. Catfish Row: Serge Sonderkine's setting for George Gershwin's opera Porgy and Bess, *1935.*

(e) **Black and Third-World Theatre:** Beyond the limited horizons of European and American fringe groups that have attracted press and media attention between the 1950s and the 1980s lies the equally notable emergence from virtual non-existence to international recognition of Third World companies from Asia, Africa, South America and the Afro-American groups in the United States. In strictly historical terms this innovation dates back to the 1930s in America with the staging of Marc Connelly's *The Green Pastures* (1930), Hal Johnson's *Run Little Chillun* (1933) and George Gershwin's opera, *Porgy and Bess* (1935), all of which were written for and presented by black casts, and in Asia to the Paris Exhibition of 1889

which brought an Indo-Chinese dance company to Europe for the first time (see p. 221 and Fig. 208).

In 1944 Philip Yordan's *Anna Lucasta*, with a cast led by the outstanding black actor Frederick O'Neill, was successfully produced in New York, reaching London in 1947. Sadly, this remarkable company folded in 1953; but by then another company, this time from Senegal in French West Africa, had appeared to dazzle European and American audiences: founded in 1949 as *Théâtre Africain*, it changed its name in 1958 to *Ballets Africains*. Touring companies of dancers from India and Indonesia were equally well received on both sides of the Atlantic.

Almost simultaneously another brilliant American black actor, James Earle Jones, teamed up with a South African playwright, Athol Fugard (1932–), to stage *Hello and Goodbye* (New York, 1965; London, 1969) and *People are Living Here* (New York, 1971; London, 1972), bringing the question of Apartheid forcefully to public notice. Fugard

209. John Kani and Winston Ntshoma in Athol Fugard's Sizwe Bansi is Dead, *Royal Court Theatre, London, 1974.*

then found two black South African actors, John Kani and Winston Ntshoma, with whom he collaborated to write and produce *Sizwe Bansi is Dead* (1972) and *The Island* (1973), both of which arrived in London at the Royal Court in 1974 (see Fig. 209). Nothing could have exposed injustices and suffering imposed upon all non-white South Africans by the white minority government more movingly than these productions. The final accolade of success was bestowed on Fugard when his *A Lesson from Aloes* was produced at the National Theatre in 1981.

Other African dramatists writing in English during the 1960s included three Nigerians – Wole Soyinka (1934-), Ola Rotimi (1936-) and John Pepper Clark (1936-) – whose plays widened European audiences' horizons by introducing them to cultures very different from their own; and in 1988 Soyinka was awarded the Nobel Prize for Literature (see Fig. 2). Their achievements were matched in the United States during the 1970s in the wake of the civil rights movement by a rapid expansion in the number of black companies and playwrights whose work could as readily be seen from coast to coast as that of white fringe groups. Two of these companies – the New Lafayette in Harlem and the Negro Ensemble based on St Mark's Playhouse, New York – quickly achieved international acclaim: the latter made its first appearance in London at the World Theatre season in 1969 (see p. 256). Among the many writers working for these and other companies was LeRoi Jones (1934-) whose *Dutchmen* (1964) and the *Death of Malcolm X* (1969) provided militantly radical portrayals of the exploitation of blacks by whites in

American society. Another was Ed Bullins (1935-), who strove as much to organize and encourage other black dramatists by publishing their work in *Black Theatre Magazine* (which he edited) as to write plays himself. However, by 1970 he had established a reputation as a playwright to watch with *Clara's Man* (1965), *The Electronic Nigger* (1968) and *The Pig Pen* (1970) in which he exposed many aspects of life within the black communities of industrial cities to public view. Finally, following the first visit of the R.S.C. to Japan in 1971, companies of Noh and Kabuki reciprocated by bringing their productions to western audiences. Thus despite the almost total disintegration of traditional dramatic theory and theatrical style as received at the start of the twentieth century which had taken place by 1980, the range of choice on offer to the public in terms of performance spaces, plays and acting companies as the new decade began was wider and more varied than it had ever been before.

4 THE ASTRINGENT EIGHTIES

A decade which began with the election of a film actor to be President of the United States and the advent of a new plague attributed to the sexual permissiveness and promiscuity of the sixties and seventies that threatened the survival of the human race, and which ended with the overthrow of the Berlin Wall and the election of a dissident playwright to be President of an Eastern bloc country can scarcely be described as dull. Yet it is still too early to pronounce with any certainty on its theatrical triumphs and shortcomings. Suffice it to say here that dramatic art continued to win wide public support but that its survival into the next century is now as severely threatened by the ubiquitous advance of television as by the equally ubiquitous withdrawal of the subsidies which have underwritten its survival since the end of the Second World War.

It was a decade in which death deprived the British theatre of three of the giants who, as actors, had sustained its fortunes through fifty years of service to stage and screen: Sir Michael Redgrave; Sir Ralph Richardson and Lord Olivier; and in which a fourth, Sir John Gielgud, returned to star in the West End at the age of 83 in Hugh Whitemore's *The Best of Friends*. It was a decade in which the R.S.C., whose ambitions had vaulted from the simple excellence of its summer seasons in Stratford in the 1950s to the unprecedented promotion of more than forty productions in ten theatres during the 1970s, finally decided to go for broke. It was a decade in which the Berliner Ensemble, the Moscow Art Theatre and even the Comédie Française dipped below the horizon of international interest and in which Broadway recovered its self-respect.

It was also a decade, moreover, in which classical actors in Britain stirred themselves into brusquely telling an earlier generation of arrogantly opinionated young directors and writers to get off their backs, and in which audiences voted to opt for fine acting and for dramatists, composers, choreographers and librettists who treated them as adults with minds of their own instead of as illiterate children in need of constant ideological instruction and frequent chastisement for inattention. Yet it remained a decade in which 'alternative theatre' could still thrive provided it could come to terms with the rapidly changing nature of its own environment.

The theatrical achievements of the 1980s thus fall broadly within the spectrum of the changes brought about within contemporary society by Reaganomics, Thatcherism and a militantly materialist 'yuppie' culture on the one hand: and, on the other, the efforts of the long-suffering citizens of Eastern bloc countries from Prague to Moscow itself to jettison their straitjacketed life-styles in favour of those flaunted in their own cities by western tourists and beamed into their homes on television from neighbouring states.

Portents of these changes in the attitudes of theatregoers had already begun to appear during the 1970s as the plays of Edward Albee (1928-), Tom Stoppard (1937-) , Michael

211. *Sailors with Greisha in Stephen Sondheim's* Pacific Overtures, *English National Opera, London Colisseum, 1989.*

Frayn (1933-), Neil Simon (1927-) and Alan Ayckbourn (1939-) and the musicals of Leonard Bernstein (1918-1990), Stephen Sondheim (1930-) and Andrew Lloyd Webber (1948-) began to win both critical and popular acclaim.

In America a high price had to be paid for the failure of Federal and State legislatures during the 1950s to protect their professional theatres against loss as the Arts Council had done in Britain (see p. 246). The supply of both outstanding new plays and musicals ground to a halt, leaving theatres dark or dependent upon imports from European sources; creative talent found itself forced to retreat from Broadway, first to Off-Broadway and then to Off-Off-Broadway locations where production and front-of-house facilities resembled those of Grotowski's 'Poor Theatre' (see p. 258). Following the establishment, however, of the National Endowment Fund for the Arts and Humanities in 1965, this deplorable situation began to improve. Leonard Bernstein's and Stephen Sondheim's *West Side Story* (1957) had already declared emphatically that all was not yet lost. Even the astonishing challenge to Broadway musicals presented by Andrew Lloyd Webber's *Jesus Christ Superstar* (1971), *Joseph and the Amazing Technicoloured Dreamcoat* (1972) and *Evita* (1978/9), if not fully answered, was at least taken up by the New York revival of Bernstein's *Candide* (1974) and first productions of Sondheim's *Company* (1970), *Follies* (1971), *A Little Night Music* (1973) and *Pacific Overtures* (1976) (see Fig. 211).

Broadway also struggled to hold its own with Edward Albee's *Zoo Story* (first produced in Berlin in 1959), *Who's Afraid of Virginia Woolf?* (1962) and *Tiny Alice* (1964), and

210. *Cartoon by Emwood (John Musgrave Wood) in* The Tatler *of John Gielgud, Ralph Richardson, Sybil Thorndike, Lewis Casson and Irene Worth in N.C.Hunter's* A Day by the Sea, *Haymarket Theatre, London 1955. University of Bristol Theatre Collection.*

212. *Susan Engel and Harry Towb in the National Theatre's production of Neil Simon's* Brighton Beach Memoirs, *London, 1987.*

1989-90. It must, however, remain an open question, where posterity is concerned, whether Andrew Lloyd Webber's *Cats* (1981) and *The Phantom of the Opera* (1986) or John Caird's and Trevor Nunn's *Les Misérables* (1986) eclipse all of them as favoured candidates for subsequent revival by amateur Light Opera companies (see Fig. 213).

A similar question arises when any comparison is attempted between the comedies of Neil Simon, Tom Stoppard, Michael Frayn and Alan Ayckbourn. All of these playwrights have chosen to reject doctrinaire approaches to the theatre in favour of a personal but objective view of the anxieties, pleasures and hang-ups of middle-class family and business life; and in doing so they

213. *Sarah Brightman and Michael Crawford in the London production of Andrew Lloyd Webber's* The Phantom of the Opera *at Her Majesty's Theatre, 1986.*

Neil Simon's sardonically comic portraits of Americans during the swinging sixties, as depicted in *Barefoot in the Park* (1963), *Plaza Suite* (1968) and *The Sunshine Boys* (1972), all of which subsequently appeared as films. Life in Mid-West and West-Coast America was likewise championed and strikingly portrayed in the acerbic and more violent plays of Sam Shephard (1943-) and David Mamet (1947-), both of whom suceeded, not only in winning a wide hearing throughout the United States, but also in seeing their plays produced in metropolitan cities in Western Europe. Shephard's *La Turista* (1967) was first produced in London in 1969, followed by *Buried Child* (New York, 1978: London, 1980) and *True West* (New York, 1980: London, 1982); Mamet's *American Buffalo* arrived in 1979 (New York, 1977).

By the middle of the 1980s Americans could safely claim that Broadway had again recovered its own sense of self-esteem: indeed Simon's *Brighton Beach Memoirs* (1983) proved so successful at the National Theatre in London in 1986 as to require transfer for an extended run to the Aldwych (see Fig. 212), while Mamet's *Speed The Plow* (1986) (about the treachery of the power-game in Hollywood) joined a brilliant revival of Tennessee William's *Cat on a Hot Tin Roof* at the National in 1988. Meantime Stephen Sondheim was reinforcing his claim to be regarded as a more creative and stimulating provider of stage musicals than anyone else, with London revivals of *Follies* (New York, 1971; London, 1987) and *A Walk in the Park with George* (New York, 1984; London, 1989) – a view confirmed by Oxford University when electing him to become its first professor of Drama for the academic year

have gained the confidence of commercial managements and the public alike with the result that a new play from any of them now possesses the same drawing power at the box-office as was formerly the case with Noël Coward, Terence Rattigan, George Kaufman or Tennessee Williams.

In the 1960s Tom Stoppard played brilliantly witty and joyous games with words, as his predecessors N.F. Simpson (1919-) and Eugene Ionesco had done respectively in *A Resounding Tinkle* (1957) and *One Way Pendulum* (1959) and in *Rhinoceros* (1960) and *Exit the King* (1963) under the general umbrella of 'Theatre of the Absurd' (see pp. 246-7 and 254-5). The new dimension that Stoppard added in *The Real Inspector Hound* (1968), *Jumpers* (1972), *Travesties* (1974) and *The Real Thing* (1982) was the distinction that he repeatedly succeeded in portraying between illusion and reality in everyday life when counter-pointed against such familiar settings as a theatre, a university, a library, or a marriage: laughter and delight ensued through his skilfully juxtaposed manipulatons of metaphysics and parody. For these remarkable achievements he was branded as élitist by his Marxist-orientated contemporaries who claimed that he had alienated (by his assumptions of literacy and a capacity for logical thought) the new, young audiences whom they were themselves aiming to recruit and convert to psycho-drama, agit-prop and other aspects of alternative community theatre. Yet the devisers of *Monty Python's Flying Circus* on television were successfully rebutting this charge as they captured the imaginations of millions of viewers in all walks of life.

Verbal *non-sequiturs* and gymnastic thought-processes had also provided comedy infused with pathos in the more poetically and symbolist-orientated plays of Samuel Beckett and Harold Pinter; but Pinter's early protagonists had had to struggle against more elusive and anonymous antagonists than Beckett's. These were never sharply defined but seemed to determine a protagonist's destiny while simultaneously opposing it, as happens to the tramp Davies in *The Caretaker* (1960), or to the mysterious matchseller standing at the gate of a large private garden in *A Slight Ache* (radio 1959; stage 1960). Yet, as with Beckett, this served as a potent emblem of the dilemma which faces all electors in modern democracies when disillusioned by their apparent inability to influence the events controlling their daily lives. Lurking within these early Pinter plays lies another theme which he, uniquely, proceeded to explore just as relentlessly in *The Homecoming* (1965), *Landscape* (1968), *No Man's Land* (1975), *Betrayal* (1980) and *Family Voices* (1982): the difficulty within all personal relationships of obtaining verification of appearances – more especially in such tightly guarded contexts as marital infidelity or the ambiguities of heterosexual and homosexual orientations.

When compared with Stoppard and Pinter, Frayn and Ayckbourn were derisively dismissed by the literary intelligentsia and the champions of 'alternative theatre' alike through the 1970s as lightweight showmen. Audiences, however, reacted differently, as they had alrady done with Peter Shaffer's *The Royal Hunt of the Sun* (1964), *Black Comedy* (1965) and *Equus* (1973), in finding that a strong story-line theatrically presented and well acted provided them with something more durable than just an evening out.

Ayckbourn, who conceived all his own plays for his own repertory company in Scarborough, followed this formula in *Relatively Speaking* (1967), *Absurd Person Singular* (1974), *The Norman Conquests* (1974), *Absent Friends* (1975) and *Bedroom Farce* (1977); all these plays swiftly moved on to other stages in London and abroad. His success is attributable to his stubborn faith in the accuracy of his own, first-hand observation, both verbal and visual, of a wide spectrum of middle-class theatregoers, and in his own ability to retail their most immediate daily concerns, frustrations, hobbies, fantasies, and social embarrassments through sharply etched and compassionately conceived characters who succeed simultaneously in provoking laughter while tugging at the heart-strings. He thus came to replace Jean Anouilh as a master of *pièces roses* (see p. 239).

In the course of the 1980s he has consolidated his claim to be a master dramatist with a succession of *pièces noires* – *A Chorus of Disapproval* (1985), *A Small Family Business* (1987), *Henceforward* (1988) and *Man of the Moment* (1989) – which employ the same techniques to handle more serious, sinister, and bleaker aspects of contemporary life, embracing the dreariness and isolation of high-rise and semi-detached terraced housing outside working hours; the insidious spread of hallucinatory and addictive drugs; the sacrifice of human values to promote technological innovation; and the power of television to manipulate and corrupt public opinion. At the end of this decade the measure of his mastery of theatrical craftsmanship is now to be gauged by his ability to accommodate these bleak observations about the state of Western civilization within the conventional requirements of an evening's entertainment in a commercial theatre. Any dramatist who can do that has to be taken seriously: and the royalties he now receives from translation and foreign performance rights prove the point. The only question remaining to be answered is whether, during the 1990s, he can provide his audiences with an equally successful sequence of *pièces brillantes* (see p. 239 and Fig. 214).

Michael Frayn with *Clouds* (1976), *Noises Off* (1982) and *Benefactors* (1984) – a play about idealistic town planners and their immediate beneficiaries who turn out to be the natural destroyers of any Utopian community – has staked a good claim to be taken as seriously as Neil Simon or Alan Ayckbourn; but whereas the former can offer twenty-five plays to date for critical scrutiny and the latter more than forty, Frayn must still be regarded as the holder of a provisional licence if classed with either of them.

This comparison applies with equal force to two other notable dramatists of the 1980s, Caryl Churchill and David Hare, both of whom graduated from the alternative theatre of the 1970s – and both of whom have since spent as much time attending rehearsals and productions of their own plays in foreign countries as in Britain. Of these, David Hare's *Pravda* (1985), *The Secret Rapture* (1988) and *Racing Demon* (1990) were all first presented at the National Theatre; Churchill's *Top Girls* (1982) and *Serious Money* (1987) were first produced at the Royal Court. All five of these plays were hailed by one dramatic critic or another as best play of the year. Both playwrights concern themselves primarily with the human costs of contemporary monetarist policies. In *Top Girls* Churchill looked searchingly at women who let their own career prospects control their life-style, and in *Serious Money* at the near-total corruption of all humane values by Stock Exchange tycoons as exemplified by the casino morality of their acolytes in metropolitan cities. Hare chose to contrast the values of newspaper proprietors with those of their readers; government ministers' pronouncements with their effects on those whom they were elected to represent (with asset-stripping as a central image); and the impending schism in the Church of England as reflected in the conflict between liturgical absolutes and evangelical priorities (see Fig. 215). Fifty years hence these plays may all be found to be 'too dated' to warrant revival: what no one can doubt today is that both of these dramatists have dared to write about the most inflammatory political and social issues of their time and have thus invited audiences to confront them directly instead of brushing them out of sight.

Another survivor from the 1970s who might have joined them was Howard Brenton. However, the staging of his *The Romans in Britain* at the National Theatre in 1980 – an allegorical alibi for a discussion of the morality of the presence of British troops in Ulster – provoked a court case arising out of a simulated act of sodomy for which the artistic director, Michael Bogdanov, was prosecuted as defendant. Although the case was withdrawn and costs

214. *Lia Williams as Angie Dell in Alan Ayckbourn's* Body Language, *Stephen Joseph Theatre, Scarborough, 1990.*

were awarded against the prosecution, nevertheless a clear message had been sent out by the judiciary to all theatrical managements: take greater care in future not to offend public decency when authorizing plays for production – a message sharply reinforced by the more general alarm signals then being raised by the rapidly increasing rate of deaths from Aids.

Now that the eighties have ended, what record is left of them in the printed plays and musicals of this decade? Not an encouraging or consoling one. The R.S.C. (which had moved from the Aldwych Theatre into the two theatres in the newly built Barbican Centre in London in 1982), having played poker with the Arts Council for thirty years, finally went broke with a deficit of millions and let these London theatres go dark at six months' notice in 1990; they reopened in 1991, but under much tighter financial

215. *Richard Pascoe as the Bishop of Southwark in David Hare's* Racing Demon, *National Theatre, London, 1990.*

the theatre has done through this decade. In this context recognition must be extended to the many industrial firms who have generously sponsored production of plays, operas and ballets that would not have gone forward without their financial help. It is noticeable, however, that the majority of television companies have done next to nothing during these difficult ten years to support and protect a profession on which they are themselves directly dependent for an adequate supply of versatile actors and actresses to retain their position in the viewer ratings. Yet it is these ratings which determine their own revenues from advertisers. This charge is frequently fobbed off by the reply, 'All drama is *very* expensive' – a response which deftly conceals a logic that has already committed quality

216. *John Carlisle as Macready and Anton Lesser as Forrest in the R.S.C.'s production of Richard Nelson's* Two Shakespearean Actors *at the Barbican Theatre, London, 1991 (see p. 196).*

control. Reaganomics in the United States and Thatcherism in Britain finally killed the golden goose of ever larger subsidies that had kept so many theatres afloat through the previous two decades. They brought with them, moreover, a brand of cultural philistinism (born as much of apathy as of hostility) that started with education and spread to embrace all the arts. Television was the only real gainer, claiming the allegiance of millions of viewers nightly with streams of soap-operas, police melodramas, and domestic 'sit-com' farces requiring nothing more of its clients than a willingness to switch on the set in their living rooms. This staple diet was leavened with occasional and mildly apologetic concessions to the principal performing arts (see Fig. 217). These entertainments, however, have kept as many if not more actors and actresses gainfully employed, even in frequently repeated commercials, than

217. Peggy Ashcroft in Stephen Poliakoff's Caught on a Train, *shown on BBC television, 31 October 1980; repeated 18 September 1989.*

drama to the waste-bin if cheaper programming can keep viewing ratings high and advertisers happy.

With that said, the major burden of blame for the blurred and erratic profile of the theatre's fortunes in all Western countries during the 1980s rests squarely with its managers. Loss of nerve in both subsidized and commercial sectors at managerial level alone explains the collapse of coherent policies consistently pursued that had underpinned the theatrical renaissance of the sixties and seventies. In Britain, the principal casualty has been the much-vaunted 'right-to-fail' at the taxpayers' expense. But why did the Governors of the R.S.C. allow its companies to stray into a world as alien to its own Charter as that of Musicals? And why did the Governors of so many outstanding provincial repertory theatres fail to prevent the take-over of their stages by political ideologists and polemicists with little or no previous knowledge of either the theatre or sound financial management? In continental Europe and America, a similar lack of managerial foresight has begged as many questions during this decade. Why, for instance, did Broadway producers, given the resources of a continent as large as the United States, allow themselves to become so heavily dependent on foreign imports as they did? Why did the French Government pour millions of francs into the building of an unwanted second Opera

House while failing to maintain the prestige of its major acting companies and their repertoires? Why have the huge subsidies poured by the Germans into their State Theatres both east and west of the Iron Curtain failed to provide any plays thought to be worth translating into other languages and performed on stages other than their own? These unanswered questions are all items on the debit side of the balance sheets for the 1980s.

The credit side reveals modest signs, during the latter half of the decade, of a recovery of managerial nerve and a more realistic approach to the budgetary aspects of their activities. This has been achieved through according a higher priority to the expressed wishes of articulate theatre-goers than to those of dogmatically minded (and often in-experienced) directors, writers and dramatic critics. Much of the credit for this recovery rests with the actors who have slowly begun to regain control of artistic policy as the surest way to survive in their chosen profession. In Britain the previous dominance of the R.S.C. and the National Theatre, where production of Shakespeare is concerned, was challenged successfully by four independently managed and actor-led companies – Declan Donovan's Cheek by Jowl, Kenneth Branagh's Renaissance Theatre Company, Michael Pennington and Michael Bogdanov's English Shakespeare Company, and Compass Theatre, created by the late Sir Anthony Quayle and now led by Tim Piggot-Smith. In the United States, Joseph Papp has performed the same service with his summer seasons in New York's Central Park, supported by other centres like those in San Diego, Ashland, Oregon, Montgomery, Alabama, and the Folger Library in Washington D.C. This phenomenon has been reinforced by blazing star performances from front-rank actors and actresses led by Ian McKellan, Simon Callow, Dustin Hoffman, Judi Dench, Vanessa Redgrave, Derek Jacobi, Janet Suzman, Maggie Smith, Anthony Hopkins, Anthony Sher, Maria Aitken and Michael Gambon in both classical revivals and new plays. Today's young theatregoers are thus as likely to remember McKellan's Coriolanus, Sher's King Richard III, Hoffman's Shylock or Piggot-Smith's Leontes as vividly as yesterday's still recall Gielgud's Hamlet, Olivier's Richard III and Archie Rice, Edith Evans's Lady Bracknell, Ralph Richardson's Peer Gynt, Peggy Ashcroft's Duchess of Malfi or Michael Redgrave's Uncle Vanya (see Figs. 210 and 217).

Thus far history seems merely to be repeating itself: dramatic art, by ensuring a supply of performers able to excel in revivals of major classical and modern plays, enables the theatre to survive an era lacking major dramatists until such time as changed political and social circumstances favour the return of writers to control its fortunes. Even so, on this occasion a noticeable difference is discernible: the eighties have created a new golden calf for all to worship, described as 'wealth creation'. It is a god that regards all previously accepted humane values – literary, musical, pictorial and histrionic – as, if not wholly irrelevant, then so insignificant to its own explicit interests as to leave secular 'free-market' forces to take over responsibility for their survival. This is a view that has been sharply challenged in the theatre during the eighties (see p. 260 and 270); and rightly so, since it is a counsel of despair. Throughout recorded time, enlightened patronage has been the mainstay of civilized values in society: to let that wither now would be tantamount to issuing an open invitation to a new wave of Goths, Visigoths, Huns and Vandals to usher in a second Dark Age.

As the pages of this short History record, it was the enlightened practice of the Greek city *polis*, the rulers of the Roman Empire, and the Roman Catholic Church throughout the Middle Ages to accord a place of major significance to all the arts in ways that made it possible for them to be accessible for all to see and hear. This was a policy maintained through the sixteenth and seventeenth centuries by Renaissance princes throughout Christendom for a limited clientele, but carried beyond the shores of Europe to New Worlds both East and West by their explorers, missionaries and colonial administrators. During the eighteenth and nineteenth centuries this responsibility was faithfully taken over at first by the bourgeois merchant princes and then by those of industry with equally notable results. Indeed, Western civilisation, as it is understood today – at least in terms of the architectural, pictorial, musical, literary and theatrical treasures of the world that form the basis of today's hugely lucrative tourist industry – rests on this achievement.

Since the end of the Second World War this responsibility has been effectively transferred, in varying degrees, to the State. In the West, however, political self-interest and monetarist ethics have combined to debase the currency of all cultural values to museum status. By doing this they have plunged all practising artists into raging seas of doubt about their future. In the theatre they now find themselves (whether as playwrights, actors, designers, directors or managers) thrown back on their own imaginative resources and under growing pressure to avoid any risk of offending potential sponsors. In financial terms, the younger members of the profession have also to consider whether they can afford to stay in it, more especially when contemplating marriage and a family, and thus to ask themselves whether they ought to seek a career in films and

television instead, or quit. Audiences have likewise begun to ponder whether the horrendous expense of metropolitan theatre attendance, with all its accompanying inconvenience and anxieties about car-parking, muggings, bar and meal prices, drink-driving and so on, can possibly justify late-night journeys to and from Broadway, London's West End or central Paris and other major cities. Yet the theatre still possesses an escape route from this dilemma: a rapid expansion of regional centres nearer home; a consequent lowering of costs, and the pleasure of live performances shared with other people as an alternative to the nightly isolation and impassivity of fireside television.

This is the challenge presented to the theatre of the 1990s. Already many theatrical companies, whether metropolitan or provincial, recognize that it has become

218. *Poster for* 'Show of Strength, Pub Theatre' *advertising its production of Norman Brock's* Here is the Monster *at the Hen and Chicken Public House, Bedminster, Bristol, 1991.*

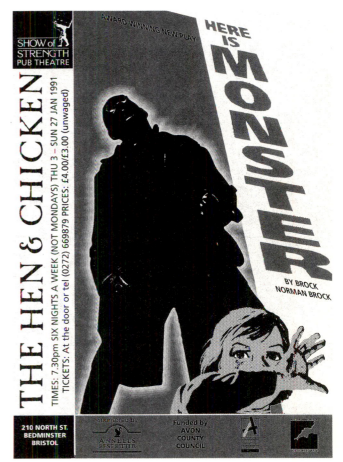

219. *For children theatrical performance still retains those qualities of the marvellous which have attracted audiences throughout history.*

imperative to equip their booking offices with computerized credit-card facilities to save patrons the need to make a special journey to acquire tickets: this not only saves the client time, but also halves the transport and parking problems associated with attending a performance. Artistic directors have also recognized that employment of actors and actresses who have already made a name for themselves on television can double the number of seats sold for each performance in their theatre whether the play on offer be old or new, and no matter who wrote it or who directed it. In addition many managements have chosen to provide restaurant facilities for meals before and after performances together with a variety of leisure pursuits in their foyers (if they are large enough) at all times of day. The need for such amenities has become so compelling as to make it doubtful whether many of the Victorian and Edwardian theatre buildings still in use can survive financially beyond the end of the century: here conservationists who insist on their preservation as architectural and cultural monuments are certain to find themselves engaged in

bitter conflicts with managements, property developers, ground-landlords and local and central government authorities alike within the next ten to twenty years. The battle presently raging over the future of the Royal Opera House, Covent Garden, admirably illustrates both the seriousness and the intractability of this problem.

The brightest omen for theatre in the nineties, however, is the number and calibre of actors and actresses spanning three generations, from those now in their seventies to those still in their twenties, who still possess courage enough to fight for the survival of dramatic art despite the threatening storm clouds that now surround it. Thus even if the luxuriously regular supply of adventurous and stimulating new plays to which we have become accustomed during the past forty years were to dwindle to a trickle, the repertoire of classics ancient and modern is large enough to enable them to charm and excite audiences in both custom-built playhouses or modest, open spaces in parks, pubs and leisure playgrounds at least until the year 2000.

Epilogue

Readers, who, like myself, are fortunate enough to have been born into a great age of theatrical experiment and achievement which embraces an international catalogue of outstanding dramatists, directors, actors and actresses must be forgiven if they think at times that they have been more favoured than either their grandparents were or their grandchildren are likely to be.

What earlier generation has had the chance to see the entire canon of Shakespeare's plays performed not just once, but two or three times? Yet that has been the experience of any regular theatregoer in England between 1935 and 1990. What other generation has been able to see so many new plays, translated and transferred from one country to another within the same period? Yet all, or nearly all, of them – whether French, German, British, Italian, Spanish, American and even Eastern European – have been as accessible in Amsterdam as in Vienna, in Berlin as in New York, and in London as in Paris. And when before have Western audiences found it so easy to encounter Oriental and African theatre at first hand, and vice versa? (see Figs. 209 and 220).

When, too, have so many definitive characterizations of classical title roles from those of Marlowe and Shakespeare to those of Ibsen, Wilde, Chekhov, and O'Neill been offered to the public as during this period? And which of those readers who recall the revues and cabaret shows devised by André Charlot, C.B. Cochran, Herbert Farjeon and others, which kept audiences enthralled from the 1920s to the 1950s with the mordant bitter-sweet wit, humour and pathos of Beatrice Lillie, Joyce Grenfell, the two Hermiones (Gingold and Baddeley), Max Adrian, Leonard Sachs, Bob Hope, Jimmy Durante, Ella Fitzgerald, Lotte Lenya, Marlene Dietrich, Maurice Chevalier, Edith Piaf and Charles Trenet, can regard today's theatrical world as anything but a duller and sadder place without them?

Here a personal apology is due to the many equally distinguished character-actors whose performances in supporting roles during the past forty years have constantly enriched the texture of those productions mentioned in the preceding two chapters, but whose names are not. Nor should the many directors, designers and theatre architects be overlooked who, between them, have created new actor-audience relationships through the last four decades, since many of these have been imaginatively enough deployed to offer theatregoers a sense of occasion at the time and a host of cherished memories thereafter. Moreover, theatre schools and *conservatoires*, in preserving the foundations of a great inherited theatrical tradition, have given younger actors, actresses and designers the firm support needed to help them to develop their personal skills and to produce fresh insights with which to enrich this tradition and thus their successors. Radio and television have also done much between them to extend public interest in plays, opera and ballet, notwithstanding the absence of direct contact between performers and their living-room audiences, and have brought many young people into theatres for the first time.

Even so, those privileged to regard themselves as participants in this extraordinary renaissance in dramatic art must be pardoned when, on surveying the contemporary scene and questioning the future, they become afflicted by a grave sense of doubt. Many openly express misgivings about a diminished scale of creativity which, at worst, heralds a descent towards the artistic standards of the amateur or, at best, must hasten the advent of a new *commedia erudita* where theory and special pleading (under agit-prop banners as blatant as those of many medieval and Tudor moral interludes) will smother professional competence in didacticism. No less worrying for practising

220. In 1990 British audiences were able to compare four productions of Shakespeare's King Lear: (a) Brian Cox as King Lear, National Theatre Company; (b) John Wood as King Lear, Royal Shakespeare Company; (c) Richard Briars as King Lear, Renaissance Theatre Company; (d) Nelliyode Vasuderan Namhoodiri preparing for his role as Goneril in the Kathakali Dance Company's King Lear from Southern India at the Edinburgh Festival.

artists and audiences alike is the grim knowledge that should the subsidies on which so many theatres and opera houses now rely to keep their doors open to the public be further reduced or withdrawn altogether, then such apparent prosperity as currently surrounds live theatrical performances will vanish with them. Nowhere are these doubts so acutely felt as in Eastern bloc countries as they try to adjust their economies to Western free-market forces; yet in Britain recent experiences of the English and Welsh opera companies reinforce this foreboding as does the threatened closure of the Bristol Old Vic in 1992.

Yet those who feel disposed to adopt this pessimistic outlook and then proceed to argue that the theatre must again succumb before this century is out to the rival attractions of television, video-recorders and heavily commercialized sporting events of every description (as was the case with tragedy and comedy in imperial Rome) would be well advised to turn their attention to the exuberance of those youthful 'fringe' groups at work in the 'poor theatres' of the world. These are now to be seen wherever tourists congregate – on the Stephanplatz in Vienna, in Covent Garden Market, on Pier 39 in San Francisco (Fig. 221), or on the Circular Quay near Sydney's spectacular Opera House. There and elsewhere, a new and genuinely active relationship is being worked out between live performer and spectator as an alternative to the generally passive 'take-it-or-leave-it' attitude adopted out of a sense of politeness in most Western theatres today.

This educational process is a slow one since, as yet, most of these performances are unstructured: but once the technique of mastering monologue so as to attract and then retain the attention of mobile audiences has been learned, it is not difficult to extend it to mastery of dialogue, whether improvised or scripted, and so to larger ensembles. Such, we should recall, was the history of the Indian and Chinese story-teller (see Fig. 11), of the medieval minstrel troupes, and after them of the 'players of interludes' and the *commedia dell'arte*. We do not know, and it is useless to try to predict, into what forms these at present unstructured entertainments will develop; but we can be sure that they will develop so long as these young performing artists remain alert and sufficiently self-critical to absorb what audiences (especially the children among them) appear to enjoy, and then build on what they have learned (see Fig. 219). Indeed, the world over they have begun to do so in parks, in streets, in pubs and in schools. Whether such optimism is warranted in the face of the philistine attitude adopted towards the funding of all the Arts throughout the English-speaking world today is another matter.

221. Street theatre comedians entertaining tourists on Pier 39, San Francisco, in September 1983.

Nevertheless, what is particularly significant about this feature of dramatic art in our times is its return to almost wholesale dependence upon the personality and talent of the actor; and actors, as remarked in the Prologue (pp. 14-15) are the life-force of the art. In other words – words, moreover, that would have been understood in ancient Greece – Dionysus has shaken off the chains binding him to writers, technicians, financial speculators and the politicians who allocate the subsidies underpinning most formally organized theatres, and has reverted instead to dance, song and mime as the indispensable nucleus of his profession. So, once again, like Shakespeare's Ariel, the actor is all air and fire, a spirit free to wander where he pleases and to make new friends wherever he can find them in the great theatre of the world: and that is a development most opportunely timed to cut through all previously existing barriers of race, colour and creed. With English rapidly becoming the universal *lingua franca*, even those barriers of language which in the past have delayed or denied transfer of theatrical forms of expression across national frontiers (as repeatedly noted in earlier chapters of this book) may shortly collapse. To date, carnivals provide the best example.

If the price to be paid for this, however, were to be the drowning of the playwright's voice in a sea of pantomime – as happened in Imperial Rome after Seneca's death – then the ancient Mummer's Play still exists to remind us, through the symbolic death and revival of its hero, of the regenerative power incarnate in nature. We should thus recall that it was out of humble beginnings like those of

222. Catherine the Great's theatre in the Winter Palace in St. Petersburg, restored and reopened by the Government of the USSR in February 1991 (see p.172).

today's market-place and fairground entertainers that the professional theatre in all Oriental countries evolved, and that the dramatic literature of the High Middle Ages reached fruition: and when *commedia erudita* in Renaissance Italy became so theoretical, stuffy and boring as to be unendurable, then *commedia dell'arte* – spontaneous, improvised, topical and inexpensive – replaced it, and both *opera seria* and ballet – lyrical, festive and up till then undreamt of – were born. Likewise, as the elegant, neo-classical and élitist court theatres of the sixteenth and seventeenth centuries collapsed under the tide of romantic and revolutionary fervour that gripped Germany, North America and France towards the close of the eighteenth century, so melodrama – raucous, unstructured and proletarian in its appeal – arose to command the allegiance of audiences larger and more widespread than ever before, and to generate yet another new art form – cinema.

In short, just as role-playing can never fail to occupy the thoughts and actions of human beings in real life, so the story of theatre is certain to require new writers to structure new dramatic forms and to record their progress; and this will be true so long as there are human beings willing to take the risks implicit in devoting their lives to mastering the actor's art. And now that schools, colleges and universites have at long last awoken to their responsibility to help in providing a continuing supply of soundly motivated theatre artists, the outlook can only be viewed as rather brighter and more secure than the prophets of doom are tempted to suppose. And who knows but that the theatre of the future may establish its roots on shores bordering the Pacific Ocean rather than on those around the Mediterranean, the Baltic, or the Atlantic as in previous centuries?

Further Reading

General

JAMES AGATE (ed.), *The English Dramatic Critics: An Anthology, 1660-1932* (New York, 1932)

MICHAEL ANDERSON, JACQUES GUICHARNAUD, and others (eds.), *Crowell's Handbook of Contemporary Drama; A Critical Handbook of Plays and Playwriting since the Second World War (New York, 1971)*

MARTIN BANHAM (ed.), *The Cambridge Guide to World Theatre* (Cambridge, 1988)

ERIC BENTLEY, *The Life of the Drama* (London, 1965)

TRAVIS BOGARD, RICHARD MOODY and WALTER J. RESERVE, *American Drama*, ed. T. W. Craik for the Revels History of Drama in English, vol. VIII (London and New York, 1977)

GERALD BORDMAN, *American Musical Theatre: A Chronicle* (New York and Oxford, 1978)

OSCAR G. BROCKETT and ROBERT R. FINDLAY, *Century of Innovation: A History of European and American Theatre and Drama since 1870* (Englewood Cliffs, 1973)

JOHN CAVANAGH, *British Theatre – A Bibliography; 1901-1985* (London, 1986)

ALAN S. DOWNER (ed.), *American Drama and its Critics: A Collection of Critical Essays* (Chicago and London, 1965)

RICHARD FINDLATER, *Banned! A Review of Theatrical Censorship in Britain* (London and Letchworth, 1967)

BAMBER GASCOIGNE, *World Theatre* (London, 1968)

PHYLLIS HARTNOLL (ed.), *The Oxford Companion to the Theatre* (Oxford, 1983)

RONALD HAYMAN, *The Set-up* (London, 1973)

HUGH HUNT, *The Live Theatre: An Introduction to the History and Practice of the Stage* (London, 1962)

HUGH HUNT, KENNETH RICHARDS and JOHN RUSSELL TAYLOR, *English Drama 1880 to the Present Day*, ed. T. W. Craik for the Revels History of Drama in English, vol. VII (London and New York, 1978)

JAMES LAVER, *Drama: Its Costume and Décor* (London and New York, 1951)

RAYMOND MANDER and JOE MITCHENSON, *A Picture History of the British Theatre* (London, 1957)

RICHARD SOUTHERN, *Changeable Scenery: Its Origins and Development* (London, 1952)

J. L. STYAN, *Drama, Stage and Audience* (Cambridge, 1975)

DAVID THOMSON, *A Biographical Dictionary of the Cinema* (London, 1975)

Part I
Introduction

WILLIAM RIDGEWAY, *The Dramas and Dramatic Dances of Non-European Races* (Cambridge, 1915; reprint New York, 1964)

Chapter 1: Oriental Drama and Theatre

FAUBIAN BOWERS, *Dance in India* (New York and Toronto, 1953)

FAUBIAN BOWERS, *Theatre in the East: A Survey of Asian Dance and Drama* (New York and Toronto, 1956)

F. T. INMOOS, *Japanese Theatre* (London, 1977)

YOSHINOBU INOURA and TOSHIO KAWATAKE, *The Traditional Theater of Japan* (Tokyo, 1981)

KHON AND LAKON, *Dance Dramas of Thailand* (Bangkok, 1963)

A. C. SCOTT, *The Classical Theatre of China* (London, 1957)

A. C. SCOTT, *The Theatre in Asia* (London, 1972)

BERYL DE ZOETE and WALTER SPIES, *Dance and Drama in Bali* (London, 1938)

Chapter 2: Greece
Chapter 3: Rome

PETER ARNOTT, *The Ancient Greek and Roman Theatre* (New York and Toronto, 1971)

PETER ARNOTT, *An Introduction to the Greek Theatre* (Bloomington, 1953; reprint 1959)

WILLIAM BEARE, *The Roman Stage* (London, 1950; reprint 1977)

MARGARETE BIEBER, *The History of the Greek and Roman Theater* (Princeton, 1939)

IRIS BROOKE, *Costume in Greek Classical Drama* (New York, 1962)

H. D. F. KITTO, *Greek Tragedy* (London, 1939; reprint 1961)

SIR ARTHUR PICKARD-CAMBRIDGE, *The Dramatic Festivals of Athens,* 2nd edn. (Oxford, 1968)

ERIC SEGAL, *Roman Laughter: The Comedy of Plautus* (Harvard, 1968)

A. D. TRENDALL and T. B. L. WEBSTER, *Illustrations of Greek Drama* (London, 1971)

DAVID WILES, *The Masks of Menander* (Cambridge, 1991)

Chapter 4: The Roman Phoenix

GREGORY DIX, *The Shape of the Liturgy* (London, 1945; reprint, New York, 1982)

O. B. HARDISON, jun., *Christian Rite and Christian Drama in the Middle Ages* (Baltimore, 1965)

ALLARDYCE NICOLL, *Masks, Mimes and Miracles* (New York, 1931; reprint 1963)

SANDRO STICCA, *The Latin Passion Play: Its Origins and Development* (Albany, 1970)

Part II
Chapter 5: Christian Europe 1000-1300 and
Chapter 6: Christian Europe 1300-the Reformation

M. D. ANDERSON, *Drama and Imagery in English Medieval Churches* (Cambridge, 1963)

RICHARD AXTON, *European Drama of the Early Middle Ages* (London, 1974)

BRENDA BOLTON, *The Medieval Reformation* (London, 1983)

ALAN BRODY, *The English Mummers and their Play* (London, 1970)

NEVILLE DENNY (ed.), *Medieval Drama,* for Stratford-upon-Avon Studies 16 (London, 1973)

SIMON ECKEHARD, *The Theatre of Medieval Europe* (Cambridge, 1991)

GRACE FRANK, *The French Medieval Drama* (Oxford, 1954)

H. C. GARDNER, *Mysteries' End* (Yale, 1946; reprint 1967)

R. D. S. JACK, *Patterns of Divine Comedy: A Study of Medieval Drama* (Cambridge, 1989)

STANLEY J. KAHL, *Traditions of Medieval Drama* (London, 1974)

V. A. KOLVE, *The Play Called Corpus Christi* (Stanford, 1966)

R. POTTER, *The English Morality Play* (London, 1975)

ELEANOR PROSSOR, *Drama and Religion in the English Mystery Plays* (Stanford, 1961)

F. M. SALTER, *Medieval Drama in Chester* (Toronto, 1955)

SANDRO STICCA (ed.), *The Medieval Drama* (New York, 1972)

WILLIAM TYDEMAN, *The Theatre in the Middle Ages* (Cambridge, 1978)

G. WICKHAM, *The Medieval Theatre* (London and New York, 1974)

Part III
Chapter 7: Italy

JACOB BURCKHARDT, *The Civilization of the Renaissance in Italy* (originally published Vienna, 1937; translation reprinted Oxford, 1981)

L. B. CAMPBELL, *Scenes and Machines on the English Stage during the Renaissance: A Classical Revival* (Cambridge, 1923; reprint, New York, 1960)

PIERRE L. DUCHARTRE, *The Italian Comedy: The Improvi- sation, Scenarios, Lives, Attributes and Masks of the Illustrious Characters of the Commedia dell'Arte,* trans. R. T. Weaver (London, 1929)

FELICITY FIRTH, 'Comedy in Italy' in *Comic Drama: The European Heritage,* ed. W. D. Howarth (London, 1978)

BARNARD HEWITT (ed.), *The Renaissance Stage: Documents of Serlio, Sabbattini, and Furttenbach* (Florida, 1958)

K. M. LEA, *Italian Popular Comedy: A Study of the Com- media dell'Arte,* 2 vols. (Oxford,1934)

A. M. NAGLER, *Theatre Festivals of the Medici, 1539-1637* (Yale, 1964)

ALLARDYCE NICOLL, *The World of Harlequin* (Cambridge, 1963)

GIACOMO OREGLIA, *The Commedia dell'Arte* (London, 1971)

S. T. WORSTHORNE, *Venetian Opera in the 17th Century* (Oxford, 1954)

Chapter 8: England

J. B. BAMBOROUGH, *Ben Jonson* (London, 1970)

G. E. BENTLEY, *The Profession of Dramatist in Shakespeare's Time* (Princeton, 1971)

G. E. BENTLEY, *The Profession of Actor in Shakespeare's Time* (Princeton, 1984)

DAVID BERGERON, *English Civic Pageantry, 1558-1642* (London, 1971)

HERBERT BERRY, *Shakespeare's Playhouses* (New York, 1987)

DAVID BEVINGTON, *From Mankind to Marlowe: Growth of Structure in the Popular Drama of Tudor England* (Harvard, 1962)

DAVID BEVINGTON, *Tudor Drama and Tudor Politics: A Critical Approach to Topical Meaning* (Harvard, 1968)

M. C. BRADBROOK, *The Rise of the Common Player* (London, 1962)

L. B. CAMPBELL, *Scenes and Machines on the English Stage during the Renaissance* (Cambridge, 1923: reprint, New York, 1960)

T. W. CRAIK, *The Tudor Interlude* (Leicester, 1958)

ALAN C. DESSEN, *Elizabethan Stage Conventions and Modern Interpreters* (Cambridge, 1984)

DONALD GORDON, *The Renaissance Imagination,* essays and lectures collected and edited by Stephen Orgel (Berkeley, 1975)

ANDREW GURR, *The Shakespearean Stage* (Cambridge, 1970)

C. WALTER HODGES, *The Globe Restored* (Oxford, 1968)

ALLARDYCE NICOLL, *Stuart Masques and the Renaissance Stage* (London, 1938; reprint New York, 1963)

STEPHEN ORGEL, *The Illusion of Power: Political Theater in the English Renaissance* (Berkeley, 1975)

JOHN ORRELL, *The Theatres of Inigo Jones and John Webb* (Cambridge, 1985)

S. GORLEY PUTT, *The Golden Age of English Drama* (Woodbridge, 1981)

STANLEY WELLS, *English Drama: Select Bibliographical Guides* (Oxford, 1975)

STANLEY WELLS, *Shakespeare: Select Bibliographical Guides* (Oxford, 1975)

ENID WELSFORD, *The Court Masque* (Cambridge, 1927; reprint, New York, 1962)

G. WICKHAM, *English Moral Interludes* (London, 1976)

F. P. WILSON, *The English Drama, 1485-1585,* ed. G. K. Hunter for *The Oxford History of English Literature* (Oxford, 1969)

Chapter 10: Spain

MELVEENA MCKENDRICK, *Theatre in Spain, 1490-1700* (Cambridge, 1990)

A. A. PARKER, *The Allegorical Drama of Calderón* (Oxford, 1943)

A. H. RENNERT, *The Spanish Stage in the Time of Lope de Vega* (New York, 1963; reprint of 1st edn., 1909)

N. D. SHERGOLD, *A History of the Spanish Stage from Medieval Times until the end of the Seventeenth Century* (Oxford, 1967)

A. E. SLOMAN, *The Dramatic Craftsmanship of Calderón: His Use of Early Plays* (Oxford, 1969)

RONALD E. SURTZ, *The Birth of a Theater: Dramatic Convention from Juan del Encina to Lope de Vega* (Princeton, 1979)

T. TREVOR DAVIES, *The Golden Century of Spain, 1501-1621* (London, 1937)

Chapter 10: France

CLAUDE ABRAHAM, *Pierre Corneille* (New York, 1972)

PER BJURSTRÖM, *Giacomo Torelli and Baroque Stage Design* (Stockholm, 1961)

G. BRERETON, *French Comic Drama from the Sixteenth to the Eighteenth Century* (London, 1977)

G. BRERETON, *Jean Racine* (London, 1951)

L. GROSSMAN, *Men and Masks: A Study of Molière* (Baltimore, 1963)

W. D. HOWARTH, *Molière: A Playwright and His Audience* (Cambridge, 1982)

J. D. HUBERT, *Molière and the Comedy of Intellect* (Berkeley and Los Angeles, 1962)

B. JEFFREY, *French Renaissance Comedy, 1552-1630* (Oxford, 1969)

H. C. LANCASTER, *A History of French Dramatic Literature in the 17th Century,* vols. 2 and 3 (Baltimore, 1929-42)

T. E. LAWRENSON, *The French Stage in the XVIIth Century: A Study in the Advent of the Italian Order* (Manchester, 1957; New York, 1986)

SAMUEL SOLOMON, *The Complete Plays of Jean Racine,* 2 vols. (New York, 1967)

W. L. WILEY, *The Early Public Theatre in France* (Cambridge, Mass., 1960)

Parts IV and V
Chapter 11: Restoration and Eighteenth Century

M. BAUR-HEINHOLD, *The Baroque Theatre* (New York, 1967)

WALTER H. BRUFORD, *Theatre, Drama and Audience in Goethe's Germany* (London, 1957)

BONAMY DOBRÉE, *Restoration Tragedy* (Oxford, 1928)

KERRY DOWNES, *Sir John Vanburgh: A Biography,* (London, 1987)

FRANK H. ELLIS, *Sentimental Comedy: Dramatic Theory and Practice* (Cambridge, 1990)

CARLO GOLDONI, *Memoirs,* trans. John Black (New York, 1926)

LESLIE HOTSON, *The Commonwealth and Restoration Stage* (Harvard, 1928)

ELEANOR JOURDAN, *Dramatic Theory and Practice in France, 1690-1808* (London, 1921)

T. E. LAWRENSON, *The French Stage and Playhouse in the Seventeenth Century* (New York, 1986)

KENNETH MUIR, *The Comedy of Manners* (London, 1970)

JOCELYN POWELL, *Restoration Theatre Production* (London, 1981)

CECIL PRICE, *Theatre in the Age of Garrick* (Oxford, 1973)

JOHN PRUDHOE, *The Theatre of Goethe and Schiller* (Oxford, 1973)

PAUL RANGER, *Gothic Drama in the London Patent Theatres, 1750-1820,* (London, 1991)

SYBIL ROSENFELD, *Georgian Scene Painters and Scene Painting* (Cambridge, 1981)

SYBIL ROSENFELD, *Strolling Players and Drama in the Provinces* (Cambridge, 1939)

DAVID THOMAS and ARNOLD HARE (eds.), *Restoration and Georgian England, 1660-1788: a documentary history* (Cambridge, 1989)

Chapters 12 and 13: Nineteenth Century

ANDRÉ ANTOINE, *Memories of the Théâtre Libre,* trans. Marvin Carlson (Miami, 1964)

MICHAEL BOOTH, *English Melodrama* (London, 1965)

MICHAEL BOOTH, *Victorian Spectacular Theatre, 1850-1910* (London, 1981)

MARVIN A. CARLSON, *The French Stage in the Nineteenth Century* (London, 1972)

MARVIN A. CARLSON, *The German Stage in the Nineteenth Century* (London, 1972)

NEMIROVITCH-DANTCHENKO, *My Life in the Russian Theatre,* trans. John Cournos (London, 1937)

JOSEPH DONOHUE, *Theatre in the Age of Kean* (Oxford, 1975)

VICTOR GLASSTONE, *Victorian and Edwardian Theatre* (London, 1975)

MORDECAI GORLICK, *New Theatres for Old* (New York, 1940)

ANTONY D. HIPPISLEY COXE, *A Seat at the Circus* (London, 1951)

RAYMOND MANDER AND JOE MITCHENSON, *Music Hall: A Story in Pictures* (London, 1971)

RAYMOND MANDER AND JOE MITCHENSON, *Pantomime: A Story in Pictures* (London, 1973)

LISE-LONE MARKER, *David Belasco: Naturalism in the Theatre* (Princeton, 1975)

LISE-LONE MARKER and FREDERICK J. MARKER *The Scandinavian Theatre: A Short History* (Oxford, 1975)

DAVID MAYER and KENNETH RICHARDS (eds.), *Western Popular Theatre* (London, 1977)

MICHAEL MEYER, *Strindberg: A Biography* (Bury St. Edmunds, Suffolk, 1985)

ANNA IRENE MILLER, *The Independent Theatre in Europe, 1887 to the Present* (New York, 1931; reprint, 1966)

ALLARDYCE NICOLL, *The World of Harlequin* (Cambridge, 1964)

FRANK RAHIL, *The World of Melodrama* (University Park and London, 1967)

JOANNA RICHARDSON, *Sarah Bernhardt and Her World* (London, 1977)

GEORGE ROWELL, *The Victorian Theatre* (Oxford, 1956; reprints, 1967, 1972)

LAURENCE SENELICK, *National Theatres in Northern and Eastern Europe, 1746-1900: A Documentary History* (Cambridge, 1990)

A. NICHOLAS VARDAC, *Stage to Screen: Theatrical Method from Garrick to Griffith* (Harvard, 1949; reprint, 1968)

Chapters 13 and 14: Twentieth Century 1900-1950

EDWARD BRAUN, *Meyerholdt on Theatre* (London, 1969)

JOSEPH CHAIKIN, *The Presence of the Actor* (New York, 1974)

RUBY COLN, *Dialogue in American Drama* (Bloomington and London, 1971)

MALCOLM GOLDSTEIN, *George S. Kaufman: His Life and his Theater* (New York and Oxford, 1979)

MARTIN GOTTFRIED, *Broadway Musicals* (New York, 1979)

JOHN GASSNER, *Directions in Modern Drama and Theatre* (New York and London, 1967)

JACQUES GUICHARNAUD, *Modern French Theatre from Giraudoux to Beckett* (Yale, 1961)

BERNARD HEWITT, *Theatre U. S. A. , 1668-1957* (New York, 1959)

RICHARD F. LEAVITT, *The World of Tennessee Williams* (London, 1978)

PAUL MCGUIRE, *The Australian Theatre* (London and Melbourne, 1948)

HENNING RISCHBEITER, *Art and the Stage in the 20th Century* (New York, 1968)

GEORGE ROWELL and ANTHONY JACKSON, *The Repertory Movement: A History of Regional Theatre in Britain* (Cambridge, 1984)

KENNETH TYNAN, *He That Plays the King: A View of the Theatre* (London, 1950)

J. C. TREWIN, *The Gay Twenties: A Decade of the Theatre* (London, 1958)

J. C. TREWIN, *The Edwardian Theatre* (London, 1976)

JOHN WILLET, *The Theatre of Bertolt Brecht* (London, 1959)

JOHN WILLET, *Expressionism* (New York, 1970)

Chapter 15 and Epilogue (contemporary)

DORIS E. ABRAMSON, *Negro Playwrights in the American Theatre* (New York, 1969)

ANTONIN ARTAUD, *Collected Works,* trans. Victor Corti, 4 vols. (London, 1971)

MARTIN BANHAM with CLIVE WAKE, *African Theatre Today* (London, 1976)

MICHAEL BAUME, *The Sydney Opera House* (Sydney, 1967)

DAVID BRADBY, *Modern French Drama, 1940-1990,* (Cambridge, 2nd Ed. 1991)

SALLY BEAUMAN, *The Royal Shakespeare Company: A History of Ten Decades* (Oxford, 1984)

PETER BROOK, *The Empty Space* (London, 1969)

ROBERT BRUSTEIN, *The Theatre of Revolt: An Approach to Modern Drama* (Boston, 1964)

JOHN ELSOM, *Post-War British Theatre Criticism* (London, 1971)

JOHN ELSOM, *Post-War British Theatre* (London, 1976)

JOHN ELSOM and NICHOLAS TOMALIN, *The History of the National Theatre* (London, 1978)

MARTIN ESSLIN, *Theatre of the Absurd* (New York, 1969)

RICHARD FINDLATER (ed.), *At the Royal Court: 25 Years of the English Stage Company* (Beccles and London, 1981)

ADRIAN HENRI, *Environments and Happenings* (London, 1974)

HAROLD HOBSON, *Theatre in Britain: A Personal View* (Oxford, 1984)

CATHERINE HUGHES, *American Playwrights 1945-1975* (London, 1976)

CATHERINE ITZIN, *Stages in the Revolution: Political Theatre in Britain since 1968* (London, 1980)

JAMES ROOS-EVANS, *Experimental Theatre from Stanislavsky to Peter Brook* (London, 1970; 4th ed. 1990)

KONSTANTIN RUDNITSKY, *Russian and Soviet Theatre: Tradition and the Avant Garde* (London, 1988)

RICHARD SCHECHNER, *Environmental Theatre* (New York, 1973)

HANNELORE SCHUBERT, *The Modern Theatre – Architecture, Stage Design, Lighting* (London, 1977)

ROMAN SZYDLOWSKI, *The Theatre in Poland* (Warsaw, 1972)

BAKARY TRAORÉ, *The Black African Theatre and its Social Function,* trans. with Preface by Dapo Adelugba (Ibadan, 1972)

IRVING WARDLE, *The Theatres of George Devine* (London, 1978)

ROGER WILMUT, *From Fringe to Flying Circus* (London, 1980)

Index

Italic figures indicate
numbers of illustrations
within the text. Pl. refers to
a colour plate.

Index

Credits

The author and publishers are grateful to all those museums, institutions and individuals who have provided illustrations for this book or who have given permission for works in their collections to be reproduced. Thanks are also due to Ted Colman and to Mike Bailey for supplying photographs, and to Mr David Mayer for his advice and help in tracking down some of the more elusive subjects.

Further acknowledgement is due to the following (bold type refers to colour plate numbers): Aerofilms 36; Alinari, Florence 82, 83; Alinari/Giraudon 56; Arborio Mella, Milan 84, 88; Chris Arthur 205; Mary Atkins Museum of Fine Arts, Kansas City 173 (photo: Raymond Mander and Joe Mitchenson Theatre Collection); Aukland Art Institute and Museum, New Zealand 5; Avranches Municipal Library 44 (photo: Weidenfeld & Nicolson Archives); © Mike Bailey 219; H. V. Balcom, Shreveport, Louisiana 3; © B. T. Batsford, 1943 199; BBC Copyright 1989 217; Biblioteca Nazionale, Florence 89; Bibliothèque de l'Arsenal, Paris 145 (photo: Roger-Viollet); Bibliothèque Nationale, Paris 30, 60 (MS. Fr. 146. f36v), 65 (MS. Fr. 12536, photo: Giraudon), 66, 122, 126 (photo: Giraudon), 131, 186, 189, 195; Bibliothèque de l'Opéra, Paris 86, 87; Bibliothèque Nationale, Paris 6, 8 (MS. Fr. 2813. f473v); 9; Biblioteca Palatina, Parma 92; Bildarchiv Foto Marburg 49, 54, 79, 111; Bildarchiv Österreichischen Nationalbibliothek, Vienna 150, 152, 153; Bodleian Library, Oxford 45 (MS. Bodley 264. f54v), 46 (MS. Douce .366. f109), 50 (MS. Bodley 264. f2Iv), 51 (MS. Auct. F. 2. 13. f4v), 67; Borghese Gallery, Rome 5; Bristol Old Vic 200 (Photo: Derek Balmer); British Library, London 19 (MS. Or. 9333, fI6v), 62 (Add. MS. 24098. fI9v), 63 (MS. Harley Roll 76. pt.7), 69 (MS. Harley Roll 4380. fI), 72 (MS. Cotton Titus A XVII. f40), 78 (MS. Cot. Vesp. B.II. fIo), 105 (photo: Mansell Collection), 138; Reproduced by courtesy of the Trustees of the British Museum, London 18, 97, 99, 103 (photo: University of Bristol Theatre Collection), 107 (photo: University of Bristol Theatre Collection), 125; Burgerbibliothek, Lucerne 76 (photo: Weidenfeld & Nicolson); Christian Museum, Estergom 7 (photo: Attila Mudrák); Nobby Clark 22; Col Sedo, Barcelona 112 (photo: Mas, Barcelona); Donald Cooper/Photostage 209, 211, 212, 213, 215, 216, 220a,b,c; Courtauld Institute, London 138; Dance Library 1 (photo: Robin Bath), 2 (photo: Jess Davis), 9 (photo: Derek Richards); Department of the Environment 35; Devonshire Collection, Chatsworth. Reproduced by permission of the Trustees of the Chatsworth Settlement 11; Drottningsholms Teatermuseum, Stockholm 148; By permission of the Governors of Dulwich Picture Gallery, London 95; Folger Library, Washington, DC 73; Foto Salmer, Barcelona 109, 113; Foto Vagenti, Vicenza 80; Garrick Club, London 139, 142 (photos: E-T Archive); Giraudon, Paris 37; Goethe Nationalmuseum, Weimar 171; Courtesy The Guardian/photo Alexander Nikolayev 222; Harvard Theatre Collection, Cambridge, Mass. 157, 162, 179; Honolulu Academy of Arts, Michener Collection 16; Henry E. Huntington Library & Art Gallery, San Marino, California 93; Illustrated London News, London 167, 169; Fine Arts Library, Indiana University 85; Italian State Tourist Office, London 32; Douglas H. Jeffery 203; A. F. Kersting, London 21, 40, 42; Raymond Mander and Joe Mitchenson Theatre Collection, London 151, 168, 176, 180, 183, 196; Mansell Collection, London 8, 17, 94, 158; Mansell/Alinari 38; Mas, Barcelona 108, 114, 115, 118, 119; The Metropolitan Museum of Art, New York, Rogers Fund, 1913 27; Tony and Marion Morrison 116; © Henri Mouron – ADAGP – Paris jacket; Alastair Muir, Frontispiece; Musée d'Angers 64 (photo: Giraudon); Musée Carnavalet, Paris 12 (photo: Arborio Mella, Milan); Musée de Civilisation, Lyons 34 (photo: Giraudon); Musée Cluny, Paris 47, 68 (photos: Giraudon); Musée Condé, Chantilly 71 (photo: Giraudon); Musée Guimet, Paris 10 (photo: Michael Holford); Musée du Louvre, Paris 28 (photo: Giraudon), 117; Musée du Petit Palais, Paris 41 (photo: Mansell Collection), 188 (photo: Bulloz, Paris); Museo Civico, Foligno 43 (photo: Deutsches Archäologisches Institut, Rome); Museo di Roma, Rome 10 (photo: Scala); Museo Lazaro Galdiano, Madrid 113; Museum Boymans-van Beuningen, Rotterdam 77; Museum of Modern Art, New York, Film Stills Archive 174; Nasjonalgalleriet, Oslo 190; National Art Museum, Copenhagen 52; Reproduced by courtesy of the Trustees of the National Gallery, London 147; National Monuments Record, London 96; National Museum, Naples 29, 31, 33 (photos: Mansell Collection), 36; National Palace Museum, Taiwan 13; National Portrait Gallery, London 106; Maurice Newcombe 203; New York Public Library, Library of Performing Arts 170, 109a,b, 197, 208; Phaidon Press Archive 1; Private Collection 4, 15, 16, 91, 128, 129, 221; Rijksmuseum, Amsterdam 134; Royal Library, Stockholm 99; Courtesy The Royal Shakespeare Theatre, 202; Scala, Florence 4, 55, 90; Scientific American, 5 April 1884, 155; A. C. Scott 11 (photo: Weidenfeld & Nicolson); The Shakespeare Centre, Stratford-upon-Avon, © Angus McBean, 204; Brian Shuel 6, 7; Society of Antiquaries, London 104 (photo: University of Bristol Theatre Collection); Society for Cultural Relations with the USSR, London 185; Staatliche Antikensammlungen und Glyptothek, Munich 23; Staatliche Museen, Berlin 24, 26 (photos: Mansell Collection); Courtesy Stephen Joseph Theatre/photo: Alec Russell 214; Stiftsbibliothek, St Gall 53 (photo: Weidenfeld & Nicolson); Suny-Binghamton Max Reinhardt Archive, New York 192; Times Newspapers Ltd 220d; Uffizi Gallery, Florence 81; University of Bristol Theatre Collection 3, 14, and 2 12, 14, 15a,b, 73, 74, 137, 161, 177 (Beerbohm Tree Collection), 182, 184, 187, 201, 210; Unterlinden Museum, Colmar 61; Utrecht University Library 102; Victoria and Albert Museum, London 48, 57, 58a,b, 75, 120, 135, 136 (Oskar Fischell Collection: photo courtesy of C. Walter Hodges), 141, 144, 146, 149, 156, 159, 160, 163, 164, 165, 166, 181; Martin von Wagner Museum, Würzburg 25; Weidenfeld & Nicolson 59, 70; Weimar Central Library 172; Worcester College Library, Oxford (Jones/Webb Collection) 100, 101a,b (photos: Bodleian Library); Drama Library, Yale University, New Haven, Conn. 132, 178.

Plates 13, and Figs. 127, 130, 133, 137 are reproduced from Joseph Gregor (ed.) Monumenta Scenica (Munich, 1924-31); Fig. 20a is reproduced from Margarete Bieber, The History of the Greek and Roman Theater (Copyright © 1939, 1961 by Princeton University Press, Figure 238 reprinted with permission of Princeton University Press); Fig. 20b is reproduced from W. Dorpfeld and E. Reisch, Das Griechische Theater (Athens, 1896, Fig. 93); Fig. 30 is reproduced from Tristano Martinelli, Compositions de Rhétorique de Monsieur Don Arlequin (Paris, 1928); Fig. 110 is reproduced from Jean Jacquot (ed.), Le Lieu Théâtrale à la Renaissance (Paris, 1964); Fig. 117 is reproduced from La Vie Théâtrale au Temps de la Renaissance, ed. P. Chilott, Institut Pédagogique National, Paris, 1963, opp. p. 207; Figs. 121, 123 and 124 are reproduced from S. Wilma Holsboer, L'Histoire de la Mise en Scène dans le Théâtre Français de 1600 a 1657 (Paris, 1933); Fig. 154 is reproduced from G. Moynet, La Machinerie Théâtrale (Paris, 1893); Fig. 192 is reproduced by kind permission of Herbert Marshall from his book The Pictorial History of the Russian Theatre (New York, 1977, p. 115). Photo: Library of Performing Arts, New York Public Library.